AWS
Certified Solutions Architect
Study Guide
Second Edition

AWS
Certified Solutions Architect
Study Guide
Associate (SAA-C01) Exam
Second Edition

Ben Piper

David Clinton

SYBEX®
A Wiley Brand

Senior Acquisitions Editor: Kenyon Brown
Development Editor: Kathi Duggan
Technical Editors: Shlomo Swidler and Sara Perrott
Senior Production Editor: Christine O'Connor
Copy Editor: Kim Wimpsett
Content Enablement and Operations Manager: Pete Gaughan
Production Manager: Kathleen Wisor
Executive Editor: Jim Minatel
Book Designers: Judy Fung and Bill Gibson
Proofreader: Nancy Carrasco
Indexer: Ted Laux
Project Coordinator, Cover: Brent Savage
Cover Designer: Wiley
Cover Image: Getty Images Inc. / Jeremy Woodhouse

ISBN: 978-1-119-50421-4
ISBN: 978-1-119-50419-1 (ebk.)
ISBN: 978-1-119-50417-7 (ebk.)

Manufactured in the United States of America

Library of Congress Control Number: 2018957473

C10008110_020619

For He who created all things.

Acknowledgments

We would like to thank the following people who helped us create this AWS Certified Solutions Architect Study Guide: Associate SAA-C01 Exam, Second Edition.

First, a special thanks to our friends at Wiley. Kenyon Brown, senior acquisitions editor, got the ball rolling on this project and pushed to get this book published quickly. His experience and guidance throughout the project was critical. Kathi Duggan, development editor, helped push this book forward by keeping us accountable to our deadlines. Her edits made many of the technical parts of this book more readable. Thanks also go to Katie Wisor, production manager; Christine O'Connor, production editor; Pete Gaughan, content enablement manager; and Nancy Carrasco, proofreader.

John Mueller reviewed the chapters and questions for technical accuracy. Not only did his comments and suggestions make this book more accurate, he also provided additional ideas for the chapter review questions to make them more challenging and relevant to the exam. Thanks also go to Sara Perrott and Shlomo Swidler for providing technical proofreading.

Lastly, the authors would like to thank each other!

About the Authors

David Clinton is a Linux server admin who has worked with IT infrastructure in both academic and enterprise environments. He has authored books—including Learn Amazon Web Services in a Month of Lunches (Manning Publications, 2017) and Linux in Action (Manning Publications, 2018)—and created more than 15 video courses teaching Amazon Web Services and Linux administration, server virtualization, and IT security for Pluralsight.

In a "previous life," David spent 20 years as a high school teacher. He currently lives in Toronto, Canada, with his wife and family and can be reached through his website: https://bootstrap-it.com.

Ben Piper, a native of Augusta, Georgia, is an IT consultant who works with clients in the Georgia-Carolina area. He has created more than 20 training courses covering Amazon Web Services, Cisco routing and switching, Puppet configuration management, and Windows Server Administration. He's also the author of Learn Cisco Network Administration in a Month of Lunches (Manning Publications, 2017). Over the years he has designed, implemented, and maintained a variety of technologies including VMware vSphere, Citrix XenApp, XenServer, NetScaler, and Cisco network infrastructure. You can contact Ben by visiting his website: https://benpiper.com.

Contents at a Glance

Introduction   *xxv*

Assessment Test   *xxxi*

Part I   **The Core AWS Services**   **1**

Chapter 1   Introduction to Cloud Computing and AWS   3

Chapter 2   Amazon Elastic Compute Cloud and Amazon
                   Elastic Block Store   21

Chapter 3   Amazon Simple Storage Service and Amazon
                   Glacier Storage   47

Chapter 4   Amazon Virtual Private Cloud   67

Chapter 5   Databases   95

Chapter 6   Authentication and Authorization—AWS Identity
                   and Access Management   123

Chapter 7   CloudTrail, CloudWatch, and AWS Config   141

Chapter 8   The Domain Name System and Network Routing:
                   Amazon Route 53 and Amazon CloudFront   169

Part II   **The Well-Architected Framework**   **189**

Chapter 9   The Reliability Pillar   191

Chapter 10   The Performance Efficiency Pillar   217

Chapter 11   The Security Pillar   247

Chapter 12   The Cost Optimization Pillar   277

Chapter 13   The Operational Excellence Pillar   295

Appendix   Answers to Review Questions   327

Index   *353*

Contents

Introduction   *xxv*

Assessment Test   *xxxi*

Part I   The Core AWS Services   **1**

Chapter   1   Introduction to Cloud Computing and AWS   **3**

Cloud Computing and Virtualization   4
    Cloud Computing Architecture   5
    Cloud Computing Optimization   5
The AWS Cloud   6
AWS Platform Architecture   11
AWS Reliability and Compliance   13
    The AWS Shared Responsibility Model   13
    The AWS Service Level Agreement   14
Working with AWS   14
    The AWS CLI   15
    AWS SDKs   15
    Technical Support and Online Resources   15
    Support Plans   15
    Other Support Resources   16
Summary   16
Exam Essentials   17
Exercise   17
Review Questions   18

Chapter   2   Amazon Elastic Compute Cloud and Amazon Elastic Block Store   **21**

Introduction   22
EC2 Instances   22
    Provisioning Your Instance   23
    Configuring Instance Behavior   28
    Instance Pricing   28
    Instance Lifecycle   29
    Resource Tags   30
    Service Limits   30
EC2 Storage Volumes   31
    Elastic Block Store Volumes   31
    Instance Store Volumes   33
Accessing Your EC2 Instance   33

Securing Your EC2 Instance   35
    Security Groups   35
    IAM Roles   36
    NAT Devices   36
    Key Pairs   37
Other EC2-Related Services   37
    AWS Systems Manager   37
    Placement Groups   37
    AWS Elastic Beanstalk   37
    Amazon Elastic Container Service and AWS Fargate   38
    AWS Lambda   38
    VM Import/Export   38
    Elastic Load Balancing and Auto Scaling   38
AWS CLI Example   39
Summary   40
Exam Essentials   40
Review Questions   42

Chapter   3   **Amazon Simple Storage Service and Amazon
                Glacier Storage   47**

Introduction   48
S3 Service Architecture   49
    Prefixes and Delimiters   49
    Working with Large Objects   49
    Encryption   50
    Logging   51
S3 Durability and Availability   51
    Durability   52
    Availability   52
    Eventually Consistent Data   53
S3 Object Lifecycle   53
    Versioning   53
    Lifecycle Management   54
Accessing S3 Objects   54
    Access Control   55
    Presigned URLs   56
    Static Website Hosting   56
    S3 and Glacier Select   57
Amazon Glacier   57
Storage Pricing   58
Other Storage-Related Services   59
    Amazon Elastic File System   59
    AWS Storage Gateway   59
    AWS Snowball   59

AWS CLI Example   60
Summary   61
Exam Essentials   61
Review Questions   63

Chapter   4   Amazon Virtual Private Cloud   67

Introduction   68
VPC CIDR Blocks   68
    Secondary CIDR Blocks   69
    IPv6 CIDR Blocks   69
Subnets   70
    Subnet CIDR Blocks   70
    Availability Zones   71
    IPv6 CIDR Blocks   72
Elastic Network Interfaces   72
    Primary and Secondary Private IP Addresses   72
    Attaching Elastic Network Interfaces   73
Internet Gateways   73
Route Tables   74
    Routes   74
    The Default Route   75
Security Groups   76
    Inbound Rules   76
    Outbound Rules   77
    Sources and Destinations   78
    Stateful Firewall   78
    Default Security Group   78
Network Access Control Lists   79
    Inbound Rules   79
    Outbound Rules   80
    Using Network Access Control Lists and Security
        Groups Together   81
Public IP Addresses   82
Elastic IP Addresses   82
Network Address Translation   83
Network Address Translation Devices   84
    Configuring Route Tables to Use NAT Devices   85
    NAT Gateway   86
    NAT Instance   87
VPC Peering   87
Summary   88
Exam Essentials   89
Review Questions   91

Chapter	5	**Databases**	**95**

Introduction   96
Relational Databases   96
    Columns and Attributes   96
    Using Multiple Tables   97
    Structured Query Language   98
    Online Transaction Processing vs. Online
        Analytic Processing   99
Amazon Relational Database Service   99
    Database Engines   100
    Licensing Considerations   101
    Database Option Groups   101
    Database Instance Classes   102
    Storage   103
    Read Replicas   106
    High Availability (Multi-AZ)   108
    Backup and Recovery   109
    Automated Snapshots   109
    Maintenance Items   110
Amazon Redshift   110
    Compute Nodes   110
    Data Distribution Styles   111
Nonrelational (No-SQL) Databases   111
    Storing Data   111
    Querying Data   112
    Types of Nonrelational Databases   112
DynamoDB   112
    Partition and Hash Keys   113
    Attributes and Items   113
    Throughput Capacity   114
    Reading Data   116
Summary   117
Exam Essentials   117
Review Questions   119

Chapter	6	**Authentication and Authorization—AWS Identity and Access Management**	**123**

Introduction   124
IAM Identities   125
    IAM Policies   125
    User and Root Accounts   126
    Access Keys   129
    Groups   130
    Roles   131

Authentication Tools	131
Amazon Cognito	132
AWS Managed Microsoft AD	132
AWS Single Sign-On	132
AWS Key Management Service	133
AWS Secrets Manager	133
AWS CloudHSM	133
AWS CLI Example	134
Summary	135
Exam Essentials	136
Review Questions	137

Chapter 7   CloudTrail, CloudWatch, and AWS Config   141

Introduction	142
CloudTrail	143
Management Events	143
Data Events	144
Event History	144
Trails	144
Log File Integrity Validation	146
CloudWatch	147
CloudWatch Metrics	147
Graphing Metrics	149
Metric Math	150
CloudWatch Logs	152
Log Streams and Log Groups	153
Metric Filters	153
CloudWatch Agent	153
Sending CloudTrail Logs to CloudWatch Logs	154
CloudWatch Alarms	155
Data Point to Monitor	155
Threshold	155
Alarm States	156
Data Points to Alarm and Evaluation Period	156
Missing Data	157
Actions	157
AWS Config	158
The Configuration Recorder	159
Configuration Items	159
Configuration History	159
Configuration Snapshots	160
Monitoring Changes	161
Summary	162
Exam Essentials	162
Review Questions	164

**Chapter 8   The Domain Name System and Network Routing:
Amazon Route 53 and Amazon CloudFront   169**

Introduction   170
The Domain Name System   170
  Namespaces   170
  Name Servers   171
  Domains and Domain Names   171
  Domain Registration   172
  Domain Layers   172
  Fully Qualified Domain Names   172
  Zones and Zone Files   173
  Record Types   173
  Alias Records   174
Amazon Route 53   174
  Domain Registration   174
  DNS Management   175
  Availability Monitoring   176
  Routing Policies   177
  Traffic Flow   180
Amazon CloudFront   181
AWS CLI Example   182
Summary   183
Exam Essentials   183
Review Questions   185

Part II   The Well-Architected Framework   189

Chapter 9   The Reliability Pillar   191

Introduction   192
Calculating Availability   192
  Availability Differences in Traditional vs. Cloud-Native
    Applications   193
  Know Your Limits   196
  Increasing Availability   196
EC2 Auto Scaling   197
  Launch Configurations   197
  Launch Templates   199
  Auto Scaling Groups   200
  Auto Scaling Options   204
Data Backup and Recovery   204
  S3   205
  Elastic File System   205
  Elastic Block Storage   205
  Database Resiliency   205

Creating a Resilient Network   206
    VPC Design Considerations   206
    External Connectivity   207
Designing for Availability   207
    Designing for 99 Percent Availability   208
    Designing for 99.9 Percent Availability   209
    Designing for 99.99 Percent Availability   210
Summary   211
Exam Essentials   211
Review Questions   213

Chapter 10   The Performance Efficiency Pillar   217

Introduction   218
Optimizing Performance for the Core AWS Services   218
    Compute   219
    Storage   223
    Database   226
    Network Optimization and Load Balancing   227
Infrastructure Automation   230
    CloudFormation   230
    Third-Party Automation Solutions   232
    Continuous Integration and Continuous Deployment   232
Reviewing and Optimizing Infrastructure Configurations   234
    Load Testing   235
    Visualization   235
Optimizing Data Operations   236
    Caching   237
    Partitioning/Sharding   238
    Compression   239
Summary   239
Exam Essentials   240
Review Questions   242

Chapter 11   The Security Pillar   247

Introduction   248
Identity and Access Management   248
    Protecting AWS Credentials   248
    Fine-Grained Authorization   249
    Permissions Boundaries   251
    Roles   252
    Enforcing Service-Level Protection   258

Chapter 10

Detective Controls   258
    CloudTrail   258
    CloudWatch Logs   259
    Searching Logs with Athena   260
    Auditing Resource Configurations with AWS Config   262
    Amazon GuardDuty   264
    Amazon Inspector   265
Protecting Network Boundaries   267
    Network Access Control Lists and Security Groups   267
    AWS Web Application Firewall   267
    AWS Shield   268
Data Encryption   268
    Data at Rest   268
    Data in Transit   270
Summary   270
Exam Essentials   271
Review Questions   272

Chapter   12   The Cost Optimization Pillar   277

Introduction   278
Planning, Tracking, and Controlling Costs   278
    AWS Budgets   279
    Monitoring Tools   280
    AWS Organizations   281
    AWS Trusted Advisor   282
    Online Calculator Tools   282
Cost-Optimizing Compute   284
    Maximizing Server Density   284
    EC2 Reserved Instances   285
    EC2 Spot Instances   285
    Auto Scaling   288
    Elastic Block Store Lifecycle Manager   288
Summary   288
Exam Essentials   289
Review Questions   290

Chapter   13   The Operational Excellence Pillar   295

Introduction   296
CloudFormation   296
    Creating Stacks   297
    Deleting Stacks   298
    Using Multiple Stacks   298

Stack Updates 301
Preventing Updates to Specific Resources 302
Overriding Stack Policies 303
CodeCommit 303
Creating a Repository 304
Repository Security 304
Interacting with a Repository Using Git 305
CodeDeploy 307
The CodeDeploy Agent 308
Deployments 308
Deployment Groups 308
Deployment Types 308
Deployment Configurations 309
Lifecycle Events 310
The Application Specification File 311
Triggers and Alarms 312
Rollbacks 312
CodePipeline 313
Continuous Integration 313
Continuous Delivery 313
Creating the Pipeline 314
Artifacts 315
AWS Systems Manager 316
Actions 316
Insights 318
Summary 320
Exam Essentials 320
Review Questions 322

Appendix   **Answers to Review Questions**   **327**

Chapter 1: Introduction to Cloud Computing and AWS 328
Chapter 2: Amazon Elastic Compute Cloud and Amazon
Elastic Block Store 329
Chapter 3: Amazon Simple Storage Service and Amazon
Glacier Storage 331
Chapter 4: Amazon Virtual Private Cloud 332
Chapter 5: Databases 334
Chapter 6: Authentication and Authorization—AWS Identity
and Access Management 336
Chapter 7: CloudTrail, CloudWatch, and AWS Config 338
Chapter 8: The Domain Name System and Network Routing:
Amazon Route 53 and Amazon CloudFront 340

Chapter 9: The Reliability Pillar   342
Chapter 10: The Performance Efficiency Pillar   344
Chapter 11: The Security Pillar   346
Chapter 12: The Cost Optimization Pillar   348
Chapter 13: The Operational Excellence Pillar   349

Index   *353*

Table of Exercises

Exercise	1.1	Use the AWS CLI	17
Exercise	2.1	Launch an EC2 Linux Instance and Log in Using SSH	27
Exercise	2.2	Assess the Free Capacity of a Running Instance and Change Its Instance Type	27
Exercise	2.3	Assess Which Pricing Model Will Best Meet the Needs of a Deployment	29
Exercise	2.4	Create and Launch an AMI Based on an Existing Instance Storage Volume	32
Exercise	2.5	Install the AWS CLI and Use It to Launch an EC2 Instance	39
Exercise	2.6	Clean Up Unused EC2 Resources	39
Exercise	3.1	Create a New S3 Bucket and Upload a File	50
Exercise	3.2	Enable Versioning and Lifecycle Management for an S3 Bucket	54
Exercise	3.3	Generate and Use a Presigned URL	56
Exercise	3.4	Enable Static Website Hosting for an S3 Bucket	57
Exercise	3.5	Calculate the Total Lifecycle Costs for Your Data	59
Exercise	4.1	Create a New VPC	69
Exercise	4.2	Create a New Subnet	72
Exercise	4.3	Create and Attach a Primary ENI	73
Exercise	4.4	Create an Internet Gateway and Default Route	75
Exercise	4.5	Create a Custom Security Group	78
Exercise	4.6	Create an Inbound Rule to Allow Remote Access from Any IP Address	80
Exercise	4.7	Allocate and Use an Elastic IP Address	83
Exercise	5.1	Create an RDS Database Instance	104
Exercise	5.2	Create a Read Replica	107
Exercise	5.3	Promote the Read Replica to a Master	108
Exercise	5.4	Create a Table in DynamoDB	115
Exercise	6.1	Lock Down the Root User	127
Exercise	6.2	Assign and Implement an IAM Policy	127
Exercise	6.3	Create, Use, and Delete an AWS Access Key	130
Exercise	6.4	Create and Configure an IAM Group	131
Exercise	7.1	Create a Trail	145
Exercise	7.2	Create a Graph Using Metric Math	151
Exercise	7.3	Deliver CloudTrail Logs to CloudWatch Logs	154

Exercise **8.1** Create a Hosted Zone on Route 53 for an EC2 Web Server 175

Exercise **8.2** Set Up a Health Check 177

Exercise **8.3** Configure a Route 53 Routing Policy 179

Exercise **8.4** Create a CloudFront Distribution for Your S3-Based
Static Website 182

Exercise **9.1** Create a Launch Template 198

Exercise **10.1** Configure and Launch an Application Using Auto Scaling 221

Exercise **10.2** Sync Two S3 Buckets as Cross-Region Replicas. 224

Exercise **10.3** Upload to an S3 Bucket Using Transfer Acceleration. 225

Exercise **10.4** Create and Deploy an EC2 Load Balancer 229

Exercise **10.5** Launch a Simple CloudFormation Template 231

Exercise **10.6** Create a CloudWatch Dashboard 236

Exercise **11.1** Create a Limited Administrative User 251

Exercise **11.2** Create and Assume a Role as an IAM User 256

Exercise **11.3** Configure VPC Flow Logging. 259

Exercise **11.4** Encrypt an EBS Volume 269

Exercise **12.1** Create an AWS Budget to Send an Alert 280

Exercise **12.2** Build Your Own Stack in Simple Monthly Calculator 283

Exercise **12.3** Request a Spot Fleet Using the AWS CLI. 286

Exercise **13.1** Create a Nested Stack 299

Exercise **13.2** Create and Interact with a CodeCommit Repository 305

Introduction

Studying for any certification always involves deciding how much of your studying should be practical hands-on experience and how much should be simply memorizing facts and figures. Between the two of us, we've taken more than 20 different IT certification exams, so we know how important it is to use your study time wisely. We've designed this book to help you discover your strengths and weaknesses on the AWS platform so that you can focus your efforts properly. Whether you've been working with AWS for a long time or whether you're relatively new to it, we encourage you to carefully read this book from cover to cover.

Passing the AWS Certified Solutions Architect – Associate exam requires understanding the components and operation of the core AWS services as well as how those services interact with each other. Read through the official documentation for the various AWS services. Amazon offers HTML, PDF, and Kindle documentation for many of them. Use this book as a guide to help you identify your strengths and weaknesses so that you can focus your study efforts properly.

Hands-on experience is crucial for exam success. Each chapter in this *AWS Certified Solutions Architect Study Guide: Associate SAA-C01 Exam, Second Edition* contains hands-on exercises that you should strive to complete during or immediately after your reading of the chapter. It's vital to understand that the exercises don't cover every possible scenario for every AWS service. In fact, it's quite the opposite. The exercises provide you with a foundation to build on. Use them as your starting point, but don't be afraid to venture out on your own. Feel free to modify them to match the variables and scenarios you might encounter in your own organization. Keep in mind that some of the exercises and figures use the AWS web console, which is in constant flux. As such, screenshots and step-by-step details of exercises may change. Use these eventualities as excuses to dig into the AWS online documentation and browse around the web console on your own. Also remember that although you can complete many of the exercises within the bounds of the AWS Free Tier, getting enough practice to pass the exam will likely require you to spend some money. But it's money well spent, as getting certified is an investment in your career and your future.

Each chapter contains review questions to thoroughly test your understanding of the services and concepts covered in that chapter. They also test your ability to integrate the concepts with information from preceding chapters. Although the difficulty of the questions varies, rest assured that they are not "fluff." We've designed the questions to help you realistically gauge your understanding and readiness for the exam. Avoid the temptation to rush through the questions to just get to the answers. Once you complete the assessment in each chapter, referring to the answer key will give you not only the correct answers but a detailed explanation as to why they're correct. It will also explain why the other answers are incorrect.

The book also contains a self-assessment exam with 39 questions, two practice exams with 50 questions each to help you gauge your readiness to take the exam, and flashcards to help you learn and retain key facts needed to prepare for the exam.

This *AWS Certified Solutions Architect Study Guide: Associate SAA-C01 Exam, Second Edition* is divided into two parts: "The Core AWS Services" and "The Well-Architected Framework."

Part I, "The Core AWS Services"

The first part of the book dives deep into each of the core AWS services. These services include ones you probably already have at least a passing familiarity with: Elastic Compute Cloud (EC2), Virtual Private Cloud (VPC), Identity and Access Management (IAM), Route 53, and Simple Storage Service (S3), to name just a few.

Some AWS services seem to serve similar or even nearly identical purposes. You'll learn about the subtle but important differences between seemingly similar services and, most importantly, when to use each.

Part II, "The Well-Architected Framework"

The second part of the book is a set of best practices and principles aimed at helping you design, implement, and operate systems in the cloud. Part II focuses on the following five pillars of good design:

- Reliability
- Performance efficiency
- Security
- Cost optimization
- Operational excellence

Each chapter of Part II revisits the core AWS services in light of a different pillar. Also, because not every AWS service is large enough to warrant its own chapter, Part II simultaneously introduces other services that, although less well known, may still show up on the exam.

Achieving the right balance among these pillars is a key skill you need to develop as a solutions architect. Prior to beginning Part II, we encourage you to peruse the Well-Architected Framework white paper, which is available for download at https://d0.awsstatic.com/whitepapers/architecture/AWS_Well-Architected_Framework.pdf.

What Does This Book Cover?

This book covers topics you need to know to prepare for the Amazon Web Services (AWS) Certified Solutions Architect – Associate exam:

Chapter 1: Introduction to Cloud Computing and AWS   This chapter overviews the AWS Cloud computing platform and its core services and concepts.

Chapter 2: Amazon Elastic Compute Cloud and Amazon Elastic Block Store   This chapter covers EC2 instances—the virtual machines that you can use to run Linux and Windows workloads on AWS. It also covers the Elastic Block Store service that EC2 instances depend on for persistent data storage.

Chapter 3: Amazon Simple Storage Service and Amazon Glacier Storage   In this chapter, you'll learn about Simple Storage Service (S3) and Glacier, which provide unlimited data storage and retrieval for AWS services, your applications, and the Internet.

Chapter 4: Amazon Virtual Private Cloud   This chapter explains Amazon Virtual Private Cloud (Amazon VPC), a virtual network that contains network resources for AWS services.

Chapter 5: Databases   In this chapter, you will learn about some different managed database services offered by AWS, including Relational Database Service (RDS), DynamoDB, and Redshift.

Chapter 6: AWS Identity and Access Management   This chapter covers AWS Identity and Access Management (IAM), which provides the primary means for protecting the AWS resources in your account.

Chapter 7: CloudTrail, CloudWatch, and AWS Config   In this chapter, you'll learn how to log, monitor, and audit your AWS resources.

Chapter 8: The Domain Name System and Network Routing: Amazon Route 53 and Amazon CloudFront   This chapter focuses on the domain name system (DNS) and Route 53, the service that provides public and private DNS hosting for both internal AWS resources and the Internet. It also covers CloudFront, Amazon's global content delivery network.

Chapter 9: The Reliability Pillar   This chapter will show you how to architect and integrate AWS services to achieve a high level of reliability for your applications. You'll learn how to plan around and recover from inevitable outages to keep your systems up and running.

Chapter 10: The Performance Efficiency Pillar   This chapter covers how to build highly performing systems and use the AWS elastic infrastructure to rapidly scale up and out to meet peak demand.

Chapter 11: The Security Pillar   In this chapter, you'll learn how to use encryption and security controls to protect the confidentiality, integrity, and availability of your data and systems on AWS. You'll also learn about the various security services such as GuardDuty, Inspector, Shield, and Web Application Firewall.

Chapter 12: The Cost Optimization Pillar   This chapter will show you how to estimate and control your costs in the cloud.

Chapter 13: The Operational Excellence Pillar   In this chapter, you'll learn how to keep your systems running smoothly on AWS. You'll learn how to implement a DevOps mind-set using CloudFormation, Systems Manager, and the AWS Developer Tools.

Interactive Online Learning Environment and Test Bank

The authors have worked hard to provide some really great tools to help you with your certification process. The interactive online learning environment that accompanies this *AWS Certified Solutions Architect Study Guide: Associate SAA-C01 Exam, Second Edition* provides a test bank with study tools to help you prepare for the certification exam—and increase your chances of passing it the first time! The test bank includes the following:

Sample Tests   All the questions in this book are provided, including the assessment test at the end of this Introduction and the chapter tests that include the review questions at the end of each chapter. In addition, there are two practice exams with 50 questions each. Use these questions to test your knowledge of the study guide material. The online test bank runs on multiple devices.

Flashcards   The online text banks include 100 flashcards specifically written to hit you hard, so don't get discouraged if you don't ace your way through them at first. They're there to ensure that you're really ready for the exam. And no worries—armed with the review questions, practice exams, and flashcards, you'll be more than prepared when exam day comes. Questions are provided in digital flashcard format (a question followed by a single correct answer). You can use the flashcards to reinforce your learning and provide last-minute test prep before the exam.

Resources   You'll find some AWS CLI and other code examples from the book for you to cut and paste for use in your own environment. A glossary of key terms from this book is also available as a fully searchable PDF.

Go to www.wiley.com/go/sybextestprep to register and gain access to this interactive online learning environment and test bank with study tools.

Exam Objectives

The AWS Certified Solutions Architect – Associate exam is intended for people who have experience in designing distributed applications and systems on the AWS platform. In general, you should have the following before taking the exam:

- A minimum of one year of hands-on experience designing systems on AWS
- Hands-on experience using the AWS services that provide compute, networking, storage, and databases
- Ability to define a solution using architectural design principles based on customer requirements.
- Ability to provide implementation guidance

- Ability to identify which AWS services meet a given technical requirement
- An understanding of the five pillars of the Well-Architected Framework
- An understanding of the AWS global infrastructure, including the network technologies used to connect them
- An understanding of AWS security services and how they integrate with traditional on-premises security infrastructure

The exam covers five different domains, with each domain broken down into objectives.

Objective Map

The following table lists each domain and its weighting in the exam, along with the chapters in the book where that domain's objectives are covered.

Domain	Percentage of Exam	Chapter
Domain 1: Design Resilient Architectures	34%	
1.1 Choose reliable/resilient storage.		2, 3, 5, 9, 10
1.2 Determine how to design decoupling mechanisms using AWS services.		5, 9, 10
1.3 Determine how to design a multitier architecture solution.		3, 4, 5, 8, 9, 10
1.4 Determine how to design high availability and/or fault tolerant architectures.		2, 3, 5, 7, 8, 9, 10
Domain 2: Define Performant Architectures	24%	
2.1 Choose performant storage and databases.		2, 3, 5, 10
2.2 Apply caching to improve performance.		8, 10
2.3 Design solutions for elasticity and scalability.		2, 3, 5, 7, 8, 10
Domain 3: Specify Secure Applications and Architectures	26%	
3.1 Determine how to secure application tiers.		2, 3, 4, 6, 7, 11
3.2 Determine how to secure data.		2, 3, 6, 7, 11

Domain	Percentage of Exam	Chapter
3.3 Define the networking infrastructure for a single VPC application.		4, 11
Domain 4: Design Cost-Optimized Architectures	10%	
4.1 Determine how to design cost-optimized storage.		2, 3, 12
4.2 Determine how to design cost-optimized compute.		2, 12
Domain 5: Define Operationally-Excellent Architectures	6%	
5.1 Choose design features in solutions that enable operational excellence.		7, 10, 13

Assessment Test

1. True/false: The Developer Support plan provides access to a support application programming interface (API).

    A. True

    B. False

2. True/false: AWS is responsible for managing the network configuration of your EC2 instances.

    A. True

    B. False

3. Which of the following services is most useful for decoupling the components of a monolithic application?

    A. SNS

    B. KMS

    C. SQS

    D. Glacier

4. An application you want to run on EC2 requires you to license it based on the number of physical CPU sockets and cores on the hardware you plan to run the application on. Which of the following tenancy models should you specify?

    A. Dedicated host

    B. Dedicated instance

    C. Shared tenancy

    D. Bring your own license

5. True/false: Changing the instance type of an EC2 instance will change its elastic IP address.

    A. True

    B. False

6. True/false: You can use a Quick Start Amazon Machine Image (AMI) to create any instance type.

    A. True

    B. False

7. Which S3 encryption option does *not* require AWS persistently storing the encryption keys it uses to decrypt data?

    A. Client-side encryption

    B. SSE-KMS

    C. SSE-S3

    D. SSE-C

8. True/false: Durability measures the percentage of likelihood that a given object will not be inadvertently lost by AWS over the course of a year.

   A. True

   B. False

9. True/false: After uploading a new object to S3, there will be a slight delay (one to two seconds) before the object is available.

   A. True

   B. False

10. You created a Virtual Private Cloud (VPC) using the Classless Inter-Domain Routing (CIDR) block 10.0.0.0/24. You need to connect to this VPC from your internal network, but the IP addresses in use on your internal network overlap with the CIDR. Which of the following is a valid way to address this problem?

    A. Remove the CIDR and use IPv6 instead.

    B. Change the VPC's CIDR.

    C. Create a new VPC with a different CIDR.

    D. Create a secondary CIDR for the VPC.

11. True/false: An EC2 instance must be in a public subnet to access the internet.

    A. True

    B. False

12. True/false: The route table for a public subnet must have a default route pointing to an Internet gateway as a target.

    A. True

    B. False

13. Which of the following use cases is well suited for DynamoDB?

    A. Running a MongoDB database on AWS

    B. Storing large binary files exceeding 1 GB in size

    C. Storing JSON documents that have a consistent structure

    D. Storing image assets for a website

14. True/false: You can create a DynamoDB global secondary index for an existing table at any time.

    A. True

    B. False

15. True/false: Enabling point-in-time RDS snapshots is sufficient to give you a recovery point objective (RPO) of less than 10 minutes.

    A. True

    B. False

16. Which of the following steps does the most to protect your AWS account?

   A. Deleting unused Identity and Access Management (IAM) policies

   B. Revoking unnecessary access for IAM users

   C. Rotating root access keys

   D. Restricting access to S3 buckets

   E. Rotating Secure Shell (SSH) key pairs

17. Which of the following can be used to encrypt the operating system of an EC2 instance?

   A. AWS Secrets Manager

   B. CloudHSM

   C. AWS Key Management Service (KMS)

   D. AWS Security Token Service (STS)

18. What is a difference between a token generated by the AWS Security Token Service (STS) and an IAM access key?

   A. The token generated by STS can't be used by an IAM principal.

   B. An IAM access key is unique.

   C. The token generated by STS can be used only once.

   D. The token generated by STS expires.

19. True/false: EC2 sends instance memory utilization metrics to CloudWatch every five minutes.

   A. True

   B. False

20. You configured a CloudWatch alarm to monitor CPU utilization for an EC2 instance. The alarm began in the INSUFFICIENT_DATA state and then entered the ALARM state. What can you conclude from this?

   A. The instance recently rebooted.

   B. CPU utilization is too high.

   C. The CPU utilization metric crossed the alarm threshold.

   D. The instance is stopped.

21. Where do AWS Config and CloudTrail store their logs?

   A. S3 buckets

   B. CloudWatch Logs

   C. CloudTrail Events

   D. DynamoDB

   E. Amazon Athena

22. True/false: An EC2 instance in a private subnet can resolve an "A" resource record for a public hosted zone hosted in Route 53.

    A. True

    B. False

23. You want to use Route 53 to send users to the application load balancer closest to them. Which of the following routing policies lets you do this with the least effort?

    A. Latency routing

    B. Geolocation routing

    C. Geoproximity routing

    D. Edge routing

24. True/false: You can use an existing domain name with Route 53 without switching its registration to AWS.

    A. True

    B. False

25. You're designing an application that takes multiple image files and combines them into a video file that users on the Internet can download. Which of the following can help you quickly implement your application in the fastest, most highly available, and most cost-effective manner?

    A. EC2 spot fleet

    B. Lambda

    C. Relational Database Service (RDS)

    D. Auto Scaling

26. You're using EC2 Auto Scaling and want to implement a scaling policy that adds one extra instance only when the average CPU utilization of each instance exceeds 90 percent. However, you don't want it to add more than one instance every five minutes. Which of the following scaling policies should you use?

    A. Simple

    B. Step

    C. Target tracking

    D. PercentChangeInCapacity

27. True/false: EC2 Auto Scaling automatically replaces group instances directly terminated by the root user.

    A. True

    B. False

28. Which ElastiCache engine can persistently store data?

   A. MySQL

   B. Memcached

   C. MongoDB

   D. Redis

29. Which of the following is *not* an AWS service?

   A. CloudFormation

   B. Puppet

   C. OpsWorks

   D. Snowball

30. True/false: S3 cross-region replication uses transfer acceleration.

   A. True

   B. False

31. Which of the following services can you deactivate on your account?

   A. Security Token Service (STS)

   B. CloudWatch

   C. Virtual Private Cloud (VPC)

   D. Lambda

32. Which of the following services can alert you to malware on an EC2 instance?

   A. AWS GuardDuty

   B. AWS Inspector

   C. AWS Shield

   D. AWS Web Application Firewall

33. True/false: If versioning is enabled on an S3 bucket, applying encryption to an unencrypted object in that bucket will create a new, encrypted version of that object.

   A. True

   B. False

34. Which instance type will, if left running, continue to incur costs?

   A. Spot

   B. Standard reserved

   C. On-demand

   D. Convertible reserved

35. True/false: The EBS Lifecycle Manager can take snapshots of volumes that were once attached to terminated instances.

   A. True

   B. False

36. Which of the following lets you spin up new web servers the quickest?

   A. Lambda

   B. Auto Scaling

   C. Elastic Container Service

   D. CloudFront

37. True/false: CloudFormation stack names are case-sensitive.

   A. True

   B. False

38. Where might CodeDeploy look for the appspec.yml file? (Choose two.)

   A. GitHub

   B. CodeCommit

   C. S3

   D. CloudFormation

39. True/false: You can use either CodeDeploy or an AWS Systems Manager command document to deploy a Lambda application.

   A. True

   B. False

Answers to Assessment Test

1. **B.** The Business plan offers access to a support API, but the Developer plan does not. See Chapter 1 for more information.

2. **B.** Customers are responsible for managing the network configuration of EC2 instances. AWS is responsible for the physical network infrastructure. See Chapter 1 for more information.

3. **C.** Simple Queue Service (SQS) allows for event-driven messaging within distributed systems that can decouple while coordinating the discrete steps of a larger process. See Chapter 1 for more information.

4. **A.** The dedicated host option lets you see the number of physical CPU sockets and cores on a host. See Chapter 2 for more information.

5. **B.** An elastic IP address will not change. A public IP address attached to an instance will change if the instance is stopped, as would happen when changing the instance type. See Chapter 2 for more information.

6. **A.** A Quick Start AMI is independent of the instance type. See Chapter 2 for more information.

7. **D.** With SSE-C you provide your own keys for Amazon to use to decrypt and encrypt your data. AWS doesn't persistently store the keys. See Chapter 3 for more information.

8. **A.** Durability corresponds to an average annual expected loss of objects stored on S3, not including objects you delete. Availability measures the amount of time S3 will be available to let you retrieve those objects. See Chapter 3 for more information.

9. **B.** S3 uses a read-after-write consistency model for new objects, so once you upload an object to S3, it's immediately available. See Chapter 3 for more information.

10. **C.** You can't change the primary CIDR for a VPC, so you must create a new one to connect it to your internal network. See Chapter 4 for more information.

11. **B.** An EC2 instance can access the Internet from a private subnet provided it uses a NAT gateway or NAT instance. See Chapter 4 for more information.

12. **A.** The definition of a public subnet is a subnet that has a default route pointing to an Internet gateway as a target. Otherwise, it's a private subnet. See Chapter 4 for more information.

13. **C.** DynamoDB is a key-value store that can be used to store items up to 400 KB in size. See Chapter 5 for more information.

14. **A.** You can create a global secondary index for an existing table at any time. You can create a local secondary index only when you create the table. See Chapter 5 for more information.

15. A. Enabling point-in-time recovery gives you an RPO of about five minutes. The recovery time objective (RTO) depends on the amount of data to restore. See Chapter 5 for more information.

16. B. Revoking unnecessary access for IAM users is the most effective of the listed measures for protecting your AWS account. See Chapter 6 for more information.

17. C. KMS can be used to encrypt Elastic Block Store (EBS) volumes that store an instance's operating system. See Chapter 6 for more information.

18. D. STS tokens expire while IAM access keys do not. An STS token can be used more than once. IAM access keys and STS tokens are both unique. An IAM principal can use an STS token. See Chapter 6 for more information.

19. B. EC2 doesn't track instance memory utilization. See Chapter 7 for more information.

20. C. The transition to the ALARM state simply implies that the metric crossed a threshold but doesn't tell you what the threshold is. Newly created alarms start out in the INSUFFICIENT_DATA state. See Chapter 7 for more information.

21. A. Both store their logs in S3 buckets. See Chapter 7 for more information.

22. A. An EC2 instance in a private subnet still has access to Amazon's private DNS servers, which can resolve records stored in public hosted zones. See Chapter 8 for more information.

23. C. Geoproximity routing routes users to the location closest to them. Geolocation routing requires you to create records for specific locations or create a default record. See Chapter 8 for more information.

24. A. Route 53 is a true DNS service in that it can host zones for any domain name. You can also register domain names with or transfer them to Route 53. See Chapter 8 for more information.

25. B. Lambda is a highly available, reliable, "serverless" compute platform that runs functions as needed and scales elastically to meet demand. EC2 spot instances can be shut down on short notice. See Chapter 9 for more information.

26. A. A simple scaling policy changes the group size and then has a cooldown period before doing so again. Step scaling policies don't have cooldown periods. Target tracking policies attempt to keep a metric at a set value. PercentChangeInCapacity is a simple scaling adjustment type, not a scaling policy. See Chapter 9 for more information.

27. A. Auto Scaling always attempts to maintain the minimum group size or, if set, the desired capacity. See Chapter 9 for more information.

28. D. ElastiCache supports Memcached and Redis, but only the latter can store data persistently. See Chapter 10 for more information.

29. B. Puppet is a configuration management platform that AWS offers via OpsWorks but is not itself an AWS service. See Chapter 10 for more information.

30. B. S3 cross-region replication transfers objects between different buckets. Transfer acceleration uses a CloudFront edge location to speed up transfers between S3 and the Internet. See Chapter 10 for more information.

31. A. You can deactivate STS for all regions except US East. See Chapter 11 for more information.

32. A. GuardDuty looks for potentially malicious activity. Inspector looks for vulnerabilities that may result in compromise. Shield and Web Application Firewall protect applications from attack. See Chapter 11 for more information.

33. A. Applying encryption to an unencrypted object will create a new, encrypted version of that object. Previous versions remain unencrypted. See Chapter 11 for more information.

34. C. On-demand instances will continue to run and incur costs. Reserved instances cost the same whether they're running or stopped. Spot instances will be terminated when the spot price exceeds your bid price. See Chapter 12 for more information.

35. A. The EBS Lifecycle Manager can take scheduled snapshots of any EBS volume, regardless of attachment state. See Chapter 12 for more information.

36. C. Elastic Container Service lets you run containers that can launch in a matter of seconds. EC2 instances take longer. Lambda is "serverless," so you can't use it to run a web server. CloudFront provides caching but isn't a web server. See Chapter 12 for more information.

37. A. Almost everything in CloudFormation is case sensitive. See Chapter 13 for more information.

38. A, C. CodeDeploy looks for the `appspec.yml` file with the application files it is to deploy, which can be stored in S3 or on GitHub. See Chapter 13 for more information.

39. B. You can use CodeDeploy to deploy an application to Lambda or EC2 instances. But an AWS Systems Manager command document works only on EC2 instances. See Chapter 13 for more information.

The Core AWS Services

Chapter

1

Introduction to Cloud Computing and AWS

The cloud is where much of the serious technology innovation and growth happens these days, and Amazon Web Services (AWS), more than any other, is the platform of choice for business and institutional workloads. If you want to be successful as an AWS solutions architect, you'll first need to make sure you understand what the cloud really is and how Amazon's end of it works.

To make sure you've got the big picture, this chapter will explore the basics:

What makes cloud computing different from other applications and client-server models

How the AWS platform provides secure and flexible virtual networked environments for your resources

How AWS provides such a high level of service reliability

How to access and manage your AWS-based resources

Where you can go for documentation and help with your AWS deployments

Cloud Computing and Virtualization

The technology that lies at the core of all cloud operations is virtualization. As illustrated in Figure 1.1, virtualization lets you divide the hardware resources of a single physical server into smaller units. That physical server could therefore host multiple virtual machines running their own complete operating systems, each with its own memory, storage, and network access.

FIGURE 1.1   A virtual machine host

Virtualization's flexibility makes it possible to provision a virtual server in a matter of seconds, run it for exactly the time your project requires, and then shut it down. The resources released will become instantly available to other workloads. The usage density you can achieve lets you squeeze the greatest value from your hardware and makes it easy to generate experimental and sandboxed environments.

Cloud Computing Architecture

Major cloud providers like AWS have enormous server farms where hundreds of thousands of servers and data drives are maintained along with the network cabling necessary to connect them. A well-built virtualized environment could provide a virtual server using storage, memory, compute cycles, and network bandwidth collected from the most efficient mix of available sources it can find.

A cloud computing platform offers on-demand, self-service access to pooled compute resources where your usage is metered and billed according to the volume you consume. Cloud computing systems allow for precise billing models, sometimes involving fractions of a penny for an hour of consumption.

Cloud Computing Optimization

The cloud is a great choice for so many serious workloads because it's scalable, elastic, and, often, a lot cheaper than traditional alternatives. Effective deployment provisioning will require some insight into those three features.

Scalability

A scalable infrastructure can efficiently meet unexpected increases in demand for your application by automatically adding resources. As Figure 1.2 shows, this most often means dynamically increasing the number of virtual machines (or *instances* as AWS calls them) you've got running.

FIGURE 1.2   Copies of a machine image are added to new VMs as they're launched.

AWS offers its autoscaling service through which you define a machine image that can be instantly and automatically replicated and launched into multiple instances to meet demand.

Elasticity

The principle of elasticity covers some of the same ground as scalability—both address managing changing demand. However, while the images used in a scalable environment let you ramp up capacity to meet rising demand, an elastic infrastructure will automatically *reduce* capacity when demand drops. This makes it possible to control costs, since you'll run resources only when they're needed.

Cost Management

Besides the ability to control expenses by closely managing the resources you use, cloud computing transitions your IT spending from a capital expenditure (capex) framework into something closer to operational expenditure (opex).

In practical terms, this means you no longer have to spend $10,000 up front for every new server you deploy—along with associated electricity, cooling, security, and rack space costs. Instead, you're billed much smaller incremental amounts for as long as your application runs.

That doesn't necessarily mean your long-term cloud-based opex costs will always be less than you'd pay over the lifetime of a comparable data center deployment. But it does mean you won't have to expose yourself to risky speculation about your long-term needs. If, sometime in the future, changing demand calls for new hardware, AWS will be able to deliver it within a minute or two.

To help you understand the full implications of cloud compute spending, AWS provides a free Total Cost of Ownership (TCO) Calculator at `https://aws.amazon.com/tco-calculator/`. This calculator helps you perform proper "apples-to-apples" comparisons between your current data center costs and what an identical operation would cost you on AWS.

The AWS Cloud

Keeping up with the steady stream of innovative new services showing up on the AWS Console can be frustrating. But as a solutions architect, your main focus should be on the core service categories. This section briefly summarizes each of the core categories (as shown in Table 1.1) and then does the same for key individual services. You'll learn much more about all of these (and more) services through the rest of the book, but it's worth focusing on these short definitions, as they lie at the foundation of everything else you're going to learn.

TABLE 1.1   AWS service categories

Category	Function
Compute	Services replicating the traditional role of local physical servers for the cloud, offering advanced configurations including autoscaling, load balancing, and even serverless architectures (a method for delivering server functionality with a very small footprint)
Networking	Application connectivity, access control, and enhanced remote connections
Storage	Various kinds of storage platforms designed to fit a range of both immediate accessibility and long-term backup needs
Database	Managed data solutions for use cases requiring multiple data formats: relational, NoSQL, or caching
Application management	Monitoring, auditing, and configuring AWS account services and running resources
Security and identity	Services for managing authentication and authorization, data and connection encryption, and integration with third-party authentication management systems
Application integration	Tools for designing loosely coupled, integrated, and API-friendly application development processes

Table 1.2 describes the functions of some core AWS services, organized by category.

TABLE 1.2   Core AWS services (by category)

Category	Service	Function
Compute	Elastic Compute Cloud (EC2)	EC2 server instances provide virtual versions of the servers you would run in your local data center. EC2 instances can be provisioned with the CPU, memory, storage, and network interface profile to meet any application need, from a simple web server to one part of a cluster of instances providing an integrated multitiered fleet architecture. Since EC2 instances are virtual, they're much more resource-efficient and deploy nearly instantly.

TABLE 1.2   Core AWS services (by category) *(continued)*

Category	Service	Function
	Lambda	Serverless application architectures like the one provided by Amazon's Lambda service allow you to provide responsive public-facing services without the need for a server that's actually running 24/7. Instead, network events (like consumer requests) can trigger the execution of a predefined code-based operation. When the operation (which can currently run for as long as 15 minutes) is complete, the Lambda event ends, and all resources automatically shut down.
	Auto Scaling	Copies of running EC2 instances can be defined as image templates and automatically launched (or *scaled up*) when client demand can't be met by existing instances. As demand drops, unused instances can be terminated (or *scaled down*).
	Elastic Load Balancing	Incoming network traffic can be directed between multiple web servers to ensure that a single web server isn't overwhelmed while other servers are underused or that traffic isn't directed to failed servers.
	Elastic Beanstalk	Beanstalk is a managed service that abstracts the provisioning of AWS compute and networking infrastructure. You are required to do nothing more than push your application code, and Beanstalk automatically launches and manages all the necessary services in the background.
Networking	Virtual Private Cloud (VPC)	VPCs are highly configurable networking environments designed to host your EC2 (and RDS) instances. You use VPC-based tools to closely control inbound and outbound network access to and between instances.
	Direct Connect	By purchasing fast and secure network connections to AWS through a third-party provider, you can use Direct Connect to establish an enhanced direct tunnel between your local data center or office and your AWS-based VPCs.

Category	Service	Function
	Route 53	Route 53 is the AWS DNS service that lets you manage domain registration, record administration, routing protocols, and health checks, which are all fully integrated with the rest of your AWS resources
	CloudFront	CloudFront is Amazon's distributed global content delivery network (CDN). When properly configured, a CloudFront distribution can store cached versions of your site's content at edge locations around the world so they can be delivered to customers on request with the greatest efficiency and lowest latency.
Storage	Simple Storage Service (S3)	S3 offers highly versatile, reliable, and inexpensive object storage that's great for data storage and backups. It's also commonly used as part of larger AWS production processes, including through the storage of script, template, and log files.
	Glacier	A good choice for when you need large data archives stored cheaply over the long term and can live with retrieval delays measuring in the hours. Glacier's lifecycle management is closely integrated with S3.
	Elastic Block Store (EBS)	EBS provides the virtual data drives that host the operating systems and working data of an EC2 instance. They're meant to mimic the function of the storage drives and partitions attached to physical servers.
	Storage Gateway	Storage Gateway is a hybrid storage system that exposes AWS cloud storage as a local, on-premises appliance. Storage Gateway can be a great tool for migration and data backup and as part of disaster recovery operations.
Database	Relational Database Service (RDS)	RDS is a managed service that builds you a stable, secure, and reliable database instance. You can run a variety of SQL database engines on RDS, including MySQL, Microsoft SQL Server, Oracle, and Amazon's own Aurora.

TABLE 1.2   Core AWS services (by category) *(continued)*

Category	Service	Function
	DynamoDB	DynamoDB can be used for fast, flexible, highly scalable, and managed nonrelational (NoSQL) database workloads.
Application management	CloudWatch	No deployment is complete without some kind of ongoing monitoring in place. And generating endless log files doesn't make much sense if there's no one keeping an eye on them. CloudWatch can be set to monitor process performance and utilization through events and, when preset thresholds are met, either send you a message or trigger an automated response.
	CloudFormation	This service enables you to use template files to define full and complex AWS deployments. The ability to script your use of any AWS resources makes it easier and more attractive to automate, standardizing and speeding up the application launch process.
	CloudTrail	CloudTrail collects records of all your account's API events. This history is useful for account auditing and troubleshooting purposes.
	Config	The Config service is designed to help you with change management and compliance for your AWS account. You first define a desired configuration state, and Config will get to work evaluating any future states against that ideal. When a configuration change pushes too far from the ideal baseline, you'll be notified.
Security and identity	Identity and Access Management (IAM)	You use IAM to administrate user and programmatic access and authentication to your AWS account. Through the use of users, groups, roles, and policies, you can control exactly who and what can access and/or work with any of your AWS resources.
	Key Management Service (KMS)	KMS is a managed service that allows you to administrate the creation and use of encryption keys to secure data used by and for any of your AWS resources.

Category	Service	Function
	Directory Service	For AWS environments that need to manage identities and relationships, Directory Service can integrate AWS resources with identity providers like Amazon Cognito and Microsoft AD domains.
Application integration	Simple Notification Service (SNS)	SNS is a notification tool that can automate the publishing of alert *topics* to other services (to an SQS Queue or to trigger a Lambda function, for instance), to mobile devices, or to recipients using email or SMS.
	Simple WorkFlow (SWF)	SWF lets you coordinate a series of tasks that must be performed using a range of AWS services or even nondigital (meaning, human) events. SWF can be the "glue" and "lubrication" that both speed a complex process and keep all the moving parts from falling apart.
	Simple Queue Service (SQS)	SQS allows for event-driven messaging within distributed systems that can decouple while coordinating the discrete steps of a larger process. The data contained in your SQS messages will be reliably delivered, adding to the fault-tolerant qualities of an application.
	API Gateway	This service enables you to create and manage secure and reliable APIs for your AWS-based applications.

AWS Platform Architecture

AWS maintains data centers for its physical servers around the world. Because the centers are so widely distributed, you can reduce your own services' network transfer latency by hosting your workloads geographically close to your users. It can also help you manage compliance with regulations requiring you to keep data within a particular legal jurisdiction.

Data centers exist within AWS regions, of which there are currently 17—not including private U.S. government AWS GovCloud regions—although this number is constantly growing. It's important to always be conscious of the particular region you have selected when you launch new AWS resources, as pricing and service availability can vary from one to the next. Table 1.3 shows a list of all 17 (nongovernment) regions along with each region's name and core endpoint addresses.

TABLE 1.3 A list of publicly accessible AWS regions

Region Name	Region	Endpoint
US East (Ohio)	us-east-2	us-east-2.amazonaws.com
US East (N. Virginia)	us-east-1	us-east-1.amazonaws.com
US West (N. California)	us-west-1	us-west-1.amazonaws.com
US West (Oregon)	us-west-2	us-west-2.amazonaws.com
Asia Pacific (Mumbai)	ap-south-1	ap-south-1.amazonaws.com
Asia Pacific (Seoul)	ap-northeast-2	ap-northeast-2.amazonaws.com
Asia Pacific (Osaka-Local)	ap-northeast-3	ap-northeast-3.amazonaws.com
Asia Pacific (Singapore)	ap-southeast-1	ap-southeast-1.amazonaws.com
Asia Pacific (Sydney)	ap-southeast-2	ap-southeast-2.amazonaws.com
Asia Pacific (Tokyo)	ap-northeast-1	ap-northeast-1.amazonaws.com
Canada (Central)	ca-central-1	ca-central-1.amazonaws.com
China (Beijing)	cn-north-1	cn-north-1.amazonaws.com.cn
EU (Frankfurt)	eu-central-1	eu-central-1.amazonaws.com
EU (Ireland)	eu-west-1	eu-west-1.amazonaws.com
EU (London)	eu-west-2	eu-west-2.amazonaws.com
EU (Paris)	eu-west-3	eu-west-3.amazonaws.com
South America (São Paulo)	sa-east-1	sa-east-1.amazonaws.com

Endpoint addresses are used to access your AWS resources remotely from within application code or scripts. Prefixes like ec2, apigateway, or cloudformation are often added to the endpoints to specify a particular AWS service. Such an address might look like this: cloudformation.us-east-2.amazonaws.com. You can see a complete list of endpoint addresses and their prefixes at https://docs.aws.amazon.com/general/latest/gr/rande.html#ec2_region.

Because low-latency access is so important, certain AWS services are offered from designated edge network locations. These services include Amazon CloudFront, Amazon Route 53, AWS Firewall Manager, AWS Shield, and AWS WAF. For a complete and up-to-date list of available locations, see https://aws.amazon.com/about-aws/global-infrastructure/regional-product-services/.

Physical AWS data centers are exposed within your AWS account as availability zones. There might be half a dozen availability zones within a region, identified using names like us-east-1a.

You organize your resources from a particular region within one or more virtual private clouds (VPCs). A VPC is effectively a network address space within which you can create network subnets and associate them with particular availability zones. When configured properly, this architecture can provide effective resource isolation and durable replication.

AWS Reliability and Compliance

AWS has a lot of the basic regulatory, legal, and security groundwork covered before you even launch your first service.

AWS has invested significant planning and funds into resources and expertise relating to infrastructure administration. Its heavily protected and secretive data centers, layers of redundancy, and carefully developed best-practice protocols would be difficult or even impossible for a regular enterprise to replicate.

Where applicable, resources on the AWS platform are compliant with dozens of national and international standards, frameworks, and certifications, including ISO 9001, FedRAMP, NIST, and GDPR. (See https://aws.amazon.com/compliance/programs/ for more information.)

The AWS Shared Responsibility Model

Of course, those guarantees cover only the underlying AWS platform. The way you decide to use AWS resources is your business—and therefore your responsibility. So, it's important to be familiar with the AWS Shared Responsibility Model.

AWS guarantees the secure and uninterrupted operation of its "cloud." That means its physical servers, storage devices, networking infrastructure, and managed services. AWS customers, as illustrated in Figure 1.3, are responsible for whatever happens *within* that cloud. This covers the security and operation of installed operating systems, client-side data, the movement of data across networks, end-user authentication and access, and customer data.

FIGURE 1.3   The AWS Shared Responsibility Model

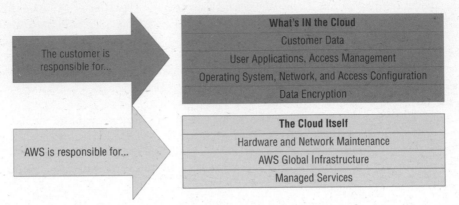

The AWS Service Level Agreement

By "guarantee," AWS doesn't mean that service disruptions or security breaches will *never* occur. Drives may stop spinning, major electricity systems may fail, and natural disasters may happen. But when something does go wrong, AWS will provide service credits to reimburse customers for their *direct* losses whenever uptimes fall below a defined threshold. Of course, that won't help you recover customer confidence or lost business.

The exact percentage of the guarantee will differ according to service. The service level agreement (SLA) rate for AWS EC2, for instance, is set to 99.99 percent—meaning that you can expect your EC2 instances, ECS containers, and EBS storage devices to be available for all but around four minutes of each month.

The important thing to remember is that it's not *if* things will fail but *when*. Build your applications to be geographically dispersed and fault tolerant so that when things do break, your users will barely notice.

Working with AWS

Whatever AWS services you choose to run, you'll need a way to manage them all. The browser-based management console is an excellent way to introduce yourself to a service's features and to how it will perform in the real world. There are few AWS administration tasks that you can't do from the console, which provides plenty of useful visualizations and helpful documentation. But as you become more familiar with the way things work, and especially as your AWS deployments become more complex, you'll probably find yourself getting more of your serious work done away from the console.

The AWS CLI

The AWS Command Line Interface (CLI) lets you run complex AWS operations from your local command line. Once you get the hang of how it works, you'll discover that it can make things much simpler and more efficient.

As an example, suppose you need to launch a half-dozen EC2 instances to make up a microservices environment. Each instance is meant to play a separate role and therefore will require a subtly different provisioning process. Clicking through window after window to launch the instances from the console can quickly become tedious and time-consuming, especially if you find yourself repeating the task every few days. But the whole process can alternatively be incorporated into a simple script that you can run from your local terminal shell or PowerShell interface using the AWS CLI.

Installing and configuring the AWS CLI on Linux, Windows, or macOS machines is not hard at all, but the details might change depending on your platform. For the most up-to-date instructions, see `https://docs.aws.amazon.com/cli/latest/userguide/installing.html`.

AWS SDKs

If you want to incorporate access to your AWS resources into your application code, you'll need to use an AWS software development kit (SDK) for the language you're working with. AWS currently offers SDKs for nine languages including Java, .NET, and Python, and a number of mobile SDKs that include Android and iOS. There are also toolkits available for Eclipse, Visual Studio, and VSTS.

You can see a full overview of AWS developer tools at `https://aws.amazon.com/tools/`.

Technical Support and Online Resources

Things won't always go smoothly for you—on AWS just as everywhere else in your life. Sooner or later, you'll need some kind of technical or account support. There's a variety of types of support, and you should understand what's available.

One of the first things you'll be asked to decide when you create a new AWS account is which support plan you'd like. Your business needs and budget will determine the way you answer this question.

Support Plans

The Basic plan is free with every account and gives you access to customer service, along with documentation, white papers, and the support forum. Customer service covers billing and account support issues.

The Developer plan starts at $29/month and adds access for one account holder to a Cloud Support associate along with limited general guidance and "system impaired" response.

For $100/month (and up), the Business plan will deliver faster guaranteed response times to unlimited users for help with "impaired" systems, personal guidance and troubleshooting, and a support API.

Finally, Enterprise support plans cover all of the other features, plus direct access to AWS solutions architects for operational and design reviews, your own technical account manager, and something called a support concierge. For complex, mission-critical deployments, those benefits can make a big difference. But they'll cost you at least $15,000 each month.

You can read more about AWS support plans at https://aws.amazon.com/premiumsupport/compare-plans/.

Other Support Resources

There's plenty of self-serve support available outside of the official support plans.

- AWS community help forums are open to anyone with a valid AWS account (https://forums.aws.amazon.com).
- Extensive and well-maintained AWS documentation is available at https://aws.amazon.com/documentation/.
- The AWS Well-Architected page (https://aws.amazon.com/architecture/well-architected/) is a hub that links to some valuable white papers and documentation addressing best practices for cloud deployment design.

Summary

Cloud computing is built on the ability to efficiently divide physical resources into smaller but flexible virtual units. Those units can be "rented" by businesses on a pay-as-you-go basis and used to satisfy just about any networked application and/or workflow's needs in an affordable, scalable, and elastic way.

Amazon Web Services provides reliable and secure resources that are replicated and globally distributed across a growing number of regions and availability zones. AWS infrastructure is designed to be compliant with best-practice and regulatory standards—although the Shared Responsibility Model leaves you in charge of what you place *within* the cloud.

The growing family of AWS services covers just about any digital needs you can imagine, with core services addressing compute, networking, database, storage, security, and application management and integration needs.

You manage your AWS resources from the management console, with the AWS CLI, or through code generated using an AWS SDK.

Technical and account support is available through support plans and through documentation and help forums. AWS also makes white papers and user and developer guides available for free as Kindle books. You can access them at this address:

```
https://www.amazon.com/default/e/B007R6MVQ6/
ref=dp_byline_cont_ebooks_1?redirectedFromKindleDbs=true
```

Exam Essentials

Understand AWS platform architecture.   AWS divides its servers and storage devices into globally distributed regions and, within regions, into availability zones. These divisions permit replication to enhance availability but also permit process and resource isolation for security and compliance purposes. You should design your own deployments in ways that take advantage of those features.

Understand how to use AWS administration tools.   While you will use your browser to access the AWS administration console at least from time to time, most of your serious work will probably happen through the AWS CLI and, from within your application code, through an AWS SDK.

Understand how to choose a support plan.   Understanding which support plan level is right for a particular customer is an important element in building a successful deployment. Become familiar with the various options.

Exercise

Use the AWS CLI

Install (if necessary) and configure the AWS CLI on your local system and demonstrate it's running properly by listing the buckets that currently exist in your account. For extra marks, create an S3 bucket and then copy a simple file or document from your machine to your new bucket. From the browser console, confirm that the file reached its target.

To get you started, here are some basic CLI commands:

```
aws s3 ls
aws s3 mb <bucketname>
aws s3 cp /path/to/file.txt s3://bucketname
```

Review Questions

1. Your developers want to run fully provisioned EC2 instances to support their application code deployments but prefer not to have to worry about manually configuring and launching the necessary infrastructure. Which of the following should they use?

    A. AWS Lambda

    B. AWS Elastic Beanstalk

    C. Amazon EC2 Auto Scaling

    D. Amazon Route 53

2. Which service would you use to most effectively reduce the latency your end users experience when accessing your application resources over the Internet?

    A. Amazon CloudFront

    B. Amazon Route 53

    C. Elastic Load Balancing

    D. Amazon Glacier

3. Which of the following is the best use-case scenario for Elastic Block Store?

    A. You need a cheap and reliable place to store files your application can access.

    B. You need a safe place to store backup archives from your local servers.

    C. You need a source for on-demand compute cycles to meet fluctuating demand for your application.

    D. You need persistent storage for the file system run by your EC2 instance.

4. Which of the following is the best tool to control access to your AWS services and administration console?

    A. AWS Identity and Access Management (IAM)

    B. Key Management Service (KMS)

    C. AWS Directory Service

    D. Simple WorkFlow (SWF)

5. For data workloads requiring more speed and flexibility than a closely defined structure offers, which service should you choose?

    A. Relational Database Service (RDS)

    B. Amazon Aurora

    C. Amazon DynamoDB

    D. Key Management Service (KMS)

6. Which of the following is the correct endpoint address for an EC2 instance running in the AWS Ireland region?

   A. `compute.eu-central-1.amazonaws.com`

   B. `ec2.eu-central-1.amazonaws.com`

   C. `elasticcomputecloud.eu-west-2.amazonaws.com`

   D. `ec2.eu-west-1.amazonaws.com`

7. What does the term *availability zone* refer to in AWS documentation?

   A. One or more isolated physical data centers within an AWS region

   B. All the hardware resources within a single region

   C. A single network subnet used by resources within a single region

   D. A single isolated server room within a data center

8. Which AWS tool lets you organize your EC2 instances and configure their network connectivity and access control?

   A. Load Balancing

   B. Amazon Virtual Private Cloud (VPC)

   C. Amazon CloudFront

   D. AWS endpoints

9. You want to be sure that the application you're building using EC2 and S3 resources will be reliable enough to meet the regulatory standards required within your industry. What should you check?

   A. Historical uptime log records

   B. The AWS Program Compliance Tool

   C. The AWS service level agreement (SLA)

   D. The AWS Shared Responsibility Model

10. Which of the following would you use to administrate your AWS infrastructure via your local command line or shell scripts?

    A. AWS Config

    B. AWS CLI

    C. AWS SDK

    D. The AWS Console

11. Your company needs direct access to AWS support for both development and IT team leaders. Which support plan should you purchase?

    A. Business

    B. Developer

    C. Basic

    D. Enterprise

Chapter

2

Amazon Elastic Compute Cloud and Amazon Elastic Block Store

THE AWS CERTIFIED SOLUTIONS ARCHITECT ASSOCIATE EXAM OBJECTIVES COVERED IN THIS CHAPTER MAY INCLUDE, BUT ARE NOT LIMITED TO, THE FOLLOWING:

Domain 1: Design Resilient Architectures

✓ 1.1 Choose reliable/resilient storage.

✓ 1.4 Determine how to design high availability and/or fault tolerant architectures.

Domain 2: Define Performant Architectures

✓ 2.1 Choose performant storage and databases.

✓ 2.3 Design solutions for elasticity and scalability.

Domain 3: Specify Secure Applications and Architectures

✓ 3.1 Determine how to secure application tiers.

✓ 3.2 Determine how to secure data.

Domain 4: Design Cost-Optimized Architectures

✓ 4.1 Determine how to design cost-optimized storage.

✓ 4.2 Determine how to design cost-optimized compute.

Introduction

The ultimate focus of a traditional data center/server room is its precious servers. But, to make those servers useful, you'll need to add racks, power supplies, cabling, switches, firewalls, and cooling.

AWS's Elastic Compute Cloud (EC2) is designed to replicate the data center/server room experience as closely as possible. At the center of it all is the EC2 virtual server, known as an *instance*. But, like the local server room I just described, EC2 provides a range of tools meant to support and enhance your instance's operations.

This chapter will explore the tools and practices used to fully leverage the power of the EC2 ecosystem, including the following:

- Provisioning an EC2 instance with the right hardware resources for your project
- Configuring the right base operating system for your application needs
- Building a secure and effective network environment for your instance
- Adding scripts to run as the instance boots to support (or start) your application
- Choosing the best EC2 pricing model for your needs
- Understanding how to manage and leverage the EC2 instance lifecycle
- Choosing the right storage drive type for your needs
- Securing your EC2 resources using key pairs, security groups, and Identity and Access Management (IAM) roles
- Accessing your instance as an administrator or end-user client

EC2 Instances

An EC2 instance may only be a virtualized and abstracted subset of a physical server, but it behaves just like the real thing. It'll have access to storage, memory, and a network interface, and its primary drive will come with a fresh and clean operating system running.

It's up to you to decide what kind of hardware resources you want your instance to have, what operating system and software stack you'd like it to run, and, ultimately, how much you'll pay for it. Let's see how all that works.

Provisioning Your Instance

You configure your instance's operating system and software stack, hardware specs (the CPU power, memory, primary storage, and network performance), and environment before launching it. The OS is defined by the Amazon Machine Image (AMI) you choose, and the hardware follows the instance type.

EC2 Amazon Machine Images

An AMI is really just a template document that contains information telling EC2 what OS and application software to include on the root data volume of the instance it's about to launch. There are four kinds of AMIs.

Amazon Quick Start AMIs   Amazon Quick Start images appear at the top of the list in the console when you start the process of launching a new instance. The Quick Start AMIs are popular choices and include various releases of Linux or Windows Server OSs and some specialty images for performing common operations (like deep learning and database). These AMIs are up-to-date and officially supported.

AWS Marketplace AMIs   AMIs from the AWS Marketplace are official, production-ready images provided and supported by industry vendors like SAP and Cisco.

Community AMIs   There are more than 100,000 images available as Community AMIs. Many of these images are AMIs created and maintained by independent vendors and are usually built to meet a specific need. This is a good catalog to search if you're planning an application built on a custom combination of software resources.

Private AMIs   You can also store images created from your own instance deployments as private AMIs. Why would you want to do that? You might, for instance, want the ability to scale up the number of instances you've got running to meet growing demand. Having a reliable instance image as an AMI makes incorporating autoscaling easy. You can also share images as AMIs or import VMs from your local infrastructure (by way of AWS S3) using the AWS VM Import/Export tool.

A particular AMI will be available in only a single region—although there will often be images with identical functionality in all regions. Keep this in mind as you plan your deployments: invoking the ID of an AMI in one region while working from within a different region will fail.

An Important Note About Billing

Besides the normal charges for running an EC2 instance, your AWS account might also be billed hourly amounts or license fees for the use of the AMI software itself. Although vendors make every effort to clearly display the charges for their AMIs, it's your responsibility to accept and honor those charges.

C5,

X1e

P3,

H1,

Compute Optimized   For more demanding web servers and high-end machine learning workloads, you'll choose from the Compute Optimized family that includes C5 and C4 types. C5 machines—currently available from the c5.large to the c5d.18xlarge—give you as much as 3.5 GHz of processor speed and strong network bandwidth.

Memory Optimized   Memory Optimized instances work well for intensive database, data analysis, and caching operations. The X1e, X1, and R4 types are available with as much as 3 terabytes of DRAM-based memory and low-latency SSD storage volumes attached.

Accelerated Computing   You can achieve higher-performing general-purpose graphics processing unit (GPGPU) performance from the P3, P2, G3, and F1 types within the Accelerated Computing group. These instances make use of various generations of high-end NVIDIA GPUs or, in the case of the F1 instances, a Xilinx Virtex UltraScale+ field-programmable gate array (FPGA—if you don't know what that is, then you probably don't need it). Accelerated Computing instances are recommended for demanding workloads such as 3D visualizations and rendering, financial analysis, and computational fluid dynamics.

Storage Optimized   The H1, I3, and D2 types currently make up the Storage Optimized family that have large, low-latency instance storage volumes—as large as 16 TB (or, in the case of D2, up to 48 TB of slower HDD storage). These instances work well with distributed file systems and heavyweight data processing applications.

The specification details and instance type names will frequently change as AWS continues to leverage new technologies to support its customers' growing computing demands. But it's important to at least be familiar with the instance type families and the naming conventions AWS uses to identify them.

Configuring an Environment for Your Instance

Deciding where your EC2 instance will live is as important as choosing a performance configuration. Here, there are three primary details to get right: geographic region, virtual private cloud (VPC), and tenancy model.

AWS Regions

As you learned earlier, AWS servers are housed in data centers around the world and organized by geographical region. You'll generally want to launch an EC2 instance in the region that's physically closest to the majority of your customers or, if you're working with data that's subject to legal restrictions, within a jurisdiction that meets your compliance needs.

EC2 resources can be managed only when you're "located within" their region. You set the active region in the console through the drop-down menu at the top of the page and through default configuration values in the AWS CLI or your SDK. You can update your CLI configuration by running `aws configure`.

Bear in mind that the costs and even functionality of services and features might vary between regions. It's always a good idea to consult the most up-to-date official documentation.

VPCs

Virtual private clouds (VPCs) are easy-to-use AWS network organizers and great tools for organizing your infrastructure. Because it's so easy to isolate the instances in one VPC from whatever else you have running, you might want to create a new VPC for each one of your projects or project stages. For example, you might have one VPC for early application development, another for beta testing, and a third for production (see Figure 2.1).

FIGURE 2.1   A multi-VPC infrastructure for a development environment

Adding a simple VPC that doesn't incorporate a NAT gateway (`https://docs.aws.amazon.com/AmazonVPC/latest/UserGuide/vpc-nat-gateway.html`) or VPN access (`https://docs.aws.amazon.com/AmazonVPC/latest/UserGuide/VPC_VPN.html`) won't cost you anything. You'll learn much more about all this in Chapter 4, "Amazon Virtual Private Cloud."

Tenancy

When launching an EC2 instance, you'll have the opportunity to choose a tenancy model. The default setting is *shared tenancy*, where your instance will run as a virtual machine on a physical server that's concurrently hosting other instances. Those other instances might well be owned and operated by other AWS customers, although the possibility of any kind of insecure interaction between instances is remote.

To meet special regulatory requirements, your organization's instances might need an extra level of isolation. The Dedicated Instance option ensures that your instance will run on its own dedicated physical server. This means that it won't be sharing the server with resources owned by a different customer account. The Dedicated Host option allows you to actually identify and control the physical server you've been assigned to meet more restrictive licensing or regulatory requirements.

Naturally, dedicated instances and dedicated hosts will cost you more than instances using shared tenancy. Exercise 2.1 will guide you through the launch of a simple EC2 Linux instance.

EXERCISE 2.1

Launch an EC2 Linux Instance and Log in Using SSH

1. From the EC2 Dashboard, click to launch a new instance and select a Linux AMI and instance type. Remember, the t2.micro is Free Tier–eligible if your AWS account is still within its first year.

2. Explore the Configure Instance Details, Add Storage, and Add Tags pages—although the default settings should work fine.

3. On the Configure Security Group page, make sure there's a rule permitting incoming SSH (port 22) traffic. It should be there by default.

4. Before letting you launch the instance, AWS will require you to select—or create—a key pair. Follow the instructions.

5. Once the instance is launched, you can return to the Instances Dashboard to wait until everything is running properly.

6. Click the Actions pull-down and then the Connect item for instructions on how to connect to the instance from your local machine. Then connect and take a look at your virtual cloud server.

In Exercise 2.2, you'll see how changing an instance's type works.

EXERCISE 2.2

Assess the Free Capacity of a Running Instance and Change Its Instance Type

1. With an instance running, open the Instances Dashboard. Select the instance you're interested in and click the Monitoring tab in the bottom half of the screen. That's a good place to see what percentage of compute and network resources you've been using over the past hours or weeks.

   Now pretend that your instance is nearly maxed out and change the instance type as follows.

2. Stop the instance. (Remember, your public IP address might be different when you start up again.)

3. From the Actions drop-down, click Instance Settings and then Change Instance Type. Select a new type.

4. Restart the instance and confirm that it's running properly.

Configuring Instance Behavior

You can optionally tell EC2 to execute commands on your instance as it boots by pointing to user data in your instance configuration (this is sometimes known as *bootstrapping*). Whether you specify the data during the console configuration process or by using the --user-data value with the AWS CLI, you can have script files bring your instance to any desired state.

User data can consist of a few simple commands to install a web server and populate its web root, or it can be a sophisticated script setting the instance up as a working node within a Puppet Enterprise–driven platform.

Instance Pricing

Use of EC2 instances can be purchased using one of three models.

For always-on deployments that you expect to run for less than 12 months, you'll normally pay for each hour your instance is running through the *on-demand model*. On-demand is the most flexible way to consume EC2 resources since you're able to closely control how much you pay by stopping and starting your instances according to your need. But, per hour, it's also the most expensive.

If you're planning to keep the lights burning 24/7 for more than a year, then you'll enjoy a significant discount by purchasing a *reserve instance*—generally over a term commitment of between one and three years. You can pay up front for the entire term of a reserve instance or, for incrementally higher rates, either partially up front and the rest in monthly charges or entirely through monthly charges. Table 2.2 gives you a sense of how costs can change between models. These estimates assume a Linux platform, all up-front payments, and default tenancy. Actual costs may vary over time and between regions.

TABLE 2.2   Pricing estimates comparing on-demand with reserve costs

Instance Type	Pricing Model	Cost/Hour	Cost/Year
t2.micro	On-demand	$0.0058	$50.81
t2.micro	Reserve (three-year term)		$38.33
g3.4xlarge	On-demand	$1.14	$9986.40
g3.4xlarge	Reserve (three-year term)		$4432.56

For workloads that can withstand unexpected disruption (like computation-intensive genome research applications), purchasing instances on Amazon's Spot market can save you a lot of money. The idea is that you enter a maximum dollar-value bid for an instance type running in a particular region. The next time an instance in that region becomes available at a per-hour rate that's equal to or below your bid, it'll be launched using the AMI and launch template you specified. Once up, the instance will keep running either until you stop it—when your workload completes, for example—or until the instance's per-hour rate rises above your maximum bid. You'll learn more about the spot market and reserve instances in Chapter 12: "The Cost Optimization Pillar."

It will often make sense to combine multiple models within a single application infrastructure. An online store might, for instance, purchase one or two reserve instances to cover its normal customer demand but also allow autoscaling to automatically launch on-demand instances during periods of unusually high demand.

Use Exercise 2.3 to dive deeper into EC2 pricing.

EXERCISE 2.3

Assess Which Pricing Model Will Best Meet the Needs of a Deployment

Imagine that your application will need to run two always-on f1.2xlarge instances (which come with instance storage and won't require any EBS volumes). To meet seasonal demand, you can expect to require as many as four more instances for a total of 100 hours through the course of a single year. How should you pay for this deployment?

Bonus: Calculate your total estimated monthly and annual costs.

Instance Lifecycle

The state of a running EC2 instance can be managed in a number of ways. Terminating the instance will shut it down and cause its resources to be reallocated to the general AWS pool.

This will, in most cases, destroy all data kept on the primary storage. The exception to this would be an Elastic Block Store (EBS) volume that has been set to persist after its instance is terminated.

If your instance won't be needed for some time but you don't want to terminate it, you can save money by simply stopping it and then restarting it when it's needed again. The data on an EBS volume will in this case not be lost, although that would not be true for an instance volume.

Later in this chapter, you'll learn about both EBS and instance store volumes and the ways they work with EC2 instances.

You should be aware that a stopped instance that had been using a nonpersistent public IP address will most likely be assigned a different address when it's restarted. If you need a predictable IP address that can survive restarts, allocate an Elastic IP address and associate it with your instance.

You can edit or change an instance's security group (which I'll discuss a bit later in this chapter) to update access policies at any time—even while an instance is running. You can also change its instance type to increase or decrease its compute, memory, and storage capacity (just try doing *that* on a physical server). You will need to stop the instance, change the type, and then restart it.

Resource Tags

The more resources you deploy on your AWS account, the harder it can be to properly keep track of things. Having constantly changing numbers of EC2—along with accompanying storage volumes, security groups, and elastic IP addresses—all spread across two or three VPCs can get complicated.

The best way to keep a lid on the chaos is to find a way to quickly identify each resource you've got running by its purpose and its relationships to other resources. The best way to do that is by establishing a consistent naming convention and applying it to tags.

AWS resource tags can be used to label everything you'll ever touch across your AWS account—they're certainly not restricted to just EC2. Tags have a key and, optionally, an associated value. So, for example, you could assign a tag with the key production-server to each element of a production deployment. Server instances could, in addition, have a value of server1, server2, and so on. A related security group could have the same production-server key but security-group1 for its value. Table 2.3 illustrates how that convention might play out over a larger deployment group.

TABLE 2.3   A sample key/value tagging convention

Key	Value
production-server	server1
production-server	server2
production-server	security-group1
staging-server	server1
staging-server	server1
staging-server	staging-security-group1
test-server	server1
test-server	test-security-group1

Applied properly, tags can improve the visibility of your resources, making it much easier to manage them effectively, control costs, and avoid costly errors.

Service Limits

By default, each AWS account has limits to the number of instances of a particular service you're able to launch. Sometimes those limits apply to a single region within an account, and others are global. If necessary, you can request AWS to raise your ceiling for a particular service. As examples, you're allowed only five VPCs per region and 5,000 key pairs across your account.

You can find up-to-date details regarding the limits of all AWS services at `https://docs .aws.amazon.com/general/latest/gr/aws_service_limits.html`.

EC2 Storage Volumes

Storage drives (or *volumes* as they're described in AWS documentation) are for the most part virtualized spaces carved out of larger physical drives. To the OS running on your instance, though, all AWS volumes will present themselves exactly as though they were normal physical drives. But there's actually more than one kind of AWS volume, and it's important to understand how each type works.

Elastic Block Store Volumes

You can attach as many Elastic Block Store (EBS) volumes to your instance as you like and use them just as you would as you would hard drives, flash drives, or USB drives with your physical server. And as with physical drives, the type of EBS volume you choose will have an impact on both performance and cost.

The AWS SLA guarantees the reliability of the data you store on its EBS volumes (promising at least 99.999 percent availability), so you don't have to worry about failure. When an EBS drive does fail, its data has already been duplicated and will probably be brought back online before anyone notices a problem. So, practically, the only thing that should concern you is how quickly and efficiently you can access your data.

There are currently four EBS volume types, two using solid-state drive (SSD) technologies and two using the older spinning hard drives (HDDs). The performance of each volume type is measured in maximum IOPS/volume (where IOPS means input/output operations per second).

EBS-Provisioned IOPS SSD

If your applications will require intense rates of I/O operations, then you should consider provisioned IOPS, which provides a maximum IOPS/volume of 32,000 and a maximum throughput/volume of 500 MB/s. Provisioned IOPS—which in some contexts is referred to as EBS Optimized—can cost $0.125/GB/month in addition to $0.065/provisioned IOPS.

EBS General-Purpose SSD

For most regular server workloads that, ideally, deliver low-latency performance, general-purpose SSDs will work well. You'll get a maximum of 10,000 IOPS/volume, and it'll cost you $0.10/GB/month. For reference, a general-purpose SSD used as a typical 8 GB boot drive for a Linux instance would, at current rates, cost you $9.60/year.

Throughput-Optimized HDD

Throughput-optimized HDD volumes can provide reduced costs with acceptable performance where you're looking for throughput-intensive workloads including log processing and big data operations. These volumes can deliver only 500 IOPS/volume but with a 500 MB/s maximum throughput/volume, and they'll cost you only $0.045/GB/month.

Cold HDD

When you're working with larger volumes of data that require only infrequent access, a 250 IOPS/volume type might meet your needs for only $0.025/GB/month.

Table 2.4 lets you compare the basic specifications and estimated costs of those types.

TABLE 2.4 Sample costs for each of the four EBS storage volume types

	EBS-Provisioned IOPS SSD	EBS General-Purpose SSD	Throughput-Optimized HDD	Cold HDD
Volume size	4 GB–16 TB	1 GB–16 TB	500 GB–16 TB	500 GB–16 TB
Max IOPS/volume	32,000	10,000	500	250
Max throughput/ volume (MB/s)	500	160	500	250
Price (/month)	$0.125/GB + $0.065/ prov IOPS	$0.10/GB	$0.045/GB	$0.025/GB

EBS Volume Features

All EBS volumes can be copied by creating a snapshot. Existing snapshots can be used to generate other volumes that can be shared and/or attached to other instances or converted to images from which AMIs can be made. You can also generate an AMI image directly from a running instance-attached EBS volume—although, to be sure no data is lost, it's best to shut down the instance first.

EBS volumes can be encrypted to protect their data while at rest or as it's sent back and forth to the EC2 host instance. EBS can manage the encryption keys automatically behind the scenes or use keys that you provide through the AWS Key Management Service (KMS).

Exercise 2.4 will walk you through launching a new instance based on an existing snapshot image.

EXERCISE 2.4

Create and Launch an AMI Based on an Existing Instance Storage Volume

1. If necessary, launch an instance and make at least some token change to the root volume. This could be something as simple as typing **touch test.txt** on a Linux instance to create an empty file.

2. Create an image from the instance's volume (you'll access the dialog through the Actions pull-down menu in the Instances Dashboard).

3. Launch an instance from the console and select the new AMI from the My AMIs tab.

4. Log into the instance and confirm that your previous change has persisted.

Instance Store Volumes

Unlike EBS volumes, instance store volumes are ephemeral. This means that when the instances they're attached to are shut down, their data is permanently lost. So, why would you want to keep your data on an instance store volume more than on EBS?

- Instance store volumes are SSDs that are physically attached to the server hosting your instance and are connected via a fast NVMe interface.

- The use of instance store volumes is included in the price of the instance itself.

- Instance store volumes work especially well for deployment models where instances are launched to fill short-term roles (as part of autoscaling groups, for instance), import data from external sources, and are, effectively, disposable.

Whether one or more instance store volumes are available for your instance will depend on the instance type you choose. This is an important consideration to take into account when planning your deployment.

Even with all the benefits of EBS and instance storage, it's worth noting that there will be cases where you're much better off keeping large data sets outside of EC2 altogether. For many use cases, Amazon's S3 service can be a dramatically less expensive way to store files or even databases that are nevertheless instantly available for compute operations.

You'll learn more about this in Chapter 3, "Amazon Simple Storage Service and Amazon Glacier Storage."

Accessing Your EC2 Instance

Like all networked devices, EC2 instances are identified by unique IP addresses. All instances are assigned at least one private IPv4 address that, by default, will fall within one of the blocks shown in Table 2.5.

TABLE 2.5   The three IP address ranges used by private networks

From:	Until:
10.0.0.0	10.255.255.255
172.16.0.0	172.31.255.255
192.168.0.0	192.168.255.255

Out of the box, you'll only be able to connect to your instance from within its subnet, and the instance will have no direct contact to the Internet.

If your instance configuration calls for multiple network interfaces (to connect to otherwise unreachable resources), you can create and then attach one or more virtual Elastic Network Interfaces to your instance. Each of these interfaces must be connected to an existing subnet and security group. You can optionally assign a static IP address within the subnet range.

Of course, an instance can also be assigned a public IP through which full Internet access is possible. As you learned earlier as part of the instance lifecycle discussion, the default public IP assigned to your instance is ephemeral and probably won't survive a reboot. Therefore, as mentioned, you'll usually want to allocate a permanent elastic IP for long-term deployments. As long as it's attached to a running instance, there's no charge for elastic IPs.

I'll talk about accessing an instance as an administrator a bit later within the context of security. But there's a lot you can learn about a running EC2 instance—including the IP addresses you'll need to connect—through the instance metadata system. Running the following curl command from the command line while logged into the instance will return a list of the kinds of data that are available:

```
$ curl http://169.254.169.254/latest/meta-data/
ami-id
ami-launch-index
ami-manifest-path
block-device-mapping/
hostname
instance-action
instance-id
instance-type
local-hostname
local-ipv4
mac
metrics/
network/
placement/
profile
public-hostname
public-ipv4
public-keys/
reservation-id
security-groups
```

You'll use the 169.254.169.254 IP for the command no matter what your instance public or private IPs happen to be.

Entries ending with a trailing slash (/) contain further sublevels of information that can also be displayed by curl. Adding a data type to that curl command will then return the information you're after. This example displays the name of the security groups used by the instance:

```
$ curl http://169.254.169.254/latest/meta-data/
security-groups launch-wizard-1
```

Securing Your EC2 Instance

You are responsible for configuring appropriate and effective access controls to protect your EC2 instances from unauthorized use. Broadly speaking, AWS provides four tools to help you with this task: security groups, Identity and Access Management (IAM) roles, network address translation (NAT) instances, and key pairs.

Security Groups

An EC2 security group plays the role of a firewall. By default, a security group will deny all incoming traffic. You define group behavior by setting policy rules that will either block or allow specified traffic types. From that point on, any data packet coming into or leaving the perimeter will be measured against those rules and processed accordingly.

Traffic is assessed by examining its source and destination, the network port it's targeting, and the protocol it's set to use. A packet that's using TCP on the SSH port 22 could, for instance, only be allowed access to a particular instance if its source IP address matches the local public IP used by computers in your office. This lets you open up SSH access on your instance without having to worry about anyone from outside your company getting in.

Using security groups, you can easily create sophisticated rule sets to finely manage access to your services. You could, say, open up a website to the whole world while blocking your backend servers to everyone besides members of your team.

If necessary, you can update your security group rules or apply them to multiple instances.

Security groups control traffic at the instance level. However, AWS also provides you with network access control lists (NACLs) that are associated with entire subnets rather than individual instances. Chapter 4, "Amazon Virtual Private Cloud," discusses both security groups and NACLs.

IAM Roles

You can also control access to AWS resources—including EC2 instances—through the use of IAM roles. You define an IAM role by giving it permissions to perform actions on specified services or resources within your AWS account. When a particular role is assigned to a user or resource, they'll gain access to whichever resources were included in the role policies.

Using roles, you can give a limited number of entities (other resources or users) exclusive access to resources like your EC2 instances. But you can also assign an IAM role *to* an EC2 instance so that processes running within it can access the external tools—like an RDS database instance—it needs to do its work.

You'll learn more about IAM in Chapter 6, "Authentication and Authorization—AWS Identity and Access Management."

NAT Devices

Sometimes you'll need to configure an EC2 instance without a public IP address to limit its exposure to the network. Naturally, that means it won't have any Internet connectivity. But that can present a problem because you'll probably still need to give it limited Internet access so it can receive security patches and software updates.

One solution is to route traffic between your private instance and the Internet through a special device. AWS gives you two ways to do that: a NAT instance and a NAT gateway (see Figure 2.2). They'll both do the job, but since a NAT gateway is a managed service, it doesn't require that you manually launch and maintain an instance. Both approaches will incur monthly charges.

FIGURE 2.2   A NAT gateway providing network access to resources in private subnets

NAT routing will be discussed at greater length in Chapter 4.

Key Pairs

As any professional administrator will know, remote login sessions on your running instances should never be initiated over unencrypted plain-text connections. To ensure properly secured sessions, you'll need to generate a key pair, save the public key to your EC2 server, and save its private half to your local machine. If you're working with a Windows AMI, you'll use the private key file to retrieve the password you'll need to authenticate into your instance. For a Linux AMI, the private key will allow you to open an SSH session.

Each key pair that AWS generates for you will remain installed within its original region and available for use with newly launched instances until you delete it. You *should* delete the AWS copy in the event your public key is lost or exposed. Just be careful before you mess with your keys: your access to an instance might depend on it.

Other EC2-Related Services

This section will briefly introduce you to a few more EC2 features. Some of these features won't necessarily play a large role in the solutions architect exam but could definitely come in handy for you in your work at some point. Others are only touched on here but will be examined in greater detail later in the book.

AWS Systems Manager

Systems Manager Services (available through the AWS console) is a collection of tools for monitoring and managing the resources you have running in the AWS cloud *and* in your own on-premises infrastructure. Through the Systems Manager portal, you can organize your AWS resources into resource groups, mine various visualization tools for insights into the health and behavior of your operations, directly execute commands or launch tasks remotely without having to log on, automate patching and other lifecycle events, and manage service parameters and access secrets.

Placement Groups

Placement groups are useful for multiple EC2 instances that require especially low-latency network interconnectivity. There are two placement group strategies.

- *Cluster* groups launch each associated instance within a single availability zone within close physical proximity to each other.
- *Spread* groups separate instances physically across hardware to reduce the risk of failure-related data or service loss.

AWS Elastic Beanstalk

Elastic Beanstalk lets you upload your application code and define a few parameters, and AWS will configure, launch, and maintain all the infrastructure necessary to keep it running.

That might include EC2 load-balanced and autoscaled instances, RDS database instances, and all the network plumbing you would otherwise have had to build yourself.

Compatible languages and platforms include .NET, Java, Node.js, Python, and Docker. Elastic Beanstalk adds no charges beyond the cost of the running infrastructure itself.

Amazon Elastic Container Service and AWS Fargate

Running Docker container-based applications at scale is the kind of thing that's a natural fit for a cloud platform like AWS. Once upon a time, if you wanted to get that done, you'd have to fire up one or more robust EC2 instances and then manually provision them as your Docker hosts.

With Amazon Elastic Container Service (ECS), however, AWS lets you launch a pre-built Docker host instance and define the way you want your Docker containers to behave (called a *task*), and ECS will make it all happen. The containers will exist within an infrastructure that's automated and fully integrated with your AWS resources.

The more recently released Fargate tool further abstracts the ECS configuration process, removing the need for you to run and configure instances for your containers. With Fargate, all you do is package your application and set your environment requirements.

AWS Lambda

"Serverless" applications are powered by programming code that's run on servers—just not servers under the control of the application owners. Instead, code can be configured to run when AWS's Lambda servers are triggered by preset events.

Lambda allows you to instantly perform almost any operation on demand at almost any time but without having to provision and pay for always-on servers.

VM Import/Export

VM Import/Export allows you to easily move virtual machine images back and forth between your on-premises VMware environment and your AWS account (via an S3 bucket). This can make it much simpler to manage hybrid environments and to efficiently migrate workloads up to the AWS cloud.

Elastic Load Balancing and Auto Scaling

A load balancer directs external user requests between multiple EC2 instances to more efficiently distribute server resources and improve user experience. Autoscaling will react to preset performance thresholds by automatically increasing or decreasing the number of EC2 instances you have running to match demand.

Both Elastic Load Balancing (ELB) and Auto Scaling can be closely integrated with your EC2 infrastructure, making for simple and seamless operation.

AWS CLI Example

The following example code shows how you can use an AWS CLI command to deploy an EC2 instance that includes many of the features you learned about in this chapter. Naturally, the image-id, security-group-ids, and subnet-id values are not real. Those you would replace with actual IDs that fit your account and region.

```
aws ec2 run-instances --image-id ami-xxxxxxxx --count 1 \
--instance-type t2.micro --key-name MyKeyPair \
--security-group-ids sg-xxxxxxxx --subnet-id subnet-xxxxxxxx \
--user-data file://my_script.sh \
--tag-specifications \
'ResourceType=instance,Tags=[{Key=webserver,Value=production}]' \
'ResourceType=volume,Tags=[{Key=cost-center,Value=cc123}]'
```

This example launches a single (--count 1) instance that's based on the specified AMI. The desired instance type, key name, security group, and subnet are all identified. A script file (that must exist locally so it can be read) is added using the user-data argument, and two tags are associated with the instance (webserver:production and cost-center:cc123).

Time to install the AWS CLI? Do Exercise 2.5.

EXERCISE 2.5

Install the AWS CLI and Use It to Launch an EC2 Instance

Need help? Learn how to install the AWS CLI for your OS here:

https://docs.aws.amazon.com/cli/latest/userguide/installing.html

Refer to the previous AWS CLI example for help launching your instance. (Hint: You will need to fill in some xxxxx placeholders with actual resource IDs.)

Never leave any resources running after you're finished using them. Exercise 2.6 can help.

EXERCISE 2.6

Clean Up Unused EC2 Resources

Since you've probably been launching resources while experimenting with AWS, you'll want to make sure you haven't accidentally left anything running that could cost you money. So, take a good look through the console and kill off what shouldn't still be alive. Here are some things to consider:

- Remember to check any other AWS regions where you might have done some work—only a single region's resources will show up in the console.

- Some resources can't be deleted because they're in use by other resources. A snapshot used by a private AMI is one example. You'll need to shut those down in the right order.

- When you're logged into your AWS account, you can check out your Billing And Cost Management Dashboard in the console (`https://console.aws.amazon.com/billing`). This Dashboard will show you whether, taking into account your current resource usage, you stand to run up a bill in the current month.

Summary

The base software stack that runs on an EC2 instance is defined by your choice of Amazon Machine Image and any scripts or user data you add at launch time, and the hardware profile is the product of an instance type. A tenancy setting determines whether your instance will share a physical host with other instances.

As with all your AWS resources, it's important to give your EC2 instances easily identifiable tags that conform to a system-wide naming convention. There are limits to the number of resources you'll be allowed to launch within a single region and account-wide. Should you hit your limit, you can always request access to additional resources.

If you plan to run an instance for a year or longer, you can save a significant amount of money over paying for on-demand by purchasing a reserve instance. If your workload can withstand unexpected shutdowns, then a spot instance could also make sense.

There are four kinds of Elastic Block Store volumes: two high IOPS and low-latency SSD types and two traditional hard drives. Your workload and budget will inform your choice. In addition, some EC2 instance types come with ephemeral instance store volumes that offer fast data access but whose data is lost when the instance is shut down.

All EC2 instances are given at least one private IP address, and should they require Internet access, they can also be given a nonpermanent public IP. Should you require a permanent public IP, you can assign an Elastic IP to the instance.

You secure access to your EC2 instances using software firewalls known as security groups and can open up secure and limited access through IAM roles, NAT instances or NAT gateways, and key pairs.

Exam Essentials

Understand how to provision and launch an EC2 instance.   You'll need to select the right AMI and instance type, configure a security group, add any extra storage volumes that might be needed, point to any necessary user data and scripts, and, ideally, tag all the elements using descriptive key values.

Understand how to choose the right hardware/software profile for your workload. Consider the benefits of building your own image against the ease and simplicity of using a marketplace, community, or official AMI. Calculate the user demand you expect your application to generate so you can select an appropriate instance type. Remember that you can always change your instance type later if necessary.

Understand EC2 pricing models and how to choose one to fit your needs. Know how to calculate whether you'll be best off on the spot market, with on-demand, or with reserve—or some combination of the three.

Understand how to configure a security group to balance access with security to match your deployment profile. Security groups act as firewalls, applying policy rules to determine which network traffic is allowed through. You can control traffic based on a packet's protocol and network port and its source and intended destination.

Know how to access a running instance. Instance data, including private and public IP addresses, can be retrieved from the AWS Console, through the AWS CLI, and from metadata queries on the instance itself. You'll need this information so you can log in to administrate the instance or access its web-facing applications.

Understand the features and behavior of storage volume types. SSD volumes can achieve higher IOPS and, therefore, lower latency but come at a cost that's higher than traditional hard drives.

Know how to create a snapshot from a storage volume and how to attach the snapshot to a different instance. Any EBS drive can be copied and either attached to a different instance or used to generate an image that, in turn, can be made into an AMI and shared or used to launch any number of new instances.

Review Questions

1. You need to deploy multiple EC2 Linux instances that will provide your company with virtual private networks (VPNs) using software called OpenVPN. Which of the following will be the most efficient solutions? (Choose two.)

    A. Select a regular Linux AMI and bootstrap it using user data that will install and configure the OpenVPN package on the instance and use it for your VPN instances.

    B. Search the community AMIs for an official AMI provided and supported by the OpenVPN company.

    C. Search the AWS Marketplace to see whether there's an official AMI provided and supported by the OpenVPN company.

    D. Select a regular Linux AMI and SSH in to manually install and configure the OpenVPN package.

2. You have a VMware virtual machine in your local infrastructure that you'd like to copy to your AWS account and run as an EC2 instance. Which of the following will be necessary steps? (Choose two.)

    A. Import the virtual machine to your AWS region using a secure SSH tunnel.

    B. Import the virtual machine using VM Import/Export.

    C. Select the imported VM from among your private AMIs and launch an instance.

    D. Select the imported VM from the AWS Marketplace AMIs and launch an instance.

3. Your AWS CLI command to launch an AMI as an EC2 instance has failed, giving you an error message that includes `InvalidAMIID.NotFound`. What of the following is the most likely cause?

    A. You haven't properly configured the `~/.aws/config` file.

    B. The AMI is being updated and is temporarily unavailable.

    C. Your key pair file has been given the wrong (overly permissive) permissions.

    D. The AMI you specified exists in a different region than the one you've currently specified.

4. The sensitivity of the data your company works with means that the instances you run must be secured through *complete* physical isolation. What should you specify as you configure a new instance?

    A. Dedicated Host Tenancy

    B. Shared Tenancy

    C. Dedicated Instance Tenancy

    D. Isolated Tenancy

5. Normally, two instances running m5.large instance types can handle the traffic accessing your online e-commerce site, but you know that you will face short, unpredictable periods of high demand. Which of the following choices should you implement? (Choose two.)

    A. Configure autoscaling.

    B. Configure load balancing.

C. Purchase two m5.large instances on the spot market and as many on-demand instances as necessary.

D. Purchase two m5.large reserve instances and as many on-demand instances as necessary.

6. Which of the following use cases would be most cost effective using spot market instances?

   A. Your e-commerce website is built using a publicly available AMI.

   B. You provide high-end video rendering services using a fault-tolerant process that can easily complete a job that was unexpectedly interrupted.

   C. You're running a backend database that must be reliably updated to keep track of critical transactions.

   D. Your deployment runs as a static website on S3.

7. Which of the following configuration details *cannot* be changed on an existing EC2 instance?

   A. AMI

   B. Instance type

   C. Security group

   D. Public IP address

8. For an account with multiple resources running as part of multiple projects, which of the following key/value combination examples would make for the most effective identification convention for resource tags?

   A. `servers:server1`

   B. `project1:server1`

   C. `EC2:project1:server1`

   D. `server1:project1`

9. Which of the following EBS options will you need to keep your data-hungry application that requires up to 20,000 IOPS happy?

   A. Cold HDD

   B. General-purpose SSD

   C. Throughput-optimized HDD

   D. Provisioned-IOPS SSD

10. If you want to generate an AMI from an existing EBS volume, which of the following steps will get you there? (Choose three.)

    A. Create an image from a detached EBS volume, use it to create a snapshot, select your new AMI from your private collection, and launch it.

    B. Create a snapshot of the EBS root volume you need, use it to create an image, select your new AMI from your private collection, and launch it.

    C. Create an image from the EBS volume attached to the instance, select your new AMI from your private collection, and launch it.

    D. Import the snapshot of an EBS root volume from a different AWS account, use it to create an image, select your new AMI from your private collection, and launch it.

11. Which of the following are benefits of instance store volumes? (Choose two.)

   A. Instance volumes are physically attached to the server that's hosting your instance, allowing faster data access.

   B. Instance volumes can be used to store data even after the instance is shut down.

   C. The use of instance volumes does not incur costs (beyond those for the instance itself).

   D. You can set termination protection so an instance volume can't be accidentally shut down.

12. According to default behavior (and AWS recommendations), which of the following IP addresses could be assigned as the private IP for an EC2 instance? (Choose two.)

   A. 54.61.211.98

   B. 23.176.92.3

   C. 172.17.23.43

   D. 10.0.32.176

13. Which of the following commands will (when run from a shell session on an EC2 instance) display the instance ID?

   A. `curl http://169.254.169.254/latest/meta-data/instance-action`

   B. `curl http://149.253.169.253/latest/meta-data/instanceaction`

   C. `curl http://169.254.169.254/latest/meta/instance-action`

   D. `curl http://169.254.169.254/meta-data/instance-action`

14. Which three attributes of an incoming data packet are used by a security group to determine whether it should be allowed through? (Choose three.)

   A. Network port

   B. Source address

   C. Datagram header size

   D. Network protocol

15. How are IAM roles commonly used to ensure secure resource access in relation to EC2 instances? (Choose two.)

   A. A role can assign processes running on the EC2 instance permission to access other AWS resources.

   B. A user can be given permission to authenticate as a role and access all associated resources.

   C. A role can be associated with individual instance-based processes (Linux instances only), giving them permission to access other AWS resources.

   D. A role can give users and resources permission to access the EC2 instance.

16. You have an instance running within a private subnet that needs external network access to receive software updates and patches. Which of the following can securely provide that access from a public subnet within the same VPC? (Choose two.)

    A. Internet gateway

    B. NAT instance

    C. Virtual private gateway

    D. NAT gateway

17. What do you have to do to securely authenticate to the GUI console of a Windows EC2 session?

    A. Use the private key of your key pair to initiate an SSH tunnel session.

    B. Use the public key of your key pair to initiate an SSH tunnel session.

    C. Use the public key of your key pair to retrieve the password you'll use to log in.

    D. Use the private key of your key pair to retrieve the password you'll use to log in.

18. Which of the following AWS tools will allow you to locate EC2 instances closer to each other to reduce network latency?

    A. Load balancing

    B. Placement groups

    C. AWS Systems Manager

    D. AWS Fargate

19. To save configuration time and money, you want your application to run only when network events trigger it but shut down immediately after. Which of the following will do that for you?

    A. AWS Lambda

    B. AWS Elastic Beanstalk

    C. Amazon Elastic Container Service (ECS)

    D. Auto Scaling

20. Which of the following will allow you to quickly copy a virtual machine image from your local infrastructure to your AWS VPC?

    A. AWS Simple Storage Service (S3)

    B. AWS Snowball

    C. VM Import/Export

    D. AWS Direct Connect

Chapter

3

Amazon Simple Storage Service and Amazon Glacier Storage

THE AWS CERTIFIED SOLUTIONS ARCHITECT ASSOCIATE EXAM OBJECTIVES COVERED IN THIS CHAPTER MAY INCLUDE, BUT ARE NOT LIMITED TO, THE FOLLOWING:

Domain 1: Design Resilient Architectures

✓ 1.1 Choose reliable/resilient storage.

✓ 1.3 Determine how to design a multitier architecture solution.

✓ 1.4 Determine how to design high availability and/or fault tolerant architectures.

Domain 2: Define Performant Architectures

✓ 2.1 Choose performant storage and databases.

✓ 2.3 Design solutions for elasticity and scalability.

Domain 3: Specify Secure Applications and Architectures

✓ 3.1 Determine how to secure application tiers.

✓ 3.2 Determine how to secure data.

Domain 4: Design Cost-Optimized Architectures

✓ 4.1 Determine how to design cost-optimized storage.

Introduction

Amazon Simple Storage Service (S3) is where individuals, applications, and a long list of AWS services keep their data. It's an excellent platform for the following:

- Maintaining backup archives, log files, and disaster recovery images
- Running analytics on big data at rest
- Hosting static websites

S3 provides inexpensive and reliable storage that can, if necessary, be closely integrated with operations running within or external to AWS.

This isn't the same as the operating system volumes you learned about in the previous chapter: those are kept on the *block storage* volumes driving your EC2 instances. S3, by contrast, provides a space for effectively unlimited *object storage*.

What's the difference between object and block storage? With block-level storage, data on a raw physical storage device is divided into individual blocks whose use is managed by a file system. NTFS is a common file system used by Windows, while Linux might use Btrfs or ext4. The file system, on behalf of the installed OS, is responsible for allocating space for the files and data that are saved to the underlying device and for providing access whenever the OS needs to read some data.

An object storage system like S3, on the other hand, provides what you can think of as a flat surface on which to store your data. This simple design avoids some of the OS-related complications of block storage and allows anyone easy access to any amount of profession-ally designed and maintained storage capacity.

When you write files to S3, they're stored along with up to 2 KB of metadata. The meta-data is made up of keys that establish system details like data permissions and the appear-ance of a file system location within nested buckets.

Through the rest of this chapter, you're going to learn the following:

- How S3 objects are saved, managed, and accessed
- How to choose from among the various classes of storage to get the right balance of durability, availability, and cost

- How to manage long-term data storage lifecycles by incorporating Amazon Glacier into your design
- What other AWS services exist to help you with your data storage and access operations

S3 Service Architecture

You organize your S3 files into buckets. By default, you're allowed to create as many as 100 buckets for each of your AWS accounts. As with other AWS services, you can ask AWS to raise that limit.

Although an S3 bucket and its contents exist within only a single AWS region, the name you choose for your bucket must be globally unique within the entire S3 system. There's some logic to this: you'll often want your data located in a particular geographical region to satisfy operational or regulatory needs. But at the same time, being able to reference a bucket without having to specify its region simplifies the process.

Here is the URL you would use to access a file called `filename` that's in a bucket called `bucketname` over HTTP:

```
https://s3.amazonaws.com/bucketname/filename
```

Naturally, this assumes you'll be able to satisfy the object's permissions requirements. This is how that same file would be addressed using the AWS CLI:

```
s3://bucketname/filename
```

Prefixes and Delimiters

As you've seen, S3 stores objects within a bucket on a flat surface without subfolder hierarchies. However, you can use prefixes and delimiters to give your buckets the *appearance* of a more structured organization.

A prefix is a common text string that indicates an organization level. For example, the word `contracts` when followed by the delimiter / would tell S3 to treat a file with a name like `contracts/acme.pdf` as an object that should be grouped together with a second file named `contracts/dynamic.pdf`.

S3 recognizes folder/directory structures as they're uploaded and emulates their hierarchical design within the bucket, automatically converting slashes to delimiters. That's why you'll see the correct folders whenever you view your S3-based objects through the console or the API.

Working with Large Objects

While there's no theoretical limit to the total amount of data you can store within a bucket, a single object may be no larger than 5 TB. Individual *uploads* can be no larger than 5 GB.

To reduce the risk of data loss or aborted uploads, AWS recommends that you use a feature called Multipart Upload for any object larger than 100 MB.

As the name suggests, Multipart Upload breaks a large object into multiple smaller parts and transmits them individually to their S3 target. If one transmission should fail, it can be repeated without impacting the others.

Multipart Upload will be used automatically when the upload is initiated by the AWS CLI or a high-level API, but you'll need to manually break up your object if you're working with a low-level API.

An application programming interface (API) is a programmatic interface through which operations can be run through code or from the command line. AWS maintains APIs as the primary method of administration for each of its services. AWS provides low-level APIs for cases when your S3 uploads require hands-on customization, and it provides high-level APIs for operations that can be more readily automated. This page contains specifics:

https://docs.aws.amazon.com/AmazonS3/latest/dev/uploadobjusingmpu.html

Work through Exercise 3.1 and create your own bucket.

EXERCISE 3.1

Create a New S3 Bucket and Upload a File

1. From the AWS S3 Dashboard, create a new bucket and use either the Dashboard or the AWS CLI (aws s3 cp mylocalfile.txt s3://mybucketname/) to upload one or more files, giving public read access to the object.

2. From the file's Overview page in the S3 Dashboard (displayed when the bucket name is clicked), copy its public link, paste it into the URL field of a browser that's not logged into your AWS account, and confirm that you can open the file.

Encryption

Unless it's intended to be publicly available—perhaps as part of a website—data stored on S3 should always be encrypted. You can use encryption keys to protect your data while it's at rest within S3 and—by using only Amazon's encrypted API endpoints for data transfers—protect data during its journeys between S3 and other locations.

Data at rest can be protected using either server-side or client-side encryption.

Server-Side Encryption

The "server-side" here is the S3 platform, and it involves having AWS encrypt your data objects as they're saved to disk and decrypt them when you send properly authenticated requests for retrieval.

You can use one of three encryption options:

▪   Server-Side Encryption with Amazon S3-Managed Keys (SSE-S3), where AWS uses its own enterprise-standard keys to manage every step of the encryption and decryption process

- Server-Side Encryption with AWS KMS-Managed Keys (SSE-KMS), where, beyond the SSE-S3 features, the use of an *envelope key* is added along with a full audit trail for tracking key usage. You can optionally import your own keys through the AWS KMS service.

- Server-Side Encryption with Customer-Provided Keys (SSE-C), which lets you provide your own keys for S3 to apply to its encryption

Client-Side Encryption

It's also possible to encrypt data before it's transferred to S3. This can be done using an AWS KMS–Managed Customer Master Key (CMK), which produces a unique key for each object before it's uploaded. You can also use a Client-Side Master Key, which you provide through the Amazon S3 encryption client.

Server-side encryption can greatly reduce the complexity of the process and is often preferred. Nevertheless, in some cases, your company (or regulatory oversight body) might require that you maintain full control over your encryption keys, leaving client-side as the only option.

Logging

Tracking S3 events to log files is disabled by default—S3 buckets can see a lot of activity, and not every use case justifies the log data that S3 can generate.

When you enable logging, you'll need to specify both a source bucket (the bucket whose activity you're tracking) and a target bucket (the bucket to which you'd like the logs saved). Optionally, you can also specify delimiters and prefixes to make it easier to identify and organize logs from multiple source buckets that are saved to a single target bucket.

S3-generated logs, which sometimes only appear after a short delay, will contain basic operation details, including the following:

- The account and IP address of the requestor
- The source bucket name
- The action that was requested (GET, PUT, etc.)
- The time the request was issued
- The response status (including error code)

S3 buckets are also used by other AWS services—including CloudWatch and CloudTrail—to store their logs or other objects (like EBS Snapshots).

S3 Durability and Availability

S3 offers more than one class of storage for your objects. The class you choose will depend on how critical it is that the data survives no matter what (durability), how quickly you might need to retrieve it (availability), and how much money you have to spend.

Durability

S3 measures durability as a percentage. For instance, the 99.999999999 percent durability guarantee for most S3 classes and Amazon Glacier is as follows:

> ". . . corresponds to an average annual expected loss of 0.000000001% of objects. For example, if you store 10,000,000 objects with Amazon S3, you can on average expect to incur a loss of a single object once every 10,000 years."

Source: https://aws.amazon.com/s3/faqs

In other words, realistically, there's pretty much no way that you can possibly lose data stored on one of the standard S3/Glacier platforms because of infrastructure failure. However, it would be irresponsible to rely on your S3 buckets as the only copies of important data. After all, there's a real chance that a misconfiguration, account lockout, or unanticipated external attack could permanently block access to your data. And, as crazy as it might sound right now, it's not unthinkable to suggest that AWS could one day go out of business. Kodak and Blockbuster Video once dominated their industries, right?

The high durability rates delivered by S3 are largely because they automatically replicate your data across at least three availability zones. That means that even if an entire AWS facility was suddenly wiped off the map, copies of your data would be restored from a different zone.

There are, however, two storage classes that aren't quite so resilient. Amazon S3 One Zone-Infrequent Access (S3 One Zone-IA), as the name suggests, stores data in only a single availability zone. Reduced Redundancy Storage (RRS) is rated at only 99.99 percent durability (because it's replicated across fewer servers than other classes). You can balance increased/decreased durability against other features like availability and cost to get the balance that's right for you. All S3 durability levels are shown in Table 3.1.

TABLE 3.1   Guaranteed reliability standards for S3 storage

	S3 Standard	S3 Standard-IA	S3 One Zone-IA	Reduced Redundancy
Durability guarantee	99.999999999%	99.999999999%	99.999999999%	99.99%
Concurrent facility fault tolerance	2	2	1	1

Availability

Object availability is also measured as a percentage, this time though, it's the percentage you can expect a given object to be instantly available on request through the course of a full year. The Amazon S3 Standard class, for example, guarantees that your data will be ready whenever you need it (meaning: it will be available) for 99.99% of the year. That means there will be less than nine hours each year of down time. If you feel down-time has exceeded that limit within a single year, you can apply for a service credit. Amazon's durability guarantee, by contrast, is designed to provide 99.999999999% data protection. This means there's practically no chance your data will be lost, even if you might sometimes not have instance access to it.

Table 3.2 illustrates the availability guarantees for all S3 classes.

TABLE 3.2 Guaranteed availability standards for S3 storage

	S3 Standard	S3 Standard-IA	S3 One Zone-IA	Reduced Redundancy
Availability guarantee	99.99%	99.9%	99.5%	99.99%

Eventually Consistent Data

It's important to bear in mind that S3 replicates data across multiple locations. As a result, there might be brief delays while updates to existing objects propagate across the system. Uploading a new version of a file or, alternatively, deleting an old file altogether can result in one site reflecting the new state with another still unaware of any changes.

To ensure that there's never a conflict between versions of a single object—which could lead to serious data and application corruption—you should treat your data according to an Eventually Consistent standard. That is, you should expect a delay (usually just two seconds or less) and design your operations accordingly.

Because there isn't the risk of corruption, S3 provides read-after-write consistency for the creation (PUT) of *new* objects.

S3 Object Lifecycle

Many of the S3 workloads you'll launch will probably involve backup archives. But the thing about backup archives is that, when properly designed, they're usually followed regularly by more backup archives. Maintaining some previous archive versions is critical, but you'll also want to retire and delete older versions to keep a lid on your storage costs.

S3 lets you automate all this with its versioning and lifecycle features.

Versioning

Within many file system environments, saving a file using the same name and location as a pre-existing file will overwrite the original object. That ensures you'll always have the most recent version available to you, but you will lose access to older versions—including versions that were overwritten by mistake.

By default, objects on S3 work the same way. But if you enable versioning at the bucket level, then older overwritten copies of an object will be saved and remain accessible indefinitely. This solves the problem of accidentally losing old data, but it replaces it with the potential for archive bloat. Here's where lifecycle management can help.

Lifecycle Management

You can configure lifecycle rules for a bucket that will automatically transition an object's storage class after a set number of days. You might, for instance, have new objects remain in the S3 Standard class for their first 30 days after which they're moved to the cheaper One Zone IA for another 30 days. If regulatory compliance requires that you maintain older versions, your files could then be moved to the low-cost, long-term storage service Glacier for 365 more days before being permanently deleted.

You can optionally use prefixes to apply lifecycle rules to only certain objects within a bucket. You should also be aware that there are minimum times (30 days, for instance) an object must remain within one class before it can be moved. In addition, you can't transition directly from S3 Standard to Reduced Redundancy.

Try it yourself with Exercise 3.2.

EXERCISE 3.2

Enable Versioning and Lifecycle Management for an S3 Bucket

1. Edit a bucket's properties to enable versioning.

2. Upload a file to that bucket, edit the copy on your local computer, and upload the new copy (keeping the filename the same). If you're working with a file from your static website, make sure you give the new file permissions allowing public access.

3. With the contents of the bucket displayed in the Dashboard, select Show versions. You should now see two versions of your file.

4. Add a couple of directories with files to your bucket.

5. From the bucket's Management tab, select Lifecycle and specify a tag that matches the directory name of one of the directories you uploaded.

6. Add a lifecycle rule by adding transitions and configuring the transition timing (in days) and target for each one.

You'll need to be patient to test this configuration because the minimum lag between transitions is 30 days.

Accessing S3 Objects

If you didn't think you'd ever need your data, you wouldn't go to the trouble of saving it to S3. So, you'll need to understand how to access your S3-hosted objects and, just as important, how to restrict access to only those requests that match your business and security needs.

Access Control

Out of the box, new S3 buckets and objects will be fully accessible to your account but to no other AWS accounts or external visitors. You can strategically open up access at the bucket and object levels using access control list (ACL) rules, finer-grained S3 bucket policies, or Identity and Access Management (IAM) policies.

There is more than a little overlap between those three approaches. In fact, ACLs are really leftovers from before AWS created IAM. As a rule, Amazon recommends applying S3 bucket policies or IAM policies instead of ACLs.

S3 bucket policies—which are formatted as JSON text and attached to your S3 bucket—will make sense for cases where you want to control access to a single S3 bucket for multiple external accounts and users. On the other hand, IAM policies—because they exist at the account level within IAM—will probably make sense when you're trying to control the way individual users and roles access multiple resources, including S3.

The following code is an example of an S3 bucket policy that allows both the root user and the user Steve from the specified AWS account to access the S3 MyBucket bucket and its contents. Both users are considered *principals* within this rule.

```
{
    "Version": "2012-10-17",
    "Statement": [
      {
        "Effect": "Allow",
        "Principal": {
          "AWS": ["arn:aws:iam::xxxxxxxxxxxx:root",
          "arn:aws:iam::xxxxxxxxxxxx:user/Steve"]
        },
        "Action": "s3:*",
        "Resource": ["arn:aws:s3:::MyBucket",
                     "arn:aws:s3:::MyBucket/*"]
      }
    ]
}
```

You can also limit access within bucket policies by specifying time of day or source CIDR IP address blocks.

When it's attached to an IAM entity (a user, group, or role), the following IAM policy will accomplish the same thing as the previous S3 bucket policy:

```
{
    "Version": "2012-10-17",
    "Statement":[{
      "Effect": "Allow",
```

```
    "Action": "s3:*",
    "Resource": ["arn:aws:s3:::MyBucket",
                 "arn:aws:s3:::MyBucket/*"]
  }
 ]
}
```

IAM roles and policies will be discussed in greater detail in Chapter 6, "Authentication and Authorization—AWS Identity and Access Management."

Presigned URLs

If you want to provide temporary access to an object that's otherwise private, you can generate a presigned URL. The URL will be usable for a specified period of time, after which it will become invalid. You can build presigned URL generation into your code to provide object access programmatically.

The following AWS CLI command will return a URL that includes the required authentication string. The authentication will become invalid after 10 minutes (600 seconds). The default expiration value is 3,600 seconds (one hour).

```
aws s3 presign s3://MyBucketName/PrivateObject --expires-in 600
```

Try it yourself with Exercise 3.3.

EXERCISE 3.3

Generate and Use a Presigned URL

1. Use the complete URL of a private object in an S3 bucket belonging to you to generate a presigned URL using a variation of this command:

    ```
    aws s3 presign s3://MyBucketName/PrivateObject --expires-in 600
    ```

2. Copy the full URL from the command output and, from a browser that's not logged into your AWS account, try to open the file.

3. Wait for the URL to expire and try again. This time, it should not work.

Static Website Hosting

S3 buckets can be used to host the HTML files for entire static websites. A website is static when the system services used to render web pages and scripts are all client rather than server-based. This architecture permits simple and lean HTML code that's designed to be executed by the client browser.

S3, because it's such an inexpensive yet reliable platform, is an excellent hosting environment for such sites. When an S3 bucket is configured for static hosting, traffic directed at the bucket's URL can be automatically made to load a specified root document, usually named index.html. Users can click links within HTML pages to be sent to the target page or media resource. Error handling and redirects can also be incorporated into the profile.

If you want requests for a DNS domain name (like mysite.com) routed to your static site, you can use Amazon Route 53 to associate your bucket's endpoint with any registered name. This will work only if your domain name is also the name of the S3 bucket. You'll learn more about domain name records in Chapter 8, "The Domain Name System (DNS) and Network Routing: Amazon Route 53 and Amazon CloudFront."

You can also get a free SSL/TLS certificate to encrypt your site by requesting a certificate from Amazon Certificate Manager (ACM) and importing it into a CloudFront distribution that specifies your S3 bucket as its origin.

Build your own static website using Exercise 3.4.

EXERCISE 3.4

Enable Static Website Hosting for an S3 Bucket

1. From the S3 Dashboard, select (or create) an S3 bucket that contains at least a file with some simple text named index.html. Any files you want to be accessible should be readable by the public.

2. From the bucket Properties tab, enable static website hosting and specify your index.html file as your index document.

3. Paste the static website endpoint into the URL field of a browser that's not logged into your AWS account and confirm you can access the website.

Note that you can also enable static website hosting from the AWS CLI using a variation of these two commands:

```
aws s3api put-bucket-acl --bucket my-bucket --acl public-read

aws s3 website s3://my-bucket/ --index-document index.html
--error-document error.html
```

S3 and Glacier Select

AWS provides a different way to access data stored on either S3 or Glacier: Select. The feature lets you apply SQL-like queries to stored objects so that only relevant data from within objects is retrieved, permitting significantly more efficient and cost-effective operations.

One possible use case would involve large CSV files containing sales and inventory data from multiple retail sites. Your company's marketing team might need to periodically analyze only sales data and only from certain stores. Using S3 Select, they'll be able to retrieve exactly the data they need—just a fraction of the full data set—while bypassing the bandwidth and cost overhead associated with downloading the whole thing.

Amazon Glacier

At first glance, Glacier looks a bit like just another S3 storage class. After all, like most S3 classes, Glacier guarantees 99.999999999 percent durability and, as you've seen, can be incorporated into S3 lifecycle configurations.

Nevertheless, there are important differences. Glacier, for example, supports archives as large as 40 TB rather than the 5 TB limit in S3. Its archives are encrypted by default, while encryption on S3 is an option you need to select; and unlike S3's "human-readable" key names, Glacier archives are given machine-generated IDs.

But the biggest difference is the time it takes to retrieve your data. Getting the objects in an existing Glacier archive can take a number of hours, compared to nearly instant access from S3. That last feature really defines the purpose of Glacier: to provide inexpensive long-term storage for data that will be needed only in unusual and infrequent circumstances.

 Glacier does offer Expedited retrievals getting you your data in minutes rather than hours. Expedited will incur a premium charge.

In the context of Glacier, the term *archive* is used to describe an object like a document, video, or a TAR or ZIP file. Archives are stored in *vaults*—the Glacier equivalent of S3's buckets. Glacier vault names do not have to be globally unique.

Storage Pricing

To give you a sense of what S3 and Glacier might cost you, here's a typical usage scenario. Imagine you make weekly backups of your company sales data that generate 5 GB archives. You decide to maintain each archive in the S3 Standard Storage and Requests class for its first 30 days and then convert it to S3 One Zone (S3 One Zone-IA), where it will remain for 90 more days. At the end of those 120 days, you will move your archives once again, this time to Glacier, where it will be kept for another 730 days (two years) and then deleted.

Once your archive rotation is in full swing, you'll have a steady total of (approximately) 20 GB in S3 Standard, 65 GB in One Zone-IA, and 520 GB in Glacier. Table 3.3 shows what that storage will cost in the US East region at rates current at the time of writing.

TABLE 3.3   Sample storage costs for data in the US East region

Class	Storage Amount	Rate/GB/Month	Cost/Month
Standard	20 GB	$0.023	$0.46
One Zone-IA	65 GB	$0.01	$0.65
Glacier	520 GB	$0.004	$2.08
Total			$3.19

Of course, storage is only one part of the mix. You'll also be charged for operations including data retrievals; PUT, COPY, POST, or LIST requests; and lifecycle transition requests. Full, up-to-date details are available at https://aws.amazon.com/s3/pricing/.

Exercise 3.5 will introduce you to an important cost-estimating tool.

EXERCISE 3.5

Calculate the Total Lifecycle Costs for Your Data

Use the AWS Simple Monthly Calculator (http://calculator.s3.amazonaws.com/index .html) to estimate the total monthly costs of the scenario described at the beginning of this section. Even better, use a scenario that fits your own business. Try to include a full usage scenario, including requests, scans, and data retrieval. Note that you access the S3 part of the calculator by clicking the Amazon S3 tab on the left, and you can keep track of your itemized estimate using the Estimate of your Monthly Bill tab along the top.

Other Storage-Related Services

It's worth being aware of some other storage-related AWS services that, while perhaps not as common as the others you've seen, can make a big difference for the right deployment.

Amazon Elastic File System

The Elastic File System (EFS) provides automatically scalable and shareable file storage. EFS-based files are designed to be accessed from within a virtual private cloud (VPC) via Network File System (NFS) mounts on EC2 instances or from your on-premises servers through AWS Direct Connect connections. The object is to make it easy to enable secure, low-latency, and durable file sharing among multiple instances.

AWS Storage Gateway

Integrating the backup and archiving needs of your local operations with cloud storage services can be complicated. AWS Storage Gateway provides software gateway appliances (based on VMware ESXi, Microsoft Hyper-V, or EC2 images) with multiple virtual connectivity interfaces. Local devices can connect to the appliance as though it's a physical backup device like a tape drive, while the data itself is saved to AWS platforms like S3 and EBS.

AWS Snowball

Migrating large data sets to the cloud over a normal Internet connection can sometimes require far too much time and bandwidth to be practical. If you're looking to move terabyte or even petabyte-scaled data for backup or active use within AWS, ordering a Snowball device might be the best option.

When requested, AWS will ship you a physical, 256-bit, encrypted Snowball storage device onto which you'll copy your data. You then ship the device back to Amazon where its data will be uploaded to your S3 bucket(s).

AWS CLI Example

This example will use the AWS CLI to create a new bucket and recursively copy the sales-docs directory to it. Then, using the low-level s3api CLI (which should have installed along with the regular AWS CLI package), you'll check for the current lifecycle configuration of your new bucket with the get-bucket-lifecycle-configuration subcommand, specifying your bucket name. This will return an error, of course, as there currently is no configuration.

Next, you'll run the put-bucket-lifecycle-configuration subcommand, specifying the bucket name. You'll also add some JSON code to the --lifecycle-configuration argument. The code (which could also be passed as a file) will transition all objects using the sales-docs prefix to the Standard-IA after 30 days and to Glacier after 60 days. The objects will be deleted (or "expire") after a full year (365 days).

Finally, you can run get-bucket-lifecycle-configuration once again to confirm that your configuration is active. Here are the commands you would need to run to make all this work:

```
$ aws s3 mb s3://bucket-name
$ aws s3 cp --recursive sales-docs/ s3://bucket-name
$ aws s3api get-bucket-lifecycle-configuration \
   --bucket bucket-name
$ aws s3api put-bucket-lifecycle-configuration \
   --bucket bucket-name \
   --lifecycle-configuration '{
  "Rules": [
      {
          "Filter": {
              "Prefix": "sales-docs/"
          },
          "Status": "Enabled",
          "Transitions": [
              {
                  "Days": 30,
                  "StorageClass": "STANDARD_IA"
              },
              {
```

```
            "Days": 60,
            "StorageClass": "GLACIER"
        }
    ],
    "Expiration": {
        "Days": 365
    },
    "ID": "Lifecycle for bucket objects."
    }
  ]
}'
$ aws s3api get-bucket-lifecycle-configuration \
  --bucket bucket-name
```

Summary

Amazon S3 provides reliable and highly available object-level storage for low-maintenance, high-volume archive and data storage. Objects are stored in buckets on a "flat" surface but, through the use of prefixes, can be made to appear as though they're part of a normal file system.

You can—and usually should—encrypt your S3 data using either AWS-provided or self-serve encryption keys. Encryption can take place when your data is at rest using either server-side or client-side encryption.

There are multiple storage classes within S3 relying on varying degrees of data replication that allow you to balance durability, availability, and cost. Lifecycle management lets you automate the transition of your data between classes until it's no longer needed and can be deleted.

You can control who and what get access to your S3 buckets—and when—through legacy ACLs or through more powerful S3 bucket policies and IAM policies. Presigned URLs are also a safe way to allow temporary and limited access to your data.

You can reduce the size and cost of your requests against S3 and Glacier-based data by leveraging the SQL-like Select feature. You can also provide inexpensive and simple static websites through S3 buckets.

Amazon Glacier stores your data archives in vaults that might require hours to retrieve but that cost considerably less than the S3 storage classes.

Exam Essentials

Understand the way S3 resources are organized. S3 objects are stored in buckets whose names must be globally unique. Buckets are associated with AWS regions. Objects are stored within buckets on a "flat" surface, but prefixes and delimiters can give data the appearance of a folder hierarchy.

Understand how to optimize your data transfers. While the individual objects you store within an S3 bucket can be as large as 5 TB, anything larger than 100 MB *should* be uploaded with Multipart Upload, and objects larger than 5 GB *must* use Multipart Upload.

Understand how to secure your S3 data. You can use server-side encryption to protect data within S3 buckets using either AWS-generated or your own privately generated keys. Data can be encrypted even before being transferred to S3 using client-side encryption.

Understand how S3 object durability and availability are measured. The various S3 classes (and Glacier) promise varying levels of infrastructure reliability, along with data availability.

Understand S3 object versioning and lifecycle management. Older versions of S3 objects can be saved even after they've been overwritten. To manage older objects, you can automate transition of objects between more accessible storage classes to less expensive but less accessible classes. You can also schedule object deletion.

Understand how to secure your S3 objects. You can control access through the legacy, bucket, and object-based ACL rules or by creating more flexible S3 bucket policies or, at the account level, IAM policies. You can also provide temporary access to an object using a presigned URL.

Understand how to create a static website. S3-based HTML and media files can be exposed as a website that, with the help of Route 53 and CloudFront, can even live behind a DNS domain name and use encrypted HTTPS pages.

Understand the differences between S3 and Glacier. Glacier is meant for inexpensive long-term storage for data archives that you're unlikely to need often.

Review Questions

1. You need a low-latency platform where you can store files to be mounted within multiple VPC-based instances. Which of the following AWS services is your best choice?

   A. AWS Storage Gateway

   B. AWS S3

   C. Amazon Elastic File System

   D. AWS Elastic Block Store

2. What is the maximum size of S3 object metadata?

   A. 2 KB

   B. 5 GB

   C. 100 MB

   D. 5 TB

3. When planning your data operations, it's important to understand the practical limitations you'll face. Which of the following will normally be available only in limited amounts?

   A. PUT requests/month against an S3 bucket

   B. The volume of data available per S3 bucket

   C. Account-wide S3 storage space

   D. The number of S3 buckets within a single account

4. You have a publicly available file called `filename` stored in an S3 bucket named `bucketname`. Which of the following addresses will successfully retrieve the file using a web browser?

   A. `https://s3.amazonaws.com/bucketname/filename`

   B. `https://filename/bucketname.s3.amazonaws.com`

   C. `s3://bucketname/filename`

   D. `s3://filename/bucketname`

5. If you want the files stored in an S3 bucket to be accessible using a familiar directory hierarchy system, you'll need to specify prefixes and delimiters. What are prefixes and delimiters?

   A. A prefix is the name common to the objects you want to group, and a delimiter is the bar character (|).

   B. A prefix is the DNS name that precedes the `amazonaws.com` domain, and a delimiter is the name you want to give your file directory.

   C. A prefix is the name common to the objects you want to group, and a delimiter is a forward slash character (/).

   D. A prefix is the name common to the file type you want to identify, and a delimiter is a forward slash character (/).

6. You want to encrypt the objects at rest in an S3 bucket using keys provided by AWS that also allows you to track related events. Which combination of tools should you use?

    A. Server-side encryption with AWS KMS-Managed Keys

    B. Service-side encryption with Amazon S3-Managed Keys

    C. Client-side encryption with AWS KMS-Managed Keys

    D. Client-side encryption with Amazon S3-Managed Keys

7. Which of the following operational details are likely to be included in S3-generated logs? (Choose three.)

    A. Source bucket name

    B. Action requested

    C. Current bucket size

    D. Response status

8. The S3 data durability guarantees cover which of the following possible threats? (Choose two.)

    A. User misconfiguration

    B. Account security breach

    C. Infrastructure failure

    D. Data center security breach

9. Which of the following explains the difference in durability between S3's S3 One Zone-IA and Reduced Redundancy classes?

    A. One Zone-IA is heavily replicated but only within a single availability zone, while reduced redundancy is only lightly replicated.

    B. Reduced redundancy is heavily replicated but only within a single availability zone, while One Zone-IA is only lightly replicated.

    C. One Zone-IA is replicated across AWS regions while reduced redundancy data is restricted to a single region.

    D. One Zone-IA data is automatically backed up to Amazon Glacier while reduced redundancy remains within S3.

10. Which of the following is the 12-month availability guarantee for the S3 Standard-IA class?

    A. 99.99 percent

    B. 99.9 percent

    C. 99.999999999 percent

    D. 99.5 percent

11. For which of the following data operations would you *not* have to worry about eventual consistency?

    A. Operations immediately preceding the deletion of an existing object

    B. Operations subsequent to the updating of an existing object

   C. Operations subsequent to the deletion of an existing object

   D. Operations subsequent to the creation of a new object

12. What must you do to protect objects in S3 buckets from being accidentally overwritten?

   A. Nothing. S3 protects existing files by default.

   B. Nothing. S3 saves older versions of your files by default.

   C. Enable versioning.

   D. Enable file overwrite protection.

13. How can you apply transitions between storage classes for only certain objects within an S3 bucket?

   A. By specifying particular prefixes when you define your lifecycle rules

   B. This isn't possible. Lifecycle rules must apply to all the objects in a bucket.

   C. By specifying particular prefixes when you create the bucket

   D. By importing a predefined lifecycle rule template

14. Which of the following classes will usually make the most sense for long-term storage when included within a sequence of lifecycle rules?

   A. Glacier

   B. Reduced Redundancy

   C. S3 One Zone-IA

   D. S3 Standard-IA

15. Which of the following are the recommended methods for providing secure and controlled access to your buckets? (Choose two.)

   A. S3 access control lists (ACLs)

   B. S3 bucket policies

   C. IAM policies

   D. Security groups

16. In the context of an S3 bucket policy, which of the following statements describes a principal?

   A. The AWS service being defined (S3 in this case)

   B. An origin resource that's given permission to alter an S3 bucket

   C. The resource whose access is being defined

   D. The user or entity to which access is assigned

17. Assuming you didn't explicitly set a value, how long will a presigned URL remain valid?

   A. 24 hours

   B. 3,600 seconds

   C. 5 minutes

   D. 360 seconds

18. Which non-S3 AWS resources can improve the security and user experience of your S3-hosted static website? (Choose two.)

 A. Amazon Certificate Manager

 B. Elastic Compute Cloud (EC2)

 C. Relational Database Service (RDS)

 D. Route 53

19. What is the largest single archive supported by Amazon Glacier?

 A. 5 GB

 B. 40 TB

 C. 5 TB

 D. 40 GB

20. Which of the following would be a good use case for Amazon Elastic File System?

 A. You need to share files from a single host source among multiple EC2 instances running within a VPC.

 B. You need an interface through which you can back up data archives from your local, on-premises infrastructure.

 C. You need a quick way to transfer large data archives to the cloud.

 D. You need a cost-effective place to store object data.

Chapter

4

Amazon Virtual Private Cloud

THE AWS CERTIFIED SOLUTIONS ARCHITECT ASSOCIATE EXAM OBJECTIVES COVERED IN THIS CHAPTER MAY INCLUDE, BUT ARE NOT LIMITED TO, THE FOLLOWING:

Domain 1: Design Resilient Architectures

✓ **1.3 Determine how to design a multitier architecture solution.**

Domain 3: Specify Secure Applications and Architectures

✓ **3.1 Determine how to secure application tiers.**

✓ **3.3 Define the networking infrastructure for a single VPC application.**

Introduction

Amazon's Virtual Private Cloud service provides the networking layer of EC2. A VPC is a virtual network that can contain EC2 instances as well as network resources for other AWS services. By default, every VPC is isolated from all other networks. You can, however, connect your VPC to other networks, including the Internet and other VPCs.

In addition to EC2, VPCs are foundational to many AWS services, so understanding how they work is fundamental to your success on the exam and as an AWS architect. Don't assume you can ignore VPCs just because you're not using EC2.

A VPC can exist only within an AWS region. When you create a VPC in a region, it won't show up in any other regions. You can have multiple VPCs in your account and create multiple VPCs in a single region. To keep things simple, I'll start by assuming only one VPC in one region. Later, I'll cover considerations for multiple VPCs.

If you're familiar with the components of a traditional network, you'll find many VPC components to be familiar. But although VPCs function like a traditional TCP/IP network, they are scalable, allowing you to expand and extend your network without having to add physical hardware. To make this scalability possible, some components that you'd find in a traditional network—such as routers, switches, and VLANs—don't exist in VPCs. Instead, they're abstracted into software functions and called by different names.

VPC CIDR Blocks

Like a traditional network, a VPC consists of at least one range of contiguous IP addresses. This address range is represented as a *Classless interdomain routing* (CIDR) block. The CIDR block determines which IP addresses may be assigned to instances and other resources within the VPC. You must assign a primary CIDR block when creating a VPC.

There are different ways to represent a range of IP addresses. The shortest way is by CIDR notation, sometimes called *slash notation*. For example, the CIDR 172.16.0.0/16 includes all addresses from 172.16.0.0 to 172.16.255.255—a total of 65,536 addresses!

You may also hear the CIDR block referred to as an *IP prefix*. The /16 portion of the CIDR is the *prefix length*. The prefix length of a VPC CIDR can range from /16 to /28. There's an inverse relationship between the prefix length and the number of IP addresses in the CIDR. The smaller the prefix length, the greater the number of IP addresses in the CIDR. A /28 prefix length gives you only 16 addresses.

The acronym IP refers to Internet Protocol version 4 or IPv4. Valid IPv4 prefix lengths range from /0 to /32. Although you can specify any valid IP range for your VPC CIDR, it's best to use one in the RFC 1918 range to avoid conflicts with public Internet addresses.

- 10.0.0.0–10.255.255.255 (10.0.0.0/8)
- 172.16.0.0–172.31.255.255 (172.16.0.0/12)
- 192.168.0.0–192.168.255.255 (192.168.0.0/16)

If you plan on connecting your VPC to another network—whether an on-premises network or another VPC—be sure the VPC CIDR you choose doesn't overlap with addresses already in use on the other network.

You can't change the primary CIDR block, so think carefully about your address requirements before creating a VPC.

Secondary CIDR Blocks

You may optionally specify secondary CIDR blocks for a VPC after you've created it. These blocks must come from either the same address range as the primary or a publicly routable range, but they must not overlap with the primary or other secondary blocks. For example, if the VPC's primary CIDR is 172.16.0.0/16, you may specify a secondary CIDR of 172.17.0.0/16. But you may not specify 192.168.0.0/16.

If you think you might ever need a secondary CIDR, be careful about your choice of primary CIDR. If you choose 192.168.0.0/16 as your primary CIDR, you won't be able to create a secondary CIDR using any of the RFC 1918 ranges.

IPv6 CIDR Blocks

You may let AWS assign an IPv6 CIDR to your VPC. Unlike the primary CIDR, which is an IP prefix of your choice, you can't choose your own IPv6 CIDR. Instead, AWS assigns one to your VPC at your request. The IPv6 CIDR will be a publicly routable prefix from the global unicast IPv6 address space. For example, AWS may assign you the CIDR 2600:1f18:2551:8900/56. Note that the prefix length of an IPv6 VPC CIDR is always /56.

Complete Exercise 4.1 to create your own VPC.

EXERCISE 4.1

Create a New VPC

Create a VPC with the primary CIDR 172.16.0.0/16.

To complete this exercise using the AWS Command Line Interface, enter the following command:

```
aws ec2 create-vpc-cidr-block 172.16.0.0/16
```

Subnets

A subnet is a logical container within a VPC that holds your EC2 instances. A subnet lets you isolate instances from each other, control how traffic flows to and from your instances, and lets you organize them by function. For example, you can create one subnet for public web servers that need to be accessible from the Internet and create another subnet for database servers that only the web instances can access. In concept, subnets are similar to virtual LANs (VLANs) in a traditional network.

Every instance must exist within a subnet. You'll often hear the phrase "launch an instance into a subnet." Once you create an instance in a subnet, you can't move it. You can, however, terminate it and create a different instance in another subnet. By extension, this also means you can't move an instance from one VPC to another.

Subnet CIDR Blocks

Each subnet has its own CIDR block that must be a subset of the VPC CIDR that it resides in. For example, if your VPC has a CIDR of 172.16.0.0/16, one of your subnets may have a CIDR of 172.16.100.0/24. This range covers 172.16.100.0–172.16.100.255, which yields a total of 256 addresses.

AWS reserves the first four and last IP addresses in every subnet. You can't assign these addresses to any instances. Assuming a subnet CIDR of 172.16.100.0/24, the following addresses would be reserved:

- 172.16.100.0–172.16.100.3
- 172.16.100.255

The restrictions on prefix lengths for a subnet CIDR are the same as VPC CIDRs. Subnet CIDR blocks in a single VPC can't overlap with each other. Also, once you assign a CIDR to a subnet, you can't change it.

It's possible for a subnet and VPC to share the same CIDR. This is uncommon and won't leave you room for additional subnets. More commonly, each subnet's prefix length will be longer than the VPC's to allow for multiple subnets to exist in the same VPC.

A subnet can't have multiple CIDRs. Unlike a VPC that can have secondary CIDRs, a subnet can have only one. However, if a VPC has a primary CIDR and a secondary CIDR, your subnet's CIDR can be derived from either. For example, if your VPC has the primary CIDR of 172.16.0.0/16 and a secondary CIDR of 172.17.0.0/16, a subnet in that VPC could be 172.17.12.0/24, as it's derived from the secondary VPC CIDR.

Availability Zones

A subnet can exist within only one *availability zone* (AZ, or *zone* for short), which is roughly analogous to a relatively small geographic location such as a data center. Although availability zones in an AWS region are connected, they are designed so that a failure in one zone doesn't cause a failure in another.

You can achieve resiliency for your applications by creating two subnets in different availability zones and then spreading your instances across those zones. Table 4.1 provides an example of two subnets in different availability zones.

TABLE 4.1   Subnets in different availability zones

Subnet	Availability Zone	Instance
web-subnet1	us-east-1a	web1
web-subnet2	us-east-1b	web2

In this example, if the us-east-1a zone fails, the instance web1 will fail because it's in that zone. But web2, which is in the us-east-1b zone, will remain available.

Having subnets in different availability zones is not a requirement. You can place all of your subnets in the same zone, but keep in mind that if that zone fails, all instances in those subnets will fail as well. Refer to Figure 4.1 for an example of two instances in different availability zones.

FIGURE 4.1   VPC with subnets and instances

Complete Exercise 4.2 to practice creating a subnet.

EXERCISE 4.2

Create a New Subnet

Create a subnet in the VPC you created earlier. Choose an availability zone and assign the CIDR block 172.16.100.0/24.

To complete this using the following AWS Command Line Interface commands, you'll need the resource ID of the VPC:

```
aws ec2 create-subnet-vpc-id [VPC resource ID] --cidr-block 172.16.100.0/24
--availability-zone us-east-1a
```

IPv6 CIDR Blocks

If you've allocated an IPv6 CIDR to your VPC, you can assign IPv6 CIDRs to subnets within that VPC. The prefix length for an IPv6 subnet is fixed at /64. If your VPC's IPv6 CIDR is 2600:1f18:2551:8900/56, you can assign a subnet the CIDR 2600:1f18:2551:8900/64 through 2600:1f18:2551:89FF/64.

> You must always assign an IPv4 CIDR block to a subnet, even if you have no plans to use it.

Elastic Network Interfaces

An *elastic network interface* (ENI) allows an instance to communicate with other network resources including AWS services, other instances, on-premises servers, and the Internet. It also makes it possible for you to connect to the operating system running on your instance to manage it. As the name suggests, an ENI performs the same basic function as a network interface on a physical server, although ENIs have more restrictions on how you can configure them.

Every instance must have a *primary network interface* (also known as the *primary ENI*), which is connected to only one subnet. This is the reason you have to specify a subnet when launching an instance. You can't remove the primary ENI from an instance.

Primary and Secondary Private IP Addresses

Each instance must have a *primary private IP address* from the range specified by the subnet CIDR. The primary private IP address is bound to the primary ENI of the instance. You can't change or remove this address, but you can assign secondary private IP addresses to the primary ENI. Any secondary addresses must come from the same subnet that the ENI is attached to.

It's possible to attach additional ENIs to an instance. Those ENIs may be in a different subnet, but they must be in the same availability zone as the instance. As always, any addresses associated with the ENI must come from the subnet to which it is attached.

Attaching Elastic Network Interfaces

An ENI can exist independently of an instance. You can create an ENI first and then attach it to an instance later. For example, you can create an ENI in one subnet and then attach it to an instance as the primary ENI when you launch the instance. If you disable the Delete on Termination attribute of the ENI, you can terminate the instance without deleting the ENI. You can then associate the ENI with another instance.

You can also take an existing ENI and attach it to an existing instance as a secondary ENI. This lets you redirect traffic from a failed instance to a working instance by detaching the ENI from the failed instance and reattaching it to the working instance. Complete Exercise 4.3 to practice creating an ENI and attaching it to an instance.

EXERCISE 4.3

Create and Attach a Primary ENI

Create an ENI in the subnet of your choice.

1. In the EC2 web console, look under the Network & Security section and click Network Interfaces.

2. Click Create Network Interface.

3. Specify the subnet in which to create the ENI, and select the default security group.

4. Launch an instance into the subnet, attaching the ENI as the primary ENI.

Internet Gateways

An *Internet gateway* gives instances the ability to receive a public IP address, connect to the Internet, and receive requests from the Internet.

When you create a VPC, it does not have an Internet gateway associated with it. You must create an Internet gateway and associate it with a VPC manually. You can associate only one Internet gateway with a VPC. But you may create multiple Internet gateways and associate each one with a different VPC.

An Internet gateway is somewhat analogous to an Internet router an Internet service provider may install on-premises. But in AWS, an Internet gateway doesn't behave exactly like a router. In a traditional network, you might configure your core router with a default gateway IP address pointing to the Internet router to give your servers access to the Internet. An Internet gateway, however, doesn't have a management IP address or network interface. Instead, AWS identifies an Internet gateway by its resource ID, which begins with igw- followed by an alphanumeric string. To use an Internet gateway, you must create a *default route* in a *route table* that points to the Internet gateway as a target.

Route Tables

Configurable virtual routers do not exist as VPC resources. Instead, the VPC infrastructure implements IP routing as a software function, and AWS calls this function an *implied router* (also sometimes called an *implicit router*). This means there's no virtual router on which to configure interface IP addresses or dynamic routing protocols. Rather, you only have to manage the route table which the implied router uses.

Each route table consists of one or more routes and at least one subnet association. Think of a route table as being connected to multiple subnets in much the same way a traditional router would be. When you create a VPC, AWS automatically creates a default route table called the *main route table* and associates it with every subnet in that VPC. You can use the main route table or create a custom one that you can manually associate with one or more subnets.

If you do not explicitly associate a subnet with a route table you've created, AWS will implicitly associate it with the main route table. A subnet cannot exist without a route table association.

Routes

Routes determine how to forward traffic from instances within the subnets associated with the route table. IP routing is destination-based, meaning that routing decisions are based only on the destination IP address, not the source.

When you create a route, you must provide the following elements:

- Destination
- Target

The destination must be an IP prefix in CIDR notation. The target must be an AWS network resource such as an Internet gateway or an ENI. It cannot be a CIDR.

Every route table contains a *local route* that allows instances in different subnets to communicate with each other. Table 4.2 shows what this route would look like in a VPC with the CIDR 172.31.0.0/16.

TABLE 4.2 The local route

Destination	Target
172.31.0.0/16	Local

The local route is the only mandatory route that exists in every route table. It's what allows communication between instances in the same VPC. Because there are no routes for any other IP prefixes, any traffic destined for an address outside of the VPC CIDR range will get dropped.

The Default Route

To enable Internet access for your instances, you must create a default route pointing to the Internet gateway. After adding a default route, you would end up with this:

Destination	Target
172.31.0.0/16	Local
0.0.0.0/0	igw-0e538022a0fddc318

The 0.0.0.0/0 prefix encompasses all IP addresses, including those of hosts on the Internet. This is why it's always listed as the destination in a default route. Any subnet that is associated with a route table containing a default route pointing to an Internet gateway is called a *public subnet*. Contrast this with a *private subnet* that does not have a default route.

Notice that the 0.0.0.0/0 and 172.31.0.0/16 prefixes overlap. When deciding where to route traffic, the implied router will route based on the closest match. Suppose an instance sends a packet to the Internet address 198.51.100.50. Because 198.51.100.50 does not match the 172.31.0.0/16 prefix but does match the 0.0.0.0/0 prefix, the implied router will use the default route and send the packet to the Internet gateway.

AWS documentation speaks of one implied router per VPC. It's important to understand that the implied router doesn't actually exist as a discrete resource. It's an abstraction of an IP routing function. Nevertheless, you may find it helpful to think of each route table as a separate implied router. Follow the steps in Exercise 4.4 to create an Internet gateway and a default route.

EXERCISE 4.4

Create an Internet Gateway and Default Route

In this exercise, you'll create an Internet gateway and attach it to the VPC you used in the previous exercises.

1. In the VPC Dashboard, click Internet Gateways.

2. Click the Create Internet Gateway button.

3. Click Create.

4. Select the Internet gateway you just created, and under the Actions menu, click Attach To VPC.

5. Select the VPC you used in the previous exercises and then click Attach.

6. To create a default route in the main route table, in the VPC Dashboard, click Route Tables.

7. Select the Main route table for the VPC.

8. Click the Routes tab, and click Edit.

9. Click the Add Another Route button.

10. For the destination, enter **0.0.0.0/0**. For the target, enter the identifier of the Internet gateway.

11. Click Save.

Security Groups

A *security group* functions as a firewall that controls traffic to and from an instance by permitting traffic to ingress or egress that instance's ENI.

Every ENI must have at least one security group associated with it. One ENI can have multiple security groups attached, and the same security group can be attached to multiple ENIs.

In practice, because most instances have only one ENI, people often think of a security group as being attached to an instance. When an instance has multiple ENIs, take care to note whether those ENIs use different security groups.

When you create a security group, you must specify a group name, description, and VPC for the group to reside in. Once you create the group, you specify inbound and outbound rules to allow traffic through the security group.

Inbound Rules

Inbound rules specify what traffic is allowed into the attached ENI. An inbound rule consists of three required elements:

▪   Source

▪   Protocol

▪   Port range

When you create a security group, it doesn't contain any inbound rules. Security groups use a default-deny approach, also called *whitelisting*, which denies all traffic that is not explicitly allowed by a rule. When you create a new security group and attach it to an instance, all inbound traffic to that instance will be blocked. You must create inbound rules to allow traffic to your instance. For this reason, the order of rules in a security group doesn't matter.

Suppose you have an instance running an HTTPS-based web application. You want to allow anyone on the Internet to connect to this instance, so you'd need an inbound rule to allow all TCP traffic coming in on port 443 (the default port and protocol for HTTPS). To manage this instance using SSH, you'd need another inbound rule for TCP port 22. However, you don't want to allow SSH access from just anyone. You need to allow SSH access only from the IP address 198.51.100.10. To achieve this, you would use a security group containing the inbound rules listed in Table 4.3.

TABLE 4.3 Inbound rules allowing SSH and HTTPS access from any IP address

Source	Protocol	Port Range
198.51.100.10/32	TCP	22
0.0.0.0/0	TCP	443

The prefix 0.0.0.0/0 covers all valid IP addresses, so using the preceding rule would allow HTTPS access not only from the Internet but from all instances in the VPC as well.

Outbound Rules

Outbound rules specify what traffic the instance may send via the attached ENI. An outbound rule mirrors an inbound rule and contains three elements.

- Destination
- Protocol
- Port range

In many cases, the outbound rules of a security group will be less restrictive than the inbound rules. When you create a security group, AWS automatically creates the outbound rule listed in Table 4.4.

TABLE 4.4 Outbound rule allowing Internet access

Destination	Protocol	Port Range
0.0.0.0/0	All	All

The main purpose of this rule is to allow the instance to access the Internet and other AWS resources. You may delete this rule, but if you do, the security group won't permit your instance to access the Internet or anything else!

Sources and Destinations

The source or destination in a rule can be any CIDR or the resource ID of a security group. If you specify a security group as the source or destination, any instance with that security group attached will be allowed by the rule. This makes it easy to allow instances to communicate with each other by simply assigning the same security group to all of them.

Stateful Firewall

A security group acts as a stateful firewall. Stateful means that when a security group allows traffic to pass in one direction, it intelligently allows reply traffic in the opposite direction. For instance, when you allow inbound HTTPS access to an instance from a client on the Internet, the security group automatically allows reply traffic from the instance to the client.

Default Security Group

Each VPC contains a default security group that you can't delete. You don't have to use it, but if you do, you can modify its rules to suit your needs. Alternatively, you may opt to create your own custom group and use it instead. Complete Exercise 4.5 to practice creating a custom security group.

EXERCISE 4.5

Create a Custom Security Group

In this exercise, you'll create a new security group that allows SSH, HTTP, and HTTPS access from any IP address.

1. From either the EC2 or VPC dashboard, click Security Groups.

2. Click Create Security Group.

3. Assign the security group a name, and select the VPC you've used in previous exercises.

4. Under the Inbound tab, click Add Rule.

5. Add rules to allow SSH, HTTP, and HTTPS access from any IP address.

6. Click Create.

Network Access Control Lists

Like a security group, a *network access control list* (NACL) functions as a firewall in that it contains inbound and outbound rules to allow traffic based on a source or destination CIDR, protocol, and port. Also, each VPC has a default NACL that can't be deleted. But the similarities end there.

A NACL differs from a security group in many respects. Instead of being attached to an ENI, a NACL is attached to a subnet. The NACL associated with a subnet controls what traffic may enter and exit that subnet. This means that NACLs can't be used to control traffic between instances in the same subnet. If you want to do that, you have to use security groups.

A subnet can have only one NACL associated with it. When you create a new subnet in a VPC, the VPC's default NACL is associated with the subnet by default. You can modify the default NACL, or you can create a new one and associate it with the subnet. You can also associate the same NACL with multiple subnets, provided those subnets are all in the same VPC as the NACL.

Unlike a security group, which is stateful, a NACL is stateless, meaning that it doesn't track the state of connections passing through it. This is much like an access control list (ACL) on a traditional switch or router. The stateless nature of the NACL is why each one is preconfigured with rules to allow all inbound and outbound traffic, as discussed in the following sections.

Inbound Rules

Inbound rules determine what traffic is allowed to ingress the subnet. Each rule contains the following elements:

- Rule number
- Protocol
- Port range
- Source
- Action

The default NACL for a VPC with no IPv6 CIDR comes prepopulated with the two inbound rules listed in Table 4.5.

TABLE 4.5   Default NACL inbound rules

Rule Number	Protocol	Port Range	Source	Action
100	All	All	0.0.0.0/0	Allow
*	All	All	0.0.0.0/0	Deny

NACL rules are processed in ascending order of the rule number. Rule 100 is the lowest-numbered rule, so it gets processed first. This rule allows all traffic from any source. You can delete or modify this rule or create additional rules before or after it. For example, if you wanted to block only HTTP (TCP port 80), you could add the following rule:

Rule Number	Protocol	Port Range	Source	Action
90	TCP	80	0.0.0.0/0	Deny

This rule denies all TCP traffic with a destination port of 80. Because it's the lowest-numbered rule in the list, it gets processed first. Any traffic not matching this rule would be processed by rule 100, which allows all traffic.

The last rule in Table 4.5 is the default rule. It's designated by an asterisk (*) instead of a number and is always the last rule in the list. You can't delete or otherwise change the default rule. The default rule causes the NACL to deny any traffic that isn't explicitly allowed by any of the preceding rules. Complete Exercise 4.6 to create a custom NACL.

EXERCISE 4.6

Create an Inbound Rule to Allow Remote Access from Any IP Address

NACL rule order matters! Create a new NACL and attach it to the subnet you used in Exercise 4.3.

1. In the VPC Dashboard, click Network ACLs.

2. Click Create Network ACL.

3. Select the VPC you used in previous exercises.

4. Select the NACL and click the Inbound Rules tab.

5. If you launched a Linux instance, add an inbound rule numbered 100 to allow SSH (TCP port 22) access from any IP address. If you launched a Windows instance, add an inbound rule to allow RDP (TCP port 3389) access from any IP address.

6. Remove any rules that allow other inbound traffic.

7. Connect to the instance and remain connected.

8. Now add another inbound rule numbered 90 that denies all traffic. Your connection to the instance should drop.

Outbound Rules

As you might expect, the outbound NACL rules follow an almost identical format as the inbound rules. Each rule contains the following elements:

- Rule number
- Protocol

- Port range
- Destination
- Action

Each default NACL comes with the outbound rules listed in Table 4.6. Notice that the rules are identical to the default inbound rules except for the Destination element.

TABLE 4.6   Default NACL outbound rules

Rule Number	Protocol	Port Range	Destination	Action
100	All	All	0.0.0.0/0	Allow
*	All	All	0.0.0.0/0	Deny

In most cases you will need these rules whether you use the default NACL or a custom one. Because a NACL is stateless, it won't automatically allow return traffic. Therefore, if you permit HTTPS traffic with an inbound rule, you must also explicitly permit the return traffic using an outbound rule. In this case, rule 100 permits the return traffic.

If you do need to restrict access from the subnet—to block Internet access, for example—you will need to create an outbound rule to allow return traffic over *ephemeral ports*. Ephemeral ports are reserved TCP or UDP ports that clients listen for reply traffic on. As an example, when a client sends an HTTPS request to your instance over TCP port 80, that client may listen for a reply on TCP port 36034. Your NACL's outbound rules must allow traffic to egress the subnet on TCP port 36034.

The range of ephemeral ports varies by client operating system. Many modern operating systems use ephemeral ports in the range of 49152–65535, but don't assume that allowing only this range will be sufficient. The range for TCP ports may differ from the range for UDP, and older or customized operating systems may use a different range altogether. To maintain compatibility, do not restrict outbound traffic using a NACL. Use a security group instead.

If your VPC includes an IPv6 CIDR, AWS will automatically add inbound and outbound rules to permit IPv6 traffic.

Using Network Access Control Lists and Security Groups Together

You may want to use a NACL in addition to a security group so that you aren't dependent upon users to specify the correct security group when they launch an instance. Because a NACL is applied to the subnet, the rules of the NACL apply to all traffic ingressing and egressing the subnet, regardless of how the security groups are configured.

When you make a change to a NACL or security group rule, that change takes effect immediately (practically, within several seconds). Avoid changing security groups and NACLs simultaneously. If your changes don't work as expected, it can become difficult to identify whether the problem is with a security group or NACL. Complete your changes on one before moving to the other. Additionally, be cautious about making changes when there are active connections to an instance, as an incorrectly ordered NACL rule or missing security group rule can terminate those connections. Refer to Exercise 4.5 for a demonstration.

Note that in a NACL rule you can specify a CIDR only as the source or destination. This is unlike a security group rule wherein you can specify another security group for the source or destination.

Public IP Addresses

A public IP address is reachable over the public Internet. This is in contrast to RFC 1918 addresses, which cannot be routed over the Internet but can be routed within private networks.

You need a public IP address for an instance if you want others to directly connect to it via the Internet. You *may* also give an instance a public IP address if you want it to have outbound-only Internet access. You *don't* need a public IP address for your instances to communicate with each other within the VPC infrastructure, as this instance-to-instance communication happens using private IP addresses.

When you launch an instance into a subnet, you can choose to automatically assign it a public IP. This is convenient, but there are a couple of potential downsides to this approach.

First, if you forget to choose this option when you launch the instance, you cannot go back and have AWS automatically assign a public IP later. Also, when you stop or terminate the instance, you will lose the public IP address. If you stop and restart the instance, it will receive a different public IP.

Even if you don't plan to stop your instance, keep in mind that AWS may perform maintenance events that cause your instance to restart. If this happens, its public IP address will change.

If your instance doesn't need to maintain the same IP address for a long period of time, this approach may be acceptable. If not, you may opt instead for an *elastic IP address*.

Elastic IP Addresses

An elastic IP address (EIP) is a type of public IP address that AWS allocates to your account when you request it. Once AWS allocates an EIP to your account, you have exclusive use of that address until you manually release it. Outside of AWS, there's no noticeable difference between an EIP and an automatically assigned public IP.

When you initially allocate an EIP, it is not bound to any instance. Instead, you must associate it with an ENI. You can move an EIP around to different ENIs, although you can associate it with only one ENI at a time. Once you associate an EIP with an ENI, it will remain associated for the life of the ENI or until you disassociate it.

If you associate an EIP to an ENI that already has an automatically assigned public IP address allocated, AWS will replace the public IP address with the EIP. Complete Exercise 4.7 to practice allocating and using an EIP.

EXERCISE 4.7

Allocate and Use an Elastic IP Address

Allocate an elastic IP address and associate it with the instance you created earlier.

1. In the VPC Dashboard, click Elastic IPs.

2. Click Allocate New Address.

3. Click Allocate.

4. Click the EIP, and under the Actions menu, click Associate Address.

5. Select the instance you created earlier.

6. Click Associate. The instance original public IP address should change to the EIP.

Network Address Translation

When you associate an ENI with a public IP address, the ENI maintains its private IP address. Associating a public IP with an ENI doesn't reconfigure the ENI with a new address. Instead, the Internet gateway maps the public IP address to the ENI's private IP address using a process called *network address translation* (NAT).

When an instance with a public IP connects to a host on the Internet, the host sees the traffic as originating from the instance's public IP. For example, assume an instance with a private IP address of 172.31.7.10 is associated with the EIP 35.168.241.48. When the instance attempts to send a packet to the Internet host 198.51.100.11, it will send the following packet to the Internet gateway:

Source IP Address	Destination IP Address
172.31.7.10	35.168.241.48

The Internet gateway will translate this packet to change the source IP address to the instance's public IP address. The translated packet, which the Internet gateway forwards to the host, looks like this:

Source IP Address	Destination IP Address
35.168.241.48	198.51.100.11

Likewise, when a host on the Internet sends a packet to the instance's EIP, the Internet gateway will perform network address translation on the incoming packet. The packet that reaches the Internet gateway from the Internet host will look like this:

Source IP Address	Destination IP Address
198.51.100.11	35.168.241.48

The Internet gateway will translate this packet, replacing the destination IP address with the instance's private IP address, as follows:

Source IP Address	Destination IP Address
198.51.100.11	172.31.7.10

Network address translation occurs automatically at the Internet gateway when an instance has a public IP address. You can't change this behavior.

Network address translation as described here is also sometimes called *one-to-one NAT* because one private IP address gets mapped to one public IP address.

Network Address Translation Devices

Although network address translation occurs at the Internet gateway, there are two other resources that can also perform NAT.

- NAT gateway
- NAT instance

AWS calls these NAT devices. The purpose of a NAT device is to allow an instance to access the Internet while preventing hosts on the Internet from reaching the instance directly. This is useful when an instance needs to go out to the Internet to fetch updates or to upload data but does not need to service requests from clients.

When you use a NAT device, the instance needing Internet access does not have a public IP address allocated to it. Incidentally, this makes it impossible for hosts on the Internet to reach it directly. Instead, only the NAT device is configured with a public IP. Additionally, the NAT device has an interface in a public subnet. Refer to Table 4.7 for an example.

TABLE 4.7   IP address configuration when using a NAT device

Name	Subnet	Private IP	Public IP
db1	Private	172.31.7.11	None
db2	Private	172.31.7.12	None
NAT device	Public	172.31.8.10	18.209.220.180

When db1 sends a packet to a host on the Internet with the address 198.51.100.11, the packet must first go to the NAT device. The NAT device translates the packet as follows:

Original Packet's Source IP Address	Original Packet's Destination IP Address	Translated Packet's Source IP Address	Translated Packet's Destination IP Address
172.31.7.11 (db1)	198.51.100.11	172.31.8.10 (NAT device)	198.51.100.11

The NAT device then takes the translated packet and forwards it to the Internet gateway. The Internet gateway performs NAT translation on this packet as follows:

NAT Device Packet's Source IP Address	NAT Device Packet's Destination IP Address	Translated Packet's Source IP Address	Translate Packet's Destination IP Address
172.31.8.10 (NAT device)	198.51.100.11	18.209.220.180 (NAT device's EIP)	198.51.100.11

Multiple instances can use the same NAT device, thus sharing the same public IP address for outbound connections. The function that NAT devices perform is also called *port address translation* (PAT).

Configuring Route Tables to Use NAT Devices

Instances that use the NAT device must send Internet-bound traffic to it, while the NAT device must send Internet-bound traffic to an Internet gateway. Hence, the NAT device and the instances that use it must use different default routes. Furthermore, they must also use different route tables and hence must reside in separate subnets.

Refer to Table 4.7 again. Notice that the instances reside in the Private subnet, and the NAT device is in the Public subnet. The default routes for these subnets would follow the pattern in Table 4.8.

TABLE 4.8   Default routes for the Private and Public subnets

Subnet	Destination	Target
Private	0.0.0.0/0	NAT device
Public	0.0.0.0/0	igw-0e538022a0fddc318

Refer to the diagram in Figure 4.2 to see the relationship between both of the route tables. Recall that a route target must be a VPC resource such as instance, Internet gateway, or ENI. The specific target you choose depends on the type of NAT device you use: a NAT gateway or a NAT instance.

FIGURE 4.2   Network address translation using a NAT device

NAT Gateway

A NAT gateway is a NAT device managed by AWS. Like an Internet gateway, it's a one-size-fits-all resource. It doesn't come in a variety of flavors, and there's nothing to manage or access. It automatically scales to accommodate your bandwidth requirements. You set it and forget it.

When you create a NAT gateway, you must assign it an EIP. A NAT gateway can reside in only one subnet, which must be a public subnet for it to access the Internet. AWS selects a private IP address from the subnet and assigns it to the NAT gateway. For redundancy, you may create additional NAT gateways in different availability zones.

After creating a NAT gateway, you must create a default route to direct Internet-bound traffic from your instances to the NAT gateway. The target you specify will be the NAT gateway ID, which follows the format `nat-0750b9c8de7e75e9f`. If you use multiple NAT gateways, you can create multiple default routes, each pointing to a different NAT gateway as the target.

Because a NAT gateway doesn't use an ENI, you can't apply a security group to it. You can, however, apply a NACL to the subnet that it resides in.

NAT Instance

A NAT instance is a normal EC2 instance that uses a preconfigured Linux-based AMI. You have to perform the same steps to launch it as you would any other instance. It functions like a NAT gateway in many respects, but there are some key differences.

Unlike a NAT gateway, a NAT instance doesn't automatically scale to accommodate increased bandwidth requirements. Therefore, it's important that you select an appropriately robust instance type. If you choose an instance type that's too small, you must manually upgrade to a larger instance type.

Also, a NAT instance has an ENI, so you must apply a security group to it. You also must remember to assign it a public IP address. Lastly, you must disable the *source/destination check* on the NAT instance's ENI. This allows the NAT instance to receive traffic addressed to an IP other than its own, and it also allows the instance to send traffic using a source IP that it doesn't own.

One advantage of a NAT instance is that you can use it as a *bastion host*, sometimes called a *jump host*, to connect to instances that don't have a public IP. You can't do this with a NAT gateway.

You must create a default route to direct Internet-bound traffic to the NAT instance. The target of the default route will be the NAT instance's ID, which follows the format `i-0a1674fe5671dcb00`.

If you want to guard against instance or availability zone failures, it's not as simple as just spinning up another NAT instance. You cannot create multiple default routes pointing to different NAT instances. If you need this level of resiliency, you're better off using NAT gateways instead.

VPC Peering

You can configure VPC peering to allow instances in one VPC to communicate with VPCs in another over the private AWS network. You may want to do this if you have instances in different regions that need to communicate. You may also want to connect your instances to another AWS customer's instances.

To enable VPC peering, you must set up a *VPC peering connection* between two VPCs. A VPC peering connection is a point-to-point connection between two and only two VPCs. You can have at most one peering connection between a pair of VPCs. Also, peered VPCs must not have overlapping CIDR blocks.

With one exception, a VPC peering connection allows only instance-to-instance communication. This means an instance in one VPC can use the peering connection only to connect to another instance in the peered VPC. You can't use it to share Internet gateways or NAT devices. You can, however, use it to share a Network Load Balancer (NLB).

If you have more than two VPCs you need to connect, you must create a peering connection between each pair. You cannot daisy-chain VPC peering connections together and route through them. This configuration is called transitive routing.

To use a peering connection, you must create new routes in both VPCs to allow traffic to travel in both directions. For each route, the destination prefix should exist within the destination VPC. The target of each route must be the peering connection's identifier, which begins with pcx-. Refer to Table 4.9 for examples of two routes you would create to enable peering between a pair of VPCs.

TABLE 4.9   Routes for VPC peering

Source VPC CIDR	Destination VPC CIDR	Target
172.31.0.0/16	10.0.0.0/16	pcx-076781cf11220b9dc
10.0.0.0/16	172.31.0.0/16	pcx-076781cf11220b9dc

Notice that the routes are mirrors of each other. Again, this is to allow traffic in both directions. The destination CIDR doesn't need to exactly match that of the destination VPC. If you want to enable peering only between specific subnets, you can specify the subnet CIDR instead.

Inter-region VPC peering is not available for some AWS regions. Peering connections between regions have a maximum transmission unit (MTU) of 1500 bytes and do not support IPv6.

Summary

The Virtual Private Cloud service provides the networking foundation for EC2 and other AWS services. AWS abstracts some networking components in such a way that their configuration is easier than in a traditional network, but you still need to have a solid grasp of networking fundamentals to architect VPCs.

In each region, AWS automatically provides a default VPC with default subnets, a main route table, a default security group, and a default NACL. Many use a default VPC for a long time without ever having to configure a VPC from scratch. This makes it all the more important that you as an AWS architect understand how to configure a virtual network infrastructure from scratch. There's a good chance you won't be allowed to modify an infrastructure that was built on top of a default VPC. Instead, you may be tasked with replicating it from the ground up—troubleshooting various issues along the way. Practice what you've learned in this chapter until creating fully functional VPCs becomes second nature to you.

In a traditional network, you're free to reconfigure server IP addresses, move them to different subnets, and even move them to different physical locations. You have tremendous flexibility to change your plans midstream. When creating a VPC, you don't have that luxury. You must carefully plan your entire application infrastructure up front, not just your network. It's therefore crucial that you understand how all of the VPC and EC2 components fit together.

You begin by defining a contiguous IP address range for the VPC and representing it as a CIDR. The primary CIDR should ideally be sufficiently large to accommodate all of your instances, but small enough to leave room for a secondary CIDR.

After that, you have to divvy up your VPC CIDR into subnets. Because a subnet is a container that resides in only one availability zone, you must make up-front decisions about where to place your instances. Once you create an instance in a subnet, you can't move it.

Prior to launching instances, you need to configure security groups, as every instance's ENI must have at least one attached. One area where you do have some flexibility is with network access control lists. You can associate a NACL with a subnet at any time or forego NACLs altogether.

If you want your instances to be accessible from the Internet, you must provision an Internet gateway, create a default route, and assign public IP addresses. Those are the basics. If you choose to use a NAT gateway or instance or a VPC peering connection, you'll have to modify multiple route tables.

Exam Essentials

Be able to determine the correct prefix length for a CIDR block based on the number of IP addresses you need in a VPC or subnet.   Allowed prefix lengths range from /16 to /28. The longer the prefix length, the fewer the number of IP addresses you'll have available.

Understand the significance of a subnet.   A subnet is a logical container that holds EC2 instances. Each subnet has a CIDR block derived from the CIDR of the VPC that it resides in. An instance in the subnet must take its private IP address from the subnet's CIDR. But AWS reserves the first four and last IP addresses in every subnet.

Know the impact of an availability zone failure.   If a zone fails, every subnet in that zone—and every instance in that subnet—will likewise fail. To tolerate a zone failure, build redundancy into your instance deployments by spreading them across different zones.

Understand the rules for creating and using elastic network interfaces (ENIs).   Every instance must have a primary network interface with a primary private IP address. Any additional ENI you attach to an instance must be in the same subnet as the primary ENI.

Be able to create, modify, and use route tables.   Know the purpose of the main route table in a VPC and its relationship to the VPC's subnets. Also understand how to create a public subnet using an Internet gateway and a default route.

Know the differences between security groups and network access control lists.   Understand why a stateful security group requires different rules than a stateless NACL to achieve the same result.

Understand how network address translation works.   Know the difference between NAT that occurs at the Internet gateway and NAT that occurs on a NAT device. NAT that occurs on a NAT device is also called port address translation (PAT). Multiple instances can share a single public IP address using a NAT device.

Be able to create and configure VPC peering among multiple VPCs.   Know the limitations of VPC peering connections. VPC peering connections do not support transitive routing or IPv6. Inter-region peering is available for some regions.

Review Questions

1. What is the range of allowed IPv4 prefix lengths for a VPC CIDR block?
   - **A.** /16 to /28
   - **B.** /16 to /56
   - **C.** /8 to /30
   - **D.** /56 only

2. You've created a VPC with the CIDR 192.168.16.0/24. You want to assign a secondary CIDR to this VPC. Which CIDR can you use?
   - **A.** 172.31.0.0/16
   - **B.** 192.168.0.0/16
   - **C.** 192.168.0.0/24
   - **D.** 192.168.16.0/23

3. You need to create two subnets in a VPC that has a CIDR of 10.0.0.0/16. Which of the following CIDRs can you assign to one of the subnets while leaving room for an additional subnet? (Choose all that apply.)
   - **A.** 10.0.0.0/24
   - **B.** 10.0.0.0/8
   - **C.** 10.0.0.0/16
   - **D.** 10.0.0.0/23

4. What is the relationship between a subnet and an availability zone?
   - **A.** A subnet can exist in multiple availability zones.
   - **B.** An availability zone can have multiple subnets.
   - **C.** An availability zone can have only one subnet.
   - **D.** A subnet's CIDR is derived from its availability zone.

5. Which is true regarding an elastic network interface?
   - **A.** It must have a private IP address from the subnet that it resides in.
   - **B.** It cannot exist independently of an instance.
   - **C.** It can be connected to multiple subnets.
   - **D.** It can have multiple IP addresses from different subnets.

6. What is true of security groups?
   - **A.** Only one security group can be attached to an ENI.
   - **B.** A security group must always be attached to an ENI.
   - **C.** A security group can be attached to a subnet.
   - **D.** Every VPC contains a default security group.

7. How does a NACL differ from a security group?

    A. A NACL is stateless.

    B. A NACL is stateful.

    C. A NACL is attached to an ENI.

    D. A NACL can be associated with only one subnet.

8. What is an Internet gateway?

    A. A resource that grants instances in multiple VPCs' Internet access

    B. An implied router

    C. A physical router

    D. A VPC resource with no management IP address

9. What is the destination for a default IPv4 route?

    A. 0.0.0.0/0

    B. ::0/0

    C. An Internet gateway

    D. The IP address of the implied router

10. You create a new route table in a VPC but perform no other configuration on it. You then create a new subnet in the same VPC. Which route table will your new subnet be associated with?

    A. The main route table

    B. The route table you created

    C. The default route table

    D. None of these

11. You create a Linux instance and have AWS automatically assign a private IP address but not a public IP address. What will happen when you stop and restart the instance?

    A. You won't be able to SSH directly to the instance from the Internet.

    B. The instance won't be able to access the Internet.

    C. The instance will receive the same private IP address.

    D. The instance will be unable to reach other instances in its subnet.

12. How can you assign a public IP address to a running instance that doesn't have one?

    A. Allocate an ENI and associate it with the instance's primary EIP.

    B. Allocate an EIP and associate it with the instance's primary ENI.

    C. Configure the instance to use an automatically assigned public IP.

    D. Allocate an EIP and change the private IP address of the instance's ENI to match.

13. When an instance with an automatically assigned public IP sends a packet to another instance's EIP, what source address does the destination instance see?

    A. The public IP

    B. The EIP

    C. The private IP

    D. 0.0.0.0

14. Why must a NAT device reside in a different subnet than an instance that uses it?

    A. Both must use different default gateways.

    B. Both must use different NACLs.

    C. Both must use different security groups.

    D. The NAT device requires a public interface and a private interface.

15. Which is a difference between a NAT instance and NAT gateway?

    A. A NAT gateway scales automatically.

    B. A NAT instance scales automatically.

    C. A NAT gateway can span multiple availability zones.

    D. There are different NAT gateway types.

16. Which VPC resource performs network address translation?

    A. Internet gateway

    B. Route table

    C. EIP

    D. ENI

17. What must you do to configure a NAT instance after creating it?

    A. Disable the source/destination check on its ENI.

    B. Enable the source/destination check on its ENI.

    C. Create a default route in its route table with a NAT gateway as the target.

    D. Assign a primary private IP address to the instance.

18. Which of the following is true regarding VPC peering?

    A. Transitive routing is not supported.

    B. A VPC peering connection requires a public IP address.

    C. You can peer up to three VPCs using a single peering connection.

    D. You can use a peering connection to share an Internet gateway among multiple VPCs.

19. You've created one VPC peering connection between two VPCs. What must you do to use this connection for bidirectional instance-to-instance communication? (Choose all that apply.)

    A. Create two routes with the peering connection as the target.

    B. Create only one default route with the peering connection as the target.

    C. Create another peering connection between the VPCs.

    D. Configure the instances' security groups correctly.

20. Which of the following is a *not* a limitation of inter-region VPC peering?

    A. You can't use IPv4.

    B. The maximum MTU is 1,500 bytes.

    C. It's not supported in some regions.

    D. You can't use IPv6.

Chapter

5

Databases

THE AWS CERTIFIED SOLUTIONS ARCHITECT
ASSOCIATE EXAM OBJECTIVES COVERED IN
THIS CHAPTER MAY INCLUDE, BUT ARE NOT
LIMITED TO, THE FOLLOWING:

Domain 1: Design Resilient Architectures

✓ 1.1   Choose reliable/resilient storage.

✓ 1.2   Determine how to design decoupling mechanisms
using AWS services.

✓ 1.3   Determine how to design a multitier architecture
solution.

✓ 1.4   Determine how to design high availability and/or
fault tolerant architectures.

Domain 2: Define Performant Architectures

✓ 2.1   Choose performant storage and databases.

✓ 2.3   Design solutions for elasticity and scalability.

Introduction

A database allows an application to store, organize, and quickly retrieve data. Although you could use flat files to store data, they become increasingly slow to search as the amount of data grows. By relying on the database to perform these tasks, developers are free to focus on the application without having to directly interact with a filesystem to store and retrieve data.

Consequently, the availability and performance of a database-backed application depend on the database you choose and how you configure it. Databases come in two flavors: relational and nonrelational. Each of these differs in the way it stores, organizes, and lets you retrieve data, so the type of database you choose depends on the needs of the application.

In this chapter, you'll learn the differences between these two database types and how to select the right one for your application. You'll also learn how to use the managed database services that AWS provides to get the level of performance and reliability your applications require, as well as how to protect your data and recover it in the event of a database failure.

This chapter will introduce three different managed database services provided by AWS.

- Relational database service (RDS)
- Redshift
- DynamoDB

Relational Databases

A *relational database* contains at least one *table*, which you can visualize as a spreadsheet with columns and rows. In a relational database table, columns may also be called *attributes*, and rows may also be called *records* or *tuples*.

Columns and Attributes

Before you can add data to a relational database table, you must predefine each column's name and what data types it can accept. Columns are ordered, and you can't change the order after you create the table. The ordering creates a relationship between attributes in the table, which is where the term *relational database* comes from. Refer to Table 5.1 for an example of a relational database table containing employee records.

TABLE 5.1   The Employees table

Employee ID (Number)	Department (String)	Last Name (String)	First Name (String)	Birthdate (Date)
101	Information technology	Smith	Charlotte	7-16-87
102	Marketing	Colson	Thomas	7-4-00

Data must match the type defined under each column. For example, the Employee ID can't be a letter, because it's defined as a numeric data type. One advantage of a relational database is that you don't have to understand up front how you're going to query the data. As long as the data is there in a consistent format, you can craft queries to get the data you want, the way you want. This makes relational databases good for applications that need to query data in arbitrary columns and customize how that data is presented. For example, you could query the database to return the birthdate of every employee whose first name is Charlotte.

You can add more columns to a table after creating it. You can also delete columns, but deleting a column entails deleting all of the data stored under the column. If you delete the First Name column, it will remove first name data for all employees in the table.

Using Multiple Tables

Storing all data in a single table can lead to unnecessary duplication, needlessly increasing the size of the database and making queries slower. Hence, it's common for applications to use multiple related tables. Using the preceding example, if 50 employees work in the information technology department, the string "Information technology" appears in the table 50 times—once for each record. To avoid this wasted space, you may create a separate table to hold department names, as shown in Table 5.2.

TABLE 5.2   The Departments table

Department ID (Number)	Department Name (String)
10	Information technology
20	Marketing

Instead of putting the department names in every employee record, you would create a single record for each department in the Departments table. The Employees table would then refer to each department using the Department ID, as shown in Table 5.3.

TABLE 5.3   The Employees table

Employee ID (Number)	Department (String)	Last Name (String)	First Name (String)	Birthdate (Date)
101	10	Smith	Charlotte	7-16-87
102	20	Colson	Thomas	7-4-00

In this relationship, the Departments table is the *parent table*, and the Employees table is the *child table*. Each value in the Department column in the Employees table refers to the Department ID in the Departments table. Notice that the data type for the Department column is still a string. Although you could change the data type to a number, it's not necessary. The Department ID in the Departments table is called the *primary key*, and it must be unique in the table so that it can uniquely identify a row. The Employees table refers to this as a *foreign key*.

You must define primary and foreign keys so that the database knows how the columns in different tables are related. The database will enforce *foreign key constraints* to ensure that when a child table references a foreign key, that key also exists in the parent.

When it comes to databases, the terminology is inconsistent. You may find that different database implementations use different terms to describe the same concept.

Structured Query Language

You use the *Structured Query Language* (SQL) with relational databases to store and query data and perform database maintenance tasks. For this reason, relational databases are often called SQL databases.

SQL statements differ slightly depending on the specific relational database management system (RDBMS) you're using. As an AWS architect, you don't need to know SQL, as all major programming languages have libraries that construct SQL statements and interact with the database. But when dealing with AWS-managed database offerings, you do need to understand the concepts behind a few common SQL terms.

Querying Data

The SELECT statement is used to query data from a SQL database. It allows you to query based on the value in any column, as well as specify the specific columns you want the database to return. Thanks to the predictable structure of tables and the enforcement of foreign key constraints, you can use a JOIN clause with a SELECT statement to join together data from different tables.

Storing Data

The INSERT statement allows you to insert data directly into a table. If you need to load a large number of records, you can use the COPY command to copy data from a properly formatted file into the table you specify.

Online Transaction Processing vs. Online Analytic Processing

Depending on its configuration, a relational database can fall into one of two categories: *online transaction processing* (OLTP) or *online analytic processing* (OLAP).

OLTP

OLTP databases are suited to applications that read and write data frequently, on the order of multiple times per second. They are optimized for fast queries, and those queries tend to be regular and predictable. Depending on the size of the database and its performance requirements, an OLTP database may have intense memory requirements so that it can store frequently accessed portions of tables in memory for quick access. Generally, a single server with ample memory and compute power handles all writes to an OLTP database. An OLTP database would be a good candidate for backing an online ordering system that processes hundreds of orders a minute.

OLAP

OLAP databases are optimized for complex queries against large data sets. As a result, OLAP databases tend to have heavy compute and storage requirements. In *data warehousing* applications, it's common to aggregate multiple OLTP databases into a single OLAP database. For example, in an OLTP database for an employee management system, employee data may be spread out across multiple tables. At regular but infrequent intervals, a data warehouse would aggregate these tables into a single table in an OLAP database. This makes it easier to write queries against the data and reduces the amount of time it takes to process such a query. With a large OLAP database, it's common for multiple database servers to share the computational load of complex queries. In a process called *partitioning*, each server gets a portion of the database for which it's responsible.

Amazon Relational Database Service

The Amazon Relational Database Service (RDS) is a managed database service that lets you run relational database systems in the cloud. RDS takes care of setting up the database system, performing backups, ensuring high availability, and patching the database software and the underlying operating system. RDS also makes it easy to recover from database failures, restore data, and scale your databases to achieve the level of performing and availability that your application requires.

To deploy a database using RDS, you start by configuring a *database instance*, which is an isolated database environment. A database instance exists in a virtual private cloud (VPC) that you specify, but unlike an EC2 instance, AWS fully manages database instances. You can't SSH into them, and they don't show up under your EC2 instances.

Database Engines

A database engine is simply the software that stores, organizes, and retrieves data in a database. Each database instance runs only one database engine. RDS offers the following six database engines to choose from:

MySQL   MySQL is designed for OLTP applications such as blogs and ecommerce. RDS offers the latest MySQL Community Edition versions, including 5.5, 5.6, and 5.7. MySQL offers two storage engines—MyISAM and InnoDB—but you should use the latter as it's the only one compatible with RDS-managed automatic backups.

MariaDB   MariaDB is a drop-in binary replacement for MySQL. It was created over concerns about MySQL's future after Oracle acquired the company that developed it. RDS offers many versions of MariaDB, ranging from 10.0.17 through 10.2. MariaDB supports the XtraDB and InnoDB storage engines, but AWS recommends using the latter for maximum compatibility with RDS.

Oracle   Oracle is one of the most widely deployed relational database management systems. Some applications expressly require an Oracle database. RDS provides the following Oracle Database editions:

- Standard Edition One (SE1)
- Standard Edition Two (SE2)
- Standard Edition (SE)
- Enterprise Edition (EE)

PostgreSQL   PostgreSQL advertises itself as the most Oracle-compatible open source database. This is a good choice when you have in-house applications that were developed for Oracle but want to keep costs down. RDS offers versions of PostgreSQL ranging from 9.3.12-R1 through 10.4-R1.

Amazon Aurora   Aurora is Amazon's drop-in binary replacement for MySQL and PostgreSQL. Aurora offers better write performance than both by using a virtualized storage layer that reduces the number of writes to the underlying storage. It provides three editions.

- MySQL 5.6-compatible
- MySQL 5.7-compatible
- PostgreSQL compatible

Depending on the edition you choose, Aurora is compatible with PostgreSQL or MySQL import and export tools and snapshots. Aurora is designed to let you seamlessly migrate from an existing deployment that uses either of those two open source databases. For MySQL-compatible editions, Aurora supports only the InnoDB storage engine. Also, the Aurora Backtrack feature for MySQL lets you, within a matter of seconds, restore your database to any point in time within the last 72 hours.

Microsoft SQL Server   RDS offers multiple Microsoft SQL Server versions: 2008 R2, 2012, 2014, 2016, and 2017. For the edition, you can choose Express, Web, Standard, and Enterprise. The variety of flavors makes it possible to migrate an existing SQL Server database from an on-prem deployment to RDS without having to perform any database upgrades.

Licensing Considerations

RDS provides two models for licensing the database engine software you run. The *license included* model covers the cost of the license in the pricing for an RDS instance. The *bring your own license* (BYOL) model requires you to obtain a license for the database engine you run.

License Included   MariaDB and MySQL use the GNU General Public License (GPL) v2.0, and PostgreSQL uses the PostgreSQL license, all of which allow for free use of the respective software.

All versions and editions of Microsoft SQL Server that you run on RDS include a license, as do Oracle Database Standard Edition One (SE1) and Standard Edition Two (SE2).

Bring Your Own License   The following Oracle Database editions allow you to bring your own license:

- Enterprise Edition (EE)
- Standard Edition (SE)
- Standard Edition One (SE1)
- Standard Edition Two (SE2)

Database Option Groups

Database engines offer various features to help you manage your databases and improve security. *Option groups* let you specify these features—called *options*—and apply them to one or more instances. Options require more memory, so make sure your instances have ample memory and enable only the options you need.

The options available for a database option group depend on the engine. Microsoft SQL Server and Oracle offer *transparent data encryption* (TDE), which causes the engine to encrypt data before writing it to storage. MySQL and MariaDB offer an audit plugin that lets you log user logons and queries run against your databases.

Database Instance Classes

When launching a database instance, you must decide how much processing power, memory, network bandwidth, and disk throughput it needs. RDS offers a variety of database instance classes to meet the diverse performance needs of different databases. If you get it wrong or if your needs change, you can switch your instance to a different class. RDS divides database instance classes into the following three types.

Standard

Standard instance classes meet the needs of most databases. The latest-generation instance class is db.m4, which provides up to:

- 256 GB memory
- 64 vCPU
- 25 Gbps network bandwidth
- 10,000 Mbps (1,280 MBps) disk throughput

Memory Optimized

Memory-optimized instance classes are for databases that have hefty performance requirements. Providing more memory to a database allows it to store more data in memory, which can result in faster query times. The latest-generation instance class is db.x1e, and it provides up to:

- 3,904 GB memory
- 128 vCPU
- 25 Gbps network bandwidth
- 14,000 Mbps (1,750 MBps) disk throughput

Database instances use EBS storage. Both the standard and memory-optimized instance class types are EBS-optimized, meaning they provide dedicated bandwidth for transfers to and from EBS storage.

Burst Capable (Burstable)

Burstable instances are for development, test, and other nonproduction databases. The only burstable instance class available is db.t2, and it gives you up to:

- 32 GB memory
- 8 vCPU

AWS indicates that the network performance is "moderate," which in most cases corresponds to less than 1 Gbps. AWS doesn't provide stats on disk throughput, but you shouldn't expect to get more than 3,200 Mbps (400 MBps).

Storage

Selecting the right storage for your database instance is about more than just ensuring you have enough disk space. You also have to decide how fast the storage must be to meet the performance requirements of your database-backed application.

Understanding Input/Output Operations Per Second

AWS measures storage performance in *input/output operations per second* (IOPS). An input/output (I/O) operation is either a read from or write to storage. All things being equal, the more IOPS you can achieve, the faster your database can store and retrieve data.

RDS allocates you a number of IOPS depending on the type of storage you select, and you can't exceed this threshold. The speed of your database storage is limited by the number of IOPS allocated to it. The amount of data you can transfer in a single I/O operation depends on the page size that the database engine uses. To understand how many IOPS you need, you first need to understand how much disk throughput you need.

MySQL and MariaDB have a page size of 16 KB. Hence, writing 16 KB of data to disk would constitute one I/O operation. Oracle, PostgreSQL, and Microsoft SQL Server use a page size of 8 KB. Writing 16 KB of data using one of those database engines would consume two I/O operations. The larger the page size, the more data you can transfer in a single I/O operation.

Assuming a 16 KB page size, suppose your database needed to read 102,400 KB (100 MB) of data every second. To achieve this level of performance, your database would have to be able to read 6,400 16 KB pages every second. Because each page read counts as one I/O operation, your storage and instance class would need to be able to sustain 6,400 IOPS. Notice the inverse relationship between IOPS and page size: The larger your page size, the fewer IOPS you need to achieve the same level of throughput.

 Things get interesting when you move beyond a 32 KB page size. If your database engine writes more than 32 KB in a single I/O operation, AWS counts that as more than one I/O operation. For example, reading or writing a 64 KB page would count as two I/O operations. A 128 KB page would count as four I/O operations.

The number of IOPS you can achieve depends on the type of storage you select. RDS offers the following three different types of storage.

General-Purpose SSD

For most databases, *general-purpose SSD* (gp2) storage is sufficient. It's fast, giving you single-digit millisecond latency. You can allocate a volume of up to 16 TB. For each gigabyte of data that you allocate to a volume, RDS allocates that volume a baseline performance of three IOPS, up to a total of 10,000 IOPS per volume. A 20 GB volume would get 60 IOPS, while a 100 GB volume would get 300 IOPS. This means that the larger your volume, the better performance you'll get. Note that the minimum storage volume you can create depends on the database engine. For SQL Server Enterprise and Standard, it's 200 GB, and for all others, it's 20 GB.

The maximum throughput the gp2 storage type offers is 1,280 Mbps (160 MBps). To achieve this, two things have to fall into place. First, your instance must support a disk throughput of at least that much. For example, the db.m4.4xlarge instance class has a maximum throughput of 2,000 Mbps, so it would suffice. Also, you must allocate a sufficient number of IOPS to sustain this throughput. Suppose you're running MariaDB with a page size of 16 KB (128 Kb or 0.128 Mb). To determine the number of IOPS you'll need to sustain 1,280 Mbps of disk throughput, you'd divide the bandwidth by the page size, as follows:

1280 Mbps/0.128 Mb = 10,000 IOPS

To achieve 1,280 Mbps disk throughput to a volume, it would need 10,000 IOPS allocated. Note that this is the maximum number of IOPS possible with gp2. To achieve this many IOPS, your volume would have to be 3,333.3 GB or about 3.34 TB.

If you think you might occasionally need up to 3000 IOPS, but don't need a lot of storage, you don't have to over-allocate storage just to get your desired number of IOPS. Volumes smaller than 1 TB can temporarily burst to 3,000 IOPS. The duration of the burst is determined by the following formula:

Burst duration in seconds = (Credit balance)/[3,000 − 3 * (storage size in GB)]

When you initially boot a database instance, you get a credit balance of 5,400,000 IOPS. Anytime your instance uses IOPS above and beyond its baseline, it will dip into the credit balance. Once the credit balance is depleted, you can no longer burst. For example, with a 200 GB volume, the burst duration would be 2,250 seconds or 37.5 minutes.

The credit balance is replenished at a rate of one baseline IOPS every second. For example, if you have a 200 GB volume with a baseline IOPS of 600, your credit balance increases by 600 IOPS per second, up to the maximum of 5,400,000.

To get some practice with these concepts, complete Exercise 5.1 to create an instance using gp2 storage.

EXERCISE 5.1

Create an RDS Database Instance

In this exercise, you'll create an RDS database instance using MariaDB as the database engine. Free Tier accounts won't incur any charges.

1. Go to the RDS Dashboard.
2. Click Create Database.
3. On the Select Engine page, select MariaDB and click Next.
4. For the use case, select Production - MariaDB. Then click Next.
5. For the DB Engine Version, stick with the default.

6. For DB Instance Class, select db.t2.micro - 1 vCPU, 1 GB RAM.

7. Choose No for Multi-AZ Deployment.

8. For Storage Type, select General Purpose (SSD).

9. Enter **20 GB** as the Allocated Storage setting. Check your entries against the example in Figure 5.1 to make sure everything matches.

FIGURE 5.1   Creating an RDS Instance

RDS > Create database

Specify DB details

Instance specifications
Estimate your monthly costs for the DB Instance using the AWS Simple Monthly Calculator

DB engine
MariaDB Community Edition

License model   Info

| general-public-license | ▼ |

DB engine version   Info

| mariadb 10.2.12 | ▼ |

DB instance class   Info

| db.t2.micro — 1 vCPU, 1 GiB RAM | ▼ |

Multi-AZ deployment   Info

○ **Create replica in different zone**
Creates a replica in a different Availability Zone (AZ) to provide data redundancy, eliminate I/O freezes, and minimize latency spikes during system backups.

◉ No

Storage type   Info

| General Purpose (SSD) | ▼ |

Allocated storage

| 20 | GiB

(Minimum: 20 GiB, Maximum: 16384 GiB) Higher allocated storage may improve IOPS performance.

10. In the Settings section, enter **mydbInstance** in the DB Instance Identifier field.

11. Enter a master username and master password of your choice and then click Next.

12. In the Network & Security section, choose the Default VPC and Default Subnet Group settings.

13. For the Public Accessible setting, choose No.

14. For Availability Zone, select No Preference.

15. For VPC Security Group(s), select Create New VPC Security Group.

16. In the Database Options section, enter **mydatabase** in the Database Name field.

17. Leave Database Port set to the default of 3306.

18. Leave all the other settings at their defaults and click Create Database.

19. Click View DB Instance Details to view the new database instance.

20. Keep the instance up and running, as you'll need it for Exercise 5.2.

Provisioned IOPS SSD (io1)

If you're not excited about the rather confusing math involved with using gp2 storage, RDS provides a more straightforward option. *Provisioned IOPS SSD* lets you simply allocate the number of IOPS you need when you create your instance. There's no concept of bursting in io1 storage. The number of IOPS you provision is what you get and what you pay for, whether you use it or not. This makes it useful for OLTP databases that require consistent low-latency performance.

If you use a standard or memory optimized instance class, RDS guarantees that you'll achieve within 10 percent of the provisioned IOPS for 99.9 percent of the year. That means you may get less than your specified number of IOPS for only about 2 hours and 45 minutes out of the year.

Assuming that you pick a standard instance with 4,000 Mbps throughput and use a database engine with a 16 KB page size, you can achieve up to 31,250 IOPS. To get this, you should provision 32,000 IOPS when you create the instance, as you must specify provisioned IOPS in increments of 1,000.

The maximum number of IOPS you can achieve and how much storage you can allocate are constrained by the database engine you select. Oracle, PostgreSQL, MariaDB, MySQL, and Aurora let you choose 100 GB to 16 TB of storage and allocate 1,000 to 40,000 provisioned IOPS. Microsoft SQL Server gives you up to 16 TB of storage and lets you choose between 1,000 and 32,000 provisioned IOPS. The ratio of storage in gigabytes to IOPS must be at least 50:1. For example, if you want 32,000 IOPS, you must provision at least 640 GB of storage.

Magnetic Storage

RDS offers magnetic storage for backward compatibility with older instances. It's limited to a maximum size of 4 TB and 1,000 IOPS.

Read Replicas

If your database instance doesn't meet your performance requirements, you have a few options, depending on where the bottleneck is.

As mentioned previously, if your memory, compute, network speed, or disk through-put are the issue, you can scale your database instance vertically by upgrading to a larger instance class. *Scaling vertically*—also called *scaling up*—is a straightforward approach. You simply throw more resources at your database instance and don't have to make any changes to your application or databases.

Scaling horizontally, also known as *scaling out*, entails creating additional database instances called *read replicas*. All database engines except for Oracle and Microsoft SQL Server support read replicas. Aurora exclusively supports a specific type of read replica called an *Aurora replica*.

A read replica is another database instance that services only queries against the data-base. A read replica takes some of the query load off of the *master database instance*, which remains solely responsible for writing data to the database. Read replicas are useful for read-heavy applications.

You can have up to five read replicas and up to fifteen Aurora replicas. Data from the master is asynchronously replicated to each read replica, meaning that there's a delay between when the data is written to the database by the master and when it shows up on the replica. This makes read replicas unsuitable for disaster recovery. For MySQL, you can set a replication delay.

When you create a read replica, RDS gives you a read-only endpoint which is a domain name that resolves only to your read replica. If you have multiple replicas, RDS will load balance the connection to one of them. If you have reporting and analysis tools that only need to read data, you would point them to a read-only endpoint.

Complete Exercise 5.2 to create a read replica for the database instance you created earlier.

EXERCISE 5.2

Create a Read Replica

1. In the RDS Dashboard, click Instances.

2. Select the instance you created earlier, click Instance Actions, and then click Create Read Replica.

3. Under the Network & Security heading, stick with the defaults, but choose No for Publicly Accessible.

4. Under the Settings section, make sure the Read Replica Source is mydbinstance.

5. Enter **mydbinstance-rr** in the Database Instance Identifier field.

6. Click the Create Read Replica button.

A read replica and the master may be in different availability zones, and even in different regions. In the event of the master instance failing, you can promote a read replica to the master. But keep in mind that because of the asynchronous nature of replication, you may lose data this way.

Complete Exercise 5.3 to promote your read replica to a stand-alone master database instance.

EXERCISE 5.3

Promote the Read Replica to a Master

1. In the RDS console, click Instances.

2. Select the read replica you created.

3. Click Instance Actions and then select Promote Read Replica.

4. Click Continue.

5. Click Promote Read Replica.

High Availability (Multi-AZ)

To keep your database continuously available in the event of a database instance outage, you can deploy multiple database instances in different availability zones using what RDS calls a *multi-AZ deployment*. In a multi-AZ deployment, you have a *primary database instance* in one availability zone that handles reads and writes to the database, and you have a *standby database instance* in a different availability zone. If the primary instance experiences an outage, it will failover to the standby instance, usually within two minutes.

Here are a few possible causes for a database instance outage:

■ Availability zone outage

■ Changing a database instance type

■ Patching of the instance's operating system

You can configure multi-AZ when you create a database instance or later. All database engines support multi-AZ but implement it slightly differently.

If you enable multi-AZ after creating your instance, you'll experience a significant performance hit, so be sure to do it during a maintenance window.

Multi-AZ with Oracle, PostgreSQL, MariaDB, MySQL, and Microsoft SQL Server

In this multi-AZ deployment, all instances must reside in the same region. RDS synchronously replicates data from the primary to the standby instance. This replication can introduce some latency, so be sure to use EBS-optimized instances and provisioned IOPS SSD storage.

The standby instance is not a read replica and cannot serve read traffic. Your application connects to the endpoint domain name for the primary. When a failover occurs, RDS changes the DNS record of the endpoint to point to the standby. The only thing your application has to do is reconnect to the endpoint.

If using the bring your own license model for Oracle, you must possess a license for both the primary and standby instances.

For MySQL and MariaDB, you can create a multi-AZ read replica in a different region. This lets you failover to a different region.

Multi-AZ with Amazon Aurora

Amazon Aurora handles multi-AZ a bit differently. An Amazon Aurora cluster consists of a primary instance. Aurora gives you a cluster endpoint that always points to the primary instance. An Aurora cluster also may include Aurora replicas.

The primary and all replicas share a single cluster volume, which is synchronously replicated across three availability zones. This cluster volume automatically expands as needed, up to 64 TB.

In the event the primary instance fails, one of two things will happen. If no Aurora replicas exist, Aurora will create a new primary instance. If an Aurora replica does exist, Aurora will promote the replica to the primary.

Backup and Recovery

RDS gives you the ability to take EBS volume snapshots of your database instances. Snapshots include all databases on the instance and are stored in S3, just like regular EBS snapshots. Snapshots are kept in multiple zones in the same region for redundancy.

Taking a snapshot suspends all I/O operations for a few seconds, unless you're using multi-AZ with a database engine other than Microsoft SQL Server. Be sure to take your snapshots during off-peak times.

When considering your backup and recovery needs, there are two metrics you should understand. The *recovery time objective* (RTO) is the maximum acceptable time to recover data and resume processing after a failure. The *recovery point objective* (RPO) is the maximum period of acceptable data loss. Consider your own RTO and RPO requirements when choosing your RDS backup options.

When you restore from a snapshot, RDS restores it to a new instance. The time to restore a snapshot can take several minutes, depending on its size. The more provisioned IOPS you allocate to your new instance, the faster the recovery time.

Automated Snapshots

RDS can automatically create snapshots of your instances daily during a 30-minute backup window. You can customize this window or let RDS choose it for you. Because taking a snapshot impacts performance, choose a time when your database is least busy. If you let RDS select the backup window, it will randomly select a 30-minute window within an 8-hour block that varies by region.

Enabling automatic backups enables *point-in-time recovery*, which archives database change logs to S3 every 5 minutes. In the event of a failure, you'll lose only up to five minutes' worth of data. Restoring to a point-in-time can take hours, depending on how much data is in the transaction logs.

RDS keeps automated snapshots for a limited period of time and then deletes them. You can choose a *retention period* between 1 day and 35 days. The default is 7 days. To disable automated snapshots, set the retention period to zero. Note that disabling automated snapshots immediately deletes all existing automated snapshots and disables point-in-time recovery. Also, if you change the retention period from zero to any other value, it will trigger an immediate snapshot.

You can also manually take a snapshot of your database instance. Unlike automated snapshots, manual snapshots stick around until you delete them. If you delete an instance, RDS will prompt you to take a final snapshot. It will also prompt you to retain automated snapshots. RDS will keep the final snapshot and all manual snapshots. If you choose not to retain automated backups, it will immediately delete any automated snapshots.

Maintenance Items

Because RDS is a managed service, it's the responsibility of AWS to handle patching and upgrades. AWS routinely performs these maintenance items on your database instances.

Maintenance items include operating system security and reliability patches. These generally occur once every few months. Database engine upgrades also may occur during a maintenance window. When AWS begins to support a new version of a database engine, you can choose to upgrade to it. Major version upgrades may contain database changes that aren't backward compatible. As such, if you want a major version upgrade, you must apply it manually. AWS may automatically apply minor version changes that are nonbreaking.

You can determine when these maintenance tasks take place by specifying a 30-minute weekly maintenance window. The window cannot overlap with the backup window. Even though the maintenance window is 30 minutes, it's possible for tasks to run beyond this.

Amazon Redshift

Redshift is a managed data warehouse solution designed for OLAP databases. Although it's based on PostgreSQL, it's not part of RDS. Redshift uses columnar storage, meaning that it stores the values for a column close together. This improves storage speed and efficiency and makes it faster to query data from individual columns. Redshift supports ODBC and JDBC database connectors.

Redshift uses compression encodings to reduce the amount of size each column takes up in storage. You can apply compression manually on a column-by-column basis. Or if you use the COPY command to import data from a file into a Redshift database, Redshift will determine which columns to compress.

Compute Nodes

A Redshift cluster contains one or more *compute nodes* that are divided into two categories. *Dense compute* nodes can store up to 326 TB of data on magnetic storage. *Dense storage* nodes can store up to 2 PB of data on fast SSDs.

If your cluster contains more than one compute node, Redshift also includes a *leader node* to coordinate communication among the compute nodes, as well as to communicate with clients. A leader node doesn't incur any additional charges.

Data Distribution Styles

Rows in a Redshift database are distributed across compute nodes. How the data is distributed depends on the distribution style. In *EVEN* distribution, the leader node spreads the data out evenly across all compute nodes. This is the default style. *KEY* distribution spreads the data according to the value in a single column. Columns with the same value are stored on the same node. In the *ALL* distribution, every table is distributed to every compute node.

Nonrelational (No-SQL) Databases

Nonrelational databases are designed to consistently handle tens of thousands of transactions per second. Although they can store the same data you'd find in a relational database, they're optimized for so-called unstructured data. Unstructured data is an unfortunate term, as all data you store in any database has some structure. A more accurate description would be multistructured data. The data you store in a nonrelational database can vary in structure, and that structure can change over time.

Nonrelational and relational databases have many elements in common. Nonrelational databases—also known as no-SQL databases—consist of collections that are confusingly also sometimes called *tables*. Within a table, you store items, which are similar to rows or tuples in a relational database. Each item consists of at least one attribute, which is analogous to a column in a SQL database. An attribute consists of a unique name called a *key*, a data type, and a value. Attributes are sometimes called *key-value pairs*.

Storing Data

One of the biggest differences between a relational and nonrelational database is that nonrelational databases are *schemaless* and don't require all items in a table to have the same attributes. Each item requires a primary key attribute whose value must be unique within the table. The purpose of the primary key is to uniquely identify an item and provide a value by which to sort items. Nonrelational databases are flexible when it comes to the type of data you can store. With the exception of the primary key attribute, you don't have to define attributes when you create a table. You create attributes on the fly when you create or modify an item. These attributes are unordered and hence have no relation to each other, which is they're called nonrelational.

Nonrelational databases do not give you a way to split data across tables and then merge it together at query time. Therefore, an application will generally keep all of its data in one table. This can lead to the duplication of data, which in a large database can incur substantial storage costs.

Querying Data

The trade-off for having flexibility to store unstructured data comes in terms of being more limited in your queries. Nonrelational databases are optimized for queries based on the primary key. Queries against other attributes are slower, making nonrelational databases inappropriate for complex or arbitrary queries. Prior to creating a table, you need to understand the exact queries that you're going to need to perform against the data. Consider the following item:

Key	Type	Value
Employee ID (primary key)	Number	101
Department	String	Information technology
Last Name	String	Smith
First Name	String	Charlotte

If you wanted to list every department that has an employee named Charlotte, it would be difficult to obtain this using a nonrelational database. Because items are sorted by Employee ID, the system would have to scan through every item to locate all items that have an attribute First Name with a value of Charlotte. And because the data in each item is unstructured, it may require searching through every attribute. It would then have to determine which of these items contain a Department attribute. Such a query would be slow and computationally expensive.

Types of Nonrelational Databases

You may hear nonrelational databases divided into categories such as key-value stores, document-oriented stores, and graph databases. But all nonrelational databases are key-value store databases.

A document-oriented store is a particular application of a nonrelational database that analyzes the contents of a document stored as a value and extracts metadata from it.

A graph database analyzes relationships between attributes in different items. This is different than a relational database that enforces relationships between records. A graph database discovers these relationships in unstructured data.

DynamoDB

DynamoDB is a managed nonrelational database service that can handle thousands of reads and writes per second. It achieves this level of performance by spreading your data across multiple *partitions*. A partition is an allocation of storage for a table, and it's backed by solid-state drives in multiple availability zones.

Partition and Hash Keys

When you create a table, you must specify a primary key and a data type. Because the primary key uniquely identifies an item in the table, its value must be unique within the table. There are two types of primary keys you can create.

A *partition key*, also known as a *hash key*, is a primary key that contains a single value. When you use only a partition key as a primary key, it's called a *simple primary key*. Good candidates for a partition key would be an email address, a unique username, or even a randomly generated identifier. A partition key can store no more than 2,048 B.

A primary key can also be a combination of two values: a partition key and a *sort (or range) key*. This is called a *composite primary key*. The partition key doesn't have to be unique, but the combination of the partition key and sort key must be unique. For example, a person's last name could be the partition key, while the first name could be the sort key. Using this approach, you could use the following values for a composite primary key for a table:

Last name (partition key)	First name (sort Key)
Lewis	Clive
Lewis	Warren
Williams	Warren

Neither the last name Lewis nor the first name Warren is unique in the table. But combining the partition and sort keys together creates a unique primary key.

DynamoDB distributes your items across partitions based on the primary key. Using the preceding example, items with the last name Lewis would all be stored on the same partition. DynamoDB would arrange the items in ascending order by the sort key. Note that a sort key can store no more than 1,024 B.

When a lot of read or write activity occurs against an item, the partition the item exists in is said to be a *hot partition*. This can negatively affect performance. To avoid hot partitions, try to make your partition keys as unique as possible. For example, if you're storing log entries, using the current date as a partition key will result in a different hot partition every day. Instead, you may consider using a timestamp that changes frequently.

Attributes and Items

Each key-value pair composes an attribute, and one or more attributes make up an item. DynamoDB can store an item size of up to 400 KB, which is roughly equivalent to 50,000 English words!

At a minimum, every item contains a primary key and corresponding value. When you create an attribute, you must define the data type. Data types fall into the following three categories:

Scalar   A *scalar data type* can have only one value. The string data type can store up to 400 KB of Unicode data with UTF-8 encoding. A string must always be greater than zero.

The number data type stores positive or negative numbers up to 38 significant digits. DynamoDB trims leading and trailing zeros.

The binary data type stores binary data in base-64 encoded format. Like the string type, it's limited by the maximum item size to 400 KB.

The Boolean data type can store a value of either true or false.

The null data type is for representing an attribute with an undefined or unknown value. Oddly, it must contain a value of null.

Set   A *set data type* holds an unordered list of scalar values. The values must be unique within a set, and a set must contain at least one value. You can create number sets, string sets, and binary sets.

Document   *Document data types* are designed to hold different types of data that fall outside the constraints of scalar and set data types. You can nest document types together up to 32 levels deep.

A list document type can store an ordered collection of values of any type. For example, you could include the following in the value of a list document:

```
Chores: ["Make coffee", Groceries: ["milk", "eggs", "cheese"], "Pay bills",
Bills: [water: [60], electric: [100]]]
```

Notice that the Chores list contains string data, numeric data, and nested lists.

A map data type can store an unordered collection of key-value pairs in a format similar to JavaScript Object Notation (JSON). As with a list, there are no restrictions on the type of data you can include. The following is an example of a map that contains a nested list and a nested map:

```
{
   Day: "Friday",
   Chores: [
     "Make coffee",
     "Groceries", {
       milk: { Quantity: 1 },
       eggs: { Quantity: 12 }
     }
     "Mow the lawn"],
}
```

Throughput Capacity

When creating a table, you must specify the number of reads and writes per second your application will require. This is called *provisioned throughput*. DynamoDB reserves partitions based on the number of *read capacity units* (RCUs) and *write capacity units* (WCUs) you specify when creating a table.

When you read an item from a table, that read may be *strongly consistent* or *eventually consistent*. A strongly consistent read always gives you the most up-to-date data, while an eventually consistent read may produce stale data that does not reflect data from a recent write operation. Whether you use strongly or eventually consistent reads depends on whether your application can tolerate reading stale data. You need to understand whether you need strongly or eventually consistent reads when deciding how much throughput to provision.

For an item up to 4 KB in size, one RCU buys you one strongly consistent read per second. To read an 8 KB item every second using a strongly consistent read, you'd need two RCUs.

If you use an eventually consistent read, one RCU buys you two eventually consistent reads per second. To read an 8 KB item every second using an eventually consistent read, you'd need only one RCU.

When it comes to writing data, one WCU gives you one write per second for an item up to 1 KB in size. This means if you need to write 100 items per second, each item being less than 1 KB, you'd need to provision 100 WCUs. If you need to write 10 items per second, each item being 2 KB, then you'd need 20 WCUs.

The throughput capacity you specify is an upper limit of what DynamoDB delivers. If you exceed your capacity, DynamoDB may throttle your request and yield an "HTTP 400 (Bad request)" error. AWS SDKs have built-in logic to retry throttled requests, so having a request throttled won't prevent your application from reading or writing data, but it will slow it down.

Complete Exercise 5.4 to create a table in DynamoDB.

EXERCISE 5.4

Create a Table in DynamoDB

1. Use the following command to create a table named Authors with a partition key named LastName and sort key named FirstName. Both keys should use the string data type. Provision the table with a WCU and RCU of 1.

    ```
    aws dynamodb create-table --table-name Authors --attribute-definitions
    AttributeName=LastName,AttributeType=S AttributeName=FirstName,AttributeType=S
    --keyschema AttributeName=LastName,KeyType=HASH
    AttributeName=FirstName,KeyType=RANGE
    --provisioned-throughput ReadCapacityUnits=1,WriteCapacityUnits=1
    ```

2. Log into the DynamoDB web console to view the table you just created.

Auto Scaling

If you're unsure exactly how much throughput you need to provision for a table or if you anticipate your throughput needs will vary over time, you can configure Auto Scaling to automatically increase your provisioned throughput when it gets close to hitting a defined threshold.

To configure Auto Scaling, you specify a minimum and maximum RCU and WCU. You also specify a desired utilization percentage. DynamoDB will automatically adjust your RCU and WCU to keep your utilization at this percentage. For example, suppose you set a utilization of 70 percent, a minimum RCU of 10, and a maximum RCU of 50. If you consume 21 RCU, Auto Scaling will adjust your provisioned capacity to around 30 RCU. If your consumption drops to 14, Auto Scaling will reduce your provisioned throughput to 20 RCU.

Setting the right utilization is a balancing act. The higher you set your utilization, the more likely you are to exceed your provisioned capacity. If that happens, your requests may get throttled. On the other hand, if you set your utilization too low, you will end up paying for capacity you don't need.

Reserved Capacity

If you need 100 or more WCU or RCU, you can purchase reserved throughput capacity to save money. You must reserve RCU and WCU separately, and you're limited to 100,000 units of each. You have to pay a one-time fee and commit to a period of one or three years.

Reading Data

DynamoDB provides two different operations to let you read data from a table. A *scan* lists all items in a table. It's a read-intensive operation and can potentially consume all of your provisioned capacity units. A *query* returns an item based on the value of the partition key. When performing a query, the value of the partition key you search for must exactly match that of an item. If your table contains a sort key, you may optionally query by the sort key as well. For the sort key, you have more flexibility. You can search by exact value, a value greater than or less than the key, a range of values, or the beginning of the value.

Secondary Indexes

Secondary indexes solve two issues with querying data from DynamoDB. When you query for a particular item, you must specify a partition key exactly. For example, the Author table you created earlier has LastName as the partition key and FirstName as the sort key. Secondary indexes let you look up data by an attribute other than the table's primary key. Think of a secondary index as a copy of some of the attributes in a table. The table that the index gets its data from is called the *base table*.

When you create a secondary index, you can choose which attributes get copied from the base table into the index. These are called *projected attributes*. A secondary index always includes the partition and sort key attributes from the base table. You can choose to copy just the partition and sort keys and their values, the keys plus other attributes, or everything. This lets you extract only the data you need. There are two types of secondary indexes.

Global Secondary Index

You can create a *global secondary index* (GSI) any time after creating a table. In a global secondary index, the partition and hash keys can be different than the base table. The same rules for choosing a primary key still apply. You want the primary key of your index to be as unique as possible. If you use a composite primary key, items having partition keys with the same value will be stored on the same partition.

When reading from a global secondary index, reads are always eventually consistent. If you add an item to a table, it may not immediately get copied to the secondary index.

Local Secondary Index

A local secondary index (LSI) must be created at the same time as the base table. You also cannot delete a local secondary index after you've created it. The partition key must always be the same as the base table, but the sort key can be different. For example, if the base table has LastName as the partition key and FirstName as the sort key, you can create a local secondary index with a partition key of LastName and a sort key of BirthYear.

Reads from a local secondary index can be strongly or eventually consistent, depending on what you specify at read time.

Summary

Whether you implement a relational or nonrelational database depends solely on the application that will use it. Relational databases have been around a long time, and many application developers default to modeling their data to fit into a relational database. Applications use database-specific SDKs to interact with the database, so often the needs of the application mandate the specific database engine required. This is why AWS RDS offers six of the most popular database engines and sports compatibility with a wide range of versions. The idea is to let you take an existing database and port it to RDS without having to make any changes to the application.

The nonrelational database is a more recent invention. DynamoDB is Amazon's proprietary nonrelational database service. Unlike applications designed for relational databases, an application designed for a nonrelational database generally cannot be ported from an on-premises deployment to DynamoDB without some code changes. You're therefore more likely to find cloud-native applications using DynamoDB. When developing or refactoring an application to use DynamoDB, there's a good chance that developers will need to consult with you regarding how to design the database. It's critical in this case that you understand how to choose partition and sort keys and data types and how to allocate throughput capacity to meet the performance needs of the application.

Regardless of which database you use, as with any AWS service, you as an AWS architect are responsible for determining your performance and availability requirements and implementing them properly.

Exam Essentials

Understand the differences between relational and nonrelational databases. A relational database requires you to specify attributes up front when you create a table. All data you insert into a table must fit into the predefined attributes. It uses the Structured Query Language (SQL) to read and write data, and so it's also called a SQL database. A nonrelational database only requires you to specify a primary key attribute when creating a table. All items in a table must include a primary key but can otherwise have different attributes. Nonrelational—also called no-SQL databases—store unstructured data.

Know the different database engines RDS supports.   RDS supports all of the most popular database engines—MySQL, MariaDB, Oracle, PostgreSQL, Amazon Aurora, and Microsoft SQL Server. Understand the difference between the bring-your-own-license and license-included licensing models. Know which database engines support which licensing models.

Be able to select the right instance class and storage type given specific storage requirements.   Memory and storage tend to be the constraining factors for relational databases, so it's crucial that you know how to choose the right instance class and storage type based on the performance needs of a database. Know the three different instance classes: standard, memory optimized, and burstable. Also know how these relate to the three different storage types: general-purpose SSD (gp2), provisioned IOPS SSD (io1), and magnetic.

Understand the differences between multi-AZ and read replicas.   Both multi-AZ and read replicas involve creating additional database instances, but there are some key differences. A read replica can service queries, while a standby instance in a multi-AZ deployment cannot. A master instance asynchronously replicates data to read replicas, while in a multi-AZ configuration, the primary instance synchronously replicates data to the standby. Understand how Aurora replicas work and how Aurora multi-AZ differs from multi-AZ with other database engines.

Be able to determine the appropriate primary key type for a DynamoDB table.   DynamoDB tables give you two options for a primary key. A simple primary key consists of just a partition key and contains a single value. DynamoDB distributes items across partitions based on the value in the partition key. When using a simple primary key, the partition key must be unique within a table. A composite primary key consists of a partition key and a sort key. The partition key does not have to be unique, but the combination of the partition key and the sort key must be.

Know how DynamoDB throughput capacity works.   When you create a table, you must specify throughput capacity in write capacity units and read capacity units. How many read capacity units a read consumes depends on two things: whether the read is strongly or eventually consistent and how much data you read within one second. For an item of up to 4 KB in size, one strongly consistent read consumes one read capacity unit. Eventually consistent reads consume half of that. When it comes to writes, one write capacity unit lets you write up to one 1 KB item per second.

Review Questions

1. In a relational database, a row may also be called what? (Choose two.)
   A. Record
   B. Attribute
   C. Tuple
   D. Table

2. What must every relational database table contain?
   A. A foreign key
   B. A primary key
   C. An attribute
   D. A row

3. Which SQL statement would you use to retrieve data from a relational database table?
   A. QUERY
   B. SCAN
   C. INSERT
   D. SELECT

4. Which relational database type is optimized to handle multiple transactions per second?
   A. Offline transaction processing (OLTP)
   B. Online transaction processing (OLTP)
   C. Online analytic processing (OLAP)
   D. Key-value store

5. How many database engines can an RDS database instance run?
   A. Six
   B. One
   C. Two
   D. Four

6. Which database engines are compatible with existing MySQL databases? (Choose all that apply.)
   A. Microsoft SQL Server
   B. MariaDB
   C. Aurora
   D. PostgreSQL

7. Which storage engine should you use with MySQL, Aurora, and MariaDB for maximum compatibility with RDS?

   A. MyISAM

   B. XtraDB

   C. InnoDB

   D. PostgreSQL

8. Which database engine supports the bring-your-own-license (BYOL) model? (Choose all that apply.)

   A. Oracle Standard Edition Two

   B. Microsoft SQL Server

   C. Oracle Standard Edition One

   D. PostgreSQL

9. Which database instance class provides dedicated bandwidth for storage volumes?

   A. Standard

   B. Memory optimized

   C. Storage optimized

   D. Burstable

10. If a MariaDB database running in RDS needs to write 200 MB of data every second, how many IOPS should you provision using io1 storage to sustain this performance?

   A. 12,800

   B. 25,600

   C. 200

   D. 16

11. Using general-purpose SSD storage, how much storage would you need to allocate to get 600 IOPS?

   A. 200 GB

   B. 100 GB

   C. 200 TB

   D. 200 MB

12. If you need to achieve 12,000 IOPS using provisioned IOPS SSD storage, how much storage should you allocate, assuming that you need only 100 GB of storage?

   A. There is no minimum storage requirement.

   B. 200 GB

   C. 240 GB

   D. 12 TB

13. What type of database instance only accepts queries?

    A. Read replica

    B. Standby database instance

    C. Primary database instance

    D. Master database instance

14. In a multi-AZ deployment using Oracle, how is data replicated?

    A. Synchronously from the primary instance to a read replica

    B. Synchronously using a cluster volume

    C. Asynchronously from the primary to a standby instance

    D. Synchronously from the primary to a standby instance

15. Which of the following occurs when you restore a failed database instance from a snapshot?

    A. RDS restores the snapshot to a new instance.

    B. RDS restores the snapshot to the failed instance.

    C. RDS restores only the individual databases to a new instance.

    D. RDS deletes the snapshot.

16. Which Redshift distribution style stores all tables on all compute nodes?

    A. EVEN

    B. ALL

    C. KEY

    D. ODD

17. Which Redshift node type can store up to 326 TB of data?

    A. Dense memory

    B. Leader

    C. Dense storage

    D. Dense compute

18. Which is true regarding a primary key in a nonrelational database? (Choose all that apply.)

    A. It's required to uniquely identify an item.

    B. It must be unique within the table.

    C. It's used to correlate data across different tables.

    D. Its data type can vary within a table.

19. In DynamoDB table containing orders, which key would be most appropriate for storing an order date?

    A. Partition key

    B. Sort key

    C. Hash key

    D. Simple primary key

20. When creating a DynamoDB table, how many read capacity units should you provision to be able to sustain strongly consistent reads of 11 KB per second?

    A. 3

    B. 2

    C. 1

    D. 0

21. Which Redshift node type can provide the fastest read access?

    A. Dense compute

    B. Dense storage

    C. Leader

    D. KEY

22. Which DynamoDB index type allows the partition and hash key to differ from the base table?

    A. Eventually consistent index

    B. Local secondary index

    C. Global primary index

    D. Global secondary index

23. To ensure the best performance, in which of the following situations would you choose to store data in a NoSQL database instead of a relational database?

    A. You need to perform a variety of complex queries against the data.

    B. You need to query data based on only one attribute.

    C. You need to store JSON documents.

    D. The data will be used by different applications.

24. What type of database can discover how different items are related to each other?

    A. SQL

    B. Relational

    C. Document-oriented store

    D. Graph

Chapter 6

Authentication and Authorization—AWS Identity and Access Management

---

THE AWS CERTIFIED SOLUTIONS ARCHITECT ASSOCIATE EXAM OBJECTIVES COVERED IN THIS CHAPTER MAY INCLUDE, BUT ARE NOT LIMITED TO, THE FOLLOWING:

Domain 3: Specify Secure Applications and Architectures

✓ 3.1   Determine how to secure application tiers.

✓ 3.2   Determine how to secure data.

Introduction

Your AWS resources are probably your company's crown jewels, so you definitely don't want to leave them unprotected. But you also can't lock them down so tightly that even your admins and customers can't get in.

Finding the perfect balance is possible. Getting there will have a lot to do with the way you *authenticate* user requests to confirm they're legitimate and then *authorize* no more and no less than the exact access they'll need. On AWS, authentication and authorization are primarily handled by Identity and Access Management (IAM).

In this chapter, you're going to learn about IAM identities—which are sometimes described as *principals*. An identity represents an AWS user or a role. Roles are identities that can be temporarily assigned to an application, service, user, or group.

Identities can also be federated. That is, users or applications without AWS accounts can be authenticated and given temporary access to AWS resources using an external service such as Kerberos, Microsoft Active Directory, or the Lightweight Directory Access Protocol (LDAP).

Identities are controlled by attaching policies that precisely define the way they'll be able to interact with all the resources in your AWS account. You can attach policies to either principals (identity-based policies) or resources (resource-based policies).

This chapter will describe the following:

- Creating policies to closely control what your principals can do on your account
- Managing the various kinds of keys or tokens used by principals to prove their identities
- Providing single sign-on solutions for integrating IAM with external providers using identity federation
- Implementing best practices for configuring accounts and roles to properly secure your resources

IAM Identities

The one identity that comes with every new AWS account is the root user. By default, root has full rights over all the services and resources associated with your account. This makes sense since there would otherwise be no way for you to get things done with the services that lie beyond root control. On the other hand, having everything in the hands of this one user makes root an attractive target for hackers: they only need to get the root password or access keys to compromise the entire account.

To reduce your exposure to this vulnerability, AWS suggests that you heavily protect your root account and delegate specific powers for day-to-day operations to other users. Figure 6.1 shows the checklist of Amazon's recommended actions in the Security Status section of a typical account's IAM home page.

FIGURE 6.1   The Security Status checklist from the IAM page of an AWS account

IAM Resources

Users: 0   Roles: 1

Groups: 0   Identity Providers: 0

Customer Managed Policies: 0

Security Status   0 out of 5 complete.

⚠ Delete your root access keys   ⌄

⚠ Activate MFA on your root account   ⌄

⚠ Create individual IAM users   ⌄

⚠ Use groups to assign permissions   ⌄

⚠ Apply an IAM password policy   ⌄

Understanding how—and why—you can satisfy those recommendations is an important first step for successfully managing your AWS account.

IAM Policies

Your first job should be to understand how policies are used to control the behavior of IAM identities. An IAM policy is a document that identifies one or more *actions* as they relate to one or more AWS *resources*. Finally, the policy document determines the *effect* permitted by the action on the resource. The value of an effect will be either Allow or Deny.

A policy might, for instance, allow (the effect) the creation of buckets (the action) within S3 (the resource). Of course, the way resources and actions are defined will vary according to the particular service you're working with.

IAM provides hundreds of preset policies that can be viewed from the Policies page that's accessed from the IAM Dashboard. You can filter policies using key words to narrow down your search. You can also create your own policy using the tools available through the Create policy page in the Dashboard or by manually crafting your own using JSON-formatted text.

The following example is a JSON AdministratorAccess policy document from the IAM Dashboard interface. Note how it *allows* the identity holding the policy to perform any (*) action on any (*) resource in your account.

```
{
    "Version": "2012-10-17",
    "Statement": [
        {
            "Effect": "Allow",
            "Action": "*",
            "Resource": "*"
        }
    ]
}
```

Any action that's not explicitly allowed by a policy will be denied. But wait, if all actions are implicitly denied, why would you ever need to explicitly invoke "Deny" within a policy? Such policies could be useful in cases where a user requires access to most—but not all—resources within a domain. "Deny" can single out exactly those resources that should remain off-limits.

When you associate a policy document with an IAM identity, that identity will now be bound to the policy's powers and limitations. A single IAM policy can be associated with any number of identities, and a single identity can have as many as 10 managed policies (each no greater than 6,144 characters) attached to it.

This raises the potential for trouble: what happens if two policies are associated with a single identity conflict? What if, for instance, one policy permits a user to create new S3 buckets and the second forbids it? AWS always resolves such conflicts by denying the action in question.

You should also bear in mind that, in general, an explicit deny effect will always overrule an allow.

User and Root Accounts

The best way to protect your root account is to lock it down by doing the following:

- Delete any access keys associated with root.
- Assign a long and complex password and store it in a secure password vault.
- Enable multifactor authentication (MFA) for the root account.
- Wherever possible, don't use root to perform administration operations.

Before all that, however, you must create at least one new user and assign it enough authority to get the necessary work done. Typically, that will involve giving your main admin user the AdministratorAccess policy, through which you'll be able to use that user to create other users, groups, and roles—each with just enough power to perform its specific task.

 You may be forgiven for wondering why giving a user the AdministratorAccess policy is any safer than leaving your root account in active service. After all, both seem to have complete control over all your resources, right? Wrong, because there are some powers that even an AdministratorAccess holder doesn't have, including the ability to create or delete account-wide budgets and enable MFA Delete on an S3 bucket.

Once all that's done, you're ready to lock down root. You can do that right now using Exercise 6.1.

EXERCISE 6.1

Lock Down the Root User

1. If necessary, create a regular user and then assign it the AdministratorAccess policy.

2. Make sure there are no active access keys associated with your root account.

3. Enable MFA for the root account, where short-lived authentication codes are sent to software applications on preset mobile devices (including smartphones) to confirm a user's identity.

4. Update your root login to a password that's long, complex, and includes nonalphanumeric characters.

5. Confirm that you can still log in as root and then store the password safely.

Perhaps now is also a good time to work through Exercise 6.2 to create a new user for your own account, assign it a policy, and confirm that the policy has the intended effect.

EXERCISE 6.2

Assign and Implement an IAM Policy

1. Create a new user in the IAM Dashboard.

2. Attach the AmazonS3FullAccess policy that will permit your user to create, edit, and delete S3 buckets. (Hint: you can search IAM policies using s3 to display a much shorter list.)

3. Note the user login instructions that will be displayed.

EXERCISE 6.2 *(continued)*

4. Log in as your new user and try creating a new S3 bucket.

5. Just to prove everything is working, try launching an EC2 instance. Your request should be denied.

When you create a new IAM user, you'll have the option of applying a password policy. This policy can be set to enforce the minimum lengths and complexity along with the maximum lapsed time between password resets. Getting your team members to use only higher-quality passwords is an important security precaution.

Users can open the My Security Credentials page (accessed via the pull-down menu beneath the user's name in the console) to manage their security settings. As you can see in Figure 6.2, that page includes sections for the following:

▪   Updating a password

▪   Activating or managing MFA

▪   Generating or deleting access keys for managing your AWS resources through the AWS CLI or programming SDKs

▪   Generating key pairs for authenticating signed URLs for your Amazon CloudFront distributions

▪   Generating X.509 certificates to encrypt Simple Object Access Protocol (SOAP) requests to those AWS services that allow it

SOAP requests to S3 and Amazon Mechanical Turk are an exception to this rule, as they use regular access keys rather than X.509 certificates.

▪   Retrieving your 12-digit AWS Account ID and, for use with legacy S3 ACLs, your canonical user ID

FIGURE 6.2   The six action items displayed on the Your Security Credentials page

Your Security Credentials

Use this page to manage the credentials for your AWS account. To manage credentials for AWS Identity and Access Management (IAM) users, use the IAM Console.

To learn more about the types of AWS credentials and how they're used, see AWS Security Credentials in AWS General Reference.

+   Password

+   Multi-factor authentication (MFA)

+   Access keys (access key ID and secret access key)

+   CloudFront key pairs

+   X.509 certificate

+   Account identifiers

Obviously, not all of those items will be relevant to all of your users.

Access Keys

Access keys provide authentication for programmatic or CLI-based access. Rather than having to find a way for your application to input a traditional username and password, you can make your local environment aware of the access key ID and secret access key. Using that information, your application or command can pass authentication data along with each request.

You learned about access keys in action in Chapter 2, "Amazon Elastic Compute Cloud and Amazon Elastic Block Store." You should also become familiar with the AWS access key lifecycle and how it should be managed.

Deactivating Unused Keys

Each active access key is a potential source of account vulnerability. Audit the keys associated with each of your users from time to time, and if you can confirm that any of these keys are not currently being used, deactivate them. If you have no plans to use them in the future, delete them altogether.

Key Rotation

Best practices require that you regularly retire older access keys because the longer a key has been in use, the greater the chance that it's been compromised. Therefore, it makes good sense to set a limit—perhaps 30 days—beyond which keys must be deleted and replaced by new ones.

Key rotation is automated for IAM roles used by EC2 resources to access other AWS services. But if your keys are designated for your own applications, things can be more complicated. It's a good idea to follow this protocol:

1. Generate a new access key for each of your users. Users can also be given the ability to manage their own keys.

2. Update your application settings to point to the new keys.

3. Deactivate (but don't delete) the old keys.

4. Monitor your applications for a few days to make sure all the updates were successful. The CLI command
   `aws iam get-access-key-last-used --access-key-id ABCDEFGHIJKLMNOP`
   can be used to determine whether any applications are still using an old key.

5. When you're sure you have everything, delete the old keys.

Key rotation can be enforced by including rotation in the password policy associated with your IAM user accounts.

Exercise 6.3 can guide you through a simple access key lifecycle.

EXERCISE 6.3

Create, Use, and Delete an AWS Access Key

1. Create a new AWS access key, and save both the access key ID and secret access key somewhere secure.

2. Use aws configure from your local command line to add the key to your AWS CLI configuration.

    If you already have a different access key configured on your system, you can create and use multiple keys in parallel. By adding the --profile argument to the aws configure command, you can create separate profiles. You'll be prompted to enter configuration details for each new profile. Here's an example:

    $ aws configure --profile account2

    You can then invoke a profile by adding the argument to a regular command.

    $ aws s3 ls --profile account2

3. Try performing some operation—such as listing your S3 buckets—and then uploading a local file using the AWS CLI and your new key.

4. Disable (select Make Inactive) or delete the key you just created from the IAM Dashboard.

5. Confirm that you are now unable to administer your S3 buckets using the key.

Groups

Creating individual users with just the permissions they'll need to perform their duties can be a secure and efficient way to manage AWS operations. But as your account becomes busier and more complex, it can also become a nightmare to manage.

Say, for instance, you've given some level of access to a half a dozen admins and a similar number of developers. Manually assigning appropriate access policies to each user can be time-consuming. But just imagine how much fun you'll have if you need to *update* permissions across the entire team—perhaps applying one set of changes for just the developers and another for the admins.

The solution for such scenarios is to create a separate IAM group for each class of user and then associate each of your users with the group that fits their job description. You could create one group for developers, another for admins, and a third for your design team.

Now, whenever you need to make changes to a particular class's access profile, rather than having to edit each user account, you just update the appropriate group. If you're adding an Elastic Beanstalk workload, you can open it up for the entire developers' group with a single action. If you're no longer running your video content through Amazon Elastic Transcoder, you can remove access from the design group.

Exercise 6.4 is a good practical introduction to working with groups.

Create and Configure an IAM Group

1.   Make sure you have at least two IAM users in your account.

2.   Create a new IAM group and attach at least one policy—perhaps IAMUserChangePassword.

3.   Add your two users to the group.

4.   Confirm that your users can now change their own passwords.

5.   Delete the group or change its policies and then confirm that your users can no longer update their passwords.

Roles

An IAM role is a temporary identity that a user or service seeking access to your account resources can request. This kind of authorization can solve a lot of logistical problems.

You might have users who will occasionally need to shut down and restart EC2 instances after an update. To prevent accidental shutdowns, however, you'd rather they didn't normally have that power. Much the way sudo works on a Linux or macOS machine—or the runas command syntax on Windows—you can allow your user to assume an authorizing role for only as long as it's needed.

You might also want to temporarily give users from another AWS account—or users who sign in using a federated authentication service—access to resources on this account. An IAM role (which by default expires after 12 hours) is often the best mechanism for making this work.

You create a new role by defining the *trusted entity* you want given access. There are four categories of trusted entity: an AWS service; another AWS account (identified by its account ID); a web identity who authenticates using a login with Amazon, Amazon Cognito, Facebook, or Google; and SAML 2.0 federation with a SAML provider you define separately.

Once your entity is defined, you give it permissions by creating and attaching your own policy document or assigning one or more preset IAM policies. When a trusted entity assumes its new role, AWS issues it a time-limited security token using the AWS Security Token Service (STS).

Authentication Tools

AWS provides a wide range of tools to meet as many user and resource management needs as possible. The IAM functionality that you've already seen is only part of the story. The Amazon Cognito, AWS Managed Microsoft AD, and AWS Single Sign-On services are for handling user authentication, while AWS Key Management Service (KMS), AWS Secrets Manager, and AWS CloudHSM simplify the administration of encryption keys and authentication secrets.

Amazon Cognito

Cognito provides mobile and web app developers with two important functions.

▪ Through Cognito's *user pools*, you can add user sign-up and sign-in to your applications.

▪ Through Cognito's *identity pools*, you can give your application users temporary, controlled access to other services in your AWS account.

Building a new user pool involves defining how you want your users to identify themselves when they sign up (attributes such as address or birth date) and sign in (username or email address). You can also set minimum requirements for password complexity, multifactor authentication, and email verification.

When you set up an identity pool, you define the pool from which your users can come (using Cognito, AWS, federated, or even unauthenticated identities). You then create and assign an IAM role to the pool. Once your pool is live, any user whose identity matches your definition will have access to the resources specified in the role.

AWS Managed Microsoft AD

Managed Microsoft AD is actually accessed through the AWS Directory Service, as are a number of directory management tools like Amazon Cloud Directory and Cognito. (Cloud Directory is a way to store and leverage hierarchical data like lists of an organization's users or hardware assets.) What the Directory Service tools all share in common is the ability to handle large stores of data and integrate them into AWS operations.

Technically, Managed Microsoft AD is called *AWS Directory Service for Microsoft Active Directory*. But whichever way you refer to it, the goal is to have Active Directory control the way Microsoft SharePoint, .NET, and SQL Server–based workloads running in your VPC connect to your AWS resources. It's also possible to connect your AWS services to an on-premises Microsoft Active Directory using AD Connector.

Managed Microsoft AD domain controllers run in two VPC availability zones. As a managed service, AWS automatically takes care of all necessary infrastructure administration, including data replication and software updates.

AWS Single Sign-On

Single sign-on (SSO) allows you to provide users with streamlined authentication and authorization through an existing Microsoft Active Directory configured within AWS Directory Service. The service works across multiple AWS accounts within AWS Organizations. SSO also supports access to popular applications such as Salesforce, Box, and Office 365 in addition to custom apps that support Security Assertion Markup Language (SAML) 2.0.

AWS Organizations, by the way, is a service that can manage policy-based controls across multiple AWS accounts. Companies with more than one AWS account can use AWS Organizations to unify and integrate the way their assets are exposed and consumed no matter how distributed they might be.

AWS Key Management Service

As you saw regarding encryption keys for EBS volumes in Chapter 2 and relating to both server-side and client-side encryption for S3 buckets in Chapter 3, "Amazon Simple Storage Service and Amazon Glacier Storage," KMS deeply integrates with AWS services to create and manage your encryption keys.

The value of KMS lies in how it provides fully managed and centralized control over your system-wide encryption. The service lets you create, track, rotate, and delete the keys that you'll use to protect your data. For regulatory compliance purposes, KMS is integrated with AWS CloudTrail, which records all key-related events.

Key creation and administration happens through the console, AWS CLI, or SDKs. Key administration powers can be assigned to individual IAM users, groups, or roles.

AWS Secrets Manager

You already know that you can manage identity authentication to AWS services using IAM roles. However, roles won't help you securely pass credentials—referred to as *secrets* in this context—to third-party services or databases.

Instead, the passwords and third-party API keys for many of the resources your applications might need can be handled by the AWS Secrets Manager. Rather than having to hard-code secrets into your code and then having to regularly update them when they change, with Secrets Manager, you can deliver the most recent credentials to applications on request. The manager will even automatically take care of credential rotation.

AWS CloudHSM

CloudHSM (where the HSM stands for "hardware security module") launches virtual compute device clusters to perform cryptographic operations on behalf of your web server infrastructure. One typical goal is to off-load the burden of generating, storing, and managing cryptographic keys from your web servers so their resources can be focused exclusively on serving your applications.

While CloudHSM provides a service that's similar to AWS KMS, according to AWS documentation (https://aws.amazon.com/cloudhsm/faqs/), it is particularly useful for the following:

- Keys stored in dedicated, third-party validated hardware security modules under your exclusive control

- Federal Information Processing Standards (FIPS) 140-2 compliance

- Integration with applications using Public Key Cryptography Standards (PKCS)#11, Java JCE (Java Cryptography Extension), or Microsoft CNG (Cryptography API: Next Generation) interfaces
- High-performance in-VPC cryptographic acceleration (bulk crypto)

You activate an HSM cluster by running the CloudHSM client as a daemon on each of your application hosts. The client is configured to fully encrypt communication with the HSM.

AWS CLI Example

The following commands create a new user named `steve` and confirm that the user now exists:

```
$ aws iam create-user --user-name steve
$ aws iam get-user --user-name steve
```

The `list-policies` command will return a long list of the preset policies IAM provides. Among them is `AmazonEC2ReadOnlyAccess`, which permits its assignee only descriptions of running EC2 resources. You can attach a policy to a user by supplying the policy's Amazon Resource Name (ARN) as follows:

```
$ aws iam list-policies
$ aws iam attach-user-policy \
  --policy-arn arn:aws:iam::aws:policy/AmazonEC2ReadOnlyAccess \
  --user-name steve
```

Here's the `AmazonEC2ReadOnlyAccess` policy in JSON format:

```
{
  "Version": "2012-10-17",
  "Statement": [
    {
      "Effect": "Allow",
      "Action": "ec2:Describe*",
      "Resource": "*"
    },
    {
      "Effect": "Allow",
      "Action": "elasticloadbalancing:Describe*",
      "Resource": "*"
    },
    {
      "Effect": "Allow",
```

```
        "Action": [
            "cloudwatch:ListMetrics",
            "cloudwatch:GetMetricStatistics",
            "cloudwatch:Describe*"
        ],
        "Resource": "*"
    },
    {

        "Effect": "Allow",
        "Action": "autoscaling:Describe*",
        "Resource": "*"

    }
  ]
}
```

The `list-access-keys` command will return the names of any existing keys associated with the specified username. If you don't specify a name, keys belonging to root will be returned. The `create-access-key` command will create a new key (make sure you copy and save the key data that's returned), and `delete-access-key` will delete the specified key.

```
$ aws iam list-access-keys --user-name steve
$ aws iam create-access-key --user-name steve
$ aws iam delete-access-key --user-name steve --access-key-id AKIAJAP<...>
```

Summary

The IAM root user that's automatically enabled on a new AWS account should ideally be locked down and not used for day-to-day account operations. Instead, you should give individual users the precise permissions they'll need to perform their jobs.

All user accounts should be protected by strong passwords, multifactor authentication, and the use of encryption certificates and access keys for resource access.

Once authenticated, a user can be authorized to access a defined set of AWS resources using IAM policies. It's a good practice to associate users with overlapping access needs into IAM groups, where their permissions can be centrally and easily updated. Users can also be assigned temporary IAM roles to give them the access they need, when they need it.

Access keys should be regularly audited to ensure that unused keys are deleted and active keys are rotated at set intervals.

Identities (including users, groups, and roles) can be authenticated using a number of AWS services, including Cognito, Managed Microsoft AD, and single sign-on. Authentication secrets are managed by services such as AWS Key Management Service (KMS), AWS Secrets Manager, and AWS CloudHSM.

Exam Essentials

Understand how to work with IAM policies.   You can build your own custom IAM policies or select preset policies and apply them to identities to control their access to AWS resources.

Understand how to protect your AWS account's root user.   You should lock down your root user and instead delegate day-to-day tasks to specially defined users.

Understand how to effectively and securely manage user access.   This includes the efficient use of IAM groups and roles and appropriately applying both preset and custom IAM policies.

Understand how to optimize account access security.   You can use IAM administration tools to enforce the use of strong passwords and MFA, along with properly managed (rotated) access keys and tokens.

Be familiar with the various AWS authentication and integration tools.   Cognito lets you manage your application's users, and Managed Microsoft AD applies Active Directory domains to compatible applications running in your VPC. Both permit federated identities (where users using external authentication services can be authenticated for AWS resources) through external providers.

Review Questions

1. Which of the following is the *greatest* risk posed by using your AWS account root user for day-to-day operations?

   A. There would be no easy way to control resource usage by project or class.

   B. There would be no effective limits on the effect of an action, making it more likely for unintended and unwanted consequences to result.

   C. Since root has full permissions over your account resources, an account compromise at the hands of hackers would be catastrophic.

   D. It would make it difficult to track which account user is responsible for specific actions.

2. Which of the following statements is a correct description of IAM policies?

   A. The Action element refers to the way IAM will react to a request.

   B. The * character applies an element globally—as broadly as possible.

   C. The Resource element refers to the third-party identities that will be allowed to access the account.

   D. The Effect element refers to the anticipated resource state after a request is granted.

3. Which of the following will—when executed on its own—prevent an IAM user with no existing policies from launching an EC2 instance? (Choose three.)

   A. Attach no policies to the user.

   B. Attach two policies to the user with one policy permitting full EC2 access and the other permitting IAM password changes but denying EC2 access.

   C. Attach a single policy permitting the user to create S3 buckets.

   D. Attach the AdministratorAccess policy.

4. Which of the following are important steps for securing IAM user accounts? (Choose two.)

   A. Never use the account to perform any administration operations.

   B. Enable multifactor authentication (MFA).

   C. Assign a long and complex password.

   D. Delete all access keys.

5. Which of the following security credentials can be used for encrypting SOAP requests to AWS services? (Choose two.)

   A. X.509 certificates

   B. Access keys

   C. Passwords

   D. Key pairs

6. Which of the following AWS CLI commands can tell you whether an access key is still being used?

   A. `aws iam get-access-key-used --access-key-id`

   B. `aws iam --get-access-key-last-used access-key-id`

   C. `aws iam get-access-key-last-used access-last-key-id`

   D. `aws iam get-access-key-last-used --access-key-id`

7. Which of the following is the greatest benefit of organizing your users into groups?

   A. It enhances security by consolidating resources.

   B. It simplifies the management of user permissions.

   C. It allows for quicker response times to service interruptions.

   D. It simplifies locking down the root user.

8. Which of the following is *not* considered a trusted entity in the context of IAM roles?

   A. A web identity authenticating with Google

   B. An identity coming through a SAML-based federated provider

   C. An identity using an X.509 certificate

   D. A web identity authenticating with Amazon Cognito

9. Which of the following AWS services provides virtual hardware devices for managing encryption infrastructure that's FIPS 140-2 compliant?

   A. AWS CloudHSM

   B. AWS Key Management Service

   C. AWS Security Token Service

   D. AWS Secrets Manager

10. Which of the following is the best tool for authenticating access to a VPC-based MS Share-Point farm?

   A. Amazon Cognito

   B. AWS Directory Service for Microsoft Active Directory

   C. AWS Secrets Manager

   D. AWS Key Management Service

11. What is the function of Amazon Cognito identity pools?

   A. Give your application users temporary, controlled access to other services in your AWS account.

   B. Add user sign-up and sign-in to your applications.

   C. Incorporate encryption infrastructure into your application lifecycle.

   D. Deliver up-to-date credentials to authenticate RDS database requests.

12. An employee with access to the root user on your AWS account has just left your company. Since you can't be 100 percent sure that the former employee won't try to harm your company, which of the following steps should you take? (Choose two.)

    A. Change the password and MFA settings for the root account.

    B. Delete and re-create all existing IAM policies.

    C. Change the passwords for all your IAM users.

    D. Delete the former employee's own IAM user (within the company account).

13. Which of the following elements will not play any role in crafting an IAM policy?

    A. Action

    B. Region

    C. Effect

    D. Resource

14. Which of the following are necessary steps for creating an IAM role? (Choose two.)

    A. Define the action.

    B. Select at least one policy.

    C. Define a trusted entity.

    D. Define the consumer application.

15. Which of the following uses authentication based on AWS Security Token Service (STS) tokens?

    A. Policies

    B. Users

    C. Groups

    D. Roles

16. What format must be used to write an IAM policy?

    A. HTML

    B. Key/value pairs

    C. JSON

    D. XML

17. If you need to allow a user full control over EC2 instance resources, which two of the following must be included in the policy you create?

    A. `"Target": "ec2:*"`

    B. `"Action": "ec2:*"`

    C. `"Resource": "ec2:*"`

    D. `"Effect": "Allow"`

18. What is the function of Amazon Cognito user pools?
    A. Give your application users temporary, controlled access to other services in your AWS account.
    B. Add user sign-up and sign-in to your applications.
    C. Incorporate encryption infrastructure into your application lifecycle.
    D. Deliver up-to-date credentials to authenticate RDS database requests.

19. Which of the following best describe the "managed" part of AWS Managed Microsoft AD? (Choose two.)
    A. Integration with on-premises AD domains is possible.
    B. AD domain controllers are launched in two availability zones.
    C. Data is automatically replicated.
    D. Underlying AD software is automatically updated.

20. Which of the following steps are part of the access key rotation process? (Choose three.)
    A. Monitor the use of your new keys.
    B. Monitor the use of old keys.
    C. Deactivate the old keys.
    D. Delete the old keys.

Chapter

7

CloudTrail, CloudWatch, and AWS Config

THE AWS CERTIFIED SOLUTIONS ARCHITECT ASSOCIATE EXAM OBJECTIVES COVERED IN THIS CHAPTER MAY INCLUDE, BUT ARE NOT LIMITED TO, THE FOLLOWING:

Domain 1: Design Resilient Architectures

✓ 1.4 Determine how to design high availability and/or fault tolerant architectures.

Domain 2: Define Performant Architectures

✓ 2.3 Design solutions for elasticity and scalability.

Domain 3: Specify Secure Applications and Architectures

✓ 3.1 Determine how to secure application tiers.

✓ 3.2 Determine how to secure data.

Domain 5: Define Operationally Excellent Architectures

✓ 5.1 Choose design features in solutions that enable operational excellence.

Introduction

CloudTrail, CloudWatch, and AWS Config are three AWS services that can help you ensure the continuing health, performance, and security of your AWS resources and applications. These services collectively help you keep an eye on your AWS environment by performing the following operational tasks:

Tracking Performance   Understanding how your AWS resources are performing can tell you if they're powerful enough to handle the load you're throwing at them or if you need to scale up or out. By tracking performance over time, you can identify spikes in usage and determine whether those spikes are temporarily exhausting your resources. For example, if an EC2 instance maxes out its CPU utilization during times of high usage, you may need to upgrade to a larger instance type or add more instances.

Detecting Application Problems   Some application problems may be latent or hidden and go unreported by users. Checking application logs for warnings or errors can alert you to latent problems early on. For example, the words *exception* or *warning* in a log may indicate a data corruption, a timeout, or other issue that needs to be investigated before it results in a catastrophic failure.

Detecting Security Problems   Users having excessive permissions—or worse, accessing resources they're not supposed to—pose a security risk. Tracking user activities and auditing user permissions can help you reduce your risk and improve your security posture.

Logging Events   Maintaining a log of every single action that occurs against your AWS resources can be invaluable in troubleshooting and security investigations. Problems and breaches are inevitable and sometimes go undiscovered until months later. Having a detailed record of who did what and when can help you understand the cause, impact, and scope of an issue. Just as importantly, you can use this information to prevent the same problem in the future.

Maintaining an Inventory of AWS Resources   Understanding your existing resources, how they're configured, and their relationships and dependencies can help you understand how proposed changes will impact your current environment. Maintaining an up-to-date inventory can also help you ensure compliance with baselines your organization has adopted. Tracking your resource configurations over time makes it easy to satisfy auditing requirements that demand documentation on how a resource was configured at a point in time in the past.

CloudTrail, CloudWatch, and AWS Config are separate services that can be configured independently. They can also work together to provide a comprehensive monitoring solution for your AWS resources, applications, and even on-premises servers.

- CloudTrail keeps detailed logs of every read or write action that occurs against your AWS resources, giving you a trail that includes what happened, who did it, when, and even their IP address.

- CloudWatch collects numeric performance metrics from AWS and non-AWS resources such as on-premises servers. It also collects and stores log files from these resources and lets you search them easily, and it provides alarms that can send you a notification or take an action when a metric crosses a threshold.

- AWS Config tracks how your AWS resources are configured and how they change over time. You can view how your resources are related to one another and how they were configured at any time in the past. You can also compare your resource configurations against a baseline that you define and have AWS Config alert you when a resource falls out of compliance.

CloudTrail

An *event* is a record of an action that a principal performs against an AWS resource. CloudTrail logs read and write actions against AWS services in your account, giving you a detailed record including the action, the resource affected and its region, who performed the action, and when.

CloudTrail logs both API and non-API actions. Non-API actions include logging into the management console. API actions include launching an instance, creating a bucket in S3, and creating a virtual private cloud (VPC). These are API events regardless of whether they're performed in the AWS management console, with the AWS Command Line Interface, with an AWS SDK, or by another AWS service. CloudTrail classifies events into *management events* and *data events*.

Management Events

Management events include operations that a principal executes (or attempts to execute) against an AWS resource. AWS also calls management events *control plane operations*.

Management events are further grouped into write-only and read-only events. Write-only events include API operations that modify or might modify resources. For example, the RunInstances API operation may create a new EC2 instance and would be logged, regardless of whether the call was successful. Write-only events also include logging into the management console as the root or an IAM user. CloudTrail does not log unsuccessful root logins. Read-only events include API operations that read resources but can't make changes, such as the DescribeInstances API operation that returns a list of EC2 instances.

Data Events

Data events track two types of data plane operations that tend to be high volume: S3 object-level activity and Lambda function executions. For S3 object-level operations, CloudTrail distinguishes read-only and write-only events. GetObject is a read-only event, while DeleteObject and PutObject are write-only events.

Event History

By default, CloudTrail logs 90 days of management events and stores them in a viewable, searchable, and downloadable database called the *event history*. The event history does not include data events.

CloudTrail creates a separate event history for each region containing only the activities that occurred in that region. But events for global services such as IAM and Route 53 are included in the event history of every region.

Trails

If you want to store more than 90 days of event history or if you want to customize the types of events CloudTrail logs—for example, by excluding specific services or actions, or including data events—you can create a *trail*.

A trail is a configuration that records specified events and delivers them as CloudTrail log files to an S3 bucket of your choice. A log file contains one or more log entries in JavaScript Object Notation (JSON) format. A log entry represents a single action against a resource and includes detailed information about the action including, but not limited to, the following:

eventTime The date and time of the action, given in universal coordinated time (UTC). Log entries in a log file are sorted by timestamp, but events with the same timestamp are not necessarily in the order in which the events occurred.

userIdentity Detailed information about the principal that initiated the request. This may include the type of principal (e.g., IAM role or user), its Amazon resource name (ARN), and IAM username.

eventSource The global endpoint of the service against which the action was taken

eventName The name of the API operation

awsRegion The region the resource is located in. For global services, this is always us-east-1.

sourceIPAddress The IP address of the requester

Creating a Trail

You can choose to log events from a single region or all regions. If you apply the trail to all regions, then whenever AWS launches a new region, they'll automatically add it to your trail.

You can create up to five trails for a single region. A trail that applies to all regions will count against this limit in each region. For example, if you create a trail in us-east-1 and then create another trail that applies to all regions, CloudTrail will consider you to have two trails in the us-east-1 region.

After creating a trail, it can take up to 15 minutes between the time CloudTrail logs an event and the time it writes a log file to the S3 bucket.

Logging Management and Data Events

When you create a trail, you can choose whether to log management events, data events, or both. If you log management events, you must choose whether to log read-only events, write-only events, or both. This allows you to log read-only and write-only events to separate trails. Complete Exercise 7.1 to create a trail that logs write-only events in all regions.

EXERCISE 7.1

Create a Trail

In this exercise, you'll configure CloudTrail to log write-only management events in all regions.

1. Browse to the CloudTrail console and click Trails.

2. Click the Create Trail button.

3. Under Trail Name, enter a trail name of your choice. Names must be at least three characters and can't contain spaces.

4. For Apply Trail To All Regions, select Yes.

5. Under the Management Events heading, for Read/Write Events, select Write-only.

6. Under the Storage Location heading, for Create New S3 Bucket, select Yes. Enter the name of the S3 bucket you want to use. Remember that bucket names must be globally unique.

7. Click the Create button.

If you create a trail using the web console and log management events, the trail will automatically log global service events also. These events are logged as occurring in the us-east-1 region. This means that if you create multiple trails using the web console, global events will be logged to each trail. To avoid these duplicate events, you can disable logging global service events on an existing trail using the AWS CLI command `aws cloudtrail update-trail --name mytrail --no-include-global-service-events`. Alternately, if a trail is configured to log to all regions and you reconfigure it to log only to a single region, CloudTrail will disable global event logging for that trail. Another option is to forego the web console and create your trails using the AWS CLI, including the `--no-include-global-service-events` flag.

If you create a single-region trail to log data events, you can log only Lambda functions that exist in that region. If you create a trail that applies to all regions, you can log Lambda functions in any region. You're limited to selecting a total of 250 individual objects per trail, including Lambda functions and S3 buckets and prefixes. If you have more than 250 objects to log, you can instruct CloudTrail to log all Lambda functions or all S3 buckets.

Don't log data events on the bucket which is storing your CloudTrail logs. Doing so would create an infinite loop!

Log File Integrity Validation

CloudTrail provides a means to ensure that no log files were modified or deleted after creation. During quiet periods of no activity, it also gives you assurance that no log files were delivered, as opposed to being delivered and then maliciously deleted. This is useful in forensic investigations where someone with access to the S3 bucket may have tampered with the log file. For example, when an attacker hacks into a system, it's common for them to delete or modify log files to cover their tracks.

With log file integrity validation enabled, every time CloudTrail delivers a log file to the S3 bucket, it calculates a cryptographic hash of the file. This hash is a unique value derived from the contents of the log file itself. If even one byte of the log file changes, the entire hash changes. Hashes make it easy to detect when a file has been modified.

Every hour, CloudTrail creates a separate file called a *digest file* that contains the cryptographic hashes of all log files delivered within the last hour. CloudTrail places this file in the same bucket as the log files but in a separate folder. This allows you to set different permissions on the folder containing the digest file to protect it from deletion. CloudTrail also cryptographically signs the digest file using a private key that varies by region and places the signature in the file's S3 object metadata.

Each digest file also contains a hash of the previous digest file, if it exists. If there are no events to log during an hour long period, CloudTrail still creates a digest file. This lets you assert that no log files were delivered during the period.

You can validate the integrity of CloudTrail log and digest files by using the AWS CLI. You must specify the ARN of the trail and a start time. The AWS CLI will validate all log files from the starting time to the present. For example, to validate all log files written from January 1, 2018, to the present, you'd issue the following command: `aws cloudtrail validate-logs --trail-arn arn:aws:cloudtrail:us-east-1:account-id:trail/benpiper-trail --start-time 2018-01-01T00:00:00Z`.

By default, log and digest files are encrypted using Amazon server-side encryption with Amazon S3-managed encryption keys (SSE-S3). For additional security, you can choose instead to use server-side encryption with AWS KMS-managed keys (SSE-KMS) for log files. The customer master key (CMK) you use must be in the same region as the bucket. Digest files are always encrypted with SSE-S3.

CloudWatch

CloudWatch functions as a metric repository that lets you collect, retrieve, and graph numeric performance metrics from AWS and non-AWS resources. All AWS resources automatically send their metrics to CloudWatch. These metrics include EC2 instance CPU utilization, EBS volume read and write IOPS, S3 bucket sizes, and DynamoDB consumed read and write capacity units. Optionally, you can send custom metrics to CloudWatch from your applications and on-premises servers. CloudWatch Alarms can send you a notification or take an action based on the value of those metrics. CloudWatch Logs lets you collect, store, view, and search logs from AWS and non-AWS sources. You can also extract custom metrics from logs, such as the number of errors logged by an application or the number of bytes served by a web server.

CloudWatch Metrics

CloudWatch organizes metrics into *namespaces*. Metrics from AWS services are stored in AWS namespaces and use the format AWS/service to allow for easy classification of metrics. For example, AWS/EC2 is the namespace for metrics from EC2, and AWS/S3 is the namespace for metrics from S3.

You can think of a namespace as a container for metrics. Namespaces help prevent confusion of metrics with similar names. For example, CloudWatch stores the WriteOps metric from the Relational Database Service (RDS) in the AWS/RDS namespace, while the EBS metric VolumeWriteOps goes in the AWS/EBS namespace. You can create custom namespaces for custom metrics. For example, you may store metrics from an Apache web server under the custom namespace Apache. Metrics exist only in the region in which they were created.

A metric functions as a variable and contains a time-ordered set of *data points*. Each data point contains a timestamp, a value, and optionally a unit of measure. Each metric is uniquely defined by a namespace, a name, and optionally a *dimension*. A dimension is a name-value pair that distinguishes metrics with the same name and namespace from one another. For example, if you have multiple EC2 instances, CloudWatch creates a CPUUtilization metric in the AWS/EC2 namespace for each instance. To uniquely identify each metric, AWS assigns it a dimension named InstanceId with the value of the instance's resource identifier.

Basic and Detailed Monitoring

How frequently an AWS service sends metrics to CloudWatch depends on the monitoring type the service uses. Most services support basic monitoring, and some support *basic monitoring* and *detailed monitoring*.

Basic monitoring sends metrics to CloudWatch every five minutes. EC2 provides basic monitoring by default. EBS uses basic monitoring for gp2 volumes.

EC2 collects metrics every minute but sends only the five-minute average to CloudWatch. How EC2 sends data points to CloudWatch depends on the hypervisor. For instances using the Xen hypervisor, EC2 publishes metrics at the end of the five-minute interval. For example, between 13:00 and 13:05 an EC2 instance has the following CPUUtilization metric values measured in percent: 25, 50, 75, 80, and 10. The average CPUUtilization over the five-minute interval is 48. Therefore, EC2 sends the CPUUtilization metric to CloudWatch with a timestamp of 13:00 and a value of 48.

For instances using the Nitro hypervisor, EC2 sends a data point every minute during a five-minute period, but a data point is a rolling average. For example, at 13:00, EC2 records a data point for the CPUUtilization metric with a value of 25. EC2 sends this data point to CloudWatch with a timestamp of 13:00. At 13:01, EC2 records another data point with a value of 50. It averages this new data point with the previous one to get a value of 37.5. It then sends this new data point to CloudWatch, but with a timestamp of 13:00. This process continues for the rest of the five-minute interval.

Services that use detailed monitoring publish metrics to CloudWatch every minute. More than 70 services support detailed monitoring including EC2, EBS, RDS, DynamoDB, ECS, and Lambda. EBS defaults to detailed monitoring for io1 volumes.

Regular and High-Resolution Metrics

The metrics generated by AWS services have a timestamp resolution of no less than one minute. For example, a measurement of CPUUtilization taken at 14:00:28 would have a timestamp of 14:00. These are called *regular-resolution* metrics. For some AWS services, such as EBS, CloudWatch stores metrics at a five-minute resolution. For example, if EBS delivers a VolumeWriteBytes metric at 21:34, CloudWatch would record that metric with a timestamp of 21:30.

CloudWatch can store custom metrics with up to one second resolution. Metrics with a resolution of less than one minute are *high-resolution metrics*. You can create your own custom metrics using the PutMetricData API operation. When publishing a custom metric, you can specify the timestamp to be up to two weeks in the past or up to two hours into the future. If you don't specify a timestamp, CloudWatch creates one based on the time it received the metric in UTC.

Expiration

You can't delete metrics in CloudWatch. Metrics expire automatically, and when a metric expires depends on its resolution. Over time, CloudWatch aggregates higher-resolution metrics into lower-resolution metrics.

A high-resolution metric is stored for three hours. After this, all the data points from each minute-long period are aggregated into a single data point at one-minute resolution. The high-resolution data points simultaneously expire and are deleted. After 15 days, five data points stored at one-minute resolution are aggregated into a single data point stored at five-minute resolution. These metrics are retained for 63 days. At the end of this retention period, 12 data points from each metric are aggregated into a single 1-hour resolution metric and retained for 15 months. After this, the metrics are deleted.

To understand how this works, consider a VolumeWriteBytes metric stored at five-minute resolution. CloudWatch will store the metric at this resolution for 63 days, after which it will convert the data points to one-hour resolution. After 15 months, CloudWatch will delete those data points permanently.

Graphing Metrics

CloudWatch lets you visualize your metrics by graphing data points over time. This is useful for showing trends and changes over time, such as spikes in usage.

CloudWatch can perform statistical analysis on data points over a period of time and graph the results as a time series. You can choose from the following *statistics*:

Sum   The total of all data points in a period

Minimum   The lowest data point in a period

Maximum   The highest data point in a period

Average   The average of all data points in a period

Sample count   The number of data points in a period

Percentile   The data point of the specified percentile. You can specify a percentile of up to two decimal places. For example, 99.44 would yield the lowest data point that's higher than 99.44 percent of the data points in the period. You must specify a percentile statistic in the format p99.44.

To graph a metric, you must specify the metric, the statistic, and the period. The period can be from 1 second to 30 days, and the default is 60 seconds.

If you want CloudWatch to graph a metric as is, use the Sum statistic and set the period equal to the metric's resolution. For example, if you're using detailed monitoring to record the CPUUtilization metric from an EC2 instance, that metric will be stored at one-minute resolution. Therefore, you would graph the CPUUtilization metric over a period of one minute using the Sum statistic. To get an idea of how this would look, refer to Figure 7.1.

FIGURE 7.1   CPU utilization

Note that the statistic applies only to data points within a period. In the preceding example, the Sum statistic adds all data points within a one-minute period. Because CloudWatch stores the metric at one-minute resolution, there is only one data point per minute. Hence, the resulting graph shows each individual metric data point.

The *time range* in the preceding graph is set to one hour, but you can choose a range of time between 1 minute and 15 months. Choosing a different range doesn't change the time series, but only how it's displayed.

Which statistic you should choose depends on the metric and what you're trying to understand about the data. CPU utilization fluctuates and is measured as a percentage, so it doesn't make much sense to graph the sum of CPU utilization over, say, a 15 minute period. It does, however, make sense to take the average CPU utilization over the same timeframe. Hence, if you were trying to understand long-term patterns of CPU utilization, you may use the Average statistic over a 15-minute period.

The NetworkOut metric in the AWS/EC2 namespace measures the number of bytes sent by an instance during the collection interval. To understand peak hours for network utilization, you may graph the Sum statistic over a one-hour period and set the time range to one day, as shown in Figure 7.2.

FIGURE 7.2   The sum of network bytes sent out over a one-hour period

The Details column shows information that uniquely identifies the metric: the namespace, metric name, and the metric dimension, which in this case is InstanceId.

Metric Math

CloudWatch lets you perform various mathematical functions against metrics and graph them as a new time series. This is useful for when you need to combine multiple metrics into a single time series by using arithmetic functions, which include addition, subtraction, multiplication, division, and exponentiation. For example, you might divide the AWS/Lambda Invocations metrics by the Errors metric to get an error rate. Complete Exercise 7.2 to create a CloudWatch graph using *metric math*.

EXERCISE 7.2

Create a Graph Using Metric Math

In this exercise, you'll create a graph that plots the `NetworkIn` and `NetworkOut` metrics for an EC2 instance. You'll then use metric math to graph a new time series combining both metrics.

1. Browse to the CloudWatch console and click Metrics on the left-side menu.

2. On the All Metrics tab, descend into the AWS/EC2 namespace. Locate and select the `NetworkIn` and `NetworkOut` metrics for the instance of your choice.

3. Click the Graphed Metrics tab.

4. For each metric, select Sum for Statistic and 5 Minutes for Period. Refer to Figure 7.2 as needed.

5. Click Add A Math Expression. CloudWatch will add an Id column next to each metric and assign the values m1 and m2. It will also add another row with an ID of e1 and Expression1 as the label.

6. In the Details column for the e1 row, enter the expression **m1+m2**. CloudWatch will add another time series to the graph representing the sum of the `NetworkIn` and `NetworkOut` metrics. Your graph should look similar to the one in Figure 7.3.

FIGURE 7.3   Graphing the sum of data points using the SUM function

In addition to arithmetic functions, CloudWatch provides the following statistical functions that you can use in metric math expressions:

- AVG—Average
- MAX—Maximum

- MIN—Minimum
- STDDEV—Standard deviation
- SUM—Sum

Statistical functions return a scalar value, not a time series, so they can't be graphed. You must combine them with the METRICS function, which returns an array of time series of all selected metrics. For instance, referring to step 6 in Exercise 7.2, you could replace the expression m1+m2 with the expression SUM(METRICS()) to achieve the same result.

As another example, suppose you want to compare the CPU utilization of an instance with the standard deviation. You would first graph the AWS/EC2 metric CPUUtilization for the instance in question. You'd then add the metric math expression METRICS()/ STDDEV(m1) where m1 is the time series for the CPUUtilization metric. See Figure 7.4 for an example of what such as graph might look like.

FIGURE 7.4   Combining metric math functions

Keep in mind that the function STDDEV(m1) returns a scalar value—the standard deviation of all data points for the CPUUtilization metric. You must therefore use the METRICS function in the numerator to yield a time series that CloudWatch can graph.

CloudWatch Logs

CloudWatch Logs is a feature of CloudWatch that collects logs from AWS and non-AWS sources, stores them, and lets you search and even extract custom metrics from them. Some common uses for CloudWatch Logs include receiving CloudTrail logs, collecting application logs from an instance, and logging Route 53 DNS queries.

Log Streams and Log Groups

CloudWatch Logs stores *log events* that are records of activity recorded by an application or AWS resource. For CloudWatch Logs to understand a log event, the event must contain a timestamp and a UTF-8 encoded event message.

CloudWatch Logs stores log events from the same source in a *log stream*. The source may be an application or AWS resource. For example, if you have multiple instances running a web server that generates access logs, each instance would send that log to CloudTrail as a separate stream. You can manually delete log streams, but not individual log events.

CloudWatch organizes log streams into *log groups*. A stream must exist in only one log group. To organize related log streams, you can place them into the same log group. There's no limit to the number of streams in a group.

You may define the retention settings for a log group, choosing to keep log events from between 1 day to 10 years or indefinitely, which is the default setting. The retention settings apply to all log streams in a log group. You can manually export a log group to an S3 bucket for archiving.

Metric Filters

You can use *metric filters* to extract data from logs in a log group to create CloudWatch metrics. You can create a metric filter to track the occurrences of a string at a particular position in a log file. For example, you may want to track the number of 404 Not Found errors that appear in an Apache web server application log. You would create a metric filter to track the number of times the string "404" appears in the HTTP status code section of the log. Every time CloudWatch Logs receives a log event that matches the filter, it increments a custom metric. You might name such a metric **HTTP404Errors** and store it in the custom Apache namespace. Of course, you can then graph this metric in CloudWatch.

Metric values must be numeric. You can use a metric filter to extract a numeric value, such as the number of bytes transferred in a request, and store that in a metric. But you can't use a metric filter to extract a non-numeric string, such as an IP address, from a log and store it as a metric. You can, however, increment a metric when the metric filter matches a specific string.

Metric filters apply to log groups, and you can create a metric filter only after creating the group. Metric filters are not retroactive and will not generate metrics based on log events that CloudWatch recorded before the filter's creation.

CloudWatch Agent

The CloudWatch Agent collects logs from EC2 instances and on-premises servers running Linux or Windows operating systems. The agent can also collect performance metrics, including metrics that EC2 doesn't natively produce, such as memory utilization. Metrics generated by the agent are custom metrics and are stored in a custom namespace that you specify.

The CloudWatch Agent is different than the legacy CloudWatch Logs agent, which sends only logs and not metrics. AWS recommends using the CloudWatch agent.

Sending CloudTrail Logs to CloudWatch Logs

You can configure CloudTrail to send a trail log to a CloudWatch Logs log stream. This lets you search and extract metrics from your trail logs. Remember that CloudTrail generates trail logs in JSON format and stores them in an S3 bucket of your choice, but it doesn't provide a way to search those logs. CloudWatch understands JSON format and makes it easy to search for specific events. For example, to search for failed console logins, you would filter the log stream using the following syntax:

```
{$.eventSource = "signin.amazonaws.com" && $.responseElements.ConsoleLogin =
"Failure" }
```

You must specify a log group and an IAM role to use. CloudTrail can create the role for you and then assume the role to create the log group. CloudTrail then begins automatically delivering new trail logs to CloudWatch Logs. Delivery isn't instant, and it can take a few minutes before trail logs show up in CloudWatch Logs. Complete Exercise 7.3 to configure your existing CloudTrail to deliver trail logs to CloudWatch Logs.

CloudTrail does not send log events larger than 256 KB to CloudWatch Logs. Hence, a single RunInstances call to launch 500 instances would exceed this limit. Therefore, make sure you break up large requests if you want them to be available in CloudWatch Logs.

EXERCISE 7.3

Deliver CloudTrail Logs to CloudWatch Logs

In this exercise, you'll reconfigure the trail you created in Exercise 7.1 to stream events captured by CloudTrail to CloudWatch Logs.

1. Browse to the CloudTrail console and click Trails.

2. Click the name of the trail you created in Exercise 7.1.

3. Under the heading CloudWatch Logs, click the Configure button.

4. CloudTrail prompts you to use a New or Existing Log Group. It should automatically populate this field with **CloudTrail/DefaultLogGroup**. You may stick with this group or enter a name of your choice.

5. Click the Continue button.

6. CloudTrail will take you to a new screen prompting you to allow it to assume an IAM role that will give it permissions to stream logs to CloudWatch Logs. Click the Allow button.

CloudWatch Alarms

A *CloudWatch alarm* watches over a single metric and performs an action based on its value over a period of time. The action CloudWatch takes can include things such as sending an email notification, rebooting an instance, or executing an Auto Scaling action.

To create an alarm, you first define the metric you want CloudWatch to monitor. In much the same way CloudWatch doesn't graph metrics directly but graphs metric statistics over a period, CloudWatch alarms does not directly monitor metrics. Instead, it performs statistical analysis of a metric over time and monitors the result. This is called the *data point to monitor*.

Data Point to Monitor

Suppose you want to monitor the average of the AWS/EBS VolumeReadOps metric over a 15-minute period. The metric has a resolution of 5 minutes. You would choose Average for the statistic and 15 minutes for the period. Every 15 minutes CloudWatch would take three metric data points—one every 5 minutes—and would average them together to generate a single data point to monitor.

> You should set the period equal to or greater than the resolution of the metric. If you set a lower period, such as one minute, CloudWatch will look for a data point every minute, but because the metric updates only once every five minutes, it will count four of the five metrics as missing. This will result in the alarm not working properly.

If you use a percentile for the statistic, you must also select whether to ignore data points until the alarm collects a statistically significant number of data points. What constitutes statistically significant depends on the percentile. If you set the percentile to .5 (p50) or greater, you must have 10/1(1-percentile) data points to have a statistically significant sample. For instance, if you use the p80 statistic, a statistically significant number of data points would be 10/(1-.8) or 50. If the percentile is less than .5, you need 10/percentile data points to have a statistically significant sample. Supposing you were using the p25 statistic, you'd need 10/(.25) or 40 data points. If you choose to ignore data points before you have a statistically significant sampling, CloudWatch will not evaluate any of them. In other words, your alarm will be effectively disabled.

Threshold

The threshold is the value the data point to monitor must meet or cross to indicate something is wrong. You define a threshold by specifying a value and a condition. If you want to trigger an alarm when CPUUtilization meets or exceeds 50 percent, you would set the threshold for that alarm to >= 50. Or if you want to know when CPUCreditBalance falls below 800, you would set the threshold to < 800.

Alarm States

An alarm can be in one of the three following states at any given time:

ALARM   The data points to alarm have crossed and remained past a defined threshold for a period of time.

OK   The data points to alarm have not crossed and remained past a defined threshold for a period of time.

INSUFFICIENT_DATA   The alarm hasn't collected enough data to determine whether the data points to alarm have crossed a defined threshold.

New alarms always start out in an INSUFFICIENT_DATA state. It's important to remember that an ALARM state doesn't necessarily indicate a problem, and an OK state doesn't necessarily indicate the absence of a problem. Alarm states track only whether the data points to alarm have crossed and remained past a threshold for a period of time.

Data Points to Alarm and Evaluation Period

The period of time a data point to monitor must remain crossing the threshold to trigger an alarm state change depends on the *data points to alarm*. As an example, if the period is five minutes and the data points to alarm is three, then the data points to monitor must cross and remain crossing the threshold for 15 minutes before the alarm goes into an ALARM state.

There are cases where you may want to trigger the alarm if a data point to monitor crosses the threshold periodically but doesn't remain past it. For this, you can set an evaluation period that's equal to or greater than the data points to alarm. Suppose you want to trigger an alarm if the data points to monitor cross the threshold for three out of five data points. You would set the evaluation period to 5. The alarm would trigger if *any* three of the latest five data points exceed the threshold. The exceeding values don't have to be consecutive. This is called an *m out of n alarm*, where *m* is the data point to alarm and *n* is the evaluation period. The evaluation period can't exceed 24 hours.

To give an illustration, let's say you create an alarm with a threshold of >= 40. The data points to alarm is 2, and the evaluation period is 3. Now suppose CloudWatch evaluates the following three consecutive data points: 46, 39, and 41. Two of the three data points exceed the threshold, so the alarm will transition to the ALARM state.

Following that, CloudWatch evaluates the consecutive data points 45, 30, and 25. Two of the three data points fall below the threshold, so the alarm transitions to an OK state. Notice that CloudWatch must evaluate three data points (the evaluation period) before it changes the alarm state.

When monitoring metrics for EC2 instances using the Nitro hypervisor, make sure the evaluation period is at least 2. Triggering an alarm based on a single data point may cause result in false positives because of the way EC2 delivers Nitro metrics to CloudWatch.

Missing Data

Missing data can occur during an evaluation period. This may happen if you detach an EBS volume from or stop an instance. CloudWatch offers the following four options for how it evaluates periods with missing data:

As Missing   This treats the period missing data as if it never happened. For instance, if over four periods the data points are 41, no data, 50, and 25, CloudWatch will remove the period with no data from consideration. If the evaluation period is 3, it will evaluate only three periods with the data points 41, 50, and 25. It will not consider the missing data as occurring in the evaluation period. This is the default setting.

Not Breaching   Missing data points are treated as not breaching the threshold. Consider a three out of four alarm with a threshold <40, given the same data points: 41, no data, 50, and 25. Even though two values are breaching, the alarm would not trigger because the missing data is assumed to be not breaching.

Breaching   CloudWatch treats missing data as breaching the threshold. Using the preceding illustration, the alarm would trigger, as three of the four values would exceed the threshold.

Ignore   The alarm doesn't change state until it receives the number of consecutive data points specified in the data points to alarm setting.

Actions

You can configure an alarm to take an action when it transitions to a given state. You're not limited to just when an alarm goes into an ALARM state. You can also have CloudWatch take an action when the alarm transitions to an OK state. This is useful if you want to receive a notification when CPU utilization is abnormally high and another when it returns to normal. You can also trigger an action when an alarm monitoring an instance goes into an INSUFFICIENT_DATA state, which may occur when the instance shuts down. You can choose from the following actions:

Notification Using Simple Notification Service   The Simple Notification Service (SNS) uses communication channels called *topics*. A topic allows a sender or *publisher* to send a notification to one or more recipients called *subscribers*.

A subscriber consists of a protocol and an endpoint. The protocol can be HTTP, HTTPS, Simple Queue Service (SQS), Lambda, a mobile push notification, email, email-JSON, or short message service (SMS). The endpoint depends on the protocol. In the case of email or email-JSON, the endpoint would be an email address. In the case of SQS, it would be a queue. The endpoint for HTTP or HTTPS would be a URL.

When creating an alarm action, you specify an SNS topic. When the alarm triggers, it sends a notification to the topic. SNS takes care of relaying the notification to the subscribers of the topic.

Auto Scaling Action   If you're using Auto Scaling, you can create a simple Auto Scaling policy to add or remove instances. The policy must exist before you can select it as an alarm action.

EC2 Action   You can stop, terminate, reboot, or recover an instance in response to an alarm state change. You might choose to monitor the AWS/EC2 StatusCheckFailed_ Instance metric, which returns 1 if there's a problem with the instance, such as memory exhaustion, file system corruption, or incorrect network or startup configuration. Such issues could be corrected by rebooting the instance.

You might also monitor the StatusCheckedFailed_System metric, which returns 1 when there's a problem that requires AWS involvement to repair, such as a loss of network connectivity or power, hypervisor problems, or hardware failure. In response to this, the recover action migrates the instance to a new host and restarts it with the same settings. In-memory data is lost during this process.

EC2 actions are available only if the metric you're monitoring includes the InstanceId as a dimension, as the action you specify will take place against that instance. Using an EC2 action requires a service-linked role named AWSServiceRoleForCloudWatchEvents, which CloudWatch can create for you when you create the alarm.

Although a single alarm can have multiple actions, it will take those actions only upon transition to a single state that you specify when configuring the alarm. You cannot, for instance, set one action when an alarm transitions to an ALARM state and another action when it transitions to an OK state. Instead, you'd have to create two separate alarms.

AWS Config

AWS Config tracks how your AWS resources are configured at a point in time. Resources are entities that you create and manage using the management console, AWS CLI, or AWS SDKs. Think of AWS Config as a time machine. You can use it to see what a resource configuration looked like at some point in the past versus what it looks like now.

It can also show you how your resources are related to one another so that you can see how a change in one resource might impact another. For instance, suppose you create an EBS volume, attach it to an instance, and then later detach it. You can use AWS Config to see not only exactly when you created the volume but when it was attached to and detached from the instance.

CloudTrail logs events, and CloudWatch can alert on events, but only AWS Config gives you a holistic view of your resources and how they were configured at any point in time. AWS Config can help you with the following objectives:

Security   AWS Config can notify you whenever a resource configuration changes, alerting you to potential breaches. You can also see what users had which permissions at a given time.

Easy Audit Reports   You can provide a configuration snapshot report from any point in time.

Troubleshooting   You can analyze configurations around the time a problem started. AWS Config makes it easy to spot misconfigurations and how a problem in one resource might impact another.

Change Management   AWS Config lets you see how a potential change to one resource could impact another. For example, if you plan to change a security group, you can use AWS Config to quickly see all instances that use it.

The Configuration Recorder

The *configuration recorder* is the workhorse of AWS Config. It discovers your existing resources, records how they're configured, monitors for changes, and tracks those changes over time. By default, it monitors all items in the region in which you configure it. It can also monitor the resources of global services such as IAM. If you don't want to monitor all resources, you can select specific resource types to monitor, such as EC2 instances, IAM users, S3 buckets, or DynamoDB tables. You can have only one configuration recorder per region.

Configuration Items

The configuration recorder generates a *configuration item* for each resource it monitors. The configuration item contains the specific settings for that resource at a point in time, as well as the resource type, its ARN, and when it was created. The configuration item also includes the resource's relationships to other resources. For example, a configuration item for an EBS volume would include the instance ID of the instance it was attached to at the time the item was recorded. AWS Config maintains configuration items for every resource it tracks, even after the resource is deleted. Configuration items are stored internally in AWS Config, and you can't delete them manually.

Configuration History

AWS Config uses configuration items to build a configuration history for each resource. A configuration history is a collection of configuration items for a given resource over time. A configuration history includes details about the resources, such as when it was created, how it was configured at different points in time, and when it was deleted, if applicable. It also includes any related API logged by CloudTrail.

Every six hours in which a change occurs to a resource, AWS Config delivers a configuration history file to an S3 bucket that you specify. The S3 bucket is part of what AWS calls the *delivery channel*. Files are grouped by resource type. The configuration history for all EC2 instances goes into one file, while the history for EBS volumes goes into another. The files are timestamped and kept in separate folders by date. You can also view configuration history directly from the AWS Config console. You can optionally add an SNS topic to the delivery channel to have AWS Config notify you immediately whenever there's a change to a resource.

Configuration Snapshots

A configuration snapshot is a collection of all configuration items from a given point in time. Think of a configuration snapshot as a configuration backup for all monitored resources in your account.

Using the AWS CLI you can have AWS Config deliver a configuration snapshot to the bucket defined in your delivery channel. By default, the delivery channel is named default, so to deliver a configuration snapshot, you would manually issue the following command:

```
aws configservice deliver-config-snapshot --delivery-channel-name default
```

AWS Config can automatically deliver a configuration snapshot to the delivery channel at regular intervals. You can't set automatic delivery of this in the console but must configure this using the CLI. To do this, you must also specify a JSON file containing at a minimum the following items:

- Delivery channel name (default)
- S3 bucket name
- Delivery frequency of the configuration snapshot

The file may also optionally contain an SNS ARN. Let's refer to the following file as deliveryChannel.json:

```
{
  "name": "default",
  "s3BucketName": "my-config-bucket-us-east-1",
   "snsTopicARN": "arn:aws:sns:us-east-1:account-id:config-topic",
  "configSnapshotDeliveryProperties": {
    "deliveryFrequency": "TwentyFour_Hours"
  }
}
```

The delivery frequency can be every hour or every 24, 12, 6, or 3 hours. To reconfigure the delivery channel according to the settings in the deliveryChannel.json file, you'd issue the following command:

```
aws configservice put-delivery-channel --delivery-channel file://deliveryChannel
.json
```

To verify that the configuration change succeeded, issue the following command:

```
aws configservice describe-delivery-channels
```

If the output matches the configuration settings in the file, then the configuration change was successful.

Monitoring Changes

The configuration recorder generates at least one new configuration item every time a resource is created, changed, or deleted. Each new item is added to the configuration history for the resource as well as the configuration history for the account.

A change to one resource will trigger a new configuration item for not only the changed resource but also related resources. For instance, removing a rule in a security group causes the configuration recorder to create a new item for the security group and every instance that uses that security group.

Although you can't delete configuration items manually, you can configure AWS Config to keep configuration items between 30 days to 7 years. Seven years is the default. Note that the retention period does not apply to the configuration history and configuration snapshot files AWS Config delivers to S3.

Starting and Stopping the Configuration Recorder

You can start and stop the configuration recorder at any time using the web console or the CLI. During the time the configuration recorder is stopped, it doesn't monitor or record changes. But it does retain existing configuration items. To stop it using the following CLI command, you must specify the configuration recorder's name, which is default.

```
aws configservice stop-configuration-recorder --configuration-recorder-name
default
```

To start the recorder, issue the following command:

```
aws configservice start-configuration-recorder --configuration-recorder-name
default
```

Recording Software Inventory

AWS Config can record software inventory changes on EC2 instances and on-premises servers. This includes the following:

- Applications
- AWS components like the CLI and SDKs
- The name and version of the operating system
- IP address, gateway, and subnet mask
- Firewall configuration
- Windows updates

To have AWS Config track these changes, you must enable inventory collection for the server using the EC2 Systems Manager. You also must ensure AWS Config monitors the SSM: ManagedInstanceInventory resource type.

Managed and Custom Rules

In addition to monitoring resources changes, AWS Config lets you specify rules to define the optimal baseline configuration for your resources. AWS Config also provides customizable, predefined rules that cover a variety of common scenarios. For example, you may want to verify that CloudTrail is enabled, that every EC2 instance has an alarm tracking the CPUUtilization metric, that all EBS volumes are encrypted, or that multifactor authentication (MFA) is enabled for the root account. If any resources are noncompliant, AWS Config flags them and generates an SNS notification.

When you activate a rule, AWS Config immediately checks monitored resources against the rules to determine whether they're compliant. After that, how often it reevaluates resources is based on how the rule is configured. A reevaluation can be triggered by configuration changes or periodically. Periodic checks can occur every hour or every 3, 6, 12, or 24 hours. Note that even if you turn off the configuration recorder, periodic rules will continue to run.

Summary

You must configure CloudWatch and AWS Config before they can begin monitoring your resources. CloudTrail automatically logs only the last 90 days of management events even if you don't configure it. It's therefore a good idea to configure these services early on in your AWS deployment.

CloudWatch, CloudTrail, and AWS Config serve different purposes, and it's important to know the differences among them and when each is appropriate for a given use case.

CloudWatch tracks performance metrics and can take some action in response to those metrics. It can also collect and consolidate logs from multiple sources for storage and searching, as well as extract metrics from them.

CloudTrail keeps a detailed record of activities performed on your AWS account for security or auditing purposes. You can choose to log read-only or write-only management or data events.

AWS Config records resource configurations and relationships past, present, and future. You can look back in time to see how a resource was configured at any point. AWS Config can also compare current resource configurations against rules to ensure that you're in compliance with whatever baseline you define.

Exam Essentials

Know how to configure the different features of CloudWatch.   CloudWatch receives and stores performance metrics from various AWS services. You can also send custom metrics to CloudWatch. You can configure alarms to take one or more actions based on a metric. CloudWatch Logs receives and stores logs from various resources and makes them searchable.

Know the differences between CloudTrail and AWS Config.   CloudTrail tracks events, while AWS Config tracks how those events ultimately affect the configuration of a resource. AWS Config organizes configuration states and changes by resource, rather than by event.

Understand how CloudWatch Logs integrates with and complements CloudTrail. CloudTrail can send trail logs to CloudWatch Logs for storage, searching, and metric extraction.

Understand how SNS works.   CloudWatch and AWS Config send notifications to an Amazon SNS topic. The SNS topic passes these notifications on to a subscriber, which consists of a protocol and endpoint. Know the various protocols that SNS supports.

Review Questions

1. You've configured CloudTrail to log all management events in all regions. Which of the following API events will CloudTrail log? (Choose all that apply.)

   A. Logging into the AWS Console

   B. Creating an S3 bucket from the web console

   C. Uploading an object to an S3 bucket

   D. Creating a subnet using the AWS CLI

2. You've configured CloudTrail to log all read-only data events. Which of the following events will CloudTrail log?

   A. Viewing all S3 buckets

   B. Uploading a file to an S3 bucket

   C. Downloading a file from an S3 bucket

   D. Creating a Lambda function

3. Sixty days ago, you created a trail in CloudTrail to log read-only management events. Subsequently someone deleted the trail. Where can you look to find out who deleted it?

   A. The IAM user log

   B. The trail logs stored in S3

   C. The CloudTrail event history in the region where the trail was configured

   D. The CloudTrail event history in any region

4. What uniquely distinguishes two CloudWatch metrics that have the same name and are in the same namespace?

   A. The region

   B. The dimension

   C. The timestamp

   D. The data point

5. Which type of monitoring sends metrics to CloudWatch every five minutes?

   A. Regular

   B. Detailed

   C. Basic

   D. High resolution

6. You update a custom CloudWatch metric with the timestamp of 15:57:08 and a value of 3. You then update the same metric with the timestamp of 15:57:37 and a value of 6. Assuming the metric is a high-resolution metric, which of the following will CloudWatch do?

   A. Record both values with the given timestamp.

   B. Record the second value with the timestamp 15:57:37, overwriting the first value.

    C.   Record only the first value with the timestamp 15:57:08, ignoring the second value.

    D.   Record only the second value with the timestamp 15:57:00, overwriting the first value.

7. How long does CloudWatch retain metrics stored at one-hour resolution?

    A.   15 days

    B.   3 hours

    C.   63 days

    D.   15 months

8. You want to use CloudWatch to graph the exact data points of a metric for the last hour. The metric is stored at five-minute resolution. Which statistic and period should you use?

    A.   The Sum statistic with a five-minute period

    B.   The Average statistic with a one-hour period

    C.   The Sum statistic with a one-hour period

    D.   The Sample count statistic with a five-minute period

9. Which CloudWatch resource type stores log events?

    A.   Log group

    B.   Log stream

    C.   Metric filter

    D.   CloudWatch Agent

10. The CloudWatch Agent on an instance has been sending application logs to a CloudWatch log stream for several months. How can you remove old log events without disrupting delivery of new log events? (Choose all that apply.)

    A.   Delete the log stream.

    B.   Manually delete old log events.

    C.   Set the retention of the log stream to 30 days.

    D.   Set the retention of the log group to 30 days.

11. You created a trail to log all management events in all regions and send the trail logs to CloudWatch logs. You notice that some recent management events are missing from the log stream, but others are there. What are some possible reasons for this? (Choose all that apply.)

    A.   The missing events are greater than 256 KB in size.

    B.   The metric filter is misconfigured.

    C.   There's a delay between the time the event occurs and the time CloudTrail streams the event to CloudWatch.

    D.   The IAM role that CloudTrail assumes is misconfigured.

12. Two days ago, you created a CloudWatch alarm to monitor the VolumeReadOps on an EBS volume. Since then, the alarm has remained in an INSUFFICIENT_DATA state. What are some possible reasons for this? (Choose all that apply.)

    A. The data points to monitor haven't crossed the specified threshold.

    B. The EBS volume isn't attached to a running instance.

    C. The evaluation period hasn't elapsed.

    D. The alarm hasn't collected enough data points to alarm.

13. You want a CloudWatch alarm to change state when four consecutive evaluation periods elapse with no data. How should you configure the alarm to treat missing data?

    A. As Missing

    B. Breaching

    C. Not Breaching

    D. Ignore

    E. As Not Missing

14. You've configured an alarm to monitor a metric in the AWS/EC2 namespace. You want CloudWatch to send you a text message and reboot an instance when an alarm is breaching. Which two actions should you configure in the alarm? (Choose two.)

    A. SMS action

    B. Auto Scaling action

    C. Notification action

    D. EC2 action

15. In a CloudWatch alarm, what does the EC2 recover action do to the monitored instance?

    A. Migrates the instance to a different host

    B. Reboots the instance

    C. Deletes the instance and creates a new one

    D. Restores the instance from a snapshot

16. You learn that an instance in the us-west-1 region was deleted at some point in the past. To find out who deleted the instance and when, which of the following must be true?

    A. The AWS Config configuration recorder must have been turned on in the region at the time the instance was deleted.

    B. CloudTrail must have been logging write-only management events for all regions.

    C. CloudTrail must have been logging IAM events.

    D. The CloudWatch log stream containing the deletion event must not have been deleted.

17. Which of the following may be included in an AWS Config delivery channel? (Choose all that apply.)

    A. A CloudWatch log stream

    B. The delivery frequency of the configuration snapshot

    C. An S3 bucket name

    D. An SNS topic ARN

18. You configured AWS Config to monitor all of your resources in the us-east-1 region. After making several changes to the AWS resources in this region, you decided you want to delete the old configuration items. How can you accomplish this?

    A. Pause the configuration recorder.

    B. Delete the configuration recorder.

    C. Delete the configuration snapshots.

    D. Set the retention period to 30 days and wait for the configuration items to age out.

19. Which of the following metric math expressions can CloudWatch graph? (Choose all that apply.)

    A. AVG(m1)-m1

    B. AVG(m1)

    C. METRICS()/AVG(m1)

    D. m1/m2

20. You've configured an AWS Config rule to check whether CloudTrail is enabled. What could prevent AWS Config from evaluating this rule?

    A. Turning off the configuration recorder

    B. Deleting the rule

    C. Deleting the configuration history for CloudTrail

    D. Failing to specify a frequency for periodic checks

The Domain Name System and Network Routing: Amazon Route 53 and Amazon CloudFront

THE AWS CERTIFIED SOLUTIONS ARCHITECT ASSOCIATE EXAM OBJECTIVES COVERED IN THIS CHAPTER MAY INCLUDE, BUT ARE NOT LIMITED TO, THE FOLLOWING:

Domain 1: Design Resilient Architectures

✓ **1.3** Determine how to design a multitier architecture solution.

✓ **1.4** Determine how to design high availability and/or fault tolerant architectures.

Domain 2: Define Performant Architectures

✓ **2.2** Apply caching to improve performance.

✓ **2.3** Design solutions for elasticity and scalability.

Introduction

Making your cloud resources accessible to the people and machines that will consume them is just as important as creating them in the first place. Facilitating network access to your content generally has three goals: availability, speed, and accurately getting the right content to the right users.

The Domain Name System (DNS) is primarily concerned with making your resources available across a network using a human-readable name. The Internet's DNS infrastructure ensures that content living behind IP addresses can be reliably associated with human-readable domain names—like amazon.com.

Amazon's Route 53 is built to manage domain services, but it can also have a significant impact on the precision and speed with which resources are delivered.

CloudFront, Amazon's global content delivery network (CDN), can take both speed and accuracy a few steps further.

You're going to learn about how AWS addresses all three of those functions in this chapter.

The Domain Name System

DNS is responsible for mapping human-readable domain names (like example.com) to the machine-readable IP addresses (like 93.184.216.34) they represent.

Whenever you launch a new network-facing service on AWS—or anywhere else—and want it to make it accessible through a readable name, you need to satisfy some configuration requirements. But before you can learn to do that, it's important to be familiar with the basic concepts on which name services are built.

In this section, we'll define the key elements of DNS infrastructure, particularly the way they're used within Amazon Route 53.

Namespaces

The addressing structure organizing the billions of objects making up the Internet is managed through naming conventions. If, for instance, there was more than one website called amazon.com or more than one resource identified by the IP address 205.251.242.103, then things would quickly get chaotic. So, there's got to be a reliable, top-down administration authority.

The Internet naming system is maintained within the *domain name hierarchy* namespace, which controls the use of human-readable names. It's a *hierarchy* in the sense that the Internet can be segmented into multiple smaller namespaces through the assignment of blocks of public or private IP addresses or through the use of top-level domains (TLDs).

Both the Internet Protocol and the domain name hierarchy are administrated through the Internet Corporation for Assigned Names and Numbers (ICANN).

Name Servers

Associating a domain name like amazon.com with its actual IP address is the job of a *name server*. All computers will have a simple name server database available locally. That database might contain entries associating *hostnames* (like localhost) with an appropriate IP address. The following code is an example of the /etc/hosts file from a typical Linux machine. It includes a line that allows you to enter fileserver.com in your browser to open the home page of a web server running within the local network with the IP 192.168.1.5.

```
127.0.0.1    localhost
127.0.1.1    MyMachine
192.168.1.5 fileserver.com

# The following lines are desirable for IPv6 capable hosts
::1      ip6-localhost ip6-loopback
fe00::0 ip6-localnet
ff00::0 ip6-mcastprefix
ff02::1 ip6-allnodes
ff02::2 ip6-allrouters
```

If a query isn't satisfied by a local name server, it will be forwarded to one of the external DNS name servers specified in your computer's network interface configuration. Such a configuration might point to a public DNS server like Google's at 8.8.8.8 or OpenDNS at 208.67.222.222. Their job is to provide an IP address matching the domain name you entered so your application (a web browser, for instance) can complete your request.

Domains and Domain Names

In terms of Internet addressing, a *domain* is one or more servers, data repositories, or other digital resources identified by a single domain name. A *domain name* is a name that's been registered for the domain that's used to direct network requests to the domain's resources.

Domain Registration

Top-level name servers must be made aware of a new domain name before they can respond to related queries. Propagating domain name data among name servers is the job of a *domain name registrar*. Registrars work with registry operators like VeriSign so that domain registrations should be globally authoritative. Among its other roles, Amazon Route 53 acts as a domain name registrar.

Domain Layers

A domain name is made up of multiple parts. The rightmost text of every domain address (like .com or .org) indicates the *top-level domain* (TLD). The name to the left of the TLD (the *amazon* part of amazon.com) is called the *second-level domain* (SLD). This SLD designation would also refer to the unique second-level domains used by some countries, like the .co of .co.uk that's used for UK-based businesses.

A subdomain identifies a subset of a domain's resources. Web and email servers from the administration department of a college, for instance, might all use the administration .school.edu name. Thus, dean@administration.school.edu might be a valid email address, while administration.school.edu/apply.pdf could point to a file kept in the web root directory of the administration.school.edu server.

www.school.edu, api.school.edu, and ftp.school.edu are all common examples of subdomains (sometimes referred to as *hosts*). Figure 8.1 illustrates the parts of a simple subdomain.

FIGURE 8.1   A simple DNS domain broken down to its parts

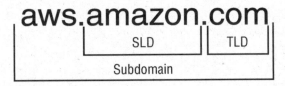

Fully Qualified Domain Names

Based on the default DNS settings on many systems, the system's default domain name will be automatically appended when resolving requests for partial domain names. As an example, a request for workstation might be resolved as workstation.localhost. If, however, you want to request a domain name as is, without anything being appended to it, you'll need to use a *fully qualified domain name* (FQDN).

An FQDN contains the absolute location of the domain including, at the least, a subdomain and the TLD. In addition, convention will often require a trailing dot after the TLD—which represents the domain root—to confirm that this is, indeed, an FQDN. Addresses in DNS zone files, for instance, will fail without a trailing dot. Here's how that might look:

administration.school.edu.

Zones and Zone Files

A *zone* (or *hosted zone* as Route 53 calls it) is a subset of a DNS domain. A *zone file* is a text file that describes the way resources within the zone should be mapped to DNS addresses within the domain. The file consists of *resource records* containing the data fields listed in Table 8.1.

TABLE 8.1 The data categories contained in a resource record from a zone file

Directive	Purpose
Name	The domain or subdomain name being defined
TTL	The time to live before the record expires
Record Class	The namespace for this record—usually IN (Internet)
Record Type	The record type defined by this record (A, CNAME, etc.)

This following example is a typical resource record defining the name server (NS) of the example.com domain as an Internet record (IN) with a one-hour TTL (1h) whose value is ns-750.awsdns-30.net.:

```
example.com. 1h IN NS ns-750.awsdns-30.net.
```

Record Types

The *record type* you enter in a zone file's resource record will determine how the record's data is formatted and how it should be used. There are currently around 40 types in active use, but Table 8.2 explains only the more common ones that also happen to be offered by Route 53.

TABLE 8.2 Some common DNS record types

Type	Function
A	Maps a hostname to an IPv4 IP address
CNAME	*Canonical name*—allows you to define one hostname as an alias for another
MX	*Mail exchange*—maps a domain to specified message transfer agents
AAAA	Maps a hostname to an IPv6 IP address

TABLE 8.2   Some common DNS record types *(continued)*

Type	Function
TXT	*Text*—contains human or machine-readable text
PTR	*Pointer*—points to another location within the domain space (This type will not be processed.)
SRV	A customizable record for service location
SPF	*Sender Policy Framework*—an email validation protocol (no longer widely supported as of RFC 7208)
NAPTR	*Name Authority Pointer*—allows regex-based domain name rewriting
CAA	*Certification Authority Authorization*—establishes authority to issue security certificates for a domain
NS	Identifies a name server to be used by a zone
SOA	*Start of authority*—Defines a zone's authoritative meta information

Alias Records

It's also possible to route traffic from one domain to another using an alias record. While the use of alias records has not yet been standardized across providers, Route 53 makes them available within record sets, allowing you to connect directly with network-facing resources running on AWS.

Amazon Route 53

With those DNS basics out of the way, it's time to turn our attention back to AWS. Route 53 provides more than just basic DNS services. In fact, it focuses on four distinct areas: domain registration, DNS management, availability monitoring (*health checks*), and *routing policies* (traffic management).

In case you're curious, the "53" in Route 53 reflects the fact that DNS traffic uses network port 53 to do its job.

Domain Registration

While there's nothing stopping you from registering your domains through any ICANN-accredited registrar—like GoDaddy—you can just as easily use Route 53. For domains that will be associated with AWS infrastructure, using Route 53 for registration can in fact help simplify your operations.

You can transfer registration of an existing domain from your current registrar by unlocking the domain transfer setting in the registrar's admin interface and then requesting an authorization code. You'll supply that code to Route 53 when you're ready to do the transfer.

If you'd prefer to leave your domain with its current registrar, you can still use Route 53 to manage your DNS configuration. Simply copy the name server addresses included in your Route 53 record set and paste them as the new name server values in your registrar's admin interface.

DNS Management

However you registered your site name, until you find some way to connect your domain with the resources it's supposed to represent, it won't do you a lot of good. On Route 53, it's the way you create and configure a hosted zone that determines what your users will be shown when they invoke your domain name in a browser, email client, or programmatically.

Within Route 53, rather than importing a preconfigured zone file (which is certainly an option), you'll usually configure your hosted zones directly via the console or AWS CLI.

When you create a new hosted zone and enter your domain name, you'll need to tell Route 53 whether you'd like this zone to be publicly or privately hosted. Routing for a privately hosted zone will be available only within the AWS VPCs that you specify. If you want your resources to be accessible to external users (which is true of most domains), then you'll create a publicly hosted zone.

Route 53 will automatically create an SOA record and provide four name server addresses. From there, it'll be your job to create new record sets defining the relationships between your domain and any subdomains you choose to create, and the resources you want made available. Exercise 8.1 guides you through the process of setting up a functioning hosted zone.

EXERCISE 8.1

Create a Hosted Zone on Route 53 for an EC2 Web Server

1. Click the Create Hosted Zone button in the GUI.

2. Enter a valid domain name that's currently not managed and select the Public Hosted Zone type. If you don't happen to already have an existing domain on Route 53 and you don't want to create a new one just for this exercise, feel free to use a fake domain—even something like example.com. Of course, you won't be able to fully test the zone if you're not using a real domain name. Either way, just remember that leaving the hosted zone up for more than 12 hours will incur a monthly hosting charge—that's currently only $0.50.

3. You'll be given name server and SOA record sets. Select those records one at a time and spend a few minutes exploring.

4. From the AWS EC2 Dashboard, create an AWS Linux AMI-based instance the way you did in Exercise 2.1 in Chapter 2, "Amazon Elastic Compute Cloud and Amazon Elastic Block Store." You're going to configure this instance as a simple web server, so you'll be able to test the domain. When configuring your security group, open HTTP port 80 so web traffic will be able to get in.

5. Log in to your instance (as you did in Exercise 2.1) and run the following commands to update the software repository, install the Apache web server, create a default index.html web page (add some text to the page when the text editor opens, and, when you're done, save and exit using Ctrl+X and then Y; this will later help you know that everything is working), and start up the Apache process.

    ```
    sudo yum update -y
    sudo yum install -y httpd
    sudo nano /var/www/html/index.html
    sudo systemctl start httpd
    ```

6. You can confirm your web server is working by pointing your browser to the instance's public IP address. You may want to keep this instance running, as it will be also helpful for the next exercise.

7. Back in the Route 53 Dashboard, click the Create Record Set button to create an A record to map your domain name to the IP address of a web server instance running on EC2. Leave the Name field to the left of the example.com value blank and enter your server's IP address (or any realistic fake address if your domain isn't real) in the Value field. Click Create.

8. Click Create Record Set once again to create a second A record. This time, you'll enter **www** in the Name field.

9. Click the Yes radio button next to Alias, click once inside the Alias Target field, and select the example.com value that should be among those that appear.

10. Domain propagation might take a few hours, but assuming you're working with an actual server, you should eventually be able to point your browser to example.com and your server's root web page should load.

Availability Monitoring

You should always be aware of the status of the resources you have running: closing your eyes and just hoping everything is fine has never been a winning strategy. Route 53 offers tools to monitor the health of the resources it's managing and ways to work around problems.

When you create a new record set, you're given the option of choosing a routing policy (which we'll discuss at length a bit later in this chapter). Selecting any policy besides

Simple will make it possible to associate your policy with a *health check*. A health check, which you create, configure, and name separately, will regularly test the resource that's represented by your record set to confirm it's healthy.

If everything's OK, Route 53 will continue routing traffic to that resource. But if a preset number of tests pass without an acceptable response, Route 53 will assume the resource is offline and can be set to redirect traffic to a backup resource. Exercise 8.2 illustrates how you can configure a health check that you can use with record sets.

EXERCISE 8.2

Set Up a Health Check

1. In the Route 53 GUI, click Create Health Check.

2. Give your check a name and select the Endpoint radio button for What To Monitor. You can use the web server you created in Exercise 8.1 as the health check endpoint.

3. With the IP address radio button selected for Specify Endpoint By, choose either HTTP or HTTPS for the protocol (this will depend on how you configured Transport Layer Security [TLS] encryption for your website—HTTP is a good bet if you're not sure).

4. Enter your server's IP address, and enter either **80** or **443** for the value of Port (again, this will depend on your site's TLS settings—80 is a good bet if you're not sure).

5. Enter the name of a file in the web root directory of your website as the value of Path. This is the resource the health check will try to load to test your site's health. You could use index.html (or index.php, if you happen to have a PHP application running), but, over the long term, that will probably cause a lot of unnecessary overhead. Instead, consider creating a small file called something like test.html and entering that for Path.

6. You can create an alarm to alert you to failed tests or simply click Create Health Check.

Routing Policies

In a world where your users all happily access a single, reliable server instance hosting your application, complicated routing policies make little sense. But since that's not the way things usually work in the real world, you'll generally want to apply flexible protocols to ensure that you're always providing the most reliable and low-latency service possible.

Route 53 routing policies provide this kind of functionality at the domain level that can be applied globally across all AWS regions. To make the most of their power, you'll need to understand what choices are available and how they work.

The simplest of the policies is, predictably, called simple. It routes all requests to the IP address or domain name you assign it. Simple is the default routing policy for new record sets.

Weighted Routing

A weighted policy will route traffic among multiple resources according to the ratio you set. To explain that better, imagine you have three servers (or load balancers representing three groups of servers) all hosting instances of the same web application. One of the servers (or server groups) has greater unused compute and memory capacity and can therefore handle far more traffic. It would be inefficient to send equal numbers of users to each of the servers. Instead, you can assign the larger server a numeric weight of, say, 50 and then 25 to the other two. That would result in half of all requests being sent to the larger server and 25 percent to each of the others.

To configure a weighted policy in Route 53, you would create a separate record set for each of your servers, give the same value for the set ID of each of the record sets, and then enter an instance-appropriate numeric value for the weight. The matching set IDs tell Route 53 that those record sets are meant to work together.

Latency Routing

Latency-based routing lets you leverage resources running in multiple AWS regions to provide service to clients from the instances that will deliver the best experience. Practically this means that, for an application used by clients in both Asia and Europe, you could place parallel resources in, say, the ap-southeast-1 and eu-west-1 regions. You then create a record set for each resource using latency-based policies in Route 53, with one pointing to your ap-southeast-1 resource and the other to eu-west-1.

Assuming you gave both record sets the same value for Set ID, Route 53 will know to direct requests for those resources to the instance that will provide the lowest latency for each client.

Failover Routing

A failover routing policy will direct traffic to the resource you identify as *primary* as long as health checks confirm that the resource is running properly. Should the primary resource go offline, subsequent traffic will be sent to the resource defined within a second record set and designated as *secondary*. As with other policies, the desired relationship between record sets is established by using matching set ID values for each set.

Geolocation Routing

Unlike latency policies that route traffic to answer data requests as *quickly* as possible, geolocation uses the continent, country, or U.S. state where the request originated to decide *what resource to send*. This can help you focus your content delivery, allowing you to deliver web pages in customer-appropriate languages, restrict content to regions where it's legally permitted, or generate parallel sales campaigns.

You should be aware that Route 53 will sometimes fail to identify the origin of a requesting IP address. You might want to configure a default record to cover those cases.

Multivalue Answer Routing

It's possible to combine a health check configuration with multivalue routing to make a deployment more highly available. Each multivalue-based record set points to a single resource and can be associated with a health check.

As many as eight records can be pointed to parallel resources and connected to each other through matching set ID values. Route 53 will use the health checks to monitor resource status and randomly route traffic among the healthy resources.

Working through Exercise 8.3 will show you the way the failover routing policy process works.

EXERCISE 8.3

Configure a Route 53 Routing Policy

1. Make sure you have two separate web-facing resources running. You could create a second Apache web server instance in addition to the one you launched in Exercise 8.1, or perhaps create a simple static website in S3 the way you did in Exercise 3.2 in Chapter 3, "Amazon Simple Storage Service and Amazon Glacier Storage." In this case, though, your bucket name will have to exactly match the domain name. That might mean something like secondary.example.com.

2. Configure a health check for each of your resources. You create a health check for an S3 static website by selecting Domain Name for Specify Endpoint By. Note that you'll need to strip off the http:// and trailing / characters from the endpoint before the health check configuration will accept it.

3. Assuming you have an active hosting zone (perhaps the one from Exercise 8.1), use the Route 53 GUI to create a record set for each of your instances. You might enter domain names like **server1.example.com** and **server2.example.com**—it's up to you.

4. Create a regular A record type if you're pointing to an EC2 instance, and enter the instance's IP address as the record's Value. If you're using an S3 static website for one or both of your resources, click Yes for Alias in the record set, click once within the Alias Target box that will appear, and select the appropriate S3 resource from among those that appear. Your static website must live in the same AWS account.

5. For Routing Policy, select Failover and choose either Primary or Secondary for the Failover Record Type radio buttons. The Set ID value will automatically change according to your choice. Make sure the record set for one of your resources is designated as Primary.

6. Select Yes for Evaluate Target Health, and select Yes for Associate With Health Check. Select the health check that matches the resource you're working with.

7. Test your configuration by first loading the primary website by its normal URL. Now, disable your primary website. You could do that by deleting or renaming its index .html file or, blocking HTTP access in the instance security group or, in the case of an S3, by disabling the static website setting. Point your browser to the same primary URL. If failover is working, you should see the index.html web page from your secondary resource.

Traffic Flow

Route 53 Traffic Flow is a console-based graphic interface that allows you to visualize complex combinations of routing policies as you build them. Figure 8.2 shows what a Traffic Flow configuration can look like.

FIGURE 8.2   A sample Traffic Flow policy

Source: https://console.aws.amazon.com/route53/trafficflow/home#/

Because it so seamlessly integrates routing policies with all the possible resource endpoints associated with your AWS account, Traffic Flow can make it simpler to quickly build a sophisticated routing structure. You can also use and customize routing templates.

Traffic Flow offers a routing policy that, as of the time of writing, is not available as a regular Route 53 policy: Geoproximity Routing. Geoproximity gives you the precision of geolocation routing but at a far finer level. Geoproximity routing rules can specify geographic areas by their relationship to either a particular longitude and latitude or to an AWS region. In both cases, setting a bias score will define how widely beyond your endpoint you want to apply your rule.

Amazon CloudFront

As you've seen, Route 53 can be used to optimize the way DNS requests are processed. But Amazon's global *content delivery network* (CDN) CloudFront can also help solve one of the primary problems addressed by Route 53: getting your content into the hands of your users as quickly as possible.

A CDN maintains a network of physical edge locations placed geographically close to the end users who are likely to request content. When you configure the way you want your content delivered—as part of what AWS calls a CloudFront distribution—you define how you want your content distributed through that network and how it should then be delivered to your users.

How do your users "know" to address their requests to your CloudFront endpoint address rather than getting it directly from your resources? Normally, they don't. But when you use Route 53 to configure your domain to direct incoming DNS requests to the CloudFront distribution, users will be automatically routed appropriately.

When a request is made, CloudFront assesses the user's location and calculates which endpoint will be available to deliver the content with the lowest latency. If this is the first time this content has been requested through the endpoint, the content will be copied from the origin server (an EC2 web server instance, perhaps, or the contents of an S3 bucket). Delivery of subsequent requests will—because the cached copy is still stored at the endpoint—be much faster.

The kind of CloudFront distribution you create will depend on the kind of media you're providing. For web pages and graphic content, you'll select a Web distribution. For video content that's stored in S3 buckets that can use Adobe's Real-Time Messaging Protocol (RTMP), CloudFront's RTMP distribution makes the most sense.

As you briefly saw in Chapter 3, when you configure your distribution, you'll have the option of adding a free *AWS Certificate Manager* (ACM) SSL/TLS encryption certificate to your distribution. This will protect your content as it moves between CloudFront and your users' devices from network sniffers and man-in-the-middle attacks.

CloudFront currently supports three categories of content origin, described in Table 8.3.

TABLE 8.3 Permitted CloudFront origins

Category	Description
Amazon S3 bucket	Any accessible S3 bucket
AWS MediaPackage channel endpoint	Video packaging and origination
AWS MediaStoreContainer endpoint	Media-optimized storage service

Exercise 8.4 will take you through steps for creating a CloudFront distribution complete with an encryption certificate.

EXERCISE 8.4

Create a CloudFront Distribution for Your S3-Based Static Website

1. Create a static website in S3 the way you did in Exercise 3.2 in Chapter 3.

2. From the CloudFront Dashboard, start a new distribution using the Web delivery method.

3. Click once inside the Origin Domain Name box, and a list of all the available resources within your account will be displayed. The S3 bucket containing your website files should be included. Select it.

4. Select a Price Class in the Distribution Settings section. Using the All Edge Locations setting will provide the best performance for the greatest number of customers, but it will also cost more. By the way, if you're only creating this as an experiment and you're unlikely to get more than a few hundred requests, then don't worry about the cost: it'll be in the low pennies.

   The next three steps will apply only if you have a valid DNS domain to work with.

5. Add the DNS domain names you want to use for this distribution to the Alternate Domain Names (CNAMES) box. Those might include **server1.example.com** and **www.example.com**. If you don't do this, your encryption certificate might not work for all content requests.

6. Click the Request Or Import A Certificate With ACM button and follow the simple instructions to request a certificate for your registered domain name. Once your request has been granted, your certificate will appear in the Custom SSL Certificate box. You can select it.

7. When you're satisfied with your settings, click Create Distribution.

8. In the Route 53 console, create (or edit) a record set that points your domain name to the CloudFront distribution you just created. Wait for the new settings to propagate and confirm that you can access the S3 content through a domain using HTTPS (encryption).

AWS CLI Example

The following command will list all the hosted zones in Route 53 within your AWS account. Among the data that will be returned is an Id for each zone. You can take the value of Id and pass it to the get-hosted-zone command to return record set details for that zone.

```
$ aws route53 list-hosted-zones
$ aws route53 get-hosted-zone --id /hostedzone/Z38LGIZCB3CSZ3
```

Summary

The DNS system manages Internet resource addressing through two top-level name spaces: the Internet Protocol (IP addresses) and the domain name hierarchy. The Internet Corporation for Assigned Names and Numbers (ICANN) administrates name servers and domain name registrars (like Route 53) through registry operators (like VeriSign).

A fully qualified domain name consists of a TLD (like org or com) and an SLD (like amazon). FQDNs are also often given a trailing dot representing "root."

DNS configuration details are organized as hosted zones, where resource record sets are created to control the way you want inbound domain traffic to be directed. That behavior can be defined through any one of a number of record types like A, CNAME, and MX.

A newly created Route 53 hosted zone will contain a start of authority (SOA) record set and a list of name servers to which requests can be directed. You'll need to create at least one record set so Route 53 will know from which domain name to expect requests.

Route 53 can be configured to regularly monitor the run status of your resources using health checks. Besides alerting you to problems, health checks can also be integrated with Route 53 routing policies to improve application availability.

Weighted routing policies let you direct traffic among multiple parallel resources proportionally according to their ability to handle it.

Latency routing policies send traffic to multiple resources to provide the lowest-latency service possible.

Failover routing monitors a resource and, on failure, reroutes subsequent traffic to a backup resource.

Geolocation routing assesses the location of a request source and directs responses to appropriate resources.

Amazon CloudFront is a CDN that caches content at edge locations to provide low-latency delivery of websites and digital media.

Exam Essentials

Understand how DNS services enable predictable and reliable network communication.   DNS registration ensures that domain names are globally unique and accessible. Domain requests are resolved using name servers—both local and remote.

Understand DNS naming conventions.   You should be familiar with "parsing" domain names. Each of the TLD, SLD, and subdomain/host sections will be read by DNS clients in a predictable way.

Be familiar with the key DNS record types.   Recognize the function of key record types, including A and AAAAA (address records for IPv4 and IPv6), CNAME (canonical name record or alias), MX (mail exchange record), NS (name server record), and SOA (start of authority record).

Be familiar with Route 53 routing policies.   Recognize the function of key routing policies, including simple (for single resources), weighted (routing among multiple resources by percentage), latency (low-latency content delivery), failover (incorporate backup resources for higher availability), and geolocation (respond to end user's location).

Understand how to create a CloudFront distribution.   CloudFront distributions can be configured to deliver content through low-latency, geographically-based content to end users.

Review Questions

1. Which of the following describes the function of a name server?
   A. Translating human-readable domain names into IP addresses
   B. Registering domain names with ICAAN
   C. Registering domain names with VeriSign
   D. Applying routing policies to network packets

2. Which of the following describes a domain?
   A. An object's FQDN
   B. Policies controlling the way remote requests are resolved
   C. One or more servers, data repositories, or other digital resources identified by a single domain name
   D. A label used to direct network requests to a domain's resources

3. Which of the following is an example of a top-level domain (TLD)?
   A. `amazon.com/documentation/`
   B. `aws.`
   C. `amazon.`
   D. `.com`

4. Which of the following categories would *not* be found in a zone file?
   A. CNAME (canonical name)
   B. TTL (time to live)
   C. Record type
   D. Record data

5. Which of the following DNS record types should you use to associate a domain name with an IP address?
   A. NS
   B. SOA
   C. A
   D. CNAME

6. Which of the following are services provided by Amazon Route 53? (Choose three.)
   A. Domain registration
   B. Content delivery network
   C. Health checks
   D. DNS management

7. For regulatory compliance, your application may only provide data to requests coming from the United States. Which of the following routing policies can be configured to do this?

   A. Simple

   B. Latency

   C. Geolocation

   D. Multivalue

8. Your web application is hosted within multiple AWS regions. Which of the following routing policies will ensure the fastest possible access for your users?

   A. Latency

   B. Weighted

   C. Geolocation

   D. Failover

9. You're testing three versions of a new application, with each version running on its own server and the current production version on a fourth server. You want to route 5 percent of your total traffic to each of the test servers and route the remaining 85 percent of traffic to the production server. Which routing policy will you use?

   A. Failover

   B. Weighted

   C. Latency

   D. Geolocation

10. You have production infrastructure sitting behind one DNS domain, and for disaster recovery purposes, you have parallel infrastructure on standby behind a second domain hosted in a second AWS region. Which routing policy will automate the switchover in the event of a failure in the production system?

    A. Latency

    B. Weighted

    C. Geolocation

    D. Failover

11. Which of the following kinds of hosted zones are real options within Route 53? (Choose two.)

    A. Public

    B. Regional

    C. VPC

    D. Private

12. Which of the following actions will you need to perform to transfer a domain from an external registrar to Route 53? (Choose two.)

   A. Unlock the domain transfer setting on the external registrar admin page.

   B. Request an authorization code from the external registrar.

   C. Copy the name server addresses from Route 53 to the external registrar admin page.

   D. Create a hosted zone CNAME record set.

13. Which of the following actions will you need to perform to use Route 53 to manage a domain that's being hosted on an external registrar?

   A. Request an authorization code from the external registrar.

   B. Copy the name server addresses from Route 53 to the external registrar admin page.

   C. Create a hosted zone CNAME record set.

   D. Unlock the domain transfer setting on the external registrar admin page.

14. How do Route 53 health checks test for the health of a resource?

   A. It periodically tries to load the `index.php` page.

   B. It periodically tries to load the `index.html` page.

   C. It periodically tries to load a specified web page.

   D. It periodically tries to log into the resource using SSH.

15. Which of the following most accurately describes the difference between geolocation and geoproximity routing policies?

   A. Geoproximity policies specify geographic areas by their relationship to either a particular longitude and latitude or to an AWS region, while geolocation policies use the continent, country, or U.S. state where the request originated to decide what resource to send.

   B Geolocation policies specify geographic areas by their relationship to either a particular longitude and latitude or to an AWS region, while geoproximity policies use the continent, country, or U.S. state where the request originated to decide what resource to send.

   C. Geolocation policies will direct traffic to the resource you identify as primary as long as health checks confirm that that resource is running properly, while geoproximity policies allow you to deliver web pages in customer-appropriate languages.

   D. Geolocation policies use a health check configuration routing to make a deployment more highly available, while geoproximity policies leverage resources running in multiple AWS regions to provide service to clients from the instances that will deliver the best experience.

16. Which of the following are problems that CloudFront is well-positioned to solve? (Choose two.)

    A. A heavily used website providing media downloads for a global audience

    B. An S3 bucket with large media files used by workers on your corporate campus

    C. A file server accessed through a corporate VPN

    D. A popular website with constantly changing content

17. Which of the following is not a permitted origin for a CloudFront distribution?

    A. Amazon S3 bucket

    B. AWS MediaPackage channel endpoint

    C. API Gateway endpoint

    D. Web server

18. What's the best way to control the costs your CloudFront distribution incurs?

    A. Select a price class that maintains copies in only a limited subset of CloudFront's edge locations.

    B. Configure a custom SSL certificate to restrict access to HTTPS requests only.

    C. Disable the use of Alternate Domain Names (CNAMES) for your distribution.

    D. Enable Compress Objects Automatically for your distribution.

19. Which of the following is not a direct benefit of using a CloudFront distribution?

    A. User requests from an edge location that's recently received the same request will be delivered with lower latency.

    B. CloudFront distributions can be directly mapped to Route 53 hosted zones.

    C. All user requests will be delivered with lower latency.

    D. You can incorporate free encryption certificates into your infrastructure.

20. Which of the following content types is the best fit for a Real-Time Messaging Protocol (RTMP) distribution?

    A. Amazon Elastic Transcoder–based videos

    B. S3-based videos

    C. Streaming videos

    D. A mix of text and media-rich digital content

The Well-Architected Framework

Chapter

9

The Reliability Pillar

THE AWS CERTIFIED SOLUTIONS ARCHITECT ASSOCIATE EXAM OBJECTIVES COVERED IN THIS CHAPTER MAY INCLUDE, BUT ARE NOT LIMITED TO THE FOLLOWING:

Domain 1: Design Resilient Architectures

✓ 1.1 Choose reliable/resilient storage.

✓ 1.2 Determine how to design decoupling mechanisms using AWS services.

✓ 1.3 Determine how to design a multitier architecture solution.

✓ 1.4 Determine how to design high availability and/or fault tolerant architectures.

Introduction

Reliability—sometimes also called *resiliency*—is the ability of an application to avoid failure and recover from it quickly when it occurs. The degree of reliability your application will achieve is proportional to the amount of effort you put into the design up front, as well as the money you spend to operate it. Achieving a high degree of reliability for your application is not a trivial matter and entails significant cost and complexity. Therefore, before you begin architecting your AWS deployment, you have to decide how much reliability you actually need. The reliability of an application is quantified in terms of *availability*—the percentage of time the application is performing as expected.

Once you decide how much availability you need, you can begin designing your AWS environment. The level of availability your application can achieve depends in part on the availability of the AWS resources it uses, including networking, compute, and storage. As you might expect, even AWS resources aren't going to be available 100 percent of the time. They'll fail, so how you plan for and handle these inevitable failures when they happen will have a significant impact on your application's availability.

In this chapter, you'll learn how to design your AWS environment to tolerate resource failures so that the failure of an instance or even an entire availability zone doesn't cause your entire application to become unavailable. You'll also learn how to recover from unavoidable failures. If all of your application's instances go down or if your application crashes because of a bug, security breach, database corruption, or just human error, you'll know how to recover quickly.

Calculating Availability

A common way of quantifying and expressing reliability is in terms of availability. Availability is the percentage of time an application is working as expected. Note that this measurement is subjective, and "working as expected" implies that you have a certain expectation of how the application should work.

Generally, you want application availability to be very high, 99 percent or greater. Table 9.1 lists the relationship between percentage availability and the amount of time an application is unavailable during the year.

TABLE 9.1   The relationship between annual availability percentage and time unavailable

Availability Percentage	Time Unavailable
99%	3 days, 15 hours, 39 minutes
99.9%	8 hours, 45 minutes
99.95%	4 hours, 22 minutes
99.99%	52 minutes
99.999%	5 minutes

You may hear availability measured in nines. For example, "2 nines" is 99 percent, "3 nines" is 99.9 percent, and so on. Some call 99.95 percent "3-1/2 nines," which isn't quite correct, but it's easier and less confusing than saying "3 and 5/9 nines!"

Availability Differences in Traditional vs. Cloud-Native Applications

As an AWS architect you must understand how application design decisions affect reliability. The applications you run in the cloud will fall into one of two broad categories: traditional or cloud-native.

Traditional Applications

Traditional applications are those written to run on and use the capabilities of traditional Linux or Windows servers. To deploy such an application on AWS, you'll need to run it on one or more EC2 instances. If the application uses a database, you'll either run and manage your own database software on an EC2 instance or use the AWS-managed equivalent. If your application requires a relational database, you can use Amazon Relational Database Service (RDS). If it uses a nonrelational database such as Redis, you can use ElastiCache for Redis. Traditional applications operate the same whether they're running on the cloud or in a data center. If you can "lift and shift" an application from the data center to the cloud without making any changes to the application's code, then it's a traditional application.

Suppose you have a traditional application running on a single EC2 instance backed by a multi-availability zone (AZ) RDS deployment. The application's availability depends on the availability of both the EC2 instance and the RDS instance. Both of these are called *hard dependencies*. To calculate the total availability of the application, you simply multiply the availability of those hard dependencies. AWS advertises the availability of the EC2 service in a region as 99.99 percent, and multi-AZ RDS as 99.95 percent. If you multiply these availabilities together (.9999 × .9995), you get 99.94 percent, which is about 5 hours and 15 minutes of downtime per year.

You might wonder why you'd use RDS with an availability of 99.95 percent when you could run your own database on the EC2 service, which has 99.99 percent availability. The reason is that the 99.99 percent availability for EC2 refers to the EC2 instance itself, not to whatever database software you may have running on it. In contrast, the 99.95 percent availability RDS offers refers to the availability of the database.

To increase availability, you can use redundant components. Let's start with EC2. Suppose that instead of one EC2 instance, you use two EC2 instances each in a different availability zone. Each EC2 instance runs the application, and an application load balancer (ALB) distributes connections to the instances in a *target group*. If the application on one instance fails or if the EC2 instance itself fails, the ALB will route connections to the remaining healthy instance. In this sense, the EC2 instances are redundant. To calculate the availability of these redundant components, you take 100 percent minus the product of the instance failure rate. If the availability of an EC2 instance is 99.99 percent then the failure rate of that instance is .01 percent. To calculate the availability for two EC2 instances, it would be as follows:

$$100\% - (0.01\% \times 0.01\%) = 99.999999\%$$

This is less than one second!

But that's just for EC2. You also have to consider the database. The database represents a hard dependency, so you must multiply the database's availability—99.95 percent—by the availability of the EC2 instances—99.999999 percent. The product would be about 99.949 percent, which is about 4 hours and 22 minutes of downtime a year. That's not a big improvement. Notice that because the RDS instance is a hard dependency and its availability is 99.95 percent, you won't be able to do better than this level of availability without introducing a redundant database. Later in this chapter, we'll show you how to do that.

Cloud-Native Applications

Cloud-native applications are written to use the resources of a specific cloud platform like AWS. These may be serverless applications written to use Lambda functions. Or they may run on EC2 instances and store objects in S3 or use DynamoDB instead of a relational database for storing data. This is especially likely to be true if the application requires low-latency access to data stored in a nonrelational data format such as JavaScript Object Notation (JSON). DynamoDB is also a popular choice for storing session state data.

Suppose you have a Linux application that runs on a single EC2 instance—just as a traditional app would—but is designed to use DynamoDB for database storage. In a single region, DynamoDB has an availability of 99.99 percent. Again, EC2 also has an availability of 99.99 percent. So considering just these two factors, the total application availability is as follows:

$$99.99\% \times 99.99\% = 99.98\%$$

This is about 1 hour and 45 minutes of downtime per year. Much better!

But suppose you want even greater availability. Instead of running one EC2 instance, you run two, each in a different AZ. Again, you'll use ALB to distribute traffic to these instances. To calculate the availability of these instances, you'd do this:

100% − (0.01% × 0.01%) = 99.999999%

To get the total application availability, multiply 99.999999 percent by the availability of DynamoDB—99.99 percent —which would give you 99.989 percent, or 57 minutes of downtime per year.

Believe it or not, you can make this even better by using two regions. In one region, you would still have two instances, each in a different AZ, and an ALB to distribute traffic to the application instances. But now you replicate this setup in a different region and then use a Route 53 weighed routing policy to distribute traffic between the two regions. Now, with a total of four instances, your calculation would be like this:

100% − (.01% × .01% × .01% × .01%)

This is about 16 nines (99.99999999999999 percent).

  Route 53 advertises an availability of 100 percent, so its failure rate is zero.

Since you'd be running the application across regions, you could take advantage of DynamoDB global tables, which replicate your DynamoDB tables across regions. DynamoDB global tables have an availability of 99.999 percent. So, to calculate the total availability for the application, you'd multiply 99.99999999999999 percent by 99.999 percent to get about 99.9989 percent, or 5 minutes of downtime per year. Being able to achieve this level of availability is one of the reasons organizations choose to use cloud-native applications instead of just running traditional applications in the cloud.

Building Serverless Applications with Lambda

Although as an AWS architect you don't need to know how to program, it's important to understand how serverless applications that run on Lambda differ from executables that run on EC2 instances. Lambda allows you to create a function written in one of a variety of languages, including the following:

- C#
- Go
- Java
- JavaScript
- PowerShell
- Python

Lambda functions are useful for performing intermittent tasks that don't warrant keeping a running EC2 instance around. For example, you can create a Lambda function that retrieves an image from an S3 source bucket, resizes it, and then uploads the processed image to a destination bucket. When a new image is uploaded to the source bucket, S3 triggers the Lambda function. You're billed only for the time the function runs.

Lambda executes functions using a highly available distributed computing platform. Unlike an EC2 instance, which can fail or be stopped or terminated, Lambda is always available.

Know Your Limits

Although one of the big selling points of the cloud is the ability to grow with you, cloud capacity is not unlimited. AWS imposes limits to prevent anyone from accidentally or intentionally consuming all resources, effectively resulting in a denial of service for other customers. The limits depend on the service and include things such as network throughput, S3 PUT requests per second, the number of instances per region, the number of elastic IP addresses per region, and so on. Many of these limits can be increased upon request.

Use the AWS Trusted Advisor to see what service limits apply to your account. You may also consider setting CloudWatch Alarms to let you know when you're getting close to hitting a limit so you can react to avoid hitting it. Avoiding hitting a limit may involve requesting a limit increase by contacting AWS support, adding another availability zone, or even shifting some of the load to another region.

Increasing Availability

The availability numbers you've looked at thus far are based only on the availability of AWS services. But the actual availability of your application could be worse. There are many things that can impact availability. For example, your app can crash, perhaps because of a bug, memory leak, or data corruption.

The best way to maximize availability is to avoid failure in the first place. Instead of having a single monster instance hosting a web application, have multiple smaller instances and spread them out across different availability zones. This way, a failure of a single instance or even an entire availability zone won't render your application unavailable. Rather than depending on one instance to be highly available, distributed application design distributes the work across multiple smaller resources that are not dependent on one another.

But that's not the whole story. If an instance fails, it means the other instances have to pick up the slack. If enough instances fail, only a few instances will be servicing a lot of traffic, resulting in poor performance and likely in those remaining instances also crashing. Therefore, you need a way to re-create failed instances when such a crash occurs.

Another issue that could arise is that increased demand could place such a load on your instances that they become unusably slow, or even crash altogether. An advantage of using a distributed application design is that it makes it easier to add capacity nondisruptively. Instead of having to upgrade to a more powerful instance class, which requires downtime, you simply add more instances. When you have a distributed system, getting more resources just involves scaling out—adding more of the same.

EC2 Auto Scaling

The *EC2 Auto Scaling* service offers a way to both avoid application failure and recover from it when it happens. Auto Scaling works by provisioning and starting on your behalf a specified number of EC2 instances. It can dynamically add more instances to keep up with increased demand. And when an instance fails or gets terminated, Auto Scaling will automatically replace it.

EC2 Auto Scaling uses either a *launch configuration* or a *launch template* to automatically configure the instances that it launches. Both perform the same basic function of defining the basic configuration parameters of the instance as well as what scripts (if any) run on it at launch time. Launch configurations have been around longer and are more familiar to you if you've been using AWS for a while. You're also more likely to encounter them if you're going into an existing AWS environment. Launch templates are newer and are what AWS now recommends. You'll learn about both, but which you use is up to you.

Launch Configurations

When you create an instance manually, you have to specify many configuration parameters, including an Amazon Machine Image (AMI), instance type, SSH key pair, security group, instance profile, block device mapping, whether it's EBS optimized, placement tenancy, and User Data, such as custom scripts to install and configure your application. A launch configuration is essentially a named document that contains the same information you'd provide when manually provisioning an instance.

You can create a launch configuration from an existing EC2 instance. Auto Scaling will copy the settings from the instance for you, but you can customize them as needed. You can also create a launch configuration from scratch.

Launch configurations are for use only with EC2 Auto Scaling, meaning you can't manually launch an instance using a launch configuration. Also, once you create a launch configuration, you can't modify it. If you want to change any of the settings, you have to create an entirely new launch configuration.

Launch Templates

Launch templates are similar to launch configurations in that you can specify the same settings. But the uses for launch templates are more versatile. You can use a launch template with Auto Scaling, of course, but you can also use it for spinning up one-off EC2 instances or even creating a Spot fleet.

Launch templates are also versioned, allowing you to change them after creation. Any time you need to make changes to a launch template, you create a new version of it. AWS keeps all versions, and you can then flip back and forth between versions as needed. This makes it easier to track your launch template changes over time. Complete Exercise 9.1 to create your own launch template.

> If you have an existing launch configuration, you can copy it to a launch template using the AWS web console. There's no need to create launch templates from scratch!

EXERCISE 9.1

Create a Launch Template

In this exercise, you'll create a launch template that installs and configures a simple web server. You'll then use the launch template to manually create an instance.

1. In the EC2 Dashboard, click Launch Templates.

2. Click the Create Launch Template button.

3. Give the launch template a name such as **MyTemplate**.

4. Click the Search For AMI link to locate one of the Ubuntu Server LTS AMIs. If you're in the us-east-1 region, you can use **ami-0ac019f4fcb7cb7e6**.

5. For Instance Type, select t2.micro.

6. Under Security Groups, select a security group that allows inbound HTTP access. Create a new security group if necessary.

7. Expand the Advanced Details section and input the following in the User Data text input field:

```
#!/bin/bash
apt-get update
apt-get install -y apache2
echo "Welcome to my website" > index.html
cp index.html /var/www/html
```

8. Click the Create Launch Template button.

9. Click the Launch Instance From This Template link.

10. Under Source Template Version, select 1 (Default).

11. Click the Launch Instance From Template button.

12. After the instance boots, browse to its public IP address. You should see a web page that says "Welcome to my website."

13. Terminate the instance when you're done with it.

Auto Scaling Groups

An *Auto Scaling group* is a group of EC2 instances that Auto Scaling manages. When creating an Auto Scaling group, you must first specify either the launch configuration or launch template you created. When you create an auto scaling group, you must specify how many running instances you want Auto Scaling to provision and maintain using the launch configuration or template you created. Specifically, you have to specify the minimum and maximum size of the Auto Scaling group. You may also optionally set the desired number of instances you want Auto Scaling to provision and maintain.

Minimum   Auto Scaling will ensure the number of healthy instances never goes below the minimum. If you set this to zero, Auto Scaling will not spawn any instances and will terminate any running instances in the group.

Maximum   Auto Scaling will make sure the number of healthy instances never exceeds this. This might seem strange, but remember that AWS imposes service limits on how many instances you can run simultaneously. Setting your maximum to less than or equal to your limit ensures you never exceed it.

Desired capacity   The desired capacity is an optional setting that must lie within the minimum and maximum values. If you don't specify a desired capacity, Auto Scaling will launch the number of instances as the minimum value. If you specify a desired capacity, Auto Scaling will add or terminate instances to stay at the desired capacity. For example, if you set the minimum to 1, maximum to 10, and desired capacity to 4, then Auto Scaling will create 4 instances. If one of those instance gets terminated—for example, because of human action or a host crash—Auto Scaling will replace it to maintain the desired capacity of 4. In the web console, desired capacity is also called the *group size*.

Specifying an Application Load Balancer Target Group

If you want to use an application load balancer to distribute traffic to instances in your Auto Scaling group, just plug in the name of the ALB target group when creating the Auto Scaling group. Whenever Auto Scaling creates a new instance, it will automatically add it to the ALB target group.

Health Checks Against Application Instances

When you create an Auto Scaling group, Auto Scaling will strive to maintain the minimum number of instances, or the desired number if you've specified it. If an instance becomes unhealthy, Auto Scaling will terminate and replace it.

By default, Auto Scaling determines an instance's health based on EC2 health checks. Recall from Chapter 7, "CloudTrail, CloudWatch, and AWS Config," that EC2 automatically performs system and instance status checks. These checks monitor for instance problems such as memory exhaustion, filesystem corruption, or an incorrect network or startup configuration, and system problems that require AWS involvement to repair. Although these checks can catch a variety of instance and host-related problems, they won't necessarily catch application-specific problems.

If you're using an application load balancer to route traffic to your instances, you can configure health checks for the load balancer's target group. Target group health checks can check for HTTP response codes from 200 to 499. You can then configure your Auto Scaling group to use the results of these health checks to determine if an instance is healthy.

If an instance fails the ALB health check, it will route traffic away from the failed instance, ensuring users don't reach it. At the same time, Auto Scaling will remove the instance, create a replacement, and add the new instance to the load balancer's target group. The load balancer will then route traffic to the new instance.

> A good design practice is to have a few recovery actions that work for a variety of circumstances. An instance may crash due to an out-of-memory condition, a bug, a deleted file, or an isolated network failure, but simply terminating and replacing the instance using Auto Scaling resolves all these cases. There's no need to come up with a separate recovery action for each cause when simply re-creating the instance solves all of them.

Auto Scaling Options

Once you create an Auto Scaling group, you can leave it be and it will continue to maintain the minimum or desired number of instances indefinitely. However, maintaining the current number of instances is just one option. Auto Scaling provides several other options to scale out the number of instances to meet demand.

Manual Scaling

If you change the minimum, desired, or maximum values at any time after creating the group, Auto Scaling will immediately adjust. For example, if you have the desired capacity set to 2 and change it to 4, Auto Scaling will launch two more instances. If you have four instances and set the desired capacity to 2, Auto Scaling will terminate two instances. Think of the desired capacity as a thermostat!

Dynamic Scaling Policies

Most AWS-managed resources are elastic; that is, they automatically scale to accommodate increased load. Some examples include S3, load balancers, Internet gateways, and network address translation (NAT) gateways. Regardless of how much traffic you throw at them, AWS is responsible for ensuring they remain available while continuing to perform well. But when it comes to your EC2 instances, you're responsible for ensuring that they're powerful and plentiful enough to meet demand.

Running out of instance resources—be it CPU utilization, memory, or disk space—will almost always result in the failure of whatever you're running on it. To ensure that your instances never become overburdened, dynamic scaling policies automatically provision more instances *before* they hit that point. Auto Scaling generates the following aggregate metrics for all instances within the group:

- Aggregate CPU utilization
- Average request count per target
- Average network bytes in
- Average network bytes out

You're not limited to using just these native metrics. You can also use metric filters to extract metrics from CloudWatch logs and use those. As an example, your application may generate logs that indicate how long it takes to complete a process. If the process takes too long, you could have Auto Scaling spin up new instances.

Dynamic scaling policies work by monitoring a CloudWatch alarm and scaling out—by increasing the desired capacity—when the alarm is breaching. There are three dynamic scaling policies to choose from: simple, step, and target tracking.

Simple Scaling Policies

With a *simple scaling policy*, whenever the metric rises above the threshold, Auto Scaling simply increases the desired capacity. How much it increases the desired capacity, however, depends on which of the following *adjustment types* you choose:

ChangeInCapacity   Increases the capacity by a specified amount. For instance, you start with a desired capacity of 4 and then have an Auto Scaling add 2 when the load increases.

ExactCapacity   Sets the capacity to a specific value, regardless of the current value. For example, suppose the desired capacity is 4. You create a policy to change the value to 6 when the load increases.

PercentChangeInCapacity   Increases the capacity by a percentage of the current amount. If the current desired capacity is 4 and you specify the percent change in capacity as 50 percent, then Auto Scaling will bump the desired capacity to 6.

For example, suppose you have four instances and create a simple scaling policy that specifies a PercentChangeInCapacity adjustment of 50 percent. When the monitored alarm triggers, Auto Scaling will increment the desired capacity by 2, which will in turn add 2 instances to the auto scaling group, giving a total of 6.

After Auto Scaling completes the adjustment, it waits a *cooldown period* before executing the policy again, even if the alarm is still breaching. The default cooldown period is 300 seconds, but you can set it as high as you want or as low as 0—effectively disabling it. Note that if an instance is unhealthy, Auto Scaling will not wait for the cooldown period before replacing the unhealthy instance.

Referring to the preceding example, suppose after the scaling adjustment completes and the cooldown period expires, the monitored alarm drops below the threshold. At this point, the desired capacity is 6. If the alarm triggers again, the simple scaling action will execute again and add three more instances. Keep in mind that Auto Scaling will never increase the desired capacity beyond the group's maximum setting.

Step Scaling Policies

If the demand on your application is rapidly increasing, a simple scaling policy may not add enough instances quickly enough. Using a *step scaling policy*, you can instead add instances based on how much the aggregate metric exceeds the threshold.

To illustrate, suppose your group starts out with four instances. You want to add more instances to the group as the average CPU utilization of the group increases. When the utilization hits 50 percent, you want to add two more instances. When it goes above 60 percent, you want to add four more instances.

You'd first create a CloudWatch Alarm to monitor the average CPU utilization and set the alarm threshold to 50 percent, since this is the utilization level at which you want to start increasing the desired capacity.

You'd must then specify at least one step adjustment. Each step adjustment consists of the following:

- A lower bound
- An upper bound
- The adjustment type
- The amount by which to increase the desired capacity

The upper and lower bound define a range that the metric has to fall within for the step adjustment to execute. Suppose for the first step you set a lower bound of 50 and an upper bound of 60, with a ChangeInCapacity adjustment of 2. When the alarm triggers, Auto Scaling will consider the metric value of the group's average CPU utilization. Suppose it's 55 percent. Because 55 is between 50 and 60, Auto Scaling will execute the action specified in this step, which is to add two instances to the desired capacity.

Suppose now that you create another step with a lower bound of 60 and an upper bound of infinity. You also set a ChangeInCapacity adjustment of 4. If the average CPU utilization increases to 62 percent, Auto Scaling will note that 60 <= 62 < infinity and will execute the action for this step, adding 4 instances to the desired capacity.

You might be wondering what would happen if the utilization were 60 percent. Step ranges can't overlap. A metric of 60 percent would fall within the lower bound of the second step.

With a step scaling policy, you can optionally specify a *warm-up time*, which is how long Auto Scaling will wait until considering the metrics of newly added instances. The default warm up time is 300 seconds. Note that there are no cooldown periods in step scaling policies.

Target Tracking Policies

If step scaling policies are too involved for your taste, you can instead use *target tracking policies*. All you do is select a metric and target value, and Auto Scaling will create a CloudWatch Alarm and a scaling policy to adjust the number of instances to keep the metric near that target.

The metric you choose must change proportionally to the instance load. Metrics like this include average CPU utilization for the group and request count per target. Aggregate metrics like the total request count for the ALB don't change proportionally to the load on an individual instance and aren't appropriate for use in a target tracking policy.

Note that in addition to scaling out, target tracking will also scale in by deleting instances to maintain the target metric value. If you don't want this behavior, you can disable scaling in. Also, just as with a step scaling policy, you can optionally specify a warm-up time.

Scheduled Actions

Scheduled actions are useful if you have a predictable load pattern and want to adjust your capacity proactively, ensuring you have enough instances *before* demand hits.

When you create a scheduled action, you must specify the following:

- A minimum, maximum, or desired capacity value
- A start date and time

You may optionally set the policy to recur at regular intervals, which is useful if you have a repeating load pattern. You can also set an end time, after which the scheduled policy gets deleted.

To illustrate how you might use a scheduled action, suppose you normally run only two instances in your Auto Scaling group during the week. But on Friday, things get busy, and you know you'll need four instances to keep up. You'd start by creating a scheduled action that sets the desired capacity to 2 and recurs every Saturday, as shown in Figure 9.1.

FIGURE 9.1 Scheduled action setting the desired capacity to 2 every Saturday

The start date is January 5, 2019, which is a Saturday. To handle the expected Friday spike, you'd create another weekly recurring policy to set the desired capacity to 4, as shown in Figure 9.2.

FIGURE 9.2   Scheduled action setting the desired capacity to 4 every Friday

This action will run every Friday, setting the desired capacity to 4, prior to the antici-pated increased load.

Note that you can combine scheduled actions with dynamic scaling policies. For exam-ple, if you're running an e-commerce site, you may use a scheduled action to increase the maximum group size during busy shopping seasons and then rely on dynamic scaling poli-cies to increase the desired capacity as needed.

Data Backup and Recovery

As you learned in Chapter 2, "Amazon Elastic Compute Cloud and Amazon Elastic Block Store," and Chapter 3, "Amazon Simple Storage Service and Amazon Glacier Storage," AWS offers several different data storage options. Although Amazon takes great pains to ensure the durability of your data stored on these services, data loss is always a possibility. AWS offers several options to help you store your data in a resilient manner as well as main-tain backups to recover from when the inevitable data loss occurs.

S3

All S3 storage classes except One Zone-Infrequent Access distribute objects across multiple availability zones. To avoid data loss from the failure of a single availability zone, be sure to use one of the other storage classes.

To guard against deletion and data corruption, enable S3 versioning. With versioning enabled, S3 never overwrites or deletes an object. Instead, modifying an object creates a new version of it that you can revert to if needed. Also, instead of deleting an object, S3 inserts a delete marker and removes the object from view. But the object and all of its versions still exist.

To protect your data against multiple availability zone failures—or the failure of an entire region—you can enable cross-region replication between a source bucket in one region and destination bucket in another. Once enabled, S3 will synchronously copy every object from the source bucket to the destination. Note that cross-region replication requires versioning to be enabled on both buckets. Also, deletes on the source bucket don't get replicated.

Elastic File System

AWS Elastic File System (EFS) provides a managed Network File System (NFS) that can be shared among EC2 instances or on-premises servers. EFS filesystems are stored across multiple zones in a region, allowing you to withstand an availability zone failure.

EFS doesn't come with versioning or native backup/restore capability. To protect against data loss and corruption, you can back up individual files to an S3 bucket or another EFS filesystem in the same region.

Elastic Block Storage

EBS automatically replicates volumes across multiple availability zones in a region so they're resilient to a single availability zone failure. Even so, data corruption is always a possibility.

One of the easiest ways to back up an EBS volume is to take a snapshot of it. AWS stores EBS snapshots across multiple availability zones in S3. You can either create a snapshot manually or use the Amazon Data Lifecycle Manager to automatically create a snapshot for you at regular intervals. To use the Amazon Data Lifecycle Manager, you create a Snapshot Lifecycle Policy and specify an interval of 12 or 24 hours, as well as a snapshot creation time. You also must specify the number of automatic snapshots to retain, up to 1,000 snapshots.

One important but often overlooked piece of data that gets stored on EBS is application logs. An application may create log files on the instance it's running on, but if the instance crashes or loses connectivity, those files won't be able to tell you what's wrong. And if EC2 Auto Scaling terminates an instance and its EBS volume along with it, any log files stored locally are gone permanently. CloudWatch Logs can collect and store application logs from an instance in real time, letting you search and analyze them even after the instance is gone.

Database Resiliency

When it comes to protecting your databases, your options vary depending on whether you're using a relational database or DynamoDB.

If you're running your own relational database server, you can use the database engine's native capability to back up the database to a file. You can then store the file in S3 or Glacier for safekeeping. Restoring a database depends on the particulars of the database engine you're running but generally involves copying the backup file back to the destination instance and running an import process to copy the contents of the backup file into the database.

If you're using Amazon Relational Database Service (RDS), you always have the option of taking a simple database instance snapshot. Restoring from a database snapshot can take several minutes and always creates a new database instance.

For additional resiliency, you can use a multi-AZ RDS deployment that maintains a primary instance in one availability zone and a standby instance in another. RDS replicates data synchronously from the primary to the standby. If the primary instance fails, either because of an instance or because of availability zone failure, RDS automatically fails over to the secondary.

For maximum resiliency, use Amazon Aurora with multiple Aurora replicas. Aurora stores your database across three different availability zones. If the primary instance fails, it will fail over to one of the Aurora replicas. Aurora is the only RDS offering that lets you provision up to 15 replicas, which is more than enough to have one in each availability zone!

DynamoDB stores tables across multiple availability zones, which in addition to giving you low-latency performance also provides additional protection against an availability zone failure. For additional resiliency, you can use DynamoDB global tables to replicate your tables to different regions. You can also configure point-in-time recovery to automatically take backups of your DynamoDB tables. Point-in-time recovery lets you restore your DynamoDB tables to any point in time from 35 days until 5 minutes before the current time.

Creating a Resilient Network

All of your AWS resources depend on the network, so designing your network properly is critical. When it comes to network design, there are two different elements to consider: your virtual private cloud (VPC) design and how users will connect to your resources within your VPC.

VPC Design Considerations

When creating a VPC, make sure you choose a sufficiently large classless interdomain routing (CIDR) block to provide enough IP addresses to assign to your resources. The more redundancy you build in to your AWS deployment, the more IP addresses you'll need. Also, when you scale out by adding more resources, you must have enough IP addresses to assign to those additional resources.

When creating your subnets, leave enough unused address space within the CIDR to add additional subnets later. This is important for a couple of reasons. First, AWS occasionally adds additional availability zones to a region. By leaving additional space, you can take advantage of those new availability zones. Your availability requirements may call for only one availability zone today, but it doesn't hurt to leave room in case your needs change. Second, even if you don't ever need an additional availability zone, you may still need a separate subnet to segment your resources for security or ease of management. When you separate an application's components into multiple subnets, it's called a *multi-tier architecture*.

Leave plenty of space in each subnet. Naturally, having more instances will consume more IP addresses. Leave enough free address space in each subnet for resources to use as demand grows. If any of your instances will have multiple private IP addresses, take that into account. Also, remember that EC2 instances aren't the only resources that consume IP address space. Consider Elastic Load Balancing interfaces, database instances, and VPC interface endpoints.

External Connectivity

Your application's availability is dependent upon the availability of the network users use to access it. Remember that the definition of availability is that your application is working as expected. If users can't connect to it because of a network issue, your application is unavailable to them, even if it's healthy and operating normally. Therefore, the method your users use to connect to the AWS cloud needs to meet your availability requirements.

The most common way to connect to AWS is via the Internet, which is generally reliable, but speed and latency vary and can be unpredictable. If getting to your application is painfully slow, you may consider it to be unavailable.

To get around a slow Internet pipe or for mission-critical applications, you may choose to use Direct Connect, either as a primary connection to AWS or as a backup. If you need a fast and reliable connection to AWS—such as if you're pushing a lot of data—Direct Connect offers access speeds of 1 or 10 Gbps with consistent latency. As a secondary connection, if you can't use the Internet to reach your AWS resources, you can get through using Direct Connect.

If you're going to use Direct Connect, VPC peering, or a VPN connection to an external network, make sure your VPC addresses don't overlap with those used in the external network. Also, be sure to leave enough room to assign IP addresses to virtual private gateways and Direct Connect private virtual interfaces.

Designing for Availability

Understanding all of the different factors that go into architecting for reliability is important. But as an AWS architect, you need to be able to start with an availability requirement and design a solution that meets it. In this section, you'll learn how to start with a set of application requirements and design different AWS infrastructures to meet three common availability percentages: 99 percent, 99.9 percent, and 99.99 percent.

As you might expect, there's a proportional relationship between availability, complexity, and cost. The higher the availability, the more resources you're going to need to provision, which adds more complexity and, of course, more cost. Although most organizations *want* as much availability as possible, you as an AWS architect must strike a balance between availability and cost. Designs with lower availability may appear, from a technical standpoint, to be inferior. But at the end of the day, the needs and priorities of the organization are what matter.

In the following scenarios, you'll architect a solution for a web-based payroll application that runs as a single executable on a Linux EC2 instance. The web application connects to a backend SQL database for storing data. Static web assets are stored in a public S3 bucket. Users connect to the application by browsing to a public domain name that is hosted on Route 53.

Designing for 99 Percent Availability

In the first scenario, you're aiming for 99 percent availability, or about 3.5 days of downtime per year. Downtime is an inconvenience but certainly not the end of the world.

In this case, you'll create a single EC2 instance to run both the application and a self-hosted SQL database. For backing up data, you'll run a script to automatically back up the database to an S3 bucket with versioning enabled. To keep data sprawl under control, you'll configure S3 lifecycle policies to move older backups to the Glacier storage class.

To alert users during outages, configure a Route 53 health check to monitor the health of the application by checking for an HTTP 200 OK status code. Then create a Route 53 failover record set to direct users to the application when the health check passes and to a static informational web page when it doesn't. The static web page can be stored in either a public S3 bucket that's configured for website hosting or a CloudFront distribution.

Recovery Process

It's important to test your recovery processes regularly so that you know they work and how long they take. Don't just create a SQL dump and upload it to an S3 bucket. Regularly bring up a new instance and practice restoring a database backup to it.

To quickly build or rebuild your combination application/database instance, use CloudFormation to do the heavy lifting for you. Create a CloudFormation template to create a new instance, install and configure the web and database servers, copy application files from a repository, and set up security groups. The CloudFormation template serves two purposes: rebuilding quickly in case of an instance failure and creating a throwaway instance for practicing database restores and testing application updates.

Availability Calculation

When it comes to estimating availability, you're going to have to make some assumptions. Each failure will require 30 minutes to analyze and decide whether to initiate your recovery process. Once you decide to recover, you'll use your CloudFormation template to build a new instance, which takes about 10 minutes. Lastly, you'll restore the database, which takes about 30 minutes. The total downtime for each failure—or your recovery time objective (RTO)—is 70 minutes. Note that the recovery point objective (RPO) you can expect depends on how frequently you're backing up the database. In this case, assume that your application will suffer one failure every quarter. That's a total annual downtime of 280 minutes, or about 4.6 hours.

However, that's just for failures. You also need to consider application and operating system updates. Assuming that updates occur 6 times a year and require 4 hours of downtime each, that's additional downtime of 24 hours per year. Adding all the numbers together, between failures and updates, the total downtime per year is about 28.6 hours or 1.19 days. That's 99.67 percent availability!

Although it's tempting to round 99.67 percent up to 99.9 percent, keep in mind that the difference between those two numbers is more than seven hours per year. Providing inflated availability numbers, even if you're honestly just rounding up, can come back to bite you if those numbers turn out later to be out of line with the application's actual availability. Remember that your availability calculations are only as good as the assumptions you make about the frequency and duration of failures and scheduled outages. When it comes to availability, err on the side of caution and round down! Following that advice, the expected availability of the application is 99 percent.

Designing for 99.9 Percent Availability

When designing for 99.9 percent availability, downtime isn't the end of the world, but it's pretty close. You can tolerate about 9 hours a year, but anything beyond that is going to be a problem. To achieve 99.9 percent availability, you'll use a distributed application design.

The application itself will run on multiple instances in multiple availability zones in a single region. You'll configure an ALB to proxy traffic from users to individual instances and perform health checks against those instances. You'll create a launch template to install the application web server and copy over application files from a centralized repository. You'll then create an Auto Scaling group to ensure that you always have at least six running instances (two in each zone).

Why six instances? Suppose that you need four application instances to handle peak demand. To withstand the loss of one zone, having two instances in each zone ensures they can handle 50 percent of the peak demand. That way, if one zone fails—taking two instances with it—the remaining two zones have four instances, which is enough to handle 100 percent of the load.

Recovery Process

For most failures, recovery will be automatic. You'll configure the Auto Scaling group to use the ALB's target health checks to determine the health of each instance. If an instance fails, the ALB will route traffic away from it, and then Auto Scaling will terminate the failed instance and create a new one.

For the database, you'll use a multi-AZ RDS instance. If the primary database instance fails (perhaps because of an entire availability zone failure), RDS will failover to the secondary instance in a different zone. You'll also configure automated database instance snapshots to guard against database corruption. Enabling automated snapshots also enables point-in-time recovery, reducing your RPO to as little as five minutes.

Availability Calculation

Thanks to the resilience of the redundant, distributed architecture, you expect only two unplanned outage events per year, lasting 60 minutes each. Software and operating system updates occur 10 times a year and last 15 minutes each. Adding up the numbers, you get a total downtime of 270 minutes or 4.5 hours per year. That's 99.95 percent availability! Again, to be conservative, you want to round that down to 99.9 percent.

Designing for 99.99 Percent Availability

Mission-critical applications, often those that generate a lot of revenue or have a significant impact on human life, must be able to tolerate multiple component failures without having to allocate additional resources.

AWS takes great pains to isolate availability zone failures. However, there's always the possibility that multiple zones in a single region can fail simultaneously. To protect against these regional disruptions, you'll simultaneously run application instances in two different regions, an active region and a passive region. Just as in the preceding scenario, you'll use Auto Scaling to provision the instances into multiple availability zones in each region and ensure that each zone can handle 50 percent of the peak load.

You'll also use multi-AZ RDS; however, there's a catch. The primary and secondary database instances both must run in the same region. RDS doesn't currently allow you to have a primary database instance in one region and secondary in another. Therefore, there's no way to failover from one region to the other without the potential for data loss.

But you do have another option. If you use the MySQL or MariaDB database engine, you can create a multi-AZ read replica in a different region. You can then asynchronously replicate data from one region to the other. With this option, there's a delay between the time data is written to the primary and the time it's replicated to the read replica. Therefore, if the primary database instance fails before the replication has completed, you may lose data. For example, given a replication lag of 10 minutes, you may lose 10 minutes of data.

Recovery Process

As in the preceding example, for an application or database instance failure isolated to the active region, or even for an entire availability zone failure, recovery is automatic. But regional failures require some manual intervention.

Users will access application instances only in the active region until that region fails. You'll create a CloudWatch Alarm to monitor the health of the ALB in the active region. If the ALB in the active region fails its health check, you must then decide whether to failover to the passive region.

If you do choose to failover, you'll need to do two things. First, you'll change the Route 53 resource record to redirect users to the ALB in the standby region. Second, you'll need to promote the read replica in the passive region to be the new primary database instance.

Availability Calculation

Failures requiring manual intervention should be rare and would probably involve either a failure of the active region that requires failover to the passive region or database corruption that requires restoring from a snapshot. Assuming two failures a year, each failure lasting 20 minutes, that amounts to 40 minutes of downtime per year. That equates to just over 99.99 percent availability.

Software and operating system updates require no downtime. When you need to do an update, you simply provision more instances alongside the existing ones. You upgrade the new instances and then gracefully migrate users to the new instances. In the event that an upgrade breaks the application, directing users back to the original instances is trivial and quick.

Summary

When it comes to maximizing availability, avoiding failure in the first place is job one. To avoid catastrophic application failures, run your application on multiple EC2 instances in different availability zones and distribute the load across those instances as much as possible using an application load balancer. If one instance or even an entire availability zone fails, ALB will route users away from the failed instances, and your application will continue to be available.

Another way to avoid application failures is to not overload individual instances. This is where EC2 Auto Scaling comes in. By implementing dynamic scaling policies, you can ensure you always have enough instances to handle increased demand.

But failures are inevitable, so the next highest priority is to recover from them quickly when they occur. When you create an Auto Scaling group, Auto Scaling will ensure you always have a minimum number of healthy instances. When an instance becomes unhealthy, Auto Scaling will terminate and replace it.

One potential cause of application failures is lost or corrupt data. Take advantage of automatic S3 versioning, cross-region replication, and EBS snapshots to keep backups of your application's important data. For the database, use multi-AZ RDS and automated database instance snapshots to keep up-to-date copies of your database stored safely across multiple availability zones.

Exam Essentials

Know how to calculate total availability using both hard dependencies and redundant components. When one resource depends on another, that's a hard dependency. An example would be an application dependent upon a database. When you have resources that don't depend on one another, such as a collection of identical application instances, those components are redundant.

Understand the difference between traditional and cloud-native applications.   Traditional applications are written to run on Linux or Windows servers and often use a standard database component such as a SQL server or a nonrelational database like Redis or MongoDB. Cloud-native applications, on the other hand, use compute, database, or networking resources available only in the cloud, such as Lambda and DynamoDB.

Be able to configure EC2 Auto Scaling.   Auto Scaling can help you avoid application failures by automatically provisioning new instances when you need them, avoiding instance failures caused by resource exhaustion. When an instance failure does occur, Auto Scaling steps in and creates a replacement.

Know how application load balancers and EC2 Auto Scaling work together to increase application availability.   When Auto Scaling creates a new instance, it automatically adds it to the associated Elastic Load Balancing target group. When it removes an instance, Auto Scaling removes the instance from the associated Elastic Load Balancing target group.

Understand the different backup and recovery options for S3, EBS, and EFS   S3 offers versioning and cross-region replication. To back up data stored on EBS volumes, you can take manual or automated EBS snapshots. EFS doesn't provide any native backup capability, but you can copy files from one EFS filesystem to another.

Review Questions

1. What's the minimum level of availability you need to stay under 30 minutes of downtime per month?

   A. 99 percent

   B. 99.9 percent

   C. 99.95 percent

   D. 99.999 percent

2. Your application runs on two EC2 instances in one availability zone. An elastic load balancer distributes user traffic evenly across the healthy instances. The application on each instance connects to a single RDS database instance. Assuming each EC2 instance has an availability of 99 percent and the RDS instance has an availability of 99 percent, what is the total application availability?

   A. 98.99 percent

   B. 99 percent

   C. 99.9 percent

   D. 97 percent

3. Your organization is designing a new application to run on AWS. The developers have asked you to recommend a database that will perform well in all regions. Which database should you recommend for maximum availability?

   A. Multi-AZ RDS using MySQL

   B. DynamoDB

   C. Multi-AZ RDS using Aurora

   D. A self-hosted SQL database

4. Which of the following can help you increase the availability of a web application? (Choose all that apply.)

   A. Store web assets in an S3 bucket instead of on the application instance.

   B. Use instance classes large enough to handle your application's peak load.

   C. Scale your instances in.

   D. Scale your instances out.

5. You've configured an EC2 Auto Scaling group to use a launch configuration to provision and install an application on several instances. You now need to reconfigure Auto Scaling to install an additional application on new instances. Which of the following should you do?

   A. Modify the launch configuration.

   B. Create a launch template and configure the Auto Scaling group to use it.

   C. Modify the launch template.

   D. Modify the CloudFormation template.

6. You create an Auto Scaling group with a minimum group size of 3, a maximum group size of 10, and a desired capacity of 5. You then manually terminate two instances in the group. Which of the following will Auto Scaling do?

   A. Create two new instances

   B. Reduce the desired capacity to 3

   C. Nothing

   D. Increment the minimum group size to 5

7. Which of the following can Auto Scaling use for instance health checks? (Choose all that apply.)

   A. ELB health checks

   B. CloudWatch Alarms

   C. Route 53 health checks

   D. EC2 system checks

   E. EC2 instance checks

8. You're running an application that receives a spike in traffic on the first day of every month. You want to configure Auto Scaling to add more instances before the spike begins and then add additional instances in proportion to the CPU utilization of each instance. Which of the following should you implement? (Choose all that apply.)

   A. Target tracking policies

   B. Scheduled actions

   C. Step scaling policies

   D. Simple scaling policies

9. Which of the following provide the most protection against data corruption and accidental deletion for existing objects stored in S3? (Choose two.)

   A. Versioning

   B. Bucket policies

   C. Cross-region replication

   D. Using the Standard storage class

10. You need to maintain three days of backups for binary files stored across several EC2 instances in a spot fleet. What's the best way to achieve this?

   A. Stream the files to CloudWatch Logs.

   B. Create an Elastic File System and back up the files to it using a cron job.

   C. Create a Snapshot Lifecycle Policy to snapshot each instance every 24 hours and retain the latest three snapshots.

   D. Create a Snapshot Lifecycle Policy to snapshot each instance every 4 hours and retain the latest 18 snapshots.

11. You plan to run multi-AZ RDS across three availability zones in a region. You want to have two read replicas per zone. Which database engine should you choose?

    A. MariaDB

    B. PostgreSQL

    C. MySQL

    D. Aurora

12. You're running an RDS instance in one availability zone. What should you implement to be able to achieve a recovery point objective (RPO) of five minutes?

    A. Configure multi-AZ.

    B. Enable automated snapshots.

    C. Add a read replica in the same region.

    D. Add a read replica in a different region.

13. When creating subnets in a VPC, what are two reasons to leave sufficient space in the VPC for more subnets later? (Choose two.)

    A. You may need to add another tier for your application.

    B. You may need to implement RDS.

    C. AWS occasionally adds more availability zones to a region.

    D. You may need to add a secondary CIDR to the VPC.

14. You plan to deploy 50 EC2 instances, each with two private IP addresses. To put all of these instances in a single subnet, which subnet CIDRs could you use? (Choose all that apply.)

    A. 172.21.0.0/25

    B. 172.21.0.0/26

    C. 10.0.0.0/8

    D. 10.0.0.0/21

15. You're currently connecting to your AWS resources using a 10 Gbps Internet connection at your office. You also have end users around the world that access the same AWS resources. What are two reasons you may consider using Direct Connect in addition to your Internet connection? (Choose two.)

    A. Lower latency

    B. Higher bandwidth

    C. Better end user experience

    D. Increased security

16. Before connecting a VPC to your data center, what must you do to ensure proper connectivity?

    A. Use IAM policies to restrict access to AWS resources.

    B. Ensure the IP address ranges in the networks don't overlap.

    C. Ensure security groups on your data center firewalls are properly configured.

    D. Use in-transit encryption.

17. You plan to run a stand-alone Linux application on AWS and need 99 percent availability. The application doesn't require a database, and only a few users will access it. You will occasionally need to terminate and re-create the instance using a different AMI. Which of the following should you use? (Choose all that apply.)

    A. CloudFormation

    B. Auto Scaling

    C. User Data

    D. Dynamic scaling policies

18. You need eight instances running simultaneously in a single region. Assuming three availability zones are available, what's the minimum number of instances you must run in each zone to be able to withstand a single zone failure?

    A. 3

    B. 16

    C. 8

    D. 4

19. If your application is down for 45 minutes a year, what is its approximate availability?

    A. 99 percent

    B. 99.9 percent

    C. 99.99 percent

    D. 99.95 percent

20. You're running an application in two regions and using multi-AZ RDS with read replicas in both regions. Users normally access the application in only one region by browsing to a public domain name that resolves to an elastic load balancer. If that region fails, which of the following should you do to failover to the other region? (Choose all that apply.)

    A. Update the DNS record to point to the load balancer in the other region.

    B. Point the load balancer to the other region.

    C. Failover to the database in the other region.

    D. Restore the database from a snapshot.

The Performance Efficiency Pillar

THE AWS CERTIFIED SOLUTIONS ARCHITECT ASSOCIATE EXAM OBJECTIVES COVERED IN THIS CHAPTER MAY INCLUDE, BUT ARE NOT LIMITED TO, THE FOLLOWING:

Domain 1: Design Resilient Architectures

✓ **1.1** Choose reliable/resilient storage.

✓ **1.2** Determine how to design decoupling mechanisms using AWS services.

✓ **1.3** Determine how to design a multitier architecture solution.

✓ **1.4** Determine how to design high availability and/or fault tolerant architectures.

Domain 2: Define Performant Architectures

✓ **2.1** Choose performant storage and databases.

✓ **2.2** Apply caching to improve performance.

✓ **2.3** Design solutions for elasticity and scalability.

Domain 5: Define Operationally-Excellent Architectures

✓ **5.1** Choose design features in solutions that enable operational excellence.

Introduction

By this point in the book, you should have a pretty good feel for the way the basic AWS services are used to deploy and manage your applications. And, from reading Chapter 9, "The Reliability Pillar," you should also now understand how to respond to failures.

This chapter will teach you the design principles that'll help you squeeze the most performance possible out of your cloud resources. It's not enough to just make sure everything is running: getting full value from AWS requires that you leverage the features that set the cloud apart from legacy environments. For the purposes of this chapter, those will include the ability to:

- Quickly launch test environments to experiment and measure performance.

- Quickly and automatically scale operations up and down to meet changing demand.

- Abstract your operations by using managed services to automate infrastructure provisioning.

- Automate the use of container and serverless technologies in response to external events.

- Automate the deployment of complex, full-stack infrastructure through scripts and templates.

- Understand and optimize operations based on the smart consumption of system data.

Optimizing Performance for the Core AWS Services

Through the book's earlier chapters, you experienced the power and flexibility of Amazon's compute, storage, database, and networking services. You've seen how to tune, launch, and administrate those tools to support your applications, and you're aware of some of the many configuration options that come built-in with the platform.

In this section, you'll take all that knowledge to the next level. You'll explore the ways you can apply some key design principles to solve—and prevent—real-world performance problems.

Compute

What, ultimately, is the goal of all "compute" services? To quickly and efficiently apply *some kind of* compute resource to a workload demand. The key there is "some kind of," as it acknowledges that not every problem is best addressed by the same kind of compute resource. To get it right, you'll need to put together just the right blend of functionality and power.

EC2 Instance Types

As you saw in Chapter 2, "Amazon Elastic Compute Cloud and Amazon Elastic Block Store," the performance you'll get from a particular EC2 instance type is defined by a number of configuration variables. Your job, when building your deployment, is to match the instance type you choose as closely as possible to the workload you expect to face. Of course, you can always change the type of a running instance if necessary or just add more of the same.

Table 10.1 lists the configuration parameter categories available to help you select the instance type that's most compatible with your workload. Parameters define the resources allocated to an instance built from a particular type and the hardware capabilities of the underlying hardware.

TABLE 10.1 Instance type parameter descriptions

Instance Parameter	Description
ECUs	EC2 compute units—useful for comparing the compute power of one instance type to another
vCPUs	The number of virtual CPUs allotted an instance built from this instance type
Physical Processor	The processor family (e.g., Intel Xeon E52676v3) used by the host server
Clock Speed	The clock speed used by a host server
Memory	The amount of RAM allotted to an instance built from this instance type
Instance Storage	The size of the local (ephemeral) instance store volume used by this instance type

TABLE 10.1 Instance type parameter descriptions *(continued)*

Instance Parameter	Description
EBS-Optimized Available	Whether such an instance can be configured to use EBS optimization for dedicated I/O throughput
Network Performance	The data transfer rate allowed to instances built from this instance type
IPv6 Support	Whether IPv6 addressing support is available
Processor Architecture	Whether the hardware server uses a 32- or 64-bit processor
Intel AES-NI	Whether the hardware host uses the Advanced Encryption Standard-New Instructions (AES-NI) encryption instruction set
Intel AVX	Whether the hardware host uses a floating-point intensive instruction set for improved graphics/analytics performance
Intel Turbo	Whether the hardware host can benefit from short-term performance boosts

Auto Scaling

Can't get everything you need from a single EC2 instance? Then feel free to scale out. Scaling out (or scaling *horizontally* as it's sometimes called) involves supporting application demand by adding new resources that will run identical workloads in parallel with existing instances.

A typical scale-out scenario would involve a single EC2 instance hosting an e-commerce web server that's struggling to keep up with rising customer demand. The account administrators could take a snapshot of the EBS volume attached to the existing instance and use it to generate an image for a private EC2 AMI. They could then launch multiple instances using the AMI they've created and use a load balancer to intelligently direct customer traffic among the parallel instances. (You'll learn more about load balancing a bit later in this chapter.)

That's scaling. *Auto Scaling* is an AWS tool that can be configured to automatically launch or shut down instances to meet changing demand. As demand rises, consuming a predefined percentage of your instance's resources, EC2 will automatically launch one or more exact copies of your instance to share the burden. When demand falls, your deployment will be scaled back to ensure there aren't costly, unused resources running.

Auto Scaling groups are built around *launch configurations* that define the kind of instance you want deployed. You could specify a custom EC2 AMI preloaded with your application (the way you saw in Chapter 2), or you could choose a standard AMI that you provision by passing user data at launch time. Exercise 10.1 demonstrates how you can build your own Auto Scaling group.

EXERCISE 10.1

Configure and Launch an Application Using Auto Scaling

1. From the EC2 Dashboard, create a launch configuration using the Ubuntu Server LTS AMI on the Quick Start tab and a t2.micro instance type.

2. On the Create Launch Configuration page, name your configuration. You don't need to select an IAM role or enable monitoring for this demo.

3. Save the following commands to a file on your local computer, name the file **start.sh**, expand the Advanced Details section, click the As File radio button, and select your start.sh script from your computer. This will install the Apache web server and create a simple index.html web page.

   ```
   #!/bin/bash
   apt-get update
   apt-get install  y apache2
   echo "Welcome to my website" > index.html
   cp index.html /var/www/html
   ```

4. Choose (or create) a security group that will permit all HTTP traffic via port 80 and then create the configuration.

5. Create an Auto Scaling group that will use your new launch configuration. Give your group a name and leave the Group Size value at 1 instance.

6. Select a virtual private cloud (VPC) into which your instances will launch, click once inside the Subnet field, and select the subnet where you'd like your instances to live. Assuming you're working with your (uncorrupted) default VPC, any one of the public subnets you'll be shown should be fine.

7. On the Configure Scaling Policies page, select the "Use scaling policies to adjust the capacity of this group" radio button and edit the value to read **Scale between 1 and 2 instances**.

8. Leave the Metric Type value as Average CPU Utilization and edit its Target Value to 5 percent.

   This unusually low value will make it easier to confirm that the auto scaling is working—normally a value of 70 percent to 80 percent would make sense.

9. For this demo, you don't need to configure notifications or tags. Click Create to finish creating the group.

10. Your group will immediately try to start the first instance. It may take a couple of minutes for everything to load. When it does, point your browser to the IP address associated with the instance (you can retrieve that from the EC2 Instances Dashboard).

Considering how small the index.html page is, it might be hard to get the Auto Scaling tool to launch a second instance. You'll probably need to "cheat" by running a busywork command such as the following on the server command line to raise your CPU level high enough:

```
$ while true; do true; done
```

 Normally, you would select the "Receive traffic from one or more load balancers" option from the Configure Auto Scaling group details page so your customers would be able to access all the instances launched from the same URL. For this demo, we'll just pretend there's a balancer in place.

Serverless Workloads

You can build elastic compute infrastructure to efficiently respond to changing environments without using an EC2 instance. Container tools like Docker or code-only functions like Lambda can provide ultra-lightweight and "instant-on" compute functionality with far less overhead than you'd need to run a full server.

As you saw in Chapter 2, container management tools like the Amazon Elastic Container Service—and its front-end abstraction AWS Fargate—can maximize your resource utilization, letting you tightly pack multiple fast-loading workloads on a single instance. Containers are also designed to be scriptable so their administration can easily be automated.

Unlike EC2 instances or ECS containers, AWS Lambda works without the need to provision an ongoing server host. Lambda functions run code for brief spurts (currently up to 15 minutes) in response to network events. Lambda functions can be closely integrated with other AWS services including by exposing your function to external Application programming interface (API) requests using Amazon API Gateway.

Table 10.2 describes some use cases that are good fits with each of the three compute technology categories.

TABLE 10.2   Common use cases for compute categories

Technology	Use Cases
EC2 instances	Long-lived, more complex web applications
	Processes requiring in-depth monitoring and tracking

Technology	Use Cases
ECS containers	Highly scalable, automated applications
	Applications requiring full control over underlying resources
	Microservices deployments
	Testing environments
Lambda functions	Retrieving data from backend databases
	Parsing data streams
	Processing transactions

Storage

You've already seen how Elastic Block Store (EBS) volumes provide durable storage where IOPS, latency, and throughput settings determine your data access performance (Chapter 2). You also know about the scalable and multitiered object storage available through S3 and Glacier (Chapter 3 Amazon Simple Storage Service (S3) and Amazon Glacier Storage). Chapter 3 is also where you encountered the Amazon Elastic File System (EFS), which offers shared file storage for instances within a VPC or over an AWS Direct Connect connection.

Here, I'll discuss some performance optimizations impacting cloud storage and the services that use it.

RAID-Optimized EBS Volumes

You can optimize the performance and reliability of your disk-based data using a Redundant Array of Independent Disks (RAID). This is something admins have been doing in the data center for many years, but some RAID configurations can also make a big difference when applied to EBS disks in the AWS cloud.

RAID works by combining the space of multiple drives into a single logical drive and then spreading and/or replicating your data across the entire array. The *RAID 0* standard involves *data striping*, where data is segmented and stored across more than one device, allowing concurrent operations to bypass a single disk's access limitations. This can greatly speed up IO performance for transaction-heavy operations like busy databases. RAID 0 does not add durability.

RAID 1 creates mirrored sets of data on multiple volumes. Traditional RAID 1 arrays don't use striping or parity, so they won't provide improved performance, but they do make your data more reliable since the failure of a single volume would not be catastrophic.

RAID 1 is common for scenarios where data durability is critical and enhanced performance is not necessary.

RAID 5 and RAID 6 configurations can combine both performance and reliability features, but because of IOPS consumption considerations, they're not recommended by AWS. AWS also does not recommend using RAID-configured volumes as instance boot drives since the failure of any single drive can leave the instance unbootable.

Setting up a RAID array involves creating at least two EBS volumes of the same size and IOPS setting and attaching them to a running instance. You then use traditional OS tools on the instance—mdadm on Linux and diskpart on Windows—to configure the volumes for RAID. Make sure that the EC2 instance you're working with has enough available bandwidth to handle the extra load.

S3 Cross-Region Replication

Even though S3 is a global service, the data in your buckets has to exist within a physical AWS region. That's why you need to select a region when you create new buckets. Now, since your data is tied to a single region, there will be times when, for regulatory or performance considerations, you'll want data "boots" on the ground in more than one place. Replication can be used to minimize latency for geographically dispersed clients or to increase reliability and durability.

When configured, S3 Cross-Region Replication (CRR) will automatically sync contents of a bucket in one region with a bucket in a second region. You set up CRR by creating a *replication* rule for your source bucket (meaning the bucket whose contents will be replicated). You can choose to have all objects in your source replicated or only those whose names match a specified prefix.

The replication rule must also define a destination bucket (meaning the bucket to which your replicated objects will be sent). The destination can be a bucket in a different region in your account, or even one from a different account.

Once enabled, copies of objects saved to the source bucket will be created in the destination bucket. When an object is deleted from the source bucket, it will similarly disappear from the destination (unless versioning is enabled on the destination bucket). Exercise 10.2 will guide you through the process of syncing two buckets through CRR.

EXERCISE 10.2

Sync Two S3 Buckets as Cross-Region Replicas

1. Use the S3 Dashboard to create two buckets in two separate regions. One will be your source and the other your destination.

2. Click the name of your source bucket in the S3 Dashboard, then on the Management tab, then on the Replication button, and finally on Add Rule. If versioning wasn't already enabled for the bucket, you can click the Enable Versioning button to set it.

3. Define the objects you want replicated from your source bucket. Choose All Contents for this demo.

4. In the Destination definition page, click once in the Select Bucket field and select the second bucket you created as the destination. Note how you can have the storage class and ownership of your objects automatically changed when copies are created in the destination bucket. Leave those options unchecked for this demo.

5. Select Create New Role in the IAM Role dialog box. This will create the permissions necessary to move assets between buckets. You can then review your settings and save the rule.

6. Confirm the replication is working by uploading a file to the source bucket and then checking to see that a copy has been created in the destination bucket.

7. Delete the object in the source and confirm that the copy in the destination has now disappeared.

Amazon S3 Transfer Acceleration

If your team or customers often find themselves transferring larger files between their local PCs and S3 buckets, then you might benefit from faster transfer rates. S3 Transfer Acceleration adds a per-GB cost to transfers (often in the $0.04 range), but, by routing data through CloudFront edge locations, they can speed things up considerably.

To find out whether transfer acceleration would work for your use case, paste the following URL into your browser, specifying an existing bucket name and its AWS region:

```
http://s3-accelerate-speedtest.s3-accelerate.amazonaws.com/en/
accelerate-speed-comparsion.html?region=us-east-1&origBucketName=my-bucket-name
```

You'll land on a Speed Comparison page that will, over the course of a few minutes, calculate the estimated difference between speeds you'll get using S3 Direct (the default S3 transfer process) and S3 Accelerated Transfer. If accelerated transfer makes sense for you, you'll need to enable it for your bucket. Exercise 10.3 shows you the AWS CLI command that will do that for you.

EXERCISE 10.3

Upload to an S3 Bucket Using Transfer Acceleration

1. Enable transfer acceleration on an existing bucket (substitute the name of your bucket for *my-bucket-name*).

```
$ aws s3api put-bucket-accelerate-configuration \
  --bucket my-bucket-name \
  --accelerate-configuration Status=Enabled
```

EXERCISE 10.3 *(continued)*

2. Transfer a file by specifying the s3-accelerate endpoint. Make sure you're using the correct file and bucket names and region.

```
$ aws s3 cp filename.mp4 s3://my-bucket-name \
  --region us-east-1 \
  --endpoint-url http://s3-accelerate.amazonaws.com
```

CloudFront and S3 Origins

Besides the static website hosting you explored in Chapter 3, S3 is also an excellent platform for hosting a wide range of files, media objects, resources (like EC2 AMIs), and data. Access to those objects can be optimized using CloudFront.

One example might involve creating a CloudFront distribution that uses an S3 bucket containing videos and images as an origin rather than a load balancer sitting in front of EC2 instances. Your EC2-based application could point to the distribution to satisfy client requests for media files, avoiding the bottlenecks and extra costs associated with hosting them locally.

Your job as a solutions architect is to assess the kinds of data your deployments will generate and consume and where that data will be most efficiently and affordably kept. More often than you might at first imagine, the answer to that second question will be S3. The trick is to keep an open mind and be creative.

Database

When designing your data management environment, you'll have some critical decisions to make. For instance, should you build your own platform on an EC2 instance or leave the heavy infrastructure lifting to AWS by opting for Amazon's Relational Database Service (RDS)?

Doing it yourself can be cheaper and permits more control and customization. But on the other hand, RDS—being a fully managed service—frees you from significant administration worries such as software updates and patches, replication, and network accessibility. You're responsible only for making basic configuration choices, like these:

- Choosing the right RDS instance type
- Optimizing the database through intelligently designing schemas, indexes, and views
- Optionally configuring option groups to define database functionality that can be applied to RDS instances
- Optionally configuring parameter groups to define finely tuned database behavior controls that can be applied to RDS instances

Building your own database solutions using EC2 resources gives you control over a much wider range of options, including the following:

Consistency, Availability, and Partition Tolerance   These are the elements that make up the CAP theorem of distributed data. To prevent data corruption, distributed data store administrators must choose between priorities, because it's impossible to maintain perfect consistency, availability, and reliability concurrently.

Latency   The storage volume type you choose—with its IOPS class and architecture (SSD or magnetic)—will go a long way to determine the read and write performance of your database.

Durability   How will you protect your data from hardware failure? Will you provision replicated and geographically diverse instances? This was discussed at length in "Chapter 9, The Reliability Pillar."

Scalability   Does your design allow for automated resource growth?

Nondatabase Hosting   Data can sometimes be most effectively hosted on nondatabase platforms such as AWS S3, where tools like the Amazon Redshift Spectrum query engine can effectively connect and consume your data.

AWS Redshift (which we discussed in Chapter 5, "Databases") isn't the only available data warehouse tool. Various integrations with third-party data management tools are commonly deployed on AWS for highly scalable SQL operations. Table 10.3 describes some of the more popular solutions.

TABLE 10.3   Third-party data warehousing and management tools

Technology	Role	Platform
Pivotal Greenplum Database	Massively parallel data warehouse for big data analytics and data science	Available as an EC2 marketplace AMI
Snowflake	Petabyte-scale data warehouse SaaS designed from the ground up for cloud environments	Available through the AWS marketplace
Presto	Distributed Hadoop-based SQL query engine for weakly structured data analytics	Deploy through Amazon Athena or Amazon EMR

Network Optimization and Load Balancing

Cloud computing workloads live and die with network connectivity. So, you've got a keen interest in ensuring your resources and customers are able to connect with and access your resources as quickly and reliably as possible. The geolocation and latency-based routing provided by Route 53 and CloudFront are important elements of a strong networking policy, as are VPC endpoints and the high-speed connectivity offered by AWS Direct Connect.

High-bandwidth EC2 instance types can also make a significant difference. When manually enabled on a compatible instance type, enhanced networking functionality can give you network speeds of up to 25 Gbps. There are two enhanced networking technologies: Intel 82599 Virtual Function (VF) interface, which can be accessed on instance types including C3, C4, and R3; and Elastic Network Adapter (ENA), which is available on types including G3, H1, and R5.

On the following web page, AWS provides clear instructions for enabling enhanced networking from within various flavors of the Linux server OS:

```
https://docs.aws.amazon.com/AWSEC2/latest/UserGuide/enhanced-networking
.html
```

But perhaps the most important network enhancing technology of them all is load balancing. Sooner or later the odds are that you'll find yourself running multiple instances of your application to keep up with demand. Adding resources to help out a popular app is great, but how are your customers going to find all those new servers? Won't they all still end up fighting their way into the poor, overworked server they've always used?

A load balancer is a software service that sits in front of your infrastructure and answers all incoming requests for content. Whether you use a DNS server like Route 53 or CloudFront, the idea is to associate a domain (like example.com) with the address used by your load balancer rather than to any one of your application servers.

When the balancer receives a request, it will, as illustrated in Figure 10.1, route it to any one of your backend application servers and then make sure that the response is sent back to the original client. When you add or remove servers, you only need to update the load balancer software with the addressing and availability status changes, and your customers won't be any the wiser.

FIGURE 10.1   The data flow of a typical load balancing operation

A load balancer created within EC2 automates much of the process for you. Because the service is scalable, you don't need to worry about unexpected and violent changes in traffic patterns, and you can design complex relationships that leverage the unique features of your particular application infrastructure.

Originally, a single EC2 load balancer type would handle HTTP, HTTPS, and TCP workloads. That Classic Load Balancer is still available, but it's been deprecated. Besides the Classic, the Elastic Load Balancing service now offers two separate balancer types: the *Application Load Balancer* for HTTP and HTTPS and the *Network Load Balancer* for TCP traffic. The new balancer types come with a number of functions unavailable to the Classic version, including the ability to register targets outside the VPC and support for containerized applications.

The Application Load Balancer operates at the application layer (layer 7 of the Open Systems Interconnection [OSI] model). Layer 7 protocols permit host and path-based routing, which means you can use this load balancer to route traffic among the multiple services of microservice or other tiered architectures.

The Network Load Balancer functions at layer four (the transport layer - TCP). Network load balancers are built to manage high volumes and traffic spikes and are tightly integrated with auto scaling, the Elastic Container Service and CloudFormation. TCP balancers should also be used for applications that don't use HTTP or HTTPS for their internal communications and for AWS managed Virtual Private Network (VPN) connections.

Try it for yourself: Exercise 10.4 will guide you through configuring and deploying a simple load balancer using EC2.

EXERCISE 10.4

Create and Deploy an EC2 Load Balancer

1. Create one instance (the way you did in Exercise 8.1 in Chapter 8, ("The Domain Name System and Network Routing: Amazon Route 53 and Amazon CloudFront") in each of two subnets. You select the subnets on the Configure Instance Details page. Make a note of the subnet designations you choose.

2. Use SSH to access your instances, install the Apache web server (again, the way you did it in Exercise 8.1), and create unique index.html files containing a short note describing the server—perhaps including the server's IP address. This will make it easier to know which instance your load balancer has loaded when you test everything out later.

3. From the EC2 Dashboard, create a load balancer. Select an Application Load Balancer, give it a name, and specify the Internet-facing scheme, IPv4 for the IP address type, and the default HTTP and port 80 values for the listener. Make sure you're using the right VPC (the default should be fine) and select (and note) two availability zones. For this demo, you can ignore the warning about using an unencrypted listener.

4.   Select (or create) a security group that allows access to port 80.

5.   When prompted, create a new target group and give it a name. Change the Target type value to IP and add a path to a file the health check can use. For this demo, enter `/index.html`.

6.   Register your two EC2 instances as targets to the group using their private IPs. You can retrieve those private IP addresses from the EC2 Instances Dashboard or from the command prompt of the instance itself using the `ip addr` command.

7.   Once your balancer is active (which can take a couple of minutes), get the DNS name of your balancer from the Load Balancers Dashboard and paste it into your browser. The `index.html` page of one of your instances should load. Refresh the browser a few times so you can confirm that both instances are being accessed.

8.   If you like, you can shut down one of the instances without causing any interruption to the load balancer service.

Infrastructure Automation

One of the biggest benefits of virtualization is the ability to describe your resources within a script. Every single service, object, and process within the Amazon cloud can be managed using textual abstractions, allowing for an Infrastructure as Code environment.

You've already seen this kind of administration through the many AWS CLI examples used in this book. But, building on the CLI and SDK foundations, sophisticated operations can be heavily automated using both native AWS and third-party tools.

CloudFormation

You can represent infrastructure resource stacks using AWS CloudFormation. CloudFormation templates are JSON or YAML-formatted text files that define the complete inventory of AWS resources you would like to run as part of a particular project.

CloudFormation templates are easy to copy or export to reliably re-create resource stacks elsewhere. This lets you design an environment to test a beta version of your application and then easily create identical environments for staging and production. Dynamic change can be incorporated into templates by parameterizing key values. This way, you could specify, say, one VPC or instance type for your test environment and a different profile for production.

Templates can be created in multiple ways.

▪   Using the browser-based drag-and-drop interface

▪   Working with prebuilt sample templates defining popular environments such as a LAMP web server or WordPress instance

▪   Manually writing and uploading a template document

A CloudFormation *stack* is the group of resources defined by your template. You can launch your stack resources by loading a template and creating the stack. AWS will report when the stack has successfully loaded or, in the event of a failure, will roll back changes.

You can update a running stack by submitting a modified version of a template. Deleting a stack will shut down and remove its resources. Try a CloudFormation on your own with Exercise 10.5.

EXERCISE 10.5

Launch a Simple CloudFormation Template

1. From the CloudFormation page, click Create New Stack.

2. Click the Select A Sample template radio button, click once inside the field, and select the Single Instance Samples – LAMP Stack option.

3. Click the View/Edit Template In Designer link and spend a few minutes reading through the template text in the bottom panel to get a feel for how all the elements are organized. Values such as the password fields will be automatically populated in later steps.

4. When you're done exploring, click the Create Stack icon at the top of the page, which will take you back to the Select Template page. Make sure the LAMP stack is selected and click Next.

5. Provide a stack name, database name, two passwords, and a DBUser name.

6. Select an instance type and provide the name of an existing, valid EC2 key pair so you'll have SSH access. Then click Next.

7. The defaults from the Options page are all fine for this demo. Click Next, review your settings, and click Create.

8. It will take a minute or two to launch the resources. While you're waiting, you can view progress in the CloudFormation Dashboard. Assuming your stack is selected in the top panel, the Outputs tab in the Dashboard will include a website URL through which you can access the site's public page. The first time you follow the link, you'll probably see the PHP site configuration page. If you plan to leave this site running, make sure that page does not remain publicly available.

9. Click the other tabs in the Dashboard including Template and Parameters (where you'll see a list of the current parameter values).

10. When you're done, make sure you delete your stack (from the Actions pull-down menu) so you're not billed for any services you're not using.

Third-Party Automation Solutions

Of course, you can also create your own infrastructure automation scripts using Bash or Windows PowerShell. Such scripts can connect directly to your AWS account and launch, manipulate, and delete resource stacks.

Besides Bash and PowerShell scripts, third-party configuration management tools such as Puppet, Chef, and Ansible can be used to closely manage AWS infrastructure. Beyond simply defining and launching resource stacks, these managers can also actively engage with your deployments through operations such as configuration enforcement (to continuously ensure your resources aren't drifting away from their configuration goals), version control (to ensure your code and software packages are kept up-to-date), and change management.

The potential value of configuration management tools for cloud deployments is so obvious that AWS has a managed service dedicated entirely to integrating Chef and Puppet tools: AWS OpsWorks.

AWS OpsWorks: Chef

Using OpsWorks, you can build an infrastructure controlled by Chef by adding a *stack* (a container for EC2 instances and related resources) and one or more *layers*. Layers are the definitions that add functionality to your stack. A stack might include a Node.js app server layer along with a load balancer, an Amazon EC2 Container Service (ECS) cluster, or an RDS database instance. Chef recipes for managing your infrastructure can also be added as layers.

OpsWorks Chef deployments also include one or more *apps*. An app points to the application code you want to install on the instances running in your stack along with some metadata providing accessibility to a remote code repository.

AWS OpsWorks: Puppet

Firing up OpsWorks for Puppet Enterprise will allow you to launch an EC2 instance as a Puppet Master server, configure the R10k environment and module toolset, and give it access to your remote code repo. Once a server is running and you've logged in using the provided credentials, you'll be ready to begin deploying your application to Puppet nodes.

Your OpsWorks experience will probably be more successful if you're already familiar with administrating either Chef or Puppet locally.

Continuous Integration and Continuous Deployment

If your organization's application is built from the code written by multiple developers and if you regularly update your application, then you're probably already using some kind of continuous integration and continuous deployment (CI/CD) process. CI/CD seeks to automate the workflow that moves a project from source code, through compiling (the build), and on to deployment. The goal is to provide a reliable, fast, and bug-free way to stay on top of application change.

The four AWS services that make up their Developer Tools (described together at https://aws.amazon.com/tools/) can facilitate CI/CD through an integrated environment for source code version control, application builds and testing, and then the final push to production—either within AWS or wherever else it needs to go.

AWS CodeCommit

CodeCommit is a Git-compatible code repository where you can safely store and access your code. Why CodeCommit and not GitHub or GitLab? It's for several reasons: because CodeCommit is deeply integrated into the AWS environment, because you can apply granular access control through AWS IAM, and because, as an AWS service, CodeCommit is highly scalable.

AWS CodeBuild

When team members are ready to commit new code versions, you'd ideally want their updates to be compiled and run within your test environment immediately. But maintaining a build server 24/7 and configuring it with access permissions appropriate for each member of your team can be an expensive and complicated process.

CodeBuild is a fully managed, virtualized build server that's scalable. That means it can handle as many resource-hungry commits and builds as you can throw at it, but it will cost you money *only* for the time you're actually using it. CodeBuild will respond to a commit by compiling, testing, and packaging your code

CodeBuild can handle code from S3, CodeCommit, Bitbucket, GitHub, and GitHub Enterprise, and it's comfortable with Java, Python, Node.js, Ruby, Go, Android, .NET Core for Linux, and Docker.

AWS CodeDeploy

You use CodeDeploy to pull code from either CodeBuild or your own build server and push it to applications running on either Amazon EC2 or AWS Lambda. EC2 instances—organized into *deployment groups*—are controlled by an installed agent that regularly polls the CodeDeploy service for pending application revisions. Revisions are executed based on the instructions in an application specification (AppSpec) file, which maps the code, source files, and scripts that make up your application with the deployment targets.

AWS CodePipeline

CodePipeline is a kind of orchestration tool that can automatically manage all the parts of your CI/CD process. As an example, the service can be set to monitor CodeCommit (or a third-party service like GitHub) for updates; push the new code through the build process using tools like CodeBuild, Jenkins, and TeamCity; and then deploy the revision using AWS services like CodeDeloy, Elastic Beanstalk, and CloudFormation.

Figure 10.2 illustrates the role played by each of the AWS Developer Tools in a typical CI/CD deployment system.

FIGURE 10.2 AWS Developer Tools as they integrate with each step of the CI/CD cycle

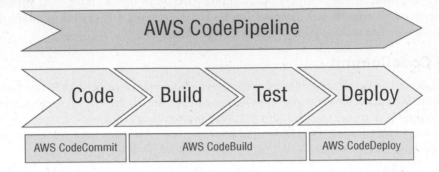

Reviewing and Optimizing Infrastructure Configurations

If you want to achieve and maintain high-performance standards for your applications, you'll need solid insights into how they're doing. To get those insights, you'll need to establish a protocol for monitoring change. Your monitoring should have these four goals:

- Watch for changes to your resource configurations. Whether a change occurred through the intervention of a member of your admin team or through an unauthorized hacker, it's important to find out fast and assess the implications. The AWS Config service—discussed in Chapter 7, "CloudTrail, CloudWatch, and AWS Config"—should give you all the information you need to get started.

- Watch AWS for announcements of changes to its services. Amazon is a busy company, and it regularly releases updates to existing services and entirely new services. To be sure your current configuration is the best one for your needs, keep up with the latest available features and functionality. One way to do that is by watching the AWS Release Notes page (https://aws.amazon.com/releasenotes/). You can subscribe to update alerts through the AWS Email Preference Center (https://pages.awscloud.com/communication-preferences.html).

- Passively monitor the performance and availability of your application. Passive monitoring is primarily concerned with analyzing historical events to understand what—if anything—went wrong and how such failures can be avoided in future. The most important tool for this kind of monitoring is system logs. On AWS, the richest source of log data is CloudWatch, as you learned in Chapter 7.

- Actively test the performance and availability of your application to proactively identify—and fix—potential problems before they can cause any damage. This will usually involve load testing.

Load Testing

One particularly useful form of active infrastructure monitoring is load—or stress—testing. The idea is to subject your infrastructure to simulated workloads and carefully observe how it handles the stress. You can try to devise some method of your own that will generate enough traffic of the right kind to create a useful simulation, but there are plenty of third-party tools available to do it for you. Search the AWS Marketplace site (`https://aws .amazon.com/marketplace`) for load testing.

In most cases—so you don't prevent your actual users from accessing your application as normal—you should run your stress tests against some kind of test environment that's configured to run at production scale. Orchestration tools like CloudFront or, for containers, Amazon Elastic Container Service (ECS), can be useful for quickly building such an environment. Your application might not respond quite the same way to requests from different parts of the world. So, you should try to simulate traffic from multiple geographical origins into your testing.

Make sure that your testing doesn't break any AWS usage rules. Before launching some kinds of vulnerability or penetration tests against your infrastructure, for instance, you need to request explicit permission from AWS. You can find out more on Amazon's Vulnerability and Penetration Testing page: `https://aws.amazon.com/security/penetration-testing`.

Of course, don't forget to set CloudWatch up in advance so you can capture the real-time results of your tests. To get the most out of your testing, it's important to establish performance baselines and consistent key performance indicators (KPIs) so you'll have an objective set of standards against which to compare your results. Knowing your normal *aggregate cumulative cost per request* or *time to first byte*, for instance, will give important context to what your testing returns.

Visualization

All the active and passive testing in the world won't do you any good if you don't have a user-friendly way to consume the data it produces. As you saw in Chapter 7, you can trigger notifications when preset performance thresholds are exceeded. Having key team members receive Simple Notification Service (SNS) messages or email alerts warning them about abnormal events can be an effective way to make your monitoring data count.

In many cases, however, there's no replacement for good, old-fashioned charts and graphs. Some AWS services have their own built-in visualizations. With an instance selected in the EC2 Instances Dashboard, as an example, you can click the Monitoring tab in the lower half of the screen and view a dozen or so metrics rendered as data charts.

But the place where you'll get the greatest visualization bang for your buck is in CloudWatch Dashboards. CloudWatch lets you create multiple Dashboards. As you'll see when you work through Exercise 10.6, a Dashboard can contain multiple *widgets*, each of which can be defined to display a customized combination of metrics pulled from individual AWS services. Keeping a well-designed Dashboard open in a browser tab where you can check on it from time to time is potentially a useful monitoring strategy.

EXERCISE 10.6

Create a CloudWatch Dashboard

1. So you'll get a better idea of how things will look, make sure you have at least one EC2 instance running and at least one S3 bucket with some files in it.

2. From the CloudWatch console, click Dashboards, click Create Dashboard, and give your Dashboard a name. Select the Line widget type and click Configure.

3. With the All Metrics tab in the bottom half of the screen selected, click EC2 and then Per-Instance Metrics. Check the boxes for a few metrics associated with your running instance. StatusCheckFailed, NetworkOut, NetworkIn, and CPUUtilization would make for a nice sample. Note how those metrics are now represented in the graph at the top of the screen. When you're satisfied with your selections, click Create Widget.

4. Your first widget will now appear in your Dashboard. You can click the widget to display it full-screen. Selecting a particular metric from the legend at the bottom of the graph will show you only that metric, making it easier to understand what the values represent.

5. If your widget is still full-screen, click Close to return to the Dashboard.

6. Click Add Widget to create a second widget. This time, select Stacked Area. Select S3 metrics and then the NumberOfObjects and BucketSizeBytes metrics for your bucket. Create the widget.

7. Once you've added all the widgets and metrics you'll need to monitor, click Save Dashboard.

    From now on, whenever you browse to CloudWatch, you'll be able to retrieve and view this Dashboard with all of its metrics. Bear in mind that, outside of the Free Tier, a single Dashboard will cost around $3 per month.

Optimizing Data Operations

Moving data efficiently is pretty much the whole story when it comes to successful applications. Your code may be a thing of great beauty, but if everything slows down while you're waiting for a large data transfer over a weak connection, then it's mostly wasted effort.

Sometimes you can't control the network connection you're working with, and sometimes you can't reduce the volume of data in play. But it's usually possible to apply some clever data management tricks to speed things up noticeably. Data caching, sharding, compression, and decoupling are good examples of the kinds of tricks you can use, so let's talk about how they work on AWS.

Caching

Does your application provide lots of frequently accessed data like a product catalog or other media that's kept in your S3 buckets or a relational database? So, why not move copies of the data closer to your clients?

A caching solution does just that. If an object is likely to be requested repeatedly, a copy can be written to system memory on a server—or a purpose-built cache database—from which it can be retrieved much more quickly. Subsequent requests for that data will see the cached copy rather than having to wait for the time it would take to read from the source. The cached copy will remain the authoritative version until its maximum *time to live* (TTL) is reached, at which point it will be flushed and replaced by an updated version that's read from the data source.

Amazon ElastiCache

An ElastiCache *cluster* consists of one or more *nodes*. As Figure 10.3 illustrates, a node is a compute instance—built from an EC2 instance type you select—that does the actual work of processing and serving data to your clients. The number of nodes and the particular instance type you choose will depend on the demands your clients are likely to place on the application. Finding the ideal configuration combination that's best for your needs will require some of the same considerations you'd use to provision for any EC2 workload.

FIGURE 10.3   A typical ElastiCache configuration with an ElastiCache cluster containing two cache nodes serving data for front-end EC2 instances

ElastiCache clusters can be created using either one of two engines: Memcached or Redis. Memcached can be simpler to configure and deploy, is easily scalable, and, because it works with multiple threads, can run faster. However, because it reads and writes only objects (blobs) as in-memory key-value data stores, Memcached isn't always flexible enough to meet the needs of all projects.

Redis, on the other hand, supports more complex data types such as strings, lists, and sets. Data can also be persisted to a disk, making it possible to snapshot data for later recovery. Redis lets you sort and rank data, allowing you to support, say, an online gaming application that maintains a leaderboard ranking the top users. The fact that Redis can persist data makes it possible to use Redis to maintain session caching, potentially improving performance.

Typically, ElastiCache will make the current version of both Redis and Memcached available, along with a few previous versions. This makes it possible to support as wide a range of application needs as possible.

Once your ElastiCache cluster is running, you can retrieve its endpoint from the ElastiCache Dashboard and connect to the cluster from your application. For a WordPress instance, for example, this can be as simple as adding a single line to the wp-config.php file containing something like the following syntax:

```
define('WP_REDIS_HOST', 'your_cluster_name.amazonaws.com');
```

You can enjoy the benefits of caching without using ElastiCache. For some use cases, you might want to save some money and simply run a reverse proxy like Varnish on your actual EC2 instance.

Other Caching Solutions

Besides caching at the application level, you can also achieve performance gains using broadly similar techniques on the data in your database.

As you saw in Chapter 5, you can add as many as five read replicas to a running database instance in RDS (RDS Aurora instances can have as many as 15). Read replicas are available for RDS MySQL, MariaDB, PostgreSQL, and Aurora. The replica will be an exact copy of the original but will be read-only. By routing some of your traffic to the replica, you lighten the load on the source database, improving response times for both copies. In addition to performance benefits, you can also, if necessary, promote a read replica to your primary database should the original fail.

Effectively, a read replica is a kind of cache that leverages relatively cheap storage overheads to provide quick and highly available copies of your data.

Another type of caching—which you saw in Chapter 8—is CloudFront. As you'll remember, a CloudFront distribution can cache copies of S3-based media on edge locations spread around the world and serve requests from the copy located closest to the client.

Partitioning/Sharding

Traffic volume on your RDS database can increase to the point that a single instance simply can't handle it. While vertical scaling may not be an option, horizontal scaling through partitioning (or sharding) can make a big difference. While not as simple a solution as the read-only read replicas just discussed, partitioning can be configured by adding appropriate logic to the application layer so client requests are directed to the right endpoints.

Sending data in real time through Amazon Kinesis Streams—using the Amazon DynamoDB Streams Kinesis Adapter—lets you process streams of data records in DynamoDB databases. Kinesis organizes records into shards that contain data along with critical meta information. If one shard hits a limit, the workload can be further distributed by subdividing it into multiple shards.

As it's highly scalable and fully managed, Kinesis streams maintain near-real-time performance and, by extension, can have a significant impact on overall data processing performance.

Compression

If bandwidth is a finite resource and it's not practical to reduce the *volume* of data you're regularly transferring, there's still hope. You can either reduce the *size* of your data or bypass the network with its built-in limits altogether.

How do you reduce data size? By borrowing a solution that, once upon a time, was a necessary part of working with expensive and limited storage space. Are you old enough to remember how we used to fit a full operating system along with our program and work files onto a 10 MB drive? Disk compression.

Storage is no longer a serious problem, but network transfers are. You can, therefore, stretch the value you get from your network connections by compressing your data before sending it. This is something that can be incorporated into your application code. But it's also used directly within some AWS services. CloudFront, for instance, can be configured to automatically compress the files sent in response to client requests, greatly reducing download times.

And bypassing the network? You can ask Amazon to send you a physical petabyte-sized storage device called a *Snowball*. You copy your archives onto the encrypted device and then ship it back to Amazon. Within a short time, your data will be uploaded to buckets in S3.

Summary

The performance and availability of EC2 instances can be managed by choosing the right instance type and by provisioning as many instances as necessary through Auto Scaling. Compute workloads can sometimes be more effectively delivered through serverless (Lambda) or container (Docker/ECS) models.

Access to EBS volume-based data and data reliability can be enhanced by configuring RAID arrays. Cross-region replication and S3 transfer acceleration can improve S3 data administration.

Carefully configuring details such as schemas, indexes, views, option groups, and parameter groups can improve the performance of your RDS databases. For manually hosted databases, latency issues can be addressed through volume class (magnetic versus SSD) and IOPS level; durability is improved through replication; and scalability can be manually configured.

Load balancers listen for incoming requests and distribute them intelligently among all available backend resources. This allows for automated health checks and request routing policies that make the best use of your resources and provide the best end-user experience possible.

Scripting resource provisioning using AWS-native tools like CloudFormation or third-party infrastructure automation tools like Chef and Puppet (working through AWS OpsWorks) can make it easy to quickly launch complicated resource stacks. This can make it possible to maintain multiple on-demand environments for testing, staging, and production.

AWS Developer Tools (AWS CodeCommit, AWS CodeBuild, AWS CodeDeploy, and AWS CodePipeline) support continuous integration and continuous deployment environments including source code version control, application builds and testing, and deployment.

You can monitor the state and performance of your resources using CloudWatch, CloudTrail, and AWS Config. It's important to incorporate load testing and report visualization (through CloudWatch Dashboards) into your administration cycles.

You can decrease data response times by replication through caching, improve data processing performance through partitioning (sharding), and transfer large data stores more quickly through compression.

Exam Essentials

Understand the way EC2 instance types are defined.   Each EC2 instance type is designed to service a different function. You should be familiar with the individual parameters that are used to measure the way each type performs.

Understand Auto Scaling.   The best way to efficiently meet changing demands on your application is to automate the process of provisioning and launching new resources as demand grows and shutting unused resources down as demand drops. Auto Scaling is the way AWS manages this functionality for EC2.

Understand the value of serverless and container computing compared with EC2 instances.   By reducing the underlying resource footprint of your service, serverless functions, such as those offered through AWS Lambda, and clusters of Docker containers (offered through AWS ECS) can provide more responsive and cost-effective compute solutions. You should understand which model will work best for a given use case.

Understand how to optimize storage performance and reliability.   Data stored on EBS volumes (using RAID) or in S3 buckets (using cross-region replication) can be replicated for greater durability and/or performance. You can also enable faster transfers in and out from S3 buckets using S3 transfer acceleration or CloudFront.

Understand how to optimize database performance.   The performance, reliability, and costs you'll experience running a database on AWS will depend on the choices you make.

How should you configure your underlying storage? Should you go with the managed RDS, build your database on an EC2 instance, or choose Redshift or a third-party integration for data warehouse management?

Understand when and how to use a load balancer.   Load balancers direct incoming client requests among multiple backend servers. This allows for scalable and reliable application delivery, as failing or overloaded instances can be automatically replaced or supported by others. Load balancing of one sort of another is a critical component of many—if not most—EC2 and RDS workloads.

Understand the value and function of infrastructure automation tools.   CloudFormation templates can be used to define and then automatically provision and launch complex resource stacks in multiple environments. Similarly, third-party solutions like Chef and Puppet can be deployed through AWS OpsWorks to script environments. Continuous integration and continuous deployment processes can also be managed through AWS developer tools.

Understand the importance of infrastructure monitoring and the tools available for the job.   It's critically important to stay on top of changes and performance trends within your infrastructure. Active load simulation testing is an important ongoing component of your administration process, as is visualizing the data that's produced using tools like CloudWatch Dashboards.

Understand how caching can be used to improve performance.   ElastiCache and CloudFront are two services that replicate data and store it to make it quickly available to consuming clients. ElastiCache can use either Memcached or Redis—you should know which will work best for a given workload.

Review Questions

1. Which of the following are parameters used to describe the performance of specific EC2 instance types? (Choose three.)

   A. ECUs (EC2 compute units)

   B. vCPUs (virtual CPUs)

   C. ACCpR (Aggregate Cumulative Cost per Request)

   D. Intel AES-NI

2. Which of the following are normally necessary components for successful Auto Scaling? (Choose three.)

   A. Launch configuration

   B. Load balancer

   C. Defined EC2 AMI

   D. A `start.sh` script

3. Which of the following best describes the role that launch configurations play in Auto Scaling?

   A. Define the capacity metric that will trigger a scaling change.

   B. Define the AMI to be deployed by Auto Scaling operations.

   C. Control the minimum and maximum number of instances to allow.

   D. Define the associated load balancer.

4. Which of the following is a good use case for container-based applications as opposed to EC2 instances or Lambda functions?

   A. Microservices deployments

   B. Processing transactions

   C. Long-lived, more complex web applications

   D. Processes requiring in-depth monitoring and tracking

5. Where are RAID-optimized EBS volume configurations performed?

   A. From the EBS Dashboard

   B. From the EC2 Storage Optimization Dashboard

   C. From the AWS CLI

   D. From within the EC2 instance OS

6. Which of the following tools will provide both low-latency access and resilience for your S3-based data?

   A. CloudFront

   B. RAID arrays

   C. Cross-region replication

   D. Transfer Acceleration

7. Which of the following tools uses CloudFront edge locations to speed up data transfers?

   A. Amazon S3 Transfer Acceleration

   B. S3 Cross-Region Replication

   C. EBS Data Transfer Wizard

   D. EC2 Auto Scaling

8. Which of the following is not a major design consideration for a managed RDS database?

   A. Optimizing indexes

   B. Optimizing scalability

   C. Optimizing schemas

   D. Optimizing views

9. Which of the following are possible advantages of hosting a relational database on an EC2 instance over using the RDS service? (Choose two.)

   A. Automated software patches

   B. Automated OS updates

   C. Cost savings

   D. Greater host control

10. You've received complaints from users that performance on your EC2-based graphics-heavy application is slower than normal. Demand has been rising over the past month or two, which could be a factor. Which of the following is the most likely to help? (Choose two.)

   A. Switching to an EC2 instance that supports enhanced graphics

   B. Deploying ElasticSearch in front of your instance

   C. Increasing the instance limit on your Auto Scaling group

   D. Putting your application behind a CloudFront distribution

11. Which of the following load balancer types is optimized for handling layer four (the transport layer) routing?

   A. Application Load Balancer

   B. Classic Load Balancer

   C. Network Load Balancer

   D. Dynamic Load Balancer

12. Which of the following can be used to configure a CloudFormation template? (Choose three.)

   A. The CloudFormation drag-and-drop interface

   B. Selecting a prebuilt sample template

   C. Importing a template from AWS CloudDeploy

   D. Creating your own JSON template document

13. Which of the following details is not a necessary component of a CloudFormation configuration?

    A. Default node name

    B. Stack name

    C. Database name

    D. DBUser name

14. Which of the following can be integrated into your AWS workflow through AWS OpsWorks? (Choose two.)

    A. Ansible

    B. Chef

    C. Terraform

    D. Puppet

15. Which of the following are important elements of a successful resource monitoring protocol? (Choose two.)

    A. CloudWatch Dashboards

    B. CloudWatch OneView

    C. SNS alerts

    D. AWS Config Dashboards

16. Which of the following will most enhance the value of the CloudWatch data your resources generate? (Choose two.)

    A. Predefined performance baselines

    B. Predefined key performance indicators (KPIs)

    C. Advanced permission from AWS

    D. A complete record of your account's resource configuration changes

17. Which of the following can be used to audit the changes made to your account and resource configurations?

    A. AWS CloudTrail

    B. AWS CloudWatch

    C. AWS CodePipeline

    D. AWS Config

18. Which of the following caching engines can be integrated with Amazon ElastiCache? (Choose two.)

    A. Varnish

    B. Redis

    C. Memcached

    D. Nginx

19. Which of the following use case scenarios are a good fit for caching using Redis and Elasti-Cache? (Choose two.)

    A. Your online application requires users' session states to be saved and the behavior of all active users to be compared.

    B. Your online application needs the fastest operation available.

    C. Your admin is not familiar with caching and is looking for a relatively simple setup for a straightforward application performance improvement.

    D. You're not sure what your application needs might be in a month or two, so you want to leave open as many options as possible.

20. Which of the following database engines is not a candidate for read replicas within Amazon RDS?

    A. MySQL

    B. Oracle

    C. MariaDB

    D. PostgreSQL

Chapter

11

The Security Pillar

THE AWS CERTIFIED SOLUTIONS ARCHITECT ASSOCIATE EXAM OBJECTIVES COVERED IN THIS CHAPTER MAY INCLUDE, BUT ARE NOT LIMITED TO, THE FOLLOWING:

Domain 3: Specify Secure Applications and Architectures

✓ **3.1 Determine how to secure application tiers.**

✓ **3.2 Determine how to secure data.**

✓ **3.3 Define the networking infrastructure for a single VPC application.**

Introduction

The primary goal of information security is to protect data, which of course entails protecting the resources that store and provide access to that data. To effectively protect data, there are three elements of the data you need to ensure: confidentiality, integrity, and availability.

Confidentiality   The only people or systems that can access data are those authorized to access it. Encryption and access control lists (ACLs) are two common mechanisms for enforcing confidentiality.

Integrity   The data has not been maliciously or accidentally changed. Cryptographic hashing and logging provide two ways to help validate the integrity of data.

Availability   The data is available to those who need it when they need it. Although the data itself may be safe and sound, if an attacker carries out a denial-of-service (DoS) attack to prevent access to that data, then the data is not available to those who need it.

In this chapter, you'll learn how to apply security controls to every system that touches your data—storage, compute, and networking—to ensure the confidentiality, integrity, and availability of your data throughout its lifecycle.

Identity and Access Management

Your AWS credentials let you log into the AWS management console, manage services, view and edit resources, and so on. Security in AWS begins with the foundation of identity, which is managed by the Identity and Access Management (IAM) service. Because your AWS credentials are the keys to the kingdom, the first order of business is to protect them from accidental exposure and unauthorized use. The second step is to ensure that users have only the permissions they need, and no more.

Protecting AWS Credentials

With some exceptions, if anyone is to interact with your AWS resources, they must be authenticated using a set of credentials. An entity that can take an action on an AWS resource is called a *principal*. You'll sometimes see a principal also referred to as an *identity*. A principal can include the following:

- The root user
- An IAM user
- An IAM role

The root user has unrestricted access to your AWS account, so it's a best practice to avoid using it for routine administrative tasks. Instead, create an IAM user and attach the AdministratorAccess AWS managed policy. For a detailed guide on securing the root user and creating an administrative IAM user, refer to Exercise 6.1 in Chapter 6, "AWS Identity and Access Management."

Another crucial step in securing the root user is to enable multifactor authentication (MFA). When you enable MFA, in addition to entering a username and password to log into the root account, you must also enter a one-time passcode. This one-time passcode is generated by a physical or virtual MFA device, which is just an application you can install on your smartphone. Use caution when enabling MFA on the root account, as losing your MFA device means being unable to log in as the root user! If this happens, you will need to contact AWS Support to get back in.

For IAM users, you can choose to enforce a password policy to ensure that all IAM users with access to the AWS Management Console have a secure password. A password policy can require any or all of the following:

- Password complexity requirements such as minimum length, the use of lower and uppercase, numbers, and nonalphanumeric characters
- Password expiration
- Preventing password reuse
- Requiring an administrator to reset an expired password

When you create an IAM user, you can choose whether to give that user AWS Management Console access, programmatic access, or both. AWS Management Console access requires a username and password. You may optionally assign an MFA token that the user must possess to sign in. Programmatic access via the AWS API, command-line interface (CLI), or an SDK requires an access key ID and secret access key.

Fine-Grained Authorization

A fundamental concept in information security is the principle of least privilege. You should give IAM principals permissions to only the resources they need and no more. By following this principle, you limit the impact that compromised credentials or malicious users can have on your AWS resources. You achieve tight control over your IAM principals through the use of policies.

IAM principals have no permissions by default. In other words, simply creating an IAM user or role doesn't grant that principal any ability to do anything in your AWS account. IAM users and roles derive their permissions only from IAM policies. An IAM policy is effectively an ACL.

You define the permissions a principal has by associating the principal with one or more policies. A policy contains one or more permission statements. Each permission statement consists of, at minimum, four elements.

Effect   The effect can be allow or deny. The effect controls whether to allow or deny an action on a resource.

Action/Operation   Each AWS service has a set of actions or operations that it can perform on its resources. For example, the EC2 service includes a RunInstances action that creates a new instance.

Resource   An action may require you to specify one or more resources. For example, the EC2 RunInstances action requires an Amazon Machine Image (AMI) ID. By specifying a resource in a permission statement, you can restrict access on a per-resource basis. For example, you can specify an AMI ID so that the RunInstances operation can be performed using only the specified image.

Condition   You may specify conditions that must be met for the permission to be granted. For example, you can allow only users from a particular IP address to perform the specified action. You can also require multifactor authentication or impose time-based restrictions on when an action can be performed.

Remember that an IAM group is not a principal. It's not possible to perform actions under the auspices of a group in the way that you would a role.

AWS Managed Policies

AWS provides hundreds of prepackaged policies called AWS *managed policies*. These cover a variety of permissions commonly required by common job roles, including network administrators, database administrators (DBAs), and security auditors. AWS updates these policies periodically to include new services.

Customer Managed Policies

A *customer managed policy* is a stand-alone policy that you create and can attach to principals in your AWS account. When you update a Customer Managed Policy, the changes immediately apply to all of the principals that the policy is attached to. Also, IAM doesn't overwrite your existing policy but creates a new version and maintains the last five versions so you can revert if needed.

Inline Policies

An *inline policy* is a set of permissions that's embedded in an IAM principal or group. Unlike AWS and customer managed policies that exist independently of any principals, an inline policy is a part of the principal itself. Inline policies are useful when you want to ensure a policy is not inadvertently attached to the wrong principal.

Permissions Boundaries

When you attach a policy to a principal to grant that principal access, the policy is called a *permissions policy*. However, you can also use a policy to define permissions boundaries. Permissions boundaries let you limit the maximum permissions an IAM principal can be assigned. This can prevent you from accidentally giving a user too many permissions by inadvertently attaching the wrong permissions policy. You set permissions boundaries for a principal by selecting a managed policy that defines the maximum permissions for the principal. For example, you may create the following policy that allows all actions for the EC2 service and then attach that policy to an IAM user as a permissions boundary:

```
{
    "Version": "2012-10-17",
    "Statement": [
        {
            "Effect": "Allow",
            "Action": [
                "ec2:*"
            ],
            "Resource": "*"
        }
    ]
}
```

If you then attach to the user the AdministratorAccess policy—which grants full access to all AWS services—the user will still only be able to perform actions in EC2. The permissions boundary limits the user to performing only those actions laid out in the permissions boundary policy. Complete Exercise 11.1 to create an IAM user whose permissions are limited by a permissions boundary policy.

EXERCISE 11.1

Create a Limited Administrative User

In this exercise, you'll create an IAM user with limited administrative privileges. You'll use policy boundary permissions to allow the user to perform only actions in the EC2 service.

1. Create a customer managed policy called **LimitedAdminPolicyBoundary**. Populate the policy document with the following content:

   ```
   {
       "Version": "2012-10-17",
       "Statement": [
           {
   ```

```
                    "Effect": "Allow",
                    "Action": "ec2:*",
                    "Resource": "*"
            }
        ]
    }
```

2. Create an IAM user with the name of your choice, such as LimitedAdmin.

3. In the IAM Dashboard, click the Users option and then click the username you created.

4. Under Permissions Boundary, click the Set Boundary button.

5. Select the LimitedAdminPolicyBoundary option and click the Set Boundary button.

6. Under Permissions Policy, click Add Permissions.

7. Click the Attach Existing Policies Directly button.

8. Select the AdministratorAccess policy and click the Next: Review button.

9. Click the Add Permissions button.

Even though the AdministratorAccess permissions policy allows full access to all AWS services, the permissions boundary policy overrides that policy and only allows the user to perform actions in EC2.

Roles

A *role* is an IAM principal that doesn't have a password or access key. Like any other IAM principal, a role may have permissions policies and a permissions boundary associated with it. An IAM user or AWS resource can assume a role and inherit the permissions associated with that role.

Roles are particularly useful for allowing applications running on EC2 instances to access AWS resources without having an access key. For example, if you're running an application that requires access to DynamoDB, you can create a role that contains a permissions policy granting the appropriate access to DynamoDB. Such a permissions policy may look like this:

```
{
    "Version": "2012-10-17",
    "Statement": [
        {
            "Effect": "Allow",
```

```
        "Action": [
            "dynamodb:CreateTable",
            "dynamodb:PutItem",
            "dynamodb:ListTables",
            "dynamodb:DescribeTable",
            "dynamodb:DeleteItem",
            "dynamodb:GetItem",
            "dynamodb:Query",
            "dynamodb:UpdateItem",
            "dynamodb:UpdateTable"
        ],
        "Resource": "*"
    }
  ]
}
```

Instance Profiles

Recall that in addition to containing permissions policies, a role also contains a trust policy that specifies which AWS resource may assume the role. Because the application that needs access to DynamoDB is running on an EC2 instance, the trust policy must grant EC2 permission to assume the role. Such a trust policy would look like this:

```
{
  "Version": "2012-10-17",
  "Statement": [
    {
      "Effect": "Allow",
      "Principal": {
        "Service": "ec2.amazonaws.com"
      },
      "Action": "sts:AssumeRole"
    }
  ]
}
```

A trust policy is an example of a resource-based policy.

When you create a role that grants EC2 access to assume it, IAM automatically creates an instance profile with the same name as the role. For example, suppose you used the previous permissions policy and trust policy documents to create a role named MyAppRole. IAM would automatically create an instance profile also named MyAppRole. You could then associate this instance profile with an EC2 instance, thereby granting the instance permission to assume the role.

To view the instance profile tied to this role, use the AWS CLI to issue the following command:

```
aws iam list-instance-profiles-for-role --role-name MyAppRole
```

You should see something like the following:

```
{
    "InstanceProfiles": [
        {
            "InstanceProfileId": "AIPAJGKR6VR52WTHHXOR6",
            "Roles": [
                {
                    "AssumeRolePolicyDocument": {
                        "Version": "2012-10-17",
                        "Statement": [
                            {
                                "Action": "sts:AssumeRole",
                                "Effect": "Allow",
                                "Principal": {
                                    "Service": "ec2.amazonaws.com"
                                }
                            }
                        ]
                    },
                    "RoleId": "AROAIV2GSBS4E4HAEFTJA",
                    "CreateDate": "2018-10-13T03:20:46Z",
                    "RoleName": "MyAppRole",
                    "Path": "/",
                    "Arn": "arn:aws:iam::xxxxxxxxxxxx:role/MyAppRole"
                }
            ],
            "CreateDate": "2018-10-13T03:20:46Z",
            "InstanceProfileName": "MyAppRole",
            "Path": "/",
            "Arn": "arn:aws:iam::xxxxxxxxxxxx:instance-profile/MyAppRole"
        }
    ]
}
```

By associating an instance with an instance profile, the instance is able to acquire temporary credentials—an access key, a secret key, and a session token—using the Security Token

Service. The Security Token Service places the temporary credentials in the instance meta-data and updates them about every six hours. To view the temporary credentials granted by a role named MyAppRole, you could theoretically browse to the following URL from within the instance:

```
http://169.254.169.254/latest/meta-data/iam/security-credentials/MyAppRole
```

And you would see something like the following:

```
{
  "Code" : "Success",
  "LastUpdated" : "2018-10-14T20:47:19Z",
  "Type" : "AWS-HMAC",
  "AccessKeyId" : "ASIASJ6WQJMEE32SJ56C",
  "SecretAccessKey" : "vcAiY5Tps6U3pbr2TFjzwrrRe2ETXbi0T+mDr1Qi",
  "Token" :
"FQoGZXIvYXdzEBYaDLwVhhKEzhxBvNtRMyK3A7RpKrXELCv61rGatSWBi1Ehg3w9gOBww7jjy9mCAwTK7kA4S
IyhmyEXQR32McB4xWqjxM3/K4Ij9o5+7ALpegD5p5c0cO7BqGIb4Xb3vZcJiA0pMk7jWRb6afB8c+iAdP1PhRE
R8oJpAOmUHwC2NoT85tpUbAwPtJc4SCW9HmFvI3Hq5pBOo2c1gB75SdcmaYMR/Xl+HxkV/KM5tqyx64BypS4uA
ByW9BuoQ5GH+WKHBXOzIFuhVDpvKS2XXaoOOfz/dfdLo/t1n13KkhzXf43NFc4Lunqsd4Zo9o7yr2D+ezXNLPD
phRN3Itc9dxSaCZY7QE51fgdDUCPBPsQ17okukrcT5jI/R+rY3cL/bBxOQ4VUd47bUcASRxCag2xvDONMAqDpb
PX4j2Kbgs8avLqEFj4q4RkCOM28gETeqWxEE8XNZEfpXCupr1eeyfPul3BzcZmrTMu22ZvvySyzYJQVf9Yijpg
Wa9RcGBFQGKbWAgu5aWxdJvKjDCDjkupyhi2tnBRlRuRXgtXXN19NkDEiVus7rAnZLMRuBIIgbeWtT6BXSMMjt
HqZ6NpaagDwGHtNmvOv6AEondaO3gU=",
  "Expiration" : "2018-10-15T03:21:21Z"
}
```

Notice that the access key ID, secret access key, and session token are in plaintext. These credentials are what an application running on the instance would use to authenti-cate to the AWS API to perform operations. It is possible for a malicious user or malware to take these credentials and use them to grain unauthorized access. For example, a user may use the preceding credentials to attempt to enumerate resources using the AWS CLI, as follows:

```
[ec2-user@ip-172-31-88-201 ~]$ export AWS_ACCESS_KEY_ID=ASTASJ6WQJMEE32SJ56C
[ec2-user@ip-172-31-88-201 ~]$ export
AWS_SECRET_ACCESS_KEY=vcAiY5Tps6U3pbr2TFjzwrrRe2ETXbi0T+mDr1Qi
[ec2-user@ip-172-31-88-201 ~]$ export
AWS_SESSION_TOKEN=FQoGZXIvYXdzEBYaDLwVhhKEzhxBvNtRMyK3A7RpKrXELCv61rGatSWBi1Ehg3w9gOBw
w7jjy9mCAwTK7kA4SIyhmyEXQR32McB4xWqjxM3/K4Ij9o5+7ALpegD5p5c0cO7BqGIb4Xb3vZcJiA0pMk7jWR
b6afB8c+iAdP1PhRER8oJpAOmUHwC2NoT85tpUbAwPtJc4SCW9HmFvI3Hq5pBOo2c1gB75SdcmaYMR/Xl+HxkV
/KM5tqyx64BypS4uAByW9BuoQ5GH+WKHBXOzIFuhVDpvKS2XXaoOOfz/dfdLo/t1n13KkhzXf43NFc4Lunqsd4
Zo9o7yr2D+ezXNLPDphRN3Itc9dxSaCZY7QE51fgdDUCPBPsQ17okukrcT5jI/R+rY3cL/bBxOQ4VUd47bUcAS
RxCag2xvDONMAqDpbPX4j2Kbgs8avLqEFj4q4RkCOM28gETeqWxEE8XNZEfpXCupr1eeyfPul3BzcZmrTMu22Z
vvySyzYJQVf9YijpgWa9RcGBFQGKbWAgu5aWxdJvKjDCDjkupyhi2tnBRlRuRXgtXXN19NkDEiVus7rAnZLMRu
BIIgbeWtT6BXSMMjtHqZ6NpaagDwGHtNmvOv6AEondaO3gU=
```

The export commands set environment variables that the AWS CLI fetches the credentials from. The user may then attempt to list all DynamoDB tables, like so:

```
[ec2-user@ip-172-31-88-201 ~]$ aws dynamodb list-tables
{
    "TableNames": [
        "MySecretTable",
        "Recipes"
    ]
}
```

Because the role grants the ListTables action, the credentials generated by the Security Token Service also grant that permission. However, if the user tries to use the same credentials to enumerate EC2 instances, the action fails.

```
[ec2-user@ip-172-31-88-201 ~]$ aws ec2 describe-instances

An error occurred (UnauthorizedOperation) when calling the DescribeInstances
operation: You are not authorized to perform this operation.
```

Therefore, it's imperative that you follow the principle of least privilege and don't grant a role more permissions than it requires. As an additional precaution, you can disable the Security Token Service on a per-region basis from the Account Settings menu option in the IAM Dashboard. Later in the chapter, you'll see how Amazon GuardDuty can help you identify when credentials such as these have been compromised.

Assuming a Role

You can create a role and allow any IAM user to assume it. The IAM user that assumes the role can be in the same account as the role or in a different account. When you assume a role, you have only the permissions granted to that role. The permissions of the IAM user you're logged in as are not added to the permissions of the role you assume. For instance, if you are logged in as an IAM user with full access to all AWS services and then assume a role that has read-only access to the EC2 service, you will not have access to any other AWS services. To see how this works for yourself, complete Exercise 11.2.

EXERCISE 11.2

Create and Assume a Role as an IAM User

In this exercise, you'll create a role and assume it.

1. While logged in as an administrative IAM user, click Roles from the menu on the left side of the IAM Dashboard screen and then click the Create Role button.

2. Under Select Type Of Trusted Entity, click the Another AWS Account button.

3. Under Account ID, enter your AWS account number. Click the Next: Permissions button.

4. Select the AmazonEC2ReadOnlyAccess AWS managed policy and click the Next: Review button.

5. Enter a name for the role, such as **EC2ReadOnlyRole**.

6. Click the Create Role button.

7. On the navigation bar at the top of the AWS Management Console, click your IAM account name. A drop-down menu will appear.

8. Click the Switch Role link in the drop-down menu, as shown here.

9. Click the Switch Role button.

10. Enter your 12-digit AWS account number or alias and the name of the role you created in step 6. The following shows an example of a Switch Role screen with the account and role specified.

11. Click the Switch Role button. The name of the role followed will appear in the top navigation bar. You will now be operating under the role you created.

12. Try to launch an EC2 instance. It will fail because the assumed role doesn't have the RunInstances permission.

13. To switch back to your IAM user, click the upper-right menu bar where the name of the role followed by your AWS account number is. Then click the link that reads Back To *[your IAM username]*.

Enforcing Service-Level Protection

In addition to defining identity-based IAM policies to control access to resources, some AWS services allow you to define resource-based policies. For example, S3 offers optional bucket policies that control access to objects or entire buckets. The Key Management Service (KMS) requires you to define a key policy to specify the administrators and users of a key. SNS topics have resource policies to control who may publish messages or subscribe to a topic, as well as which delivery protocols they may use. Simple Queue Service (SQS) queues also use resource-based policies to control who can send to and receive messages from a queue.

Notice that users without AWS credentials tend to consume the AWS services that offer resource-based policies. For example, an end user of an application may receive an SNS notification via email, even though they don't have an AWS account. An anonymous user on the Internet may download a publicly accessible object stored in an S3 bucket. Resource-based policies give you control that you wouldn't have with identity-based policies alone. As with identity-based policies, use the principle of least privilege when creating resource-based policies.

Detective Controls

AWS offers a number of detective controls that can keep a record of the events that occur in your AWS environment, as well as alert you to security incidents or potential threats.

CloudTrail

It's important to carefully think about what you want to log and how you'll use the information contained in those logs. CloudTrail can log activities on your AWS account. But before configuring CloudTrail, you need to decide the scope of the logging, including whether to log any of the following:

- Management events, data events, or both
- Read-only events, write-only events, or both

- All resources or just specific ones
- All regions or just specific regions
- Global services

You'll also need to decide how many trails to create. You may decide to have one trail for read-only events and another for write-only events. Or you may choose to have a separate trail for each region.

CloudTrail stores logs in S3, so you'll want to set up bucket policies to control who can read and delete those logs. You may also consider setting up an additional trail just to log data events on the S3 bucket containing your CloudTrail management event logs. For additional security, when creating a trail, enable SSE-KMS encryption and log file integrity validation. You can optionally have CloudTrail generate a Simple Notification Service (SNS) notification when it delivers a log file to the S3 bucket. Note that it can take up to 15 minutes between the time an event occurs and when the CloudTrail creates the log file containing the event.

CloudWatch Logs

CloudWatch Logs can aggregate logs from multiple sources for easy storage and searching. The logs that CloudWatch can ingest from various AWS services include the following:

CloudTrail Logs   To easily search and view CloudTrail logs, stream them to CloudWatch Logs. To set this up, refer to the steps in Exercise 7.3 in Chapter 7, "CloudTrail, CloudWatch, and AWS Config."

VPC Flow Logs   VPC flow logs include information about traffic ingressing or egressing a VPC. Flow logs include network interface, source and destination IP addresses, ports, protocols, and packet and byte counts. Flow logs do not include DHCP traffic or traffic to the Amazon DNS server. Follow the steps in Exercise 11.3 to configure VPC flow logging and deliver the logs to CloudWatch Logs.

RDS Logs   RDS can stream logs from database engines including MariaDB, MySQL, Aurora with MySQL compatibility, and Oracle.

Route 53 DNS Queries   You can configure Route 53 to log DNS queries for a hosted zone and stream them to CloudWatch Logs.

Lambda   You can add logging statements to Lambda code. Lambda automatically streams these log events to a log group derived from the name of the function, using the format /aws/lambda/<function name>.

EXERCISE 11.3

Configure VPC Flow Logging

In this exercise, you'll configure VPC flow logging to deliver flow logs to a CloudWatch Logs log group.

1. In the VPC Dashboard, select a VPC you want to log traffic for. Click the Flow Logs tab.

2. Click the Create Flow Log button.

3. In the Destination Log Group input field, enter a name of your choice, such as FlowLogs.

4. You'll need to specify a role which AWS can create for you. Click the Set Up Permissions link.

5. A new browser tab will open. Click the Allow button. AWS will create a role called FlowlogsRole.

6. Return to the previous tab with the Create Flow Log wizard. Select the FlowlogsRole.

7. Click the Create button.

It will take up to 10 minutes for logs to begin to flow into the new log group.

Searching Logs with Athena

AWS uses S3 to store various logs, including CloudTrail logs, VPC flow logs, DNS query logs, and S3 server access logs. Athena lets you use the Structured Query Language (SQL) to search data stored in S3. Although you can use CloudWatch Logs to store and search logs, you can't format the output to show you only specific data. For example, suppose you use the following filter pattern to search for all DetachVolume, AttachVolume, and DeleteVolume events in a CloudWatch log stream containing CloudTrail logs:

```
{ $.eventName = "*tachVolume" || $.eventName = "DeleteVolume" }
```

CloudWatch Logs will display each matching event in its native JSON format, which as you can see in Figure 11.1 is inherently difficult to read.

FIGURE 11.1   CloudWatch Logs showing AttachVolume, DetachVolume, and DeleteVolume events

Additionally, you may not be interested in every property in the JSON document and want to see only a few key elements.

Amazon Athena makes it easy to achieve this. Once you bring data into Athena from S3, you can query it using SQL, sort it, and have Athena display only specific columns, as shown in Figure 11.2.

FIGURE 11.2   Athena query results

Because Athena uses SQL, you must define the structure of the data by using a CREATE TABLE Data Definition Language (DDL) statement. The DDL statement maps the values in the source file to columns in a table. AWS provides DDL statements for creating tables to store Application Load Balancer logs, CloudTrail logs, CloudFront logs, and VPC flow logs.

You can import multiple logs into a single Athena database and then use SQL JOIN statements to correlate data across those logs. The data formats that Athena supports include the following:

- Comma-separated values (CSV) and tab-separated values (TSV)

- JavaScript Object Notation (JSON)—including CloudTrail logs, VPC flow logs, and DNS query logs

- Apache ORC and Parquet—storage formats for Apache Hadoop, which is a framework for processing large data sets

Auditing Resource Configurations with AWS Config

In addition to monitoring events, your overall security strategy should include monitoring the configuration state of your AWS resources. AWS Config can alert you when a resource configuration in your AWS account changes. It can also compare your resource configurations against a baseline and alert you when the configuration deviates from it, which is useful for validating that you're in compliance with organizational and regulatory requirements.

To compare your resource configurations against a desired baseline, you can implement AWS Config rules. In a busy AWS environment where configuration changes are occurring frequently, it's important to determine which types of changes require further investigation. AWS Config Rules let you define configuration states that are abnormal or suspicious so that you can focus on analyzing and, if necessary, remediating them. AWS offers a variety of managed rules to cover such scenarios. For example, the ec2-volume-inuse-check rule looks for EBS volumes that aren't attached to any instance. With this rule in place, if you create an EBS volume and don't attach it to an instance, AWS Config will report the volume as noncompliant, as shown in Figure 11.3.

FIGURE 11.3   AWS Config showing an EBS volume as noncompliant

Note that the rule only gives the current compliance status of the resource. Suppose that an IT auditor needed to see which EC2 instances this EBS volume was previously attached to. Although you could derive this information from CloudTrail logs, it would be difficult and time-consuming. You'd have to carefully sift through the CloudTrail logs, paying attention to every AttachVolume and DetachVolume operation. Imagine how much more cumbersome this process would be if you had to do this for hundreds of instances! Instead, you could simply use AWS Config to view the configuration timeline for the resource, as shown in Figure 11.4.

FIGURE 11.4   Configuration timeline for an EBS volume

The configuration timeline shows a timestamp for each time the EBS volume was modified. You can click any box in the timeline to view the specific API events that triggered the configuration change, the before-and-after configuration details, and any relationship changes. The latest configuration and relationship changes, shown in Figure 11.5, reveal that the volume was attached to an instance and was then subsequently detached. Note that the act of detaching the volume from an instance placed the volume out of compliance with the ec2-volume-inuse-check rule.

FIGURE 11.5   EBS volume configuration and relationship changes

Amazon GuardDuty

Amazon GuardDuty analyzes VPC flow logs, CloudTrail management event logs, and Route 53 DNS query logs, looking for known malicious IP addresses, domain names, and potentially malicious activity.

You do not need to stream any logs to CloudWatch Logs for GuardDuty to be able to analyze them.

When GuardDuty detects a potential security problem, it creates a *finding*, which is a notification that details the questionable activity. GuardDuty displays the finding in the GuardDuty console and also delivers the finding to CloudWatch Events. You can configure an SNS notification to send an alert or take an action in response to such an event. Findings are classified according to the ostensible purpose of the threat, which can be one of the following finding types:

Backdoor   This indicates an EC2 instance has been compromised by malware that can be used to send spam or participate in distributed denial-of-service (DDoS) attacks. This finding may be triggered when the instance communicates on TCP port 25 or when it resolves the domain name of a known command-and-control server used to coordinate DDoS attacks.

Behavior   This indicates an EC2 instance is communicating on a protocol and port that it normally doesn't or is sending an abnormally large amount of traffic to an external host.

Cryptocurrency   An EC2 instance is exhibiting network activity indicating that it's operating at a Bitcoin node. It may be sending, receiving, or mining Bitcoin.

Pentest   A system running Kali Linux, a popular Linux distribution used for penetration testing, is making API calls against your AWS resources.

Persistence   An IAM user with no prior history of doing so has modified user or resource permissions, security groups, routes, or network access control lists.

Recon   This indicates a reconnaissance attack may be underway. Behavior that can trigger this finding may include a host from a known malicious IP address probing an EC2 instance on a port that's not blocked by a security group or network access control list. Reconnaissance behavior can also include a malicious IP attempting to invoke an API call against a resource in your AWS account. Another trigger is an IAM user with no history of doing so attempting to enumerate security groups, network access control lists, routes, AWS resources, and IAM user permissions.

ResourceConsumption   This indicates that an IAM user has launched an EC2 instance, despite having no history of doing so.

Stealth   A password policy was weakened, CloudTrail logging was disabled or modified, or CloudTrail logs were deleted.

Trojan   An EC2 instance is exhibiting behavior that indicates a Trojan may be installed. A Trojan is a malicious program that can send data from your AWS environment to an attacker or provide a way for an attacker to collect or store stolen data on your instance.

UnauthorizedAccess   Indicates a possible unauthorized attempt to access your AWS resources via an API call or console login. This finding type may also indicate someone attempting to brute force a secure shell (SSH) or Remote Desktop Protocol (RDP) session.

Notice that every finding type relates to either the inappropriate use of AWS credentials or the presence of malware on an EC2 instance. For example, in Figure 11.6, GuardDuty has detected network activity indicative of malware attempting to communicate with a command-and-control server, which is a server run by an attacker used to coordinate various types of attacks.

FIGURE 11.6   GuardDuty finding showing a possible malware infection

Remediating this finding might involve identifying and removing the malware or simply terminating the instance and creating a new one.

In the case of the potentially inappropriate use of AWS credentials, remediation would include first contacting the authorized owner of the credentials to find out whether the activity was legitimate. If the credentials were used by an unauthorized party, then you would immediately revoke the compromised credentials and issue new ones.

Amazon Inspector

Amazon Inspector is an agent-based service that looks for vulnerabilities on your EC2 instances. Whereas GuardDuty looks for security threats by inspecting network traffic to and from your instances, the Inspector agent runs an *assessment* on the instance and analyzes its network, filesystem, and process activity. Inspector determines whether any threats or vulnerabilities exist by comparing the collected data against one or more rules packages. Inspector offers five rules packages:

Common Vulnerabilities and Exposures   Common Vulnerabilities and Exposures (CVEs) are common vulnerabilities found in publicly released software, which includes both commercial and open source software for both Linux and Windows.

Center for Internet Security Benchmarks   These include security best practices for Linux and Windows operating system configurations.

Security Best Practices   These rules are a subset of the Center for Internet Security Benchmarks, providing a handful of rules against Linux instances only. Issues that these rules look for include root access via SSH, lack of a secure password policy, and insecure permissions on system directories.

Runtime Behavior Analysis   This detects the use of insecure client and server protocols, unused listening TCP ports, and, on Linux systems, inappropriate file permissions and ownership.

Network Reachability   These rules detect network configurations that make resources in your VPC vulnerable. Some examples include having an instance in a public subnet or running an application listening on a well-known port.

After an assessment runs, Inspector generates a list of findings classified by the following severity levels:

- High—The issue should be resolved immediately.
- Medium—The issue should be resolved at the next possible opportunity.
- Low—The issue should be resolved at your convenience.
- Informational—This indicates a security configuration detail that isn't likely to result in your system being compromised. Nevertheless, you may want to address it depending on your organization's requirements.

Note that the high, medium, and low severity levels indicate an issue is likely to result in a compromise of the confidentiality, integrity, or availability of information. Figure 11.7 shows a finding with a severity level of medium.

FIGURE 11.7   Inspector finding showing that root users can log in via SSH

Once you resolve any outstanding security vulnerabilities on an instance, you can create a new AMI from that instance and use it going forward when provisioning new instances.

Protecting Network Boundaries

The network can be the first line of defense against attacks. All AWS services depend on the network, so when designing your AWS infrastructure, you should consider how your AWS resources will need to communicate with one another, with external resources, and with users.

Many AWS services have public endpoints that are accessible via the Internet. It's the responsibility of AWS to manage the network security of these endpoints and protect them from attacks. However, you can control network access to and from the resources in your VPCs, such as EC2 instances, RDS instances, and elastic load balancers.

Network Access Control Lists and Security Groups

Each resource within a VPC must reside within a subnet. Network access control lists define what traffic is allowed to and from a subnet. Security groups provide granular control of traffic to and from individual resources, such as instances and elastic load balancer listeners. You should configure your security groups and network access control lists to allow traffic to and from your AWS resources using only the protocols and ports required. If your security requirements call for it, you may also need to restrict communication to specific IP address ranges.

Consider which of your resources need to be accessible from the Internet. A VPC must have an Internet gateway for resources in the VPC to access the Internet. Also, each route table attached to each subnet must have a default route with the Internet gateway as a target. If you're running a multitier application with instances that don't need Internet access—such as database servers—consider placing those in a separate subnet that permits traffic to and from the specific resources that the instance needs to communicate with. As an added precaution, ensure the route table the subnet is associated with doesn't have a default route.

AWS Web Application Firewall

The Web Application Firewall (WAF) monitors HTTP and HTTPS requests to an application load balancer or CloudFront distribution. WAF protects your applications from common exploits that could result in a denial or service or allow unauthorized access to your application.

Unlike network access control lists and security groups, which allow or deny access based solely on a source IP address or port and protocol, WAF lets you inspect application traffic for signs of malicious activity, including injection of malicious scripts used in cross-site scripting attacks, SQL statements used in SQL injection attacks, and abnormally long query strings. You can block these requests so that they never reach your application.

WAF can also block traffic based on source IP address patterns or geographic location. You can create a Lambda function to check a list of known malicious IP addresses and add them to a WAF block list. You can also create a Lambda function to analyze web server logs and identify IP addresses that generate bad or excessive requests indicative of an HTTP flood attack and add those addresses to a block list.

AWS Shield

Internet-facing applications running on AWS are of necessity vulnerable to DDoS attacks. AWS Shield is a service that helps protect your applications from such an attack. AWS Shield comes in two flavors.

AWS Shield Standard Defends against common layer 3 and 4 DDoS attacks such as SYN flood and UDP reflection attacks. Shield Standard is automatically activated for all AWS customers.

AWS Shield Advanced Provides the same protection as Shield Standard but also includes protection against layer 7 attacks, such as HTTP flood attacks that overwhelm an application with HTTP GET or POST requests. To obtain layer 7 protection for an EC2 instance, it must have an elastic IP address. You also get attack notifications, forensic reports, and 24/7 assistance from the AWS DDoS response team. AWS WAF is included at no charge.

Shield mitigates 99 percent of attacks in five minutes or less. It mitigates attacks against CloudFront and Route 53 in less than one second and Elastic Load Balancing in less than five minutes. Shield usually mitigates all other attacks in less than 20 minutes.

Data Encryption

Encrypting data ensures the confidentiality of data by preventing those without the correct key from decrypting and reading it. As a side effect, encryption also makes it infeasible for someone to modify the original data once it's been encrypted.

Data can exist in one of two states: at rest, sitting on a storage medium such as an EBS volume or S3 bucket, and in transit across the network. How you encrypt data differs according to its state.

Data at Rest

How you encrypt data at rest depends on where it's stored. On AWS, the bulk of your data will probably reside in S3, Elastic Block Store (EBS) volumes, or an Elastic File System (EFS) or a Relational Database Service (RDS) database. Each of these services integrates with KMS and gives you the option of using your own customer-managed customer master key (CMK) or an AWS-managed customer master key.

When you use your own CMK, you can configure key policies to control who may use the key to encrypt and decrypt data. You can also rotate, disable, and revoke keys. Using a customer-managed CMK gives you maximum control over your data.

An AWS-managed CMK automatically rotates once a year. You can't disable, rotate, or revoke it. You can view existing CMKs and create new ones by browsing to the Encryption Keys link in the IAM Dashboard.

Most AWS services offer encryption of data at rest using KMS-managed keys, although a few including DynamoDB support using only AWS-managed keys. Note that enabling encryption for some services such as CloudWatch Logs requires using the AWS CLI.

S3

If your data is stored in an S3 bucket, you have a number of encryption options.

- Server-side encryption with S3-managed Keys (SSE-S3)
- Server-side encryption with KMS-managed keys (SSE-KMS)
- Server-side encryption with customer-provided keys (SSE-C)
- Client-side encryption

Remember that encryption applies per object, so it's possible to have a bucket containing objects using different encryption options or no encryption at all. Applying default encryption at the bucket level does not automatically encrypt existing objects in the bucket but only those created moving forward.

Elastic Block Store

You can encrypt an EBS volume using a KMS-managed key. You can encrypt a volume when you initially create it. However, you cannot directly encrypt a volume created from an unencrypted snapshot or unencrypted AMI. You must first create a snapshot of the unencrypted volume and then encrypt the snapshot. To encrypt an existing unencrypted volume, follow the steps in Exercise 11.4.

EXERCISE 11.4

Encrypt an EBS Volume

For this exercise, you'll encrypt an unencrypted volume attached to a running EC2 instance.

1. Create an EC2 instance from an unencrypted snapshot or AMI. If you already have one you can bear to part with, you may use that.

2. At the EC2 Dashboard, click Volumes in the left-side menu.

3. Select the volume attached to your instance.

4. Under the Actions menu, click Create Snapshot. EBS will begin creating an unencrypted snapshot of the volume.

5. On the left side menu, click Snapshots. Wait for the snapshot to complete.

6. Select the snapshot and under the Actions menu, click Copy.

7. Check the Encrypt This Snapshot checkbox.

8. Next to the Master Key dropdown, select the KMS key you'd like to use to encrypt the snapshot. You can use your own customer master key, or the default aws/ebs key.

9. Click the Copy button. EBS will begin creating an encrypted copy of the snapshot. The larger the volume, the longer the encryption process takes. A good rule of thumb is about 3 gigabytes per minute.

10. Select the encrypted snapshot and under the Actions menu, click Create Volume.

11. Choose the volume type, size, and availability zone, which can be different than the original volume.

12. Click the Create Volume button. The new volume will be encrypted using the same key that was used to encrypt the snapshot.

You can now detach the unencrypted volume from your instance and attach the new encrypted volume.

When you copy a snapshot, you have the option of choosing the destination region. The key you use to encrypt the destination snapshot must exist in the destination region.

Elastic File System

You can enable encryption for an EFS filesystem when you create it. EFS encryption uses KMS customer master keys to encrypt files, and an EFS-managed key to encrypt filesystem metadata, such as file and directory names.

Data in Transit

Encrypting data in transit is enabled through the use of a Transport Layer Security (TLS) certificate. You can use the Amazon Certificate Manager (ACM) to generate a TLS certificate and then install it on an Application Load Balancer or a CloudFront distribution. Refer to Exercise 8.4 in Chapter 8, "The Domain Name System and Network Routing: Amazon Route 53 and Amazon CloudFront," for instructions on creating a TLS encryption certificate and installing it on a CloudFront distribution.

Keep in mind that you cannot export the private key for a TLS certificate generated by ACM. This means you can't install the certificate directly on an EC2 instance or on-premises server. You can, however, import an existing TLS certificate and private key into ACM. The certificate must be valid and not expired when you import it. To use an imported certificate with CloudFront, you must import it into the us-east-1 region.

Summary

Effective security controls necessarily add more complexity to your deployment and will occasionally cause things to break. But by implementing security at every level, you can resolve those issues as you go along. Then by the time you're done, you'll be starting with an effective security posture. From that point on, it will be much easier to mitigate vulnerabilities and threats as they trickle in.

It's fine to be a little lax when initially configuring a service just to make sure everything works as expected, but as soon as you do, be sure to implement your security controls. Follow the principle of least privilege, using IAM and resource-based policies and network-based controls. Configure logging early on to make troubleshooting easier. Set up encryption prior to going live so that your data is never sent or stored in the clear. Implement notifications for key events so you know immediately when a misconfiguration, attack, or error occurs. Finally, automate as much as possible using Auto Scaling, CloudFormation, and preconfigured AMIs. Automation allows you to recover more quickly from an incident. It also reduces human intervention, thus minimizing the chances of mistakes.

Exam Essentials

Be able to configure permissions policies.   Permissions policies are the foundation of identity and resource-based policies. Understand the difference between these policies and be able to understand and create them. Identity-based policies are attached to an IAM principal such as a user or role. Resource-based policies apply to a resource and don't include the "principal" element.

Know how permissions boundaries interact with permissions policies.   Permissions boundaries define the maximum permissions an IAM principal can have. You set permissions boundaries on a per-identity basis by attaching a managed policy that defines them.

Understand roles and trust policies.   A role is a set of permissions that an IAM user, AWS service, or federated user can acquire by assuming that role. Trust policies are resource-based policies that define who can assume the role and under what conditions.

Know your options for collecting, searching, and analyzing logs.   CloudWatch Logs can consolidate logs from multiple sources, including CloudTrail, VPC flow logs, DNS query logs, and logs generated by your application. You can search logs from within CloudWatch Logs using filter patterns. For logs stored in S3, you can use Athena to search them using SQL queries.

Be able to identify use cases for GuardDuty, Inspector, Shield, and WAF.   GuardDuty analyzes various logs looking for signs of an attack. Inspector uses an agent to inspect your EC2 instances for vulnerabilities. Shield identifies and blocks well-known network-based attacks as they occur. WAF allows you to configure custom rules to block suspicious or undesirable traffic.

Understand how KMS works.   Know how to create customer master keys and set key policies. A key policy defines the key users—IAM principals who can use a key to encrypt and decrypt data. A key policy also defines the administrators of a key—those who can enable and disable a key. Key administrators can also modify the key policy.

Review Questions

1. Which of the following options can you not set in a password policy? (Choose two.)

    A. Maximum length

    B. Require the use of numbers.

    C. Prevent multiple users from using the same password.

    D. Require an administrator to reset an expired password.

2. An IAM user is attached to a customer managed policy granting them sufficient access to carry out their duties. You want to require multifactor authentication (MFA) for this user to use the AWS CLI. What element should you change in the policy?

    A. Resource

    B. Condition

    C. Action

    D. Principal

3. You created an IAM policy that another administrator subsequently modified. You need to restore the policy to its original state but don't remember how it was configured. What should you do to restore the policy? (Choose two.)

    A. Consult CloudTrail global management event logs.

    B. Restore the policy from a snapshot.

    C. Consult CloudTrail data event logs.

    D. Revert to the previous policy version.

4. An IAM user with full access to all EC2 actions in all regions assumes a role that has access to only the EC2 RunInstances operation in the us-east-1 region. What will the user be able to do under the assumed role?

    A. Create a new instance in any region.

    B. Create a new instance in the us-east-1 region.

    C. Start an existing instance in the us-east-1 region.

    D. Start an existing instance in any region

5. Several objects in a S3 bucket are encrypted using a KMS customer master key. Which of the following will give an IAM user permission to decrypt these objects?

    A. Add the user to the key policy as a key user.

    B. Grant the user access to the key using an IAM policy.

    C. Add the user to the key policy as a key administrator.

    D. Add the user as a principal to the bucket policy.

6. You run a public-facing application on EC2 instances. The application is backed by a database running on RDS. Users access it using multiple domain names that are hosted in Route 53. You want to get an idea of what IP addresses are accessing your application. Which of the following would you stream to CloudWatch Logs to get this information?

    A. RDS logs

    B. DNS query logs

    C. VPC flow logs

    D. CloudTrail logs

7. You're running a web server that keeps a detailed log of web requests. You want to determine which IP address has made the most requests in the last 24 hours. What should you do to accomplish this? (Choose two.)

    A. Create a metric filter.

    B. Stream the web server logs to CloudWatch Logs.

    C. Upload the web server log to S3

    D. Use Athena to query the data.

8. An application running on an EC2 instance has been updated to send large amounts of data to a server in your data center for backup. Previously, the instance generated very little traffic. Which GuardDuty finding type is this likely to trigger?

    A. Behavior

    B. Backdoor

    C. Stealth

    D. ResourceConsumption

9. You've set up an AWS Config managed rule to check whether a particular security group is attached to every instance in a VPC. You receive an SNS notification that an instance is out of compliance. But when you check the instance a few hours later, the security group is attached. Which of the following may help explain the apparent discrepancy? (Choose two.)

    A. The AWS Config timeline

    B. Lambda logs

    C. CloudTrail management event logs

    D. VPC flow logs

10. You want to use Amazon Inspector to analyze the security posture of your EC2 instances running Windows. Which rules package should you not use in your assessment?

    A. Common Vulnerabilities and Exposures

    B. Center for Internet Security Benchmarks

    C. Runtime Behavior Analysis

    D. Security Best Practices

11. You have a distributed application running in data centers around the world. The application connects to a public Simple Queue Service (SQS) endpoint to send messages to a queue. How can you prevent an attacker from using this endpoint to gain unauthorized access to the queue? (Choose two.)

   A. Network access control lists

   B. Security groups

   C. IAM policies

   D. SQS access policies

12. You're using a public-facing application load balancer to forward traffic to EC2 instances in an Auto Scaling group. What can you do to ensure users on the Internet can reach the load balancer over HTTPS without reaching your instances directly? (Choose two.)

   A. Create a security group that allows all inbound traffic to TCP port 443.

   B. Attach the security group to the instances.

   C. Attach the security group to the load balancer.

   D. Remove the internet gateway from the VPC.

   E. Create a security group that allows all inbound traffic to TCP port 80.

13. You're running a UDP-based application on an EC2 instance. How can you protect it against a DDoS attack?

   A. Place the instance behind a network load balancer.

   B. Implement a security group to restrict inbound access to the instance.

   C. Place the instance behind an application load balancer.

   D. Enable AWS Shield Standard.

14. You're running a web application on six EC2 instances behind a network load balancer. The web application uses a MySQL database. How can you protect your application against SQL injection attacks?

   A. Enable WAF.

   B. Assign elastic IP addresses to the instances.

   C. Place the instances behind an application load balancer.

   D. Block TCP port 3306.

15. Which services protect against an HTTP flood attack?

   A. GuardDuty

   B. WAF

   C. Shield Standard

   D. Shield Advanced

16. Your security policy requires that you use a KMS key for encrypting S3 objects. It further requires this key be rotated once a year and revoked when misuse is detected. Which key type should you use? (Choose two.)

    A. Customer-managed CMK

    B. AWS-managed CMK

    C. S3-managed key

    D. Customer-provided key

17. A developer is designing an application to run on AWS and has asked for your input in deciding whether to use a SQL database or DynamoDB for storing highly transactional application data. Your security policy requires all application data to be encrypted and encryption keys to be rotated every 90 days. Which AWS service should you recommend for storing application data?

    A. KMS

    B. RedShift

    C. DynamoDB

    D. RDS

18. You need to copy the data from an unencrypted EBS volume to another region and encrypt it. How can you accomplish this? (Choose two.)

    A. Create an encrypted snapshot of the unencrypted volume.

    B. Simultaneously encrypt and copy the snapshot to the destination region.

    C. Copy the encrypted snapshot to the destination region.

    D. Create an unencrypted snapshot of the unencrypted volume.

19. An instance with an unencrypted EBS volume has an unencrypted EFS filesystem mounted on it. You need to encrypt the data on an existing EFS filesystem using a KMS key. How can you accomplish this?

    A. Encrypt the EBS volume of the instance.

    B. Create a new encrypted EFS filesystem and copy the data to it.

    C. Enable encryption on the existing EFS filesystem.

    D. Use a third-party encryption program to encrypt the data.

20. On which of the following can you not use an ACM-generated TLS certificate? (Choose two.)

    A. An S3 bucket

    B. A CloudFront distribution

    C. An Application Load Balancer

    D. An EC2 instance

Chapter

12

The Cost Optimization Pillar

THE AWS CERTIFIED SOLUTIONS ARCHITECT ASSOCIATE EXAM OBJECTIVES COVERED IN THIS CHAPTER MAY INCLUDE, BUT ARE NOT LIMITED TO, THE FOLLOWING:

Domain 4: Design Cost-Optimized Architectures

✓ 4.1   Determine how to design cost-optimized storage.

✓ 4.2   Determine how to design cost-optimized compute.

Introduction

Through the previous chapters of this book you've explored many AWS cost planning basics. In Chapter 3, "Amazon Simple Storage Service and Amazon Glacier Storage," for instance, you learned how to leverage different data storage classes to ensure the instant access you need for your newer data using, say, the S3 Standard class while using the lower costs available for high-latency, long-term storage (using S3 Reduced Redundancy or Glacier) of older objects.

You're no doubt also familiar with the Free Tier available on AWS accounts within their first year. The Free Tier makes it possible to experiment with light versions of just about any combination of AWS resources until you find the perfect stack for your application. Used right, the tier can help you build excellent solutions architect skills without costing you anything. Don't be shy: use it.

But you're not quite there yet.

Even if you do everything right and design the perfect, multitiered, scalable, and highly available application environment, it'll be a complete waste if it ends up costing too much. No plan is complete without a solid cost assessment. And even if you did make it all happen for the right price, are you sure nothing expensive has accidentally been left running on any of the accounts under your control or you haven't been compromised by hackers?

The best protection from unpleasant surprises is through understanding how you're billed for using AWS services, how you can deploy resources in the most cost-effective way, and how you can automate cost event alerting protocols.

That's what you'll learn about here.

Planning, Tracking, and Controlling Costs

The place to find account-level financial information is the Billing and Cost Management Dashboard, which is accessed via the My Billing Dashboard link in the account drop-down menu at the top of the console. That's where you can view past bills, manage credits, and enter your tax registration information. The page also includes a quick visual overview of the current month's cost activities.

Right now, however, you're more interested in how the Billing and Cost Management Dashboard also links you to tools you'll use to monitor and control your AWS spending. The precise function of these tools—and even the names AWS gives them—will probably change over time. But their overall goal is clear: to provide deep insight into what your running resources are costing you and how you can closely track them.

AWS Budgets

The Preferences link takes you to a simple page where you choose the way you'd like to consume billing information. You can tell AWS to send ongoing *billing reports* to an S3 bucket you specify. You can also have AWS email you *billing alerts* created through either Amazon CloudWatch Alarms (as you saw in Chapter 7, "CloudTrail, CloudWatch, and AWS Config") or the newer AWS Budgets.

Budgets are meant to track your ongoing resource-related usage and costs and alert you if projected usage levels fall outside of a predefined threshold. You could, for instance, have an email sent alerting you when the total quarterly costs of transferring S3-based data between regions threatens to rise above a certain dollar amount. Or you could create a budget to tell you when the total volume of outbound data transferred to the Internet from On Demand EC2 instances running in a specified AWS region exceeds, say, 100GB.

You can create and apply *cost allocation tags* to your resources and use them in your budgets as filters. This will let you limit your alerts to only those resources belonging to a particular class. You could use this kind of filtering to track only your staging or development environments, but not production.

You can activate and manage tags from the Cost Allocation Tags page, which is accessed by clicking the Cost Allocation Tags link in Billing. User-defined tags can be created and managed using the Tag Editor accessed through the Resource Groups drop-down menu in the AWS Console. You use that page to find active resources such as EC2 instances and S3 buckets and then create and/or edit tags for those resources. Note the following:

- Tags can take up to 24 hours before they appear in the Billing and Cost Management Dashboard.

- Tags can't be applied to resources that were launched before the tags were created.

You're allowed two free budgets per account. Subsequent tags will cost around $0.02 each per month.

You configure a budget by defining whether you want to track resource cost, usage, or—to be sure you're getting optimal value from your EC2 reserve instances—reserve instance utilization or reserve instance coverage. You can narrow the scope of a budget by filtering it using parameters such as services, regions, tags, and usage type. Notification triggers are defined when thresholds are met (for instance, "Forecasted usage is greater than 80 percent of the budgeted amount") and are sent to Simple Notification Service (SNS) or email addresses.

Exercise 12.1 shows you how to configure a simple budget to protect an account from unexpected, unauthorized, and expensive activity.

EXERCISE 12.1

Create an AWS Budget to Send an Alert

1. Click the Budgets link in the Billing and Cost Management console and then click Create Budget.

2. Select the Cost budget option and click Set your budget.

3. Give your budget a name (something descriptive like "Monthly-Limit" might work well). Select Monthly for the Period and select the Recurring Budget radio button. That will run the budget each month indefinitely. For this exercise, enter, say 100 for as the Budgeted Amount. That will be interpreted as a dollar value. Similarly, leave all the Aggregate Costs values checked. When you're done, click Configure alerts.

4. Set the Actual Costs radio button for Send alert based on, and enter 80 in the Alert threshold, while selecting % of budgeted amount from the drop down menu. Type your email address in the Email Contacts field, and click Create.

    Once you've set this up, you'll receive an email alert whenever your account resources have generated more than $80 (80% of your $100 value for the Budgeted Amount).

    If you don't need the budget you just created, select its entry in the Dashboard and delete it to make sure you're not billed for it.

Monitoring Tools

You've seen how to set limits to control your AWS spending using budget alerts. But the busier and more complicated your resource stacks get, the more you'll need to dive deeply into spending patterns so you can understand and, if necessary, adjust developing trends. Cost Explorer and Reports can help with that.

Cost Explorer

Clicking Cost Explorer from the Billing and Cost Management Dashboard, and then on Launch Cost Explorer, takes you to a detailed visualization of your historical AWS usage and costs. The default view covers the last six months and, by clicking the Explore costs link, can be filtered by a prominent Usage Type Group metric (like EC2: Running Hours).

The more you have running, you more you'll want to drill down into the weeds of the data. You can adjust the view, filtering by things such as grouping or service, or download the data as a CSV file.

Clicking New Report lets you open a report template, including Reserve Instance (RI) Utilization or RI Coverage—relevant, obviously, only if you've purchased reserve instances.

AWS Cost and Usage Reports

At first glance, the content delivered by Cost and Usage Reports seems to overlap a bit with Cost Explorer. After all, they both provide data covering your billing costs, rates, and product and pricing attributes.

However, the unique value proposition of Reports is hinted to in the Select Content page of the Report creation process. There, you can choose to enable support for either Redshift or QuickSight. Redshift, as you know, is a serious tool for handling serious amounts of data. And Amazon QuickSight is a pay-per-session tool for squeezing business intelligence out of data stores.

So, AWS Reports are meant for accounts that are so busy you struggle to keep track of many moving parts. Reports are optimized for this kind of analytics through their normalized data model that organizes discrete cost components in individual columns.

Reports are configured to be regularly written to an S3 bucket in your account for which you've previously added appropriate permissions. Sample bucket policies are available from the Create Report dialog.

The Report configuration process replaces a few deprecated (and soon to be removed) "other" reports.

AWS Organizations

You can consolidate the management of multiple AWS accounts using AWS Organizations. Why bother? Because it's not uncommon for larger organizations to have so many projects and resources running on AWS that they need some degree of resource isolation to keep a handle on them. It can also be hugely convenient to maintain some level of bird's-eye-view supervision over the whole thing—and to channel billing through a single payer.

AWS Organizations lets you create new accounts and invite existing accounts into an organization. Once your accounts are connected, the organization administration can create global access policies much the same way as you might for individual users within a single account.

Account security for an organization is even more critical than for a single account since a breach could potentially impact all the resources in all member accounts. You should therefore be especially careful to enforce all the normal security best practices, including multifactor authorization (MFA), strong passwords, and secured root accounts.

AWS Organizations has replaced the old and deprecated Consolidated Billing tool.

AWS Trusted Advisor

You can get a quick view of how closely your account configurations are currently following AWS best practices from the Trusted Advisor Dashboard (accessed from the main AWS service menu). The compliance and health data is divided into five categories.

- Cost Optimization checks for underutilized or running but idle resources that might be costing you money.

- Performance checks for configuration mismatches—such as excessive use of EBS magnetic volumes—that might unnecessarily impact performance.

- Security checks for potentially vulnerable configurations, such as wide open S3 bucket permissions or security groups.

- Fault Tolerance checks for appropriate replication and redundancy configurations to ensure that a single service failure would be unlikely to cause you a catastrophic loss.

- Service Limits checks for your usage of AWS services to make sure you're not approaching default limits.

The results of each check are color coded to tell you whether you're compliant and are accompanied by a helpful description of the issue. Sometimes, for an S3 bucket-hosted static website that needs open permissions, for instance, you'll want to ignore the warning. But it's nevertheless important to regularly check in with Trusted Advisor to see whether it's caught anything new.

The first thing you'll notice when you visit Trusted Advisor is that most of the metrics are disabled unless you upgrade your support—to either the Business or Enterprise plan.

Online Calculator Tools

One powerful way to model the cost of multiple resource stacks is by gathering comprehensive pricing information and using it to calculate the price tag for each element of a stack. However, when you consider just how many permutations and combinations of services and price levels can coexist within a single stack—and how often those prices change—then accurate *cost modeling* can feel impossibly complicated.

Fortunately, AWS provides two regularly updated calculators that do all the number crunching for you: the Simple Monthly Calculator and the AWS TCO Calculator.

Simple Monthly Calculator

The Simple Monthly Calculator (https://calculator.s3.amazonaws.com/index.html) lets you select service resources at a fine detail (three EC2 instances built on a Linux m4.large instance type with a 500 GB Provisioned IOPS SSD EBS volume set for 1,000 IOPS in the US East N. Virginia region, for example). You can also enter the portion of a month you expect your instance to actually be running.

You should be aware that costs can differ between AWS regions, so make sure you price resources within each of the regions that would, practically, work for your application. The same applies to different EBS and RDS storage types: explore pricing for SSD, Provisioned IOPS, and other storage types.

When you're done entering the stack resources from every relevant service your project will use, the estimated monthly bill will appear in the tab at the top of the page. Clicking that tab will provide a fully itemized breakdown of the monthly cost of your stack, which can be downloaded in CSV format. Saving your estimate will generate a URL that can be shared with colleagues or clients.

The beautiful thing about the monthly calculator—as you'll see for yourself while working through Exercise 12.2—is how closely it mirrors the experience of selecting and then running AWS resources. If you haven't built an accurate cost simulation of a complicated stack you're planning, then you're probably setting yourself up for some surprises later when painful monthly billing statements show up.

EXERCISE 12.2

Build Your Own Stack in Simple Monthly Calculator

1. Start a fresh calculation at https://calculator.s3.amazonaws.com/index.html. Click Reset All if necessary and deselect the FREE USAGE TIER box at the top

2. Within the US West (Oregon region), click the Amazon EC2 tab on the left and click the plus sign next to the first Add New Row. Select two instances running **120** hours (5 days) a week of a Linux c5d.xlarge instance type. Leave the Billing Option setting as On-Demand.

3. Add two general-purpose EBS volumes of **100** GB each and, in the Data Transfer section, add **200** GB of Data Transfer In and **400** GB of Data Transfer Out. Feel free to click the Estimate tab at the top.

4. From the Services tab once again, click the Amazon S3 link on the left. Enter **200** GB of storage, **250000** PUT Requests, and **1000000** GET Requests for S3 Standard Storage And Requests. Enter **600** GB of storage, and use 10 Lifecycle Transitions for S3 Standard – Infrequent Access (S3 Standard-IA) Storage & Requests.

5. Enter **400** GB/month of Data Transfer Out on the Amazon CloudFront tab.

6. On the Amazon Elastic Load Balancing tab, enter **1** for Number Of Application LBs, **5** for Avg Number Of New Connections/sec Per ALB, **300** seconds for Avg Connection Duration, and **400** GB for Total Data Processed Per ALB.

7. Now take a good look at the itemized bill in the Estimate tab. Just for comparison, my total came to around $320/month.

AWS Total Cost of Ownership Calculator

The "other" AWS calculator (https://aws.amazon.com/tco-calculator/) estimates the total cost of ownership (TCO) to help you make an apples-to-apples comparison of what a complex workload would cost on-premises as opposed to what it would cost on the AWS cloud. The interface asks you to define the infrastructure you'd need to run your application locally. You'll enter the number and size of the servers, whether they're physical or virtual, which virtualization hypervisor you'll be using (if applicable), and the total storage capacity you'll need.

When you run the calculation you'll be shown a highly detailed itemized cost sheet calculated over 3 years. The output will include estimates of on-premises networking and hardware acquisition costs along with AWS support costs, and a detailed explanation of the calculator's methodology and assumptions.

Cost-Optimizing Compute

Perhaps more than anything else, the virtualization revolution makes greatly increased server density possible. That is, you can run more compute workloads sharing the physical assets of a single server than ever before. And of course, getting "more production out of a server" is just another way of saying "getting more value for your investment."

Since cloud computing platforms like AWS live and breathe virtualization, you might assume that following AWS best practices can help you get the most out of your assets. And you'd be correct.

Here's where I'll spend some time talking about squeezing every drop of digital goodness out of your AWS infrastructure. You'll explore some basic server density tricks such as selecting the EC2 instance type that's the best match for your workload, and, although I introduced them in Chapter 2, "Amazon Elastic Compute Cloud and Amazon Elastic Block Store," I'll dive a bit deeper into effectively using reserved and spot instances.

Maximizing Server Density

You have a keen interest in getting the most out of a server instance—whether it's for an application running on EC2 or a database with AWS Relational Database Service (RDS). Matching your workload to the right instance type can make a big difference not only in performance but also in overall cost.

The M5 instance type family, for instance, is optimized to take advantage of the higher core counts found on Intel Xeon Scalable processors. You can typically pack multiple resource-hungry workloads onto a single, high-end M5 instance (like the m5.24xlarge type), potentially requiring fewer instances overall. Similarly, the high-performing and parallel processing NVIDIA K80 GPU cores, enhanced networking, and default EBS optimization of a single P2 instance can often replace multiple instances of other families for high-demand analytics and machine learning workloads.

The features unique to each EC2 instance type are detailed and compared at https://aws.amazon.com/ec2/instance-types/.

AWS Lambda also provides a kind of server density: it may not be *your* server resources you're conserving by running Lambda functions, but you're certainly getting a lot more value from your compute dollar by following the "serverless" model.

The flexibility potential of virtualization is nowhere more obvious than with container technologies like Docker. Whether you're running Docker clusters on Amazon's Elastic Container Service (ECS—see Chapter 2), running the Amazon Elastic Container Service for Kubernetes (Amazon EKS), or manually provisioning your own EC2 instances as Docker hosts, you'll be able to tightly pack virtual applications or microservices into every corner of your host hardware.

EC2 Reserved Instances

You learned about purchasing reserved instances (RIs) for 24/7 compute needs lasting at least 12 months in Chapter 2. But spending a few extra minutes on some of the finer details will help you make smarter and more effective choices.

The basics are straightforward: you can have AWS set aside lower-cost, long-term compute capacity for you by purchasing a reserved instance. (You're not actually "purchasing" something called a *reserved instance*; instead, you're just buying the right to use a regular EC2 instance.) You can also purchase an instance through the Amazon EC2 Reserved Instance Marketplace, where you effectively take over the time remaining on a reserved instance owned by other AWS users who have changed their usage plans. Just as you would when launching a normal EC2 instance, you select an RI that matches the configuration details you're after. Therefore, you'll search by tenancy (default or dedicated), instance type, and platform (choosing from OSs including Linux, SUSE, RHEL, Microsoft Windows Server, and Microsoft SQL Server).

However, exactly how much money you'll save on your instance and how much flexibility it'll give you depends on decisions you make up front. You can, for example, pay a bit more for a *Convertible* RI that will allow you to exchange your instance later as long as the new instance has equal or great value than the original. Convertible RIs provide a discount of up to 54 percent less than on-demand. A Standard RI can save you up to 75 percent off on-demand, while, obviously, locking you in for the duration of the term to the instance profile you initially selected.

Optionally, you can also specify a single availability zone or, for a cost premium, maintain the flexibility to run your RI in any AZ within your selected region.

You can also schedule an RI to launch within a specified recurring time window. You purchase on a schedule from the Scheduled Instances link in the EC2 Dashboard (rather than the regular Reserved Instances link).

Finally, you can pay for your RI using any one of three payment options: All Upfront (the lowest price), Partial Upfront, and No Upfront (billed hourly).

EC2 Spot Instances

In Chapter 2, you also learned about EC2 spot instances—short-term "rentals" of EC2 instances that offer very low prices in exchange for volatile lifecycles and unpredictable shutdowns. As you just did with RIs, let's look at the details. I'll begin with a few important definitions.

- **Spot Price**—The current going rate for spot instances of a given set of launch specifications (type, region, and profile values). Spot prices can rise or fall without warning, sometimes forcing a running instance to shut down.

- **Spot Instance Interruption**—You can choose one of three ways for EC2 to react when your maximum price is exceeded by the spot price: Terminate (permanently delete all associated resources and volumes), Stop (possible only when you're using an EBS-backed AMI), and Hibernate.

- **Spot Instance Pool**—All the unused EC2 instances matching a particular set of launch specifications. Spot fleets are drawn from matching spot instance pools.

- **Spot Fleet**—A group of spot instances (sometimes including on-demand instances) that is launched to meet a spot fleet request. A spot fleet can be made up of instances using multiple launch specifications drawn from multiple spot instance pools.

- **Request Type**—When you configure your request from the Request Spot Instances page, you're offered three request types: Request (a one-time instance request), Request And Maintain (to maintain target capacity using a fleet), and Reserve For Duration (request an uninterrupted instance for between one and six hours).

You can configure your request for spot instances from the EC2 Dashboard. You use the Request Spot Instances page to set details such as your total target capacity (the maximum instances or vCPUs you want running), the AMI and instance type you want launched, whether you want to incorporate load balancing, and any user data you want to pass to your instances at launch time.

You can define your workload by using a private AMI you built for the task or by passing user data (the way you did for yourself in Exercise 10.1 from Chapter 10, "The Performance Efficiency Pillar").

The Spot Advisor, which is available from the Spot Instances Dashboard, can helpfully recommend sample configuration profiles for a few common tasks. Once you accept a recommendation, you can either customize it or send it right to the fleet configuration stage with a single click.

Why not work through Exercise 12.3 to see how you can request a simple spot fleet using the AWS CLI?

EXERCISE 12.3

Request a Spot Fleet Using the AWS CLI

1. Before you'll be able to launch your spot request using the AWS CLI, you'll need to gather some information from your AWS account.

2. From the Quick Start tab in the EC2 Launch Instance dialog, copy the AMI ID of, say, the Ubuntu LTS AMI and save it: you'll need it later.

3. From the VPC Dashboard, click the Subnets link on the left and then note the subnet IDs of two subnets in a VPC (your default VPC should work fine). While still in the VPC

Dashboard, click Security Groups and note the group ID of a security group that fits the permissions your spot instances will require. Since this is only a simple demo, anything will do. If there aren't any existing groups, create a new one.

4. Now you'll need to create an IAM role that will give the spot manager permission to start and stop EC2 instances. From the IAM Roles page, click Create Role, select AWS Service, select EC2, and then select EC2 – Fleet. Then click Next: Permissions.

5. You'll see the AWSEC2FleetServiceRolePolicy on the next screen. Click Next: Review. You can add a suffix to the role name if you like and then create the role. You'll see your new role in the list of IAM roles. Click it and copy its ARN.

6. With all that done, create a `Config.json` file that looks something like this (using the correct values from your account):

```
{
    "SpotPrice": "0.04",
    "TargetCapacity": 2,
    "IamFleetRole": "arn:aws:iam::123456789012:role/my-spot-fleet-role",
    "LaunchSpecifications": [
        {
            "ImageId": "ami-1a2b3c4d",
            "SecurityGroups": [
                {
                    "GroupId": "sg-1a2b3c4d"
                }
            ],
            "InstanceType": "t2-micro",
            "SubnetId": "subnet-1a2b3c4d, subnet-3c4d5e6f",
        }
    ]
}
```

7. Now run this CLI command pointing to the `Config.json` file you just created:

```
aws ec2 request-spot-fleet \
    --spot-fleet-request-config file://Config.json
```

8. The AWS CLI may complain about errors, so carefully read the messages and go back to figure out what went wrong. When the command returns only a spot fleet ID that looks something like the following output example, you'll know you were successful:

```
{
    "SpotFleetRequestId": "sfr-6b8225fe-b6d2-4c58-94d7-d14fdd7877be"
}
```

9. That alone is no proof that everything is running properly. You should head over to the Spot Requests page of the EC2 Dashboard and select the entry for your fleet. Click the History tab in the bottom half of the page and look for messages. Correct any errors that might appear and, if necessary, cancel your request and launch a new one with your corrected configuration.

10. Don't forget to shut down your resources when you're done with them.

Auto Scaling

You've already learned about efficiently increasing your compute resources to meet demand using Auto Scaling. But don't forget that an Auto Scaling configuration should also be set to scale your instances *down* as demand drops. You do this by configuring the scaler to decrease the group size when the average usage of your running instances drops below a set threshold. This can make a big difference to your costs and is one of the greatest benefits of the entire cloud computing model.

Elastic Block Store Lifecycle Manager

The EBS volumes attached to your EC2 instances are well protected by replication, but, like all technology, there's no guarantee that *nothing* bad will ever happen. The best practice has always been to back up your volumes by making snapshots, but adding a new snapshot every few hours can, over time, add up to some intimidating storage costs.

The obvious solution is to delete older snapshots, leaving only fresher copies online. Since, however, you're not likely to get around to regularly doing that on your own, you're better off automating. The EBS Lifecycle Manager (accessed through the EC2 Dashboard) lets you create a rotation policy where you set the frequency at which new snapshots will be created and the maximum number of snapshots to retain.

Summary

AWS budgets can be created to watch all or selected areas of your account usage and alert you when costs approach specified thresholds. You can use cost allocation tags to efficiently focus your budgets on subsets of your running resources.

You can track historical billing costs, rates, and product attributes using both Cost Explorer and Cost and Usage Reports. Reports, however, is designed for the kind of big data analytics needed by particular large-scale operations.

You can consolidate billing and access management administration of multiple accounts belonging to a single owner using AWS Organizations.

AWS Trusted Advisor monitors and reports on your account configuration status as it relates to best practices and account limits. The Simple Monthly Calculator and AWS Total Cost of Ownership are important tools for helping you find the most cost-effective and efficient way to build your application stack.

Matching the right EC2 instance type and, where appropriate, running container workloads, are effective ways to maximize your use—and minimize the costs—of server resources.

Your use of EC2 reserved instances can be optimized by selecting a convertible RI for greater long-term flexibility and by scheduling reserve availability for recurring blocks of time.

Spot instances can be requested individually or as a fleet and can be set to react to shutdowns in ways that best fit your specific application needs.

Exam Essentials

Know how to effectively monitor costs incurred by your AWS account resource use.   AWS offers multiple tools to track your billing and usage activity to help you anticipate and prevent overages, spot and understand usage trends, and deeply analyze usage data. Tracking tools include Budgets, Cost Explorer, Cost and Usage Reports, and Trusted Advisor.

Know how to simulate and anticipate the costs of AWS application stacks.   The Simple Monthly Calculator lets you quickly model multiple alternative resource stacks to accurately estimate and compare costs. The AWS Total Cost of Ownership calculator is built to closely compare the cost of deploying an application stack on AWS versus the costs you'd face doing it on-premises.

Understand how to match your application to the right EC2 instance type.   An EC2 instance type is built on a hardware profile that makes it particularly efficient for certain kinds of workloads. You should be familiar with at least the general instance family categories and their use cases.

EC2 reserved instances can be configured for a wide range of uses.   You can reserve RIs as Convertible to allow you to exchange your instance type with another one during the reservation term or to permit use in any availability zone within your region. You can also schedule recurring time blocks for your RI.

Spot fleets can be requested to provide multiple concurrent instances.   Complex combinations of multiple customized spot instances can be configured using prebuilt AMIs, durable capacity preferences, and lifecycle behavior.

Review Questions

1. Which of the following best describes the AWS Free Tier?
    A. Free access to AWS services for a new account's first month
    B. Free access to all instance types of AWS EC2 instances for new accounts
    C. Free access to basic levels of AWS services for a new account's first year
    D. Unlimited and open-ended access to the "free tier" of most AWS services

2. Which of the following storage classes provides the least expensive storage *and* transfer rates?
    A. Amazon Glacier
    B. Amazon S3 Standard-Infrequent Access
    C. Amazon S3 Standard
    D. Amazon S3 One Zone-Infrequent Access

3. Which AWS service is best suited to controlling your spending by sending email alerts?
    A. Cost Explorer
    B. Budgets
    C. Organizations
    D. TCO Calculator

4. Which AWS service is best suited to analyzing account usage data at scale?
    A. Trusted Advisor
    B. Cost Explorer
    C. Budgets
    D. Cost and Usage Reports

5. Your company wants to more closely coordinate the administration of its multiple AWS accounts, and AWS Organizations can help it do that. How does that change your security profile? (Choose three.)
    A. An organization-level administration account breach is potentially more damaging.
    B. User permissions can be controlled centrally at the organization level.
    C. You should upgrade to use only specially hardened organization-level VPCs.
    D. Standard security best practices such as MFA and strong passwords are even more essential.

6. Which of the following resource states are monitored by AWS Trusted Advisor? (Choose two.)
    A. Route 53 routing failures
    B. Running but idle EC2 instances
    C. S3 buckets with open permissions
    D. EC2 Linux instances that allow root account SSH access

7. You're planning a new AWS deployment, and your team is debating whether they'll be better off using an RDS database or one run on an EC2 instance. Which of the following tools will be most helpful?

    A. TCO Calculator

    B. Simple Monthly Calculator

    C. Trusted Advisor

    D. Cost and Usage Reports

8. Which of the following is not a metric you can configure an AWS budget to track?

    A. EBS volume capacity

    B. Resource usage

    C. Reserve instance coverage

    D. Resource cost

9. Which of the following statements are true of cost allocation tags? (Choose two.)

    A. Tags can take up to 24 hours before they appear in the Billing and Cost Management Dashboard.

    B. Tags can't be applied to resources that were launched before the tags were created.

    C. You're allowed five free budgets per account.

    D. You can activate and manage cost allocation tags from the Tag Editor page.

10. Your online web store normally requires three EC2 instances to handle traffic but experiences double the load each year for the two summer months. Which of the following approaches makes the most sense?

    A. Run three on-demand instances 12 months per year and schedule six reserve instances for the summer months.

    B. Run three spot instances for the summer months and three reserve instances 12 months/year.

    C. Run nine reserve instances for 12 months/year.

    D. Run three reserve instances 12 months/year and schedule six reserve instances for the summer months.

11. Which of the following settings do you *not* need to provide when configuring a reserved instance?

    A. Payment option

    B. Standard or Convertible RI

    C. Interruption policy

    D. Tenancy

12. Which of the following payment options is the most expensive when configuring a reserve instance?

    A. All Upfront

    B. Partial Upfront

    C. No Upfront

    D. Monthly

13. Which of the following benefits of containers such as Docker can significantly reduce your AWS compute costs? (Choose two.)

    A. Containers can launch quickly.

    B. Containers can deliver increased server density.

    C. Containers make it easy to reliably replicate server environments.

    D. Containers can run using less memory than physical machines.

14. Which of the following EC2 instance use-case scenarios makes the best use case for a reserved instance?

    A. An application that will run continuously for six months straight

    B. An application that will run continuously for 36 months straight

    C. An application that runs only during local business hours

    D. An application that runs at unpredictable times and can survive unexpected shutdowns

15. Which of the following describes "unused EC2 instances matching a particular set of launch specifications"?

    A. Request type

    B. Spot instance interruption

    C. Spot fleet

    D. Spot instance pool

16. Which of the following best describes a spot instance interruption?

    A. A spot instance interruption occurs when the spot price rises above your maximum.

    B. A spot instance interruption is the termination of a spot Instance when its workload completes.

    C. A spot instance interruption occurs when a spot request is manually restarted.

    D. A spot instance interruption is the result of a temporary outage in an AWS data center.

17. Which of the following describes the maximum instances or vCPUs you want running?

    A. Spot instance pool

    B. Target capacity

    C. Spot maximum

    D. Spot cap

18. Which of the following best describes the function of the Spot Advisor?

    A. To recommend sample configuration profiles for a few common tasks

    B. To help you choose the best Amazon Machine Image (AMI)

    C. To guide you to the right EBS volume profile

    D. To help you set up an instance health check

19. Which of these AWS CLI commands will launch a spot fleet?

   A. `aws ec2 request-fleet --spot-fleet-request-config file://Config.json`

   B. `aws ec2 spot-fleet --spot-fleet-request-config file://Config.json`

   C. `aws ec2 launch-spot-fleet --spot-fleet-request-config file://Config.json`

   D. `aws ec2 request-spot-fleet --spot-fleet-request-config file://Config.json`

20. Which of the following elements is not something you'd include in your spot fleet request?

   A. Availability zone

   B. Target capacity

   C. Platform (the instance OS)

   D. AMI

Chapter 13

The Operational Excellence Pillar

THE AWS CERTIFIED SOLUTIONS ARCHITECT ASSOCIATE EXAM OBJECTIVES COVERED IN THIS CHAPTER MAY INCLUDE, BUT ARE NOT LIMITED TO, THE FOLLOWING:

Domain 5: Define Operationally-Excellent Architectures

✓ 5.1 Choose design features in solutions that enable operational excellence.

Introduction

Operations include the ongoing activities required to keep your applications running smoothly and securely on AWS. Achieving operational excellence requires automating some or all of the tasks that support your organization's workloads, goals, and compliance requirements.

The key prerequisite to automating is to define your infrastructure and operations as annotated code. Unlike manual tasks, which can be time-consuming and are prone to human error, tasks embodied in code are repeatable and can be carried out rapidly. It's also easier to track code changes over time and repurpose it for testing and experimentation. For us humans, annotated code also functions as de facto documentation of your infrastructure configurations and operational workflows.

In this chapter, you'll learn how to leverage the following AWS services to automate the deployment and operation of your AWS resources:

- CloudFormation
- AWS Developer Tools, which include the following:
  - CodeCommit
  - CodeDeploy
  - CodePipeline
- AWS Systems Manager

CloudFormation

As you learned in Chapter 10, "The Performance Efficiency Pillar," CloudFormation uses templates to let you simultaneously deploy, configure, and document your infrastructure as code. Because CloudFormation templates are code, you can store them in a version-controlled repository just as you would any other codebase. The resources defined by a template compose a *stack*. When you create a stack, you must give it a name that's unique within the account.

One advantage of CloudFormation is that you can use the same template to build multiple identical environments. For example, you can use a single template to define and deploy two different stacks for an application, one for production and another for development. This would ensure both environments are as alike as possible.

In this section, we'll consider two templates: `network-stack.json` and `web-stack.json`. To download these templates, visit `https://www.wiley.com/go/sybextestprep`, follow the instructions to log in, and then click to the resource page for this book.

Creating Stacks

In a CloudFormation template, you define your resources in the Resources section of the template. You give each resource an identifier called a *logical ID*. For example, the following snippet of the `network-stack.json` template defines a VPC with the logical ID of `PublicVPC`:

```
"Resources": {
        "PublicVPC": {
            "Type": "AWS::EC2::VPC",
            "Properties": {
                "EnableDnsSupport": "true",
                "EnableDnsHostnames": "true",
                "CidrBlock": "10.0.0.0/16"
            }
        }
    }
```

The logical ID, also sometimes called the *logical name*, must be unique within a template. The VPC created by CloudFormation will have a VPC ID, such as `vpc-0380494054677f4b8`, also known as the *physical ID*.

CloudFormation can read templates only from an S3 bucket. You can keep your templates anywhere, but for CloudFormation to use them, they must be in an S3 bucket. To create a stack named `Network` using a template stored in an S3 bucket, you can issue the AWS command-line interface (CLI) command in the following format:

```
aws cloudformation create-stack --stack-name Network --template-url
https://s3.amazonaws.com/cf-templates-c23z8b2vpmbb-us-east-1/network-stack.json
```

You can optionally define *parameters* in a template. A parameter lets you pass custom values to your stack when you create it, as opposed to hard-coding values into the template. For instance, instead of hard-coding the Classless Interdomain Routing (CIDR) block into a template that creates a VPC, you can define a parameter that will prompt for a CIDR when creating the stack.

Stack names and logical IDs are case-sensitive.

Deleting Stacks

You can delete a stack from the web console or the AWS command-line interface (CLI). For instance, to delete the stack named Network, issue the following command:

```
aws cloudformation delete-stack --stack-name Network
```

If termination protection is not enabled on the stack, CloudFormation will immediately delete the stack and all resources that were created by it.

Using Multiple Stacks

You don't have to define all of your AWS infrastructure in a single stack. Instead, you can break your infrastructure across different stacks. A best practice is to organize stacks by lifecycle and ownership. For example, the network team may create a stack named Network to define the networking infrastructure for a web-based application. The network infrastructure would include a virtual private cloud (VPC), subnets, Internet gateway, and a route table. The development team may create a stack named Web to define the runtime environment, including a launch template, Auto Scaling group, application load balancer, IAM roles, instance profile, and a security group. Each of these teams can maintain their own stack.

When using multiple stacks with related resources, it's common to need to pass values from one stack to another. For example, an application load balancer in the Web stack needs the logical ID of the VPC in the Network stack. You therefore need a way to pass the VPC's logical ID from the Network stack to the Web stack. There are two ways to accomplish this: using nested stacks and exporting stack output values.

Nesting Stacks

Because CloudFormation stacks are AWS resources, you can configure a template to create additional stacks. These additional stacks are called *nested stacks*, and the stack that creates them is called the *parent stack*. To see how this works, we'll consider the network-stack.json and web-stack.json templates.

In the template for the Web stack (web-stack.json), you'd define the template for the Network stack as a resource, as shown by the following snippet:

```
"Resources": {
      "NetworkStack" : {
          "Type" : "AWS::CloudFormation::Stack",
          "Properties" : {
              "TemplateURL" : "https://s3.amazonaws.com/cf-templates-
c23z8b2vpmbb-us-east-1/network-stack.json"
          }
      },
```

The logical ID of the stack is NetworkStack, and the TemplateURL indicates the location of the template in S3. When you create the Web stack, CloudFormation will also automatically create the Network stack first.

The templates for your nested stacks can contain an Outputs section where you define which values you want to pass back to the parent stack. You can then reference these values in the template for the parent stack. For example, the network-stack.json template defines an output with the logical ID VPCID and the value of the VPC's physical ID, as shown in the following snippet:

```
"Outputs": {
        "VPCID": {
            "Description": "VPC ID",
            "Value": {
                "Ref": "PublicVPC"
            }
        },
```

The Ref intrinsic function returns the physical ID of the PublicVPC resource. The parent web-stack.json template can then reference this value using the Fn::GetAtt intrinsic function, as shown in the following snippet from the Resources section:

```
"ALBTargetGroup": {
  "Type": "AWS::ElasticLoadBalancingV2::TargetGroup",
  "Properties": {
    "VpcId": { "Fn::GetAtt" : [ "NetworkStack", "Outputs.VPCID" ] },
```

Follow the steps in Exercise 13.1 to create a nested stack.

EXERCISE 13.1

Create a Nested Stack

In this exercise, you'll create a nested stack that creates an EC2 Auto Scaling group and the supporting network infrastructure. To complete this exercise, you'll need to know the name of a secure shell (SSH) key pair in the region you're using.

1. Visit https://www.wiley.com/go/sybextestprep and click Resources. Download the web-stack.json and network-stack.json CloudFormation templates.

2. Create an S3 bucket and upload the network-stack.json template to the bucket.

3. Edit the web-stack.json template and locate the NetworkStack resource. Change the TemplateURL value to the URL of the network-stack.json template in S3.

4. Upload the web-stack.json template to the same S3 bucket you used in step 2.

5. Run the following AWS CLI command:

```
aws cloudformation create-stack --stack-name web-stack --template-url
[URL of the web-stack.json template]  --parameters ParameterKey=KeyName,
ParameterValue=[the name of your SSH keypair] --capabilities CAPABILITY_
NAMED_IAM
```

6. CloudFormation will begin to create the web stack and the nested network stack. Enter the following command to view the stacks:

```
aws cloudformation describe-stacks
```

7. To delete the stacks, run the following command:

```
aws cloudformation delete-stack --stack-name web-stack
```

Exporting Stack Output Values

If you want to share information with stacks outside of a nested hierarchy, you can selectively export a stack output value by defining it in the Export field of the Output section, as follows:

```
"Outputs": {
        "VPCID": {
            "Description": "VPC ID",
            "Value": {
                "Ref": "PublicVPC"
            },
            "Export": {
                "Name": {
                    "Fn::Sub": "${AWS::StackName}-VPCID"
                }
            }
        }
    },
```

> **NOTE** AWS::StackName is a pseudoparameter that returns the name of the stack.

Any other template in the same account and region can then import the value using the Fn::ImportValue intrinsic function, as follows:

```
"ALBTargetGroup": {
        "Type": "AWS::ElasticLoadBalancingV2::TargetGroup",
        "Properties": {
            "VpcId": { "Fn::ImportValue" :  {"Fn::Sub":
"${NetworkStackName}-VPCID" } },
```

Keep in mind that you can't delete a stack if another stack is referencing any of its outputs.

Stack Updates

If you need to reconfigure a resource in a stack, the best way is to modify the resource configuration in the source template and then either perform a *direct update* or create a *change set*.

Direct Update

To perform a direct update, upload the updated template. CloudFormation will ask you to enter any parameters the template requires. CloudFormation will deploy the changes immediately, modifying only the resources that changed in the template.

Change Set

If you want to understand exactly what changes CloudFormation will make, create a change set instead. You submit the updated template, and once you create the change set, CloudFormation will display a list of every resource it will add, remove, or modify. You can then choose to execute the change set to make the changes immediately, delete the change set, or do nothing. You can create multiple change sets using different templates, compare them, and then choose which one to execute. This is useful if you want to compare multiple different configurations without having to create a new stack each time.

 You can also use change sets to create new stacks.

Update Behavior

How CloudFormation updates a resource depends on the update behavior of the resource's property that you're updating. Update behaviors can be one of the following:

Update with No Interruption   The resource is updated with no interruption and without changing its physical ID. For example, changing the IAM instance profile attached to an EC2 instance doesn't require an interruption to the instance.

Update with Some Interruption   The resource encounters a momentary interruption but retains its physical ID. This happens when, for example, you change the instance type for an EBS-backed EC2 instance.

Replacement   CloudFormation creates a new resource with a new physical ID. It then points dependent resources to the new resource and deletes the original resource. For example, if you change the availability zone for an instance defined in a template, CloudFormation will create a new instance in the availability zone defined in the updated template and then delete the original instance.

Preventing Updates to Specific Resources

To prevent specific resources in a stack from being modified by a stack update, you can create a *stack policy* when you create the stack. If you want to modify a stack policy or apply one to an existing stack, you can do so using the AWS CLI. You can't remove a stack policy.

A stack policy follows the same format as other resource policies and consists of the same Effect, Action, Principal, Resource, and Condition elements. The Effect functions the same as in other resource policies, but the Action, Principal, Resource, and Condition elements differ as follows:

Action   The action must be one of the following:

Update:Modify   Allows updates to the specific resource only if the update will modify and not replace or delete the resource

Update:Replace   Allows updates to the specific resource only if the update will replace the resource

Update:Delete   Allows updates to the specific resource only if the update will delete the resource

Update:*   Allows all update actions

Principal   The principal must always be the wildcard (*). You can't specify any other principal.

Resource   This specifies the logical ID of the resource to which the policy applies. You must prefix this with the text LogicalResourceId/.

Condition   This specifies the resource types, such as AWS::EC2::VPC. You can use wildcards to specify multiple resource types within a service, such as AWS::EC2::* to match all EC2 resources. If you use a wildcard, you must use the StringLike condition. Otherwise, you can use the StringEquals condition.

The following stack policy document allows all stack updates except for those that would replace the PublicVPC resource. Such an update would include changing the VPC CIDR.

```
{
  "Statement" : [
    {
      "Effect" : "Allow",
      "Action" : "Update:*",
      "Principal": "*",
      "Resource" : "*"
    },
    {
```

```
      "Effect" : "Deny",
      "Action" : "Update:Replace",
      "Principal": "*",
      "Resource" : "LogicalResourceId/PublicVPC",
      "Condition" : {
        "StringLike" : {
            "ResourceType" : ["AWS::EC2::VPC"]
        }
      }
    }
  ]
}
```

 A stack policy cannot prevent a principal from updating a resource directly, deleting a resource, or deleting an entire stack. If you need to control which principals can modify a stack or resource, you should use IAM policies.

CloudFormation doesn't preemptively check whether an update will violate a stack policy. If you attempt to update a stack in such a way that's prevented by the stack policy, CloudFormation will still attempt to update the stack. The update will fail only when CloudFormation attempts to perform an update prohibited by the stack policy. Therefore, when updating a stack, it's important to verify that the update succeeded. Don't just start the update and walk away.

Overriding Stack Policies

You can temporarily override a stack policy when doing a direct update. When you perform a direct update, you can specify a stack policy that overrides the existing one. CloudFormation will apply the updated policy during the update. Once the update is complete, CloudFormation will revert to the original policy.

CodeCommit

Git (https://git-scm.com) is a free and open-source version control system invented by Linus Torvalds to facilitate collaborative software development projects. However, people often use Git to store and track a variety of file-based assets, including source code, scripts, documents, and binary files. Git stores these files in a *repository*, colloquially referred to as a *repo*.

The AWS CodeCommit service hosts private Git-based repositories for version-controlled files, including code, documents, and binary files. CodeCommit provides advantages over other private Git repositories, including the following:

- Encryption at rest using an AWS-managed key stored in KMS
- Encryption in transit using HTTPS or SSH
- No size limitation for repositories
- 2 GB size limitation for a single file
- Integration with other AWS services

A Git repository and S3 have some things in common. They both store files and provide automatic versioning, allowing you to revert to a previous version of a deleted or overwritten file. But Git tracks changes to individual files using a process called *differencing*, allowing you to see what changed in each file, who changed it, and when. It also allows you to create additional *branches*, which are essentially snapshots of an entire repository. For example, you could take an existing source code repository, create a new branch, and experiment on that branch without causing any problems in the original or master branch.

Creating a Repository

You create a repository in CodeCommit using the AWS management console or the AWS CLI. When you create a new repository in CodeCommit, it is always empty. You can add files to the repository in three ways.

- Upload files using the CodeCommit management console.
- Use Git to clone the empty repository locally, add files to it, commit those changes, and then push those changes to CodeCommit.
- Use Git to push an existing local repository to CodeCommit.

Repository Security

CodeCommit uses IAM policies to control access to repositories. To help you control access to your repositories, AWS provides three managed policies. Each of the following policies allows access to all CodeCommit repositories using both the AWS Management Console and Git.

AWSCodeCommitFullAccess   This policy provides unrestricted access to CodeCommit. This is the policy you'd generally assign to repository administrators.

AWSCodeCommitPowerUser   This policy provides near full access to CodeCommit repositories but doesn't allow the principal to delete repositories. This is the policy you'd assign to users who need both read and write access to repositories.

AWSCodeCommitReadOnly   This grants read-only access to CodeCommit repositories.

If you want to restrict access to a specific repository, you can copy one of these policies to your own customer-managed policy and specify the ARN of the repository.

Interacting with a Repository Using Git

Most users will interact with a CodeCommit repository via the Git command-line interface, which you can download from https://git-scm.com. Many integrated development environments (IDEs) such as Eclipse, IntelliJ, Visual Studio, and Xcode provide their own user-friendly Git-based tools.

Only IAM principals can interact with a CodeCommit repository. AWS recommends generating a Git username and password for each IAM user from the IAM management console. You can generate up to two Git credentials per user. As CodeCommit doesn't use resource-based policies, it doesn't allow anonymous access to repositories.

If you don't want to configure IAM users or if you need to grant repository access to a federated user or application, you can grant repository access to a role. You can't assign Git credentials to a role, so instead you must configure Git to use the AWS CLI Credential Helper to obtain temporary credentials that Git can use.

Git-based connections to CodeCommit must be encrypted in transit using either HTTPS or SSH. The easiest option is HTTPS, as it requires inputting only one's Git credentials. However, if you can't use Git credentials—perhaps because of security requirements—you can use SSH. If you go this route, you must generate public and private SSH keys for each IAM user and upload the public key to AWS. The user must also have permissions granted by the IAMUserSSHKeys AWS-managed policy.

Follow the steps in Exercise 13.2 to create your own CodeCommit repository.

EXERCISE 13.2

Create and Interact with a CodeCommit Repository

In this exercise, you'll create a CodeCommit repository and learn how to use Git to work with it.

1. On the same machine on which you installed the AWS CLI, download Git from https://git-scm.com and install it.

2. Use the following AWS CLI command to create a repository named myrepo:

    ```
    aws codecommit create-repository --repository-name myrepo
    ```

    You should see output listing the URL and ARN of the repository, like so:

    ```
    {
        "repositoryMetadata": {
            "repositoryName": "myrepo",
            "cloneUrlSsh": "ssh://git-codecommit.us-east-1.amazonaws.com/v1/repos/
    myrepo",
            "lastModifiedDate": 1540919473.55,
            "repositoryId": "f0d6111a-db12-461c-8bc4-a3727c0e8481",
            "cloneUrlHttp": "https://git-codecommit.us-east-1.amazonaws.com/v1/
    repos/myrepo",
    ```

```
            "creationDate": 1540919473.55,
            "Arn": "arn:aws:codecommit:us-east-1:xxxxxxxxxxxx:myrepo",
            "accountId": "xxxxxxxxxxxx"
        }
    }
```

3. In the IAM management console, create a new IAM policy by importing the AWSCodeCommitPowerUser policy. For the CodeCommit service permissions, specify as the resource the repository's ARN from step 2. Give the policy a name of your choice, such as **CodeCommit-myrepo-PowerUser**.

4. Create a new IAM user with programmatic access. Assign the user the policy you created in step 3.

5. In the IAM management console, click Users on the menu on the left and then click the name of the user you just created.

6. Click on the Security Credentials tab.

7. Under HTTPS Git Credentials for AWS CodeCommit, click the Generate button. Note the username and password that IAM generates.

8. At a command prompt, issue the following command to clone the myrepo repository:

    git clone https://git-codecommit.us-east-1.amazonaws.com/v1/repos/ myrepo

    This is the same URL you saw in step 2.

9. Git will prompt you for the username and password IAM generated in step 7. Enter these and you should see output indicating that Git successfully cloned the repository, as follows:

    ```
    Cloning into 'myrepo'...
    Username for 'https://git-codecommit.us-east-1.amazonaws.com': user-at-
    xxxxxxxxxxxx
    Password for 'https://user-at-xxxxxxxxxxxx@git-codecommit.us-east-1.amazonaws
    .com':
    warning: You appear to have cloned an empty repository.
    Checking connectivity... done.
    ```

10. Descend into the local repository by typing **cd myrepo**.

11. Before you can add files to the local repository, you'll need to set up Git by configuring a name and email address. These can be anything you want, but Git does require

them to be set as shown in the following two commands (replace the values in quotes to a username and email address that you prefer):

```
git config user.name "Ben Piper"
git config user.email "ben@benpiper.com"
```

12. Create a file to add to the repo by entering **echo test > file.txt**.

13. Instruct Git to stage the file for addition to the local repository by typing **git add file.txt**.

14. Commit the changes to the repository by typing **git commit -m "Add file .txt"**. The text in quotes can be whatever you want but should be a description of the changes you've made. You should see output similar to the following:

```
[master (root-commit) bc914ea] Add file.txt
 1 file changed, 1 insertion(+)
 create mode 100644 file.txt
```

15. Push the changes up to the CodeCommit repository using the command **git push**. Git will prompt you for your Git credentials. Once you've inputted them successfully, Git will display output similar to the following:

```
Counting objects: 3, done.
Writing objects: 100% (3/3), 218 bytes | 0 bytes/s, done.
Total 3 (delta 0), reused 0 (delta 0)
To https://git-codecommit.us-east-1.amazonaws.com/v1/repos/myrepo
 * [new branch]      master -> master
```

16. Go to the CodeCommit management console and click Repositories on the menu on the left.

17. Click the myrepo repository. You should see the file named file.txt.

CodeDeploy

CodeDeploy is a service that can deploy applications to EC2 or on-premises instances. You can use CodeDeploy to deploy binary executables, scripts, web assets, images, and anything else you can store in an S3 bucket or GitHub repository. You can also use CodeDeploy to deploy Lambda functions. CodeDeploy offers a number of advantages over manual deployments, including the following:

- Simultaneous deployment to multiple instances or servers
- Automatic rollback if there are deployment errors

- Centralized monitoring and control of deployments
- Deployment of multiple applications at once

The CodeDeploy Agent

The CodeDeploy agent is a service that runs on your Linux or Windows instances and performs the hands-on work of deploying the application onto an instance. You can install the CodeDeploy agent on an EC2 instance at launch using a Userdata script or you can bake it into an AMI. You can also use AWS Systems Manager to install it automatically. You'll learn about Systems Manager later in the chapter.

Deployments

To deploy an application using CodeDeploy, you must create a *deployment* that defines the compute platform, which can be EC2/On-premises or Lambda, and the location of the application source files. CodeDeploy currently only supports deployments from S3 or GitHub.

CodeDeploy doesn't automatically perform deployments. If you want to automate deployments, you can use CodePipeline, which we'll cover later in the chapter.

Deployment Groups

Prior to creating a deployment, you must create a *deployment group* to define which instances CodeDeploy will deploy your application to. A deployment group can be based on an EC2 Auto Scaling group, EC2 instance tags, or on-premises instance tags.

Deployment Types

When creating a deployment group for EC2 or on-premises instances, you must specify a *deployment type*. CodeDeploy gives you the following two different deployment types to give you control over how you deploy your applications.

In-Place Deployment

With an in-place deployment you deploy the application to existing instances. In-place deployments are useful for initial deployments to instances that don't already have the application. These instances can be stand-alone or, in the case of EC2 instances, part of an existing Auto Scaling group.

On each instance, the application is stopped and upgraded (if applicable) and then restarted. If the instance is behind an elastic load balancer, the instance is deregistered before the application is stopped and then reregistered to the load balancer after the deployment to the instance succeeds. Although an elastic load balancer isn't required to perform an in-place deployment, having one already set up allows CodeDeploy to prevent traffic from going to instances that are in the middle of a deployment.

You must use the in-place deployment type for on-premises instance deployments.

Blue/Green Deployment

A blue/green deployment is used to upgrade an existing application with minimal interruption. With Lambda deployments, CodeDeploy deploys a new version of a Lambda function and automatically shifts traffic to the new version. Lambda deployments always use the blue/green deployment type.

In a blue/green deployment against EC2 instances, the existing instances in the deployment group are left untouched. A new set of instances is created to which CodeDeploy deploys the application.

Blue/green deployments require an existing Application, Classic, or Network Load balancer. CodeDeploy registers the instances to the load balancer's target group after a successful deployment. At the same time, instances in the original environment are deregistered from the target group.

Note that if you're using an Auto Scaling group, CodeDeploy will create a new Auto Scaling group with the same configuration as the original. CodeDeploy will not modify the minimum, maximum, or desired capacity settings for an Auto Scaling group.

You can choose to terminate the original instances or keep them running. You may choose to keep them running if you need to keep them available for testing or forensic analysis.

Deployment Configurations

When creating your deployment group, you must also select a *deployment configuration*. The deployment configuration defines the number of instances CodeDeploy simultaneously deploys to, as well as how many instances the deployment must succeed on for the entire deployment to be considered successful. The effect of a deployment configuration differs based on the deployment type. There are three preconfigured deployment configurations you can choose from: OneAtATime, HalfAtATime, and AllAtOnce.

OneAtATime

For both in-place and blue/green deployments, if the deployment group has more than one instance, CodeDeploy must successfully deploy the application to one instance before moving on to the next one. The overall deployment succeeds if the application is deployed successfully to all but the last instance. For example, if the deployment succeeds to the first two instances in a group of three, the entire deployment will succeed. If the deployment fails to any instance but the last one, the entire deployment fails.

If the deployment group has only one instance, the overall deployment succeeds only if the deployment to the instance succeeds.

For blue/green deployments, CodeDeploy reroutes traffic to each instance as deployment succeeds on the instance. If unable to reroute traffic to any instance except the last one, the entire deployment fails.

HalfAtATime

For in-place and blue/green deployments, CodeDeploy will deploy to up to half of the instances in the deployment group before moving on to the remaining instances. The entire deployment succeeds only if deployment to at least half of the instances succeeds.

For blue/green deployments, CodeDeploy must be able to reroute traffic to at least half of the new instances for the entire deployment to succeed.

AllAtOnce

For in-place and blue/green deployments, CodeDeploy simultaneously deploys the application to as many instances as possible. If the application is deployed to at least one instance, the entire deployment succeeds.

For blue/green deployments, the entire deployment succeeds if CodeDeploy reroutes traffic to at least one new instance.

Custom Deployment Configurations

You can also create custom deployment configurations. This is useful if you want to customize how many instances CodeDeploy attempts to deploy to simultaneously. The deployment must complete successfully on these instances before CodeDeploy moves onto the remaining instances in the deployment group. Hence, the value you must specify when creating a custom deployment configuration is called the number of *healthy instances*. The number of healthy instances can be a percentage of all instances in the group or a number of instances.

Lifecycle Events

An instance deployment is divided into lifecycle events, which include stopping the application (if applicable), installing prerequisites, installing the application, and validating the application. During some of these lifecycle events, you can have the agent execute a *lifecycle event hook*, which is a script of your choosing. The following are all the lifecycle events during which you can have the agent automatically run a script:

ApplicationStop   You can use this hook to gracefully stop an application prior to an in-place deployment. You can also use it to perform cleanup tasks. This event occurs prior to the agent copying any application files from your repository. This event doesn't occur on original instances in a blue/green deployment, nor does it occur the first time you deploy to an instance.

BeforeInstall   This event occurs after the agent copies the application files to a temporary location on the instance, but before it copies them to their final location. If your application files require some manipulation, such as decryption or the insertion of a unique identifier, this would be the hook to use.

AfterInstall   Once the agent copies your application files to their final destination, you can perform further needed tasks such as setting file permissions.

ApplicationStart   You use this hook to start your application. For example, on a Linux instance running an Apache web server, this may be as simple as running a script that executes the `systemctl httpd start` command.

ValidateService   Here you can check that the application is working as expected. For instance, you may check that it's generating log files or that it's established a connection to a backend database. This is the final event for in-place deployments that don't use an elastic load balancer.

BeforeBlockTraffic   With an in-place deployment using an elastic load balancer, this event occurs first, before the instance is unregistered.

AfterBlockTraffic   This event occurs after the instance is unregistered from an elastic load balancer. You may hook this event to wait for user sessions or in-process transfers to complete.

BeforeAllowTraffic   For deployments using an elastic load balancer, this event occurs after the application is installed and validated. You may use this hook to perform any tasks needed to warm up the application or otherwise prepare it to accept traffic.

AfterAllowTraffic   This is the final event for deployments using an elastic load balancer.

Notice that not all of these lifecycle events can occur on all instances in a blue/green deployment. The BeforeBlockTraffic event, for example, wouldn't occur on a replacement instance since it makes no sense for CodeDeploy to unregister a replacement instance from a load balancer during a deployment.

Each script run during a lifecycle event must complete successfully before CodeDeploy will allow the deployment to advance to the next event. By default, the agent will wait one hour for the script to complete before it considers the instance deployment failed. You can optionally set the timeout to a lower value, as shown in the following section.

The Application Specification File

The application specification file defines where the agent should copy the application files onto your instance and what scripts it should run during the deployment process. You must place the file in the root of your application repository and name it `appspec.yml`. It consists of the following five sections:

Version   Currently the only allowed version of the AppSpec file is 0.0.

OS   Because the CodeDeploy agent works only on Linux and Windows, you must specify one of these as the operating system.

Files   This specifies one or more source and destination pairs identifying the files or directories to copy from your repository to the instance.

Permissions   This optionally sets ownership, group membership, file permissions, and SELinux context labels for the files after they're copied to the instance. This applies to Amazon Linux, Ubuntu, and RedHat Enterprise Linux instances only.

Hooks   This section is where you define the scripts the agent should run at each lifecycle event. You must specify the name of the lifecycle event followed by a tuple containing the following:

  Location   This must be a full path to an executable.

  Timeout   You can optionally set the time in seconds that the agent will wait for the script to execute before it considers the instance deployment failed.

  Run As   For Amazon Linux and Ubuntu instances, this lets you specify the user the script should run as.

Note that you can specify multiple locations, timeouts, and script tuples under a single lifecycle event. Keep in mind that the total timeouts for a single lifecycle event can't exceed one hour.

The following is a sample appspec.yml file:

```
version: 0.0
os: linux
files:
  - source: /index.html
    destination: /var/www/html/
hooks:
  BeforeInstall:
    - location: scripts/install_dependencies
      timeout: 300
      runas: root
```

Triggers and Alarms

You can optionally set up triggers to generate an SNS notification for certain deployment and instance events, such as when a deployment succeeds or fails.

You can also configure your deployment group to monitor up to 10 CloudWatch alarms. If an alarm exceeds or falls below a threshold you define, the deployment will stop.

Rollbacks

You can optionally have CodeDeploy *roll back*, or revert, to the last successful revision of an application if the deployment fails or if a CloudWatch alarm is triggered during deployment. Despite the name, rollbacks are actually new deployments.

CodePipeline

CodePipeline lets you automate the different *stages* of your software development and release process. These stages are often implemented using *continuous integration* (CI) and *continuous delivery* (CD) workflows or *pipelines*. Continuous integration (CI) and continuous delivery (CD) are different but related concepts.

Continuous Integration

Continuous integration is a method whereby developers use a version control system such as Git to regularly submit or check in their changes to a common repository. This first stage of the pipeline is the source stage.

Depending on the application, a build system may compile the code or build it into a binary file, such as an executable, AMI, or container image. This is called the *build stage*. One goal of continuous integration is to ensure that the code developers are adding to the repository works as expected and meets the requirements of the application. Thus, the build stage may also include unit tests, such as verifying that a function given a certain input returns the correct output. This way, if a change to an application causes something to break, the developer can learn of the error and fix it early. Not all applications require a build stage. For example, a web-based application using an interpreted language like PHP doesn't need to be compiled.

Continuous Delivery

Continuous delivery incorporates elements of the continuous integration process but also deploys the application to production. A goal of continuous delivery is to allow frequent updates to an application while minimizing the risk of failure. To do this, continuous delivery pipelines usually include a test stage. As with the build stage, the actions performed in test stage depend on the application. For example, testing a web application may include deploying it to a test web server and verifying that the web pages display the correct content. On the other hand, testing a Linux executable that you plan to release publicly may involve deploying it to test servers running a variety of different Linux distributions and versions.

The final stage is deployment in which the application is deployed to production. Although continuous delivery can be fully automated without requiring human intervention, it's common to require manual approval before releasing an application to production. You can also schedule releases to occur regularly or during opportune times such as maintenance windows.

Because continuous integration and continuous delivery pipelines overlap, you'll often see them combined into one to form the term *CI/CD pipeline*. Keep in mind that even though a CI/CD pipeline includes every stage from source to deployment, that doesn't mean you have to deploy to production every time you make a change. You can add logic to require a manual approval before deployment. Or you can disable transitions from one stage to the next. For instance, you may disable the transition from the test stage to the deployment stage until you're actually ready to deploy.

Creating the Pipeline

Every CodeDeploy pipeline must include at least two stages and can have up to 10. Within each stage, you must define at least one task or *action* to occur during the stage. An action can be one of the following types:

- Source
- Build
- Test
- Approval
- Deploy
- Invoke

CodePipeline integrates with other AWS and third-party *providers* to perform the actions. You can have up to 20 actions in the same stage, and they can run sequentially or in parallel. For example, during your testing stage you can have two separate test actions that execute concurrently. Note that different action types can occur in the same stage. For instance, you can perform build and test actions in the same stage.

Source

The source action type specifies the source of your application files. The first stage of a pipeline must include at least one source action and can't include any other types of actions. Valid providers for the source type are CodeCommit, S3, or GitHub.

If you specify CodeCommit or S3, you must also specify the ARN of a repository or bucket. AWS can use CloudWatch events to detect when a change is made to the repository or bucket. Alternatively, you can have CodePipeline periodically poll for changes.

To add a GitHub repository as a source, you'll have to grant CodePipeline permission to access your repositories. Whenever you update the repository, GitHub creates a webhook that notifies CodePipeline of the change.

Build

Not all applications require build actions. An interpreted language such as those used in shell scripts and declarative code such as CloudFormation templates doesn't require compiling. However, even noncompiled languages may benefit from a build stage that analyzes the code for syntax errors and style conventions.

The build action type can use AWS CodeBuild as well as third-party providers CloudBees, Jenkins, Solano CI, and TeamCity. AWS CodeBuild is a managed build service that lets you compile source code and perform unit tests. CodeBuild offers on-demand build environments for a variety of programming languages, saving you from having to create and manage your own build servers.

Test

The test action type can also use AWS CodeBuild as a provider. For testing against smartphone platforms, AWS DeviceFarm offers testing services for Android iOS and web applications. Other supported providers are BlazeMeter, Ghost Inspector, HPE StormRunner Load, Nouvola, and Runscope.

Approval

The approval action type includes only one action: manual approval. When pipeline execution reaches this action, it awaits manual approval before continuing to the next stage. If there's no manual approval within seven days, the action is denied, and pipeline execution halts. You can optionally send an SNS notification, which includes a link to approve or deny the request and may include a URL for the approver to review.

Deploy

For deployment, CodePipeline offers integrations with CodeDeploy, CloudFormation, Elastic Container Service, Elastic Beanstalk, OpsWorks Stacks, Service Catalog, and XebiaLabs.

Recall that CodeDeploy doesn't let you specify a CodeCommit repository as a source for your application files. But you can specify CodeCommit as the provider for the source action and CodeDeploy as the provider for the Deploy action.

Invoke

If you want to run a custom Lambda function as part of your pipeline, you can invoke it using the invoke action type. For example, you can write a function to create an EBS snapshot, perform application testing, clean up unused resources, and so on.

At least one stage must have an action that's not a source action type.

Artifacts

When you create a pipeline, you must specify an S3 bucket to store the files used during different stages of the pipeline. CodePipeline compresses these files into a ZIP file called an *artifact*. Different actions in the pipeline can take an artifact as an input, generate it as an output, or both.

The first stage in your pipeline must include a source action specifying the location of your application files. When your pipeline runs, CodePipeline compresses the files to create a source artifact.

Suppose that the second stage of your pipeline is a build stage, CodePipeline then unzips the source artifact and passes the contents along to the build provider. The build provider uses this as an input artifact. The build provider yields its output; let's say it's a binary file. CodePipeline takes that file and compresses it into another ZIP file, called an *output artifact*.

This process continues throughout the pipeline. When creating a pipeline, you must specify a service role for CodePipeline to assume. It uses this role to obtain permissions to the S3 bucket. The bucket must exist in the same region as the pipeline. You can use the same bucket for multiple pipelines, but each pipeline can use only one bucket for artifact storage.

AWS Systems Manager

AWS Systems Manager, formerly known as EC2 Systems Manager and Simple Systems Manager (SSM), lets you automatically or manually perform *actions* against your AWS resources and on-premises servers.

From an operational perspective, Systems Manager can handle many of the maintenance tasks that often require manual intervention or writing scripts. For on-premises and EC2 instances, these tasks include upgrading installed packages, taking an inventory of installed software, and installing a new application. For your AWS resources, such tasks may include creating an AMI golden image from an EBS snapshot, attaching IAM instance profiles, or disabling public read access to S3 buckets.

Systems Manager provides the following two capabilities:

- Actions
- Insights

Actions

Actions let you automatically or manually perform actions against your AWS resources, either individually or in bulk. These actions must be defined in *documents*, which are divided into three types:

- Automation—actions you can run against your AWS resources
- Command—actions you run against your Linux or Windows instances
- Policy

Automation

Automation enables you to perform actions against your AWS resources in bulk. For example, you can restart multiple EC2 instances, update CloudFormation stacks, and patch AMIs.

Automation provides granular control over how it carries out its individual actions. It can perform the entire automation task in one fell swoop, or it can perform one step at a time, enabling you to control precisely what happens and when. Automation also offers rate control, so you can specify as a number or a percentage how many resources to target at once.

Run Command

While automation enables you to automate tasks against your AWS resources, Run Commands let you execute tasks on your managed instances that would otherwise require logging in or using a third-party tool to execute a custom script.

Systems Manager accomplishes this via an agent installed on your EC2 and on-premises *managed instances*. The Systems Manager agent is installed on all Windows Server and Amazon Linux AMIs.

By default, Systems Manager doesn't have permissions to do anything on your instances. You first need to apply an instance profile role that contains the permissions in the AmazonEC2RoleforSSM policy.

AWS offers a variety of preconfigured command documents for Linux and Windows instances; for example the AWS-InstallApplication document installs software on Windows, and the AWS-RunShellScript document allows you to execute arbitrary shell scripts against Linux instances. Other documents include tasks such as restarting a Windows service or installing the CodeDeploy agent.

You can target instances by tag or select them individually. As with automation, you optionally may use rate limiting to control how many instances you target at once.

Session Manager

Session Manager lets you achieve interactive bash and PowerShell access to your Linux and Windows instances, respectively, without having to open up inbound ports on a security group or network ACL or even having your instances in a public subnet. You don't need to set up a bastion host or worry about SSH keys. All Linux versions and Windows Server 2008 R2 through 2016 are supported.

You open a session using the web console or AWS CLI. You must first install the Session Manager plugin on your local machine to use the AWS CLI to start a session. The Session Manager SDK has libraries for developers to create custom applications that connect to instances. This is useful if you want to integrate an existing configuration management system with your instances without opening ports in a security group or network ACL.

Connections made via Session Manager are secured using TLS 1.2. Session Manager can keep a log of all logins in CloudTrail and store a record of commands run within a session in an S3 bucket.

Patch Manager

Patch Manager helps you automate the patching of your Linux and Windows instances. It doesn't support all operating systems supported by other Systems Manager features but does support the following:

- All recent Amazon Linux versions
- CentOS/RHEL 6.5–7.5
- SUSE Linux Enterprise Server 12.0–12.9

- Ubuntu Server 14.04 LTS, 16.04 LTS, and 18.04 LTS

- Windows Server 2003–2016

You can individually choose instances to patch, patch according to tags, or create a *patch group*. A patch group is a collection of instances with the tag key Patch Group. For example, if you wanted to include some instances in the Webservers patch group, you'd assign tags to each instance with the tag key of Patch Group and the tag value of Webservers. Keep in mind that the tag key is case-sensitive.

Patch Manager uses *patch baselines* to define which available patches to install, as well as whether the patches will be installed automatically or require approval.

AWS offers default baselines that differ according to operating system but include patches that are classified as security-related, critical, important, or required. The patch baselines for all operating systems except Ubuntu automatically approve these patches after seven days. This is called an *auto-approval delay*.

For more control over which patches get installed, you can create your own custom baselines. Each custom baseline contains one or more approval rules that define the operating system, the classification and severity level of patches to install, and an auto-approval delay.

You can also specify approved patches in a custom baseline configuration. For Windows baselines, you can specify knowledgebase and security bulletin IDs. For Linux baselines, you can specify CVE IDs or full package names. If a patch is approved, it will be installed during a maintenance window that you specify. Alternatively, you can forego a maintenance window and patch your instances immediately. Patch Manager executes the AWS-RunPatchBaseline document to perform patching.

State Manager

While Patch Manager can help ensure your instances are all at the same patch level, State Manager is a configuration management tool that ensures your instances have the software you want them to have and are configured in the way you define. More generally, State Manager can automatically run command and policy documents against your instances, either one time only or on a schedule. For example, you may want to install antivirus software on your instances and then take a software inventory.

To use State Manager, you must create an *association* that defines the command document to run, any parameters you want to pass to it, the target instances, and the schedule. Once you create an association, State Manager will immediately execute it against the target instances that are online. Thereafter, it will follow the schedule.

There is currently only one policy document you can use with State Manager: AWS-GatherSoftwareInventory. This document defines what specific metadata to collect from your instances. Despite the name, in addition to collecting software inventory, you can also have it collect network configurations, file information, CPU information, and, for Windows, registry values.

Insights

Insights aggregate health, compliance, and operational details about your AWS resources into a single area of AWS Systems Manager. Some insights are categorized according to

AWS resource groups, which are collections of resources in an AWS region. You define a resource group based on one or more tag keys and optionally tag values. For example, you can apply the same tag key to all resources related to a particular application—EC2 instances, S3 buckets, EBS volumes, security groups, and so on. Insights are categorized as covered next.

Built-in Insights

Built-in insights are monitoring views that Systems Manager makes available to you by default. Built-in insights include the following:

AWS Config Compliance   This insight shows the total number of resources in a resource group that are compliant or noncompliant with AWS Config rules, as well as compliance by resource. It also shows a brief history of configuration changes tracked by AWS Config.

CloudTrail Events   This insight displays each resource in the group, the resource type, and the last event that CloudTrail recorded against the resource.

Personal Health Dashboard   The Personal Health Dashboard contains alerts when AWS experiences an issue that may impact your resources. For example, some service APIs occasionally experience increased latency. It also shows you the number of events that AWS resolved within the last 24 hours.

Trusted Advisor Recommendations   The AWS Trusted Advisor tool can check your AWS environment for optimizations and recommendations around cost optimization, performance, security, and fault tolerance. It will also show you when you've exceeded 80 percent of your limit for a service.

Business and Enterprise support customers get access to all Trusted Advisor checks. All AWS customers get the following security checks for free:

- Public access to an S3 bucket, particularly upload and delete access
- Security groups with unrestricted access to ports that normally should be restricted, such as TCP port 1433 (MySQL) and 3389 (Remote Desktop Protocol)
- Whether you've created an IAM user
- Whether multifactor authentication is enabled for the root user
- Public access to an EBS or RDS snapshot

Inventory Manager

The Inventory Manager collects data from your instances, including operating system and application versions. Inventory Manager can collect data for the following:

- Operating system name and version
- Applications and filenames, versions, and sizes
- Network configuration including IP and MAC addresses
- Windows updates, roles, services, and registry values
- CPU model, cores, and speed

You choose which instances to collect data from by creating a region-wide *inventory association* by executing the AWS-GatherSoftwareInventory policy document. You can choose all instances in your account or select instances manually or by tag. When you choose all instances in your account, it's called a *global inventory association*, and new instances you create in the region are automatically added to it. Inventory collection occurs at least every 30 minutes.

When you configure the Systems Manager agent on an on-premises server, you specify a region for inventory purposes. To aggregate metadata for instances from different regions and accounts, you may configure Resource Data Sync in each region to store all inventory data in a single S3 bucket.

Compliance

Compliance insights show how the patch and association status of your instances stacks up against the rules you've configured. Patch compliance shows the number of instances that have the patches in their configured baseline, as well as details of the specific patches installed. Association compliance shows the number of instances that have had an association successfully executed against them.

Summary

Automation is certainly nothing new. System administrators have been writing scripts for decades to automate common (and often mundane) tasks. But in the cloud, automation can be extended to infrastructure deployments as well. Because of the flexibility of cloud infrastructure, the line between infrastructure—which has traditionally been static—and operations is becoming more blurred. In the cloud, deploying infrastructure and operating it are essentially the same thing.

Despite this, there are some differences to keep in mind. Because the infrastructure belongs to AWS, you have to use the AWS web console, CLI, or SDKs to configure it. You can automate this using CloudFormation, or you can write your own scripts. Conversely, when it comes to configuring the operating system and applications running on instances, you can write scripts and use your own tooling, or you can use the services AWS provides, namely, the AWS Developer Tools and Systems Manager. The combination of scripts, tools, and services you use is up to you, but as an AWS architect, you need to understand all options available to you and how they all fit together.

Exam Essentials

Know how to use CloudFormation stacks. A stack is a collection of AWS resources created by a CloudFormation template. These resources can be created, updated, and deleted as a group. Stacks can also pass information to each other through the use of output exports and nested stacks.

Understand the use cases for CodeCommit and Git.   CodeCommit offers Git-based repositories for storing files. It provides automatic versioning and differencing, allowing multiple IAM users to collaborate on software development projects, document creation, and more.

Be able to decide whether to use a blue/green or in-place deployment.   In a blue/green deployment you deploy an application to a new set of instances and then route traffic to them, resulting in minimal downtime. An in-place deployment is appropriate when you're initially deploying an application to existing instances. It's also a good option when you don't want to create new instances but are able to safely take your existing application offline to update it.

Know how CodePipeline works.   CodePipeline lets you create workflows that define the different stages of software development, all the way from coding to deployment. It can integrate with other AWS and third-party tools to perform builds and unit testing.

Understand the features of Systems Manager.   Systems Manager lets you automatically or manually take actions against your AWS resources and instances in bulk or individually. It also gives you insights into the state of your resources, such as compliance status and software inventory.

Review Questions

1. When using CloudFormation to provision multiple stacks of related resources, by which of the following should you organize your resources into different stacks? (Choose two.)

   A. Cost

   B. S3 bucket

   C. Lifecycle

   D. Ownership

2. Which of the following resource properties are good candidates for definition as parameters in a CloudFormation template? (Choose two.)

   A. AMI ID

   B. EC2 key-pair name

   C. Stack name

   D. Logical ID

3. You want to use nested stacks to create an EC2 Auto Scaling group and the supporting VPC infrastructure. These stacks do not need to pass any information to stacks outside of the nested stack hierarchy. Which of the following must you add to the template that creates the Auto Scaling group?

   A. An `Export` field to the `Output` section

   B. A resource of the type `AWS::EC2::VPC`

   C. A resource of the type `AWS::CloudFormation::Stack`

   D. `Fn::ImportValue`

4. You need to update a stack that has a stack policy applied. What must you do to verify the specific resources CloudFormation will change prior to updating the stack?

   A. Create a change set.

   B. Perform a direct update.

   C. Update the stack policy.

   D. Override the stack policy.

5. You've granted a developer's IAM user permissions to read and write to a CodeCommit repository using Git. What information should you provide him to access it as his IAM user?

   A. IAM username and password

   B. Access key and secret key

   C. Git username and password

   D. SSH public key

6. You need to grant access to a specific CodeCommit repository to only one IAM user. How can you do this?

   A. Specify the repository's clone URL in an IAM policy.

   B. Generate Git credentials only for the user.

   C. Specify the user's ARN in a repository policy.

   D. Specify the repository's ARN in an IAM policy.

7. You need to store text-based documentation for your data center infrastructure. This documentation changes frequently, and auditors need to be able to see how the documents change over time. The documents must also be encrypted at rest. Which service should you use to store the documents, and why?

   A. CodeCommit because it offers differencing

   B. S3 because it offers versioning

   C. S3 because it works with customer-managed KMS keys

   D. CodeCommit because it works with customer-managed KMS keys

8. Which command will download a CodeCommit repository?

   A. `aws codecommit get-repository`

   B. `git clone`

   C. `git push`

   D. `git add`

9. You need to deploy an application using CodeDeploy. Where must you place your application files so CodeDeploy can deploy them?

   A. An EBS snapshot

   B. A CodeCommit repository

   C. A self-hosted Git repository

   D. An S3 bucket

10. Which deployment type requires an elastic load balancer?

    A. In-place instance deployment

    B. Blue/green instance deployment

    C. Blue/green Lambda deployment

    D. In-place Lambda deployment

11. You want to use CodeDeploy to perform an in-place upgrade of an application running on five instances. You consider the entire deployment successful if the deployment succeeds even on only one instance. Which preconfigured deployment configuration should you use?

    A. OneAtATime

    B. HalfAtATime

    C. AllAtOnce

    D. OnlyOne

12. You want CodeDeploy to run a shell script that performs final checks against your application after allowing traffic to it and before declaring the deployment successful. Which lifecycle event hook should you use?

    A. ValidateService

    B. AfterAllowTraffic

    C. BeforeAllowTraffic

    D. AllowTraffic

13. The build stage of your software development pipeline compiles Java source code into a binary JAR file that can be deployed to a web server. CodePipeline compresses this file and puts it in an S3 bucket. What's the term for this compressed file?

    A. An artifact

    B. A provider

    C. An asset

    D. A snapshot

14. You're designing an automated continuous integration pipeline and want to ensure developers don't accidentally trigger a release to production when checking in code. What are two ways to accomplish this?

    A. Create a separate bucket in S3 to store artifacts for deployment.

    B. Implement an approval action before the deploy stage.

    C. Disable the transition to the deploy stage.

    D. Don't allow developers access to the deployment artifact bucket.

15. You have CloudFormation templates stored in a CodeCommit repository. Whenever someone updates a template, you want a new CloudFormation stack automatically deployed. How should you design a CodePipeline pipeline to achieve this? (Choose all that apply.)

    A. Use a source action with the CodeCommit provider.

    B. Use a build action with the CloudFormation provider.

    C. Use a deploy action with the CodeCommit provider.

    D. Use a deploy action with the CloudFormation provider.

    E. Create a two-stage pipeline.

    F. Create a three-stage pipeline.

    G. Create a single-stage pipeline.

16. How many stages can you have in a pipeline?

    A. 1

    B. 10

    C. 20

    D. 21

17. You need to manually take EBS snapshots of several hundred volumes. Which type of Systems Manager document enables you to do this?

A. Command

B. Automation

C. Policy

D. Manual

18. You want to use Systems Manager to perform routine administration tasks and collect software inventory on your EC2 instances running Amazon Linux. You already have an instance profile attached to these instances. Which of the following should you do to enable you to use Systems Manager for these tasks?

A. Add the permissions from the AmazonEC2RoleforSSM managed policy to the role you're using for the instance profile.

B. Manually install the Systems Manager Agent.

C. Use Session Manager to install the Systems Manager agent.

D. Modify the instance security groups to allow access from Systems Manager.

19. You've configured Patch Manager to patch your Windows instances every Saturday. The custom patch baseline you're using has a seven-day auto-approval delay for security-related patches. On this Monday, a critical security patch was released, and you want to push it to your instances as soon as possible. You also want to take the opportunity to install all other available security-related packages. How can you accomplish this? (Choose two.)

A. Execute the AWS-RunPatchBaseline document.

B. Add the patch to the list of approved patches in the patch baseline.

C. Change the maintenance window to occur every Monday at midnight.

D. Set the patch baseline's auto-approval delay to zero days.

20. You've installed the Systems Manager agent on an Ubuntu instance and ensured the correct instance profile is applied. But Systems Manager Insights don't display the current network configuration. Which of the following must you do to be able to automatically collect and view the network configuration for this and future instances in the same region?

A. Make sure the instance is running.

B. Create a global inventory association.

C. Execute the AWS-GatherSoftwareInventory policy document against the instance.

D. Execute the AWS-SetupManagedInstance automation document against the instance.

Appendix

Answers to Review Questions

Chapter 1: Introduction to Cloud Computing and AWS

1. B. Elastic Beanstalk takes care of the ongoing underlying deployment details for you, allowing you to focus exclusively on your code. Lambda will respond to trigger events by running code a single time, Auto Scaling will ramp up existing infrastructure in response to demand, and Route 53 manages DNS and network routing.

2. A. CloudFront maintains a network of endpoints where cached versions of your application data are stored to provide quicker responses to user requests. Route 53 manages DNS and network routing, Elastic Load Balancing routes incoming user requests among a cluster of available servers, and Glacier provides high-latency, low-cost file storage.

3. D. Elastic Block Store provides virtual block devices (think: storage drives) on which you can install and run filesystems and data operations. It is not normally a cost-effective option for long-term data storage.

4. A. AWS IAM lets you create user accounts, groups, and roles and assign them rights and permissions over specific services and resources within your AWS account. KMS is a tool for generating and managing encryption keys, Directory Service allows you to integrate your resources with external users and resources through third-party authentication services, and SWF is a tool for coordinating application tasks.

5. C. DynamoDB provides a NoSQL (nonrelational) database service for workloads that can be more efficiently run without the relational schema of SQL database engines (like those, including Aurora, that are offered by RDS). KMS is a tool for generating and managing encryption keys.

6. D. EC2 endpoints will always start with an `ec2` prefix followed by the region designation (eu-west-1 in the case of Ireland).

7. A. An availability zone is an isolated physical data center within an AWS region. Regions are geographic areas that contain multiple availability zones, subnets are IP address blocks that can be used within a zone to organize your networked resources, and there can be multiple data centers within an availability zone.

8. B. VPCs are virtualized network environments where you can control the connectivity of your EC2 (and RDS, etc.) infrastructure. Load Balancing routes incoming user requests among a cluster of available servers, CloudFront maintains a network of endpoints where cached versions of your application data are stored to provide quicker responses to user requests, and AWS endpoints are URIs that point to AWS resources within your account.

9. C. The AWS service level agreement tells you the level of service availability you can realistically expect from a particular AWS service. You can use this information when assessing your compliance with external standards. Log records, while they can offer important

historical performance metrics, probably won't be enough to prove compliance. The AWS Shared Responsibility Model outlines who is responsible for various elements of your AWS infrastructure. There is no AWS Program Compliance tool.

10. B. The AWS Command Line Interface (CLI) is a tool for accessing AWS APIs from the command-line shell of your local computer. The AWS SDK is for accessing resources programmatically, the AWS Console works graphically through your browser, and AWS Config is a service for editing and auditing your AWS account resources.

11. A. Unlike the Basic and Developer plans (which allow access to a support associate to no or one user, respectively), the Business plan allows multiple team members.

Chapter 2: Amazon Elastic Compute Cloud and Amazon Elastic Block Store

1. A, C. Many third-party companies maintain official and supported AMIs running their software on the AWS Marketplace. AMIs hosted among the community AMIs are not always official and supported versions. Since your company will need multiple such instances, you'll be better off automating the process by bootstrapping rather than having to configure the software manually each time.

2. B, C. The VM Import/Export tool handles the secure and reliable transfer for a virtual machine between your AWS account and local data center. A successfully imported VM will appear among the private AMIs in the region you selected.

3. D. AMIs are specific to a single AWS region and cannot be deployed into any other region. Should your AWS CLI or its key pair not be configured properly, your connection would have failed completely. A public AMI being unavailable because it's "updating" is theoretically possible but unlikely.

4. A. Dedicated Instance tenancy instances may be hosted on the same physical server as other instances within your account, while only Dedicated Host tenancy offers full isolation.

5. A, D. Reserved instances will give you the best price for instances you know will be running 24/7, while on-demand makes the most sense for workloads that will run at unpredictable times but can't be shut down until they're no longer needed. Load balancing controls traffic routing and, on its own, has no impact on your ability to meet changing demand.

6. B. Spot market instances can be shut down with only a minimal (two-minute) warning, so they're not recommended for workloads that require reliably predictable service. Even if your AMI can be re-launched, the interrupted workload will still be lost. Static S3 websites don't run on EC2 infrastructure in the first place.

7. A. You can edit or even add or remove security groups from running instances and the changes will take effect instantly. Similarly, you can associate or release an Elastic IP

address to/from a running instance. You can change an instance type as long as you shut down the instance first. But the AMI can't be changed; you'll need to create an entirely new instance.

8. B. The first of two strings in a resource tag is the *key*—the group to which the specific resource belongs. The second string is the *value*, which identifies the resource itself.

9. D. Provisioned-IOPS SSD volumes are currently the only type that comes close to 20,000 IOPS. In fact, they can deliver up to 32,000 IOPS.

10. B, C, D. When an image is created, a snapshot is automatically created from which an AMI is built. One does not, however, create a snapshot from an image.

11. A, C. The data on instance volumes is ephemeral and will be lost as soon as the instance is shut down. There is no way to set termination protection for instance volumes as they're dependent on the lifecycle of their host instances.

12. C, D. By default, EC2 uses the standard address blocks for private subnets, so all private addresses will fall within these ranges: 10.0.0.0 to 10.255.255.255, 172.16.0.0 to 172.31.255.255, and 192.168.0.0 to 192.168.255.255.

13. A. Accept no substitutes: it's curl `http://169.254.169.254/latest/meta-data/instance-action`.

14. A, B, D. Security group rules do not take packet size into consideration.

15. A, D. IAM roles define how resources access other resources. Users cannot authenticate as an instance role, nor can a role be associated with an instance's internal system process.

16. B, D. NAT instances and NAT gateways are AWS tools for safely routing traffic between private and public subnets and from there, out to the Internet. An Internet gateway connects a VPC with the Internet, and a virtual private gateway connects a VPC with a remote site over a secure VPN.

17. D. The client computer in an encrypted operation must always provide the private key to authenticate. For EC2 instances running Windows, you retrieve the password you'll use for the GUI login using your private key.

18. B. Load balancing directs external user requests between multiple EC2 instances, Systems Manager provides tools for monitoring and managing your resources, and Fargate is an interface for administrating Docker containers on Amazon ECS.

19. A. Beanstalk launches and manages infrastructure for your application that will remain running until you manually stop it, ECS manages Docker containers but doesn't necessarily stop them when a task is done, and Auto Scaling can *add* instances to an already running deployment to meet demand.

20. C. S3 buckets are used to store an image, but they're not directly involved in the import operation. The Snowball is a physical high-capacity storage device that Amazon ships to your office for you to load data and ship back. Direct Connect uses Amazon partner providers to build a high-speed connection between your servers and your AWS VPC.

Chapter 3: Amazon Simple Storage Service and Amazon Glacier Storage

1. C. S3 can be used to share files, but it doesn't offer low-latency access—and its eventual consistency won't work well with filesystems. Storage Gateway is designed to simplify backing up archives to the AWS cloud; it's not for sharing files. EBS volumes can be used for only a single instance at a time.

2. A. Object metadata contains information used by S3 to manage an object's security profile, behavior, and the way it's exposed to client requests. Storing this information requires very little space—2 KB will normally be more than enough.

3. D. In theory, at least, there's no limit to the data you can upload to a single bucket or to all the buckets in your account or to the number of times you upload (using the PUT command). By default, however, you are allowed only 100 S3 buckets per account.

4. A. HTTP (web) requests must address the s3.amazon.aws.com domain along with the bucket and filenames.

5. C. A prefix is the name common to the objects you want to group, and a slash character (/) can be used as a delimiter. The bar character (|) would be treated as part of the name, rather than a delimiter. While DNS names can have prefixes, they're not relevant to S3 naming.

6. A. Client-side encryption addresses encryption before an object reaches the bucket (i.e., before it's at rest). Only AWS KMS-Managed Keys provide an audit trail.

7. A, B, D. Since there is no limit to the size of an S3 bucket, there would be little to gain by reporting its current size.

8. C, D. The S3 guarantee only covers the physical infrastructure owned by AWS.

9. A. One Zone-IA is heavily replicated but only within a single availability zone, while reduced redundancy is only lightly replicated.

10. B. The S3 Standard-IA (Infrequent Access) class is guaranteed to be available 99.9 percent of the time.

11. D. S3 can't guarantee instant consistency across their infrastructure for changes to existing objects, but there aren't such concerns for newly created objects.

12. C. Object versioning must be manually enabled for each bucket before older versions of objects will be saved.

13. A. S3 lifecycle rules can incorporate specifying objects by prefix. There's no such thing as a lifecycle template.

14. A. Glacier offers the least expensive and most highly resilient storage within the AWS ecosystem. Reduced Redundancy is not resilient, and S3 One Zone and S3 Standard are relatively expensive.

15. B, C. ACLs are a legacy feature that isn't as flexible as IAM or S3 bucket polices. Security groups are not used with S3 buckets.

16. D. In this context, a principal is a user or entity to which bucket access is assigned.

17. B. The default expiry value for a presigned URL is 3,600 seconds (one hour).

18. A, D. The Amazon Certificate Manager can (when used as part of a CloudFront distribution) apply an SSL/TLS encryption certificate to your website pages. You can use Route 53 to associate a DNS domain name to your site. EC2 instances and RDS database instances would never be used for static websites.

19. B. At the time of this writing, a single Glacier archive can be no larger than 40 TB.

20. A. Elastic File System is good for sharing files from a single host source among multiple EC2 instances running within a VPC. It doesn't provide cost-effective connections to your on-premises infrastructure.

Chapter 4: Amazon Virtual Private Cloud

1. A. The allowed range of prefix lengths for a VPC CIDR is between /16 and /28 inclusive. The maximum possible prefix length for an IP subnet is /32, so /56 is not a valid length.

2. C. A secondary CIDR may come from the same RFC 1918 address range as the primary, but it may not overlap with the primary CIDR. 192.168.0.0/24 comes from the same address range (192.168.0.0–192.168.255.255) as the primary and does not overlap with 192.168.16.0/24. 192.168.0.0/16 and 192.168.16.0/23 both overlap with 192.168.16.0/24. 172.31.0.0/16 is not in the same range as the primary CIDR.

3. A, D. 10.0.0.0/24 and 10.0.0.0/23 are within the VPC CIDR and leave room for a second subnet. 10.0.0.0/8 is wrong because prefix lengths less than /16 aren't allowed. 10.0.0.0/16 doesn't leave room for another subnet.

4. B. Multiple subnets may exist in a single availability zone. A subnet cannot span availability zones.

5. A. Every ENI must have a primary private IP address. It can have secondary IP addresses, but all addresses must come from the subnet the ENI resides in. Once created, the ENI cannot be moved to a different subnet. An ENI can be created independently of an instance and later attached to an instance.

6. D. Each VPC contains a default security group that can't be deleted. You can create a security group by itself without attaching it to anything. But if you want to use it, you must attach it to an ENI. You also attach multiple security groups to the same ENI.

7. A. A NACL is stateless, meaning it doesn't track connection state. Every inbound rule must have a corresponding outbound rule to permit traffic, and vice versa. A NACL is attached to a subnet, whereas a security group is attached to an ENI. A NACL can be associated with multiple subnets, but a subnet can have only one NACL.

8. D. An Internet gateway has no management IP address. It can be associated with only one VPC at a time and so cannot grant Internet access to instances in multiple VPCs. It is a logical VPC resource and not a virtual or physical router.

9. A. The destination 0.0.0.0/0 matches all IP prefixes and hence covers all publicly accessible hosts on the Internet. ::/0 is an IPv6 prefix, not an IPv4 prefix. An Internet gateway is the target of the default route, not the destination.

10. A. Every subnet is associated with the main route table by default. You can explicitly associate a subnet with another route table. There is no such thing as a default route table, but you can create a default route within a route table.

11. A. An instance must have a public IP address to be directly reachable from the Internet. The instance may be able to reach the Internet via a NAT device. The instance won't necessarily receive the same private IP address because it was automatically assigned. The instance will be able to reach other instances in the subnet because a public IP is not required.

12. B. Assigning an EIP to an instance is a two-step process. First you must allocate an EIP, and then you must associate it with an ENI. You can't allocate an ENI, and there's no such thing as an instance's primary EIP. Configuring the instance to use an automatically assigned public IP must occur at instance creation. Changing an ENI's private IP to match an EIP doesn't actually assign a public IP to the instance, as the ENI's private address is still private.

13. A. Internet-bound traffic from an instance with an automatically assigned public IP will traverse an Internet gateway that will perform NAT. The source address will be the instance's public IP. An instance with an automatically assigned public IP cannot also have an EIP. The NAT process will replace the private IP source address with the public IP. 0.0.0.0 is not a valid source address.

14. A. The NAT device's default route must point to an Internet gateway, and the instance's default route must point to the NAT device. No differing NACL configurations between subnets are required to use a NAT device. Security groups are applied at the ENI level. A NAT device doesn't require multiple interfaces.

15. A. A NAT gateway is a VPC resource that scales automatically to accommodate increased bandwidth requirements. A NAT instance can't do this. A NAT gateway exists in only one availability zone. There are not multiple NAT gateway types. A NAT instance is a regular EC2 instance that comes in different types.

16. A. An Internet gateway performs NAT for instances that have a public IP address. A route table defines how traffic from instances is forwarded. An EIP is a public IP address and can't perform NAT. An ENI is a network interface and doesn't perform NAT.

17. A. The source/destination check on the NAT instance's ENI must be disabled to allow the instance to receive traffic not destined for its IP and to send traffic using a source address that it doesn't own. The NAT instance's default route must point to an Internet gateway as the target. You can't assign a primary private IP address after the instance is created.

18. A. You cannot route through a VPC using transitive routing. Instead, you must directly peer the VPCs containing the instances that need to communicate. A VPC peering connection uses the AWS internal network and requires no public IP address. Because a peering connection is a point-to-point connection, it can connect only two VPCs. A peering connection can be used only for instance-to-instance communication. You can't use it to share other VPC resources.

19. A, D. Each peered VPC needs a route to the CIDR of its peer; therefore, you must create two routes with the peering connection as the target. Creating only one route is not sufficient to enable bidirectional communication. Additionally, the instances' security groups must allow for bidirectional communication. You can't create more than one peering connection between a pair of VPCs.

20. A. Inter-region VPC peering connections aren't available in all regions and support a maximum MTU of 1,500 bytes. You can use IPv4 across an inter-region peering connection but not IPv6.

Chapter 5: Databases

1. A, C. Different relational databases use different terminology. A row, record, and tuple all describe an ordered set of columns. An attribute is another term for column. A table contains rows and columns.

2. C. A table must contain at least one attribute or column. Primary and foreign keys are used for relating data in different tables, but they're not required. A row can exist within a table, but a table doesn't need a row in order to exist.

3. D. The SELECT statement retrieves data from a table. INSERT is used for adding data to a table. QUERY and SCAN are commands used by DynamoDB, which is a nonrelational database.

4. B. Online transaction processing databases are designed to handle multiple transactions per second. Online analytics processing databases are for complex queries against large data sets. A key-value store such as DynamoDB can handle multiple transactions per second, but it's not a relational database. There's no such thing as an offline transaction processing database.

5. B. Although there are six database engines to choose from, a single database instance can run only one database engine. If you want to run more than one database engine, you will need a separate database instance for each engine.

6. B, C. MariaDB and Aurora are designed as binary drop-in replacements for MySQL. PostgreSQL is designed for compatibility with Oracle databases. Microsoft SQL Server does not support MySQL databases.

7. C. InnoDB is the only storage engine Amazon recommends for MySQL and MariaDB deployments in RDS and the only engine Aurora supports. MyISAM is another storage engine that works with MySQL but is not compatible with automated backups. XtraDB is

another storage engine for MariaDB, but Amazon no longer recommends it. The PostgreSQL database engine uses its own storage engine by the same name and is not compatible with other database engines.

8. A, C. All editions of the Oracle database engine support the bring-your-own-license model in RDS. Microsoft SQL Server and PostgreSQL only support the license included model.

9. B. Memory-optimized instances are EBS optimized, providing dedicated bandwidth for EBS storage. Standard instances are not EBS optimized and top out at 10,000 Mbps disk throughput. Burstable (burst capable) instances are designed for development and test workloads and provide the lowest disk throughput of any instance class. There is no instance class called storage optimized.

10. A. MariaDB has a page size of 16 KB. To write 200 MB (204,800 KB) of data every second, it would need 12,800 IOPS. Oracle, PostgreSQL, or Microsoft SQL Server, which all use an 8 KB page size, would need 25,600 IOPS to achieve the same throughput. When provisioning IOPS, you must specify IOPS in increments of 1,000, so 200 and 16 IOPS—which would be woefully insufficient anyway—are not valid answers.

11. A. General-purpose SSD storage allocates three IOPS per gigabyte, up to 10,000 IOPS. Therefore, to get 600 IOPS, you'd need to allocate 200 GB. Allocating 100 GB would give you only 300 IOPS. The maximum storage size for gp2 storage is 16 TB, so 200 TB is not a valid value. The minimum amount of storage you can allocate depends on the database engine, but it's no less than 20 GB, so 200 MB is not valid.

12. C. When you provision IOPS using io1 storage, you must do so in a ratio no greater than 50 IOPS for 1 GB. Allocating 240 GB of storage would give you 12,000 IOPS. Allocating 200 GB of storage would fall short, yielding just 10,000 IOPS. Allocating 12 TB would be overkill for the amount of storage required.

13. A. A read replica only services queries and cannot write to a database. A standby database instance in a multi-AZ deployment does not accept queries. Both a primary and master database instance can service both queries and writes.

14. D. Multi-AZ deployments using Oracle, PostgreSQL, MariaDB, MySQL, or Microsoft SQL Server replicate data synchronously from the primary to a standby instance. Only a multi-AZ deployment using Aurora uses a cluster volume and replicates data to a specific type of read replica called an Aurora replica.

15. A. When you restore from a snapshot, RDS creates a new instance and doesn't make any changes to the failed instance. A snapshot is a copy of the entire instance, not just a copy of the individual databases. RDS does not delete a snapshot after restoring from it.

16. B. The ALL distribution style ensures every compute node has a complete copy of every table. The EVEN distribution style splits tables up evenly across all compute nodes. The KEY distribution style distributes data according to the value in a specified column. There is no distribution style called ODD.

17. D. The dense compute type can store up to 326 TB of data on magnetic storage. The dense storage type can store up to 2 PB of data on solid state drives. A leader node coordinates communication among compute nodes but doesn't store any databases. There is no such thing as a dense memory node type.

18. A, B. In a nonrelational database, a primary key is required to uniquely identify an item and hence must be unique within a table. All primary key values within a table must have the same data type. Only relational databases use primary keys to correlate data across different tables.

19. B. An order date would not be unique within a table, so it would be inappropriate for a partition (hash) key or a simple primary key. It would be appropriate as a sort key, as DynamoDB would order items according to the order date, which would make it possible to query items with a specific date or within a date range.

20. A. A single strongly consistent read of an item up to 4 KB consumes one read capacity unit. Hence, reading 11 KB of data per second using strongly consistent reads would consume three read capacity units. Were you to use eventually consistent reads, you would need only two read capacity units, as one eventually consistent read gives you up to 8 KB of data per second. Regardless, you must specify a read capacity of at least 1, so 0 is not a valid answer.

21. B. The dense storage node type uses fast SSDs, while the dense compute node uses slower magnetic storage. The leader node doesn't access the database but coordinates communication among compute nodes. KEY is a data distribution strategy Redshift uses, but there is no such thing as a key node.

22. D. When you create a table, you can choose to create a global secondary index with a different partition and hash key. A local secondary index can be created after the table is created, but the partition key must be the same as the base table, although the hash key can be different. There is no such thing as a global primary index or eventually consistent index.

23. B. NoSQL databases are optimized for queries against a primary key. If you need to query data based only one on attribute, you'd make that attribute the primary key. NoSQL databases are not designed for complex queries. Both NoSQL and relational databases can store JSON documents, and both database types can be used by different applications.

24. D. A graph database is a type of nonrelational database that discovers relationships among items. A document-oriented store is a nonrelational database that analyzes and extracts data from documents. Relational databases can enforce relationships between records but don't discover them. A SQL database is a type of relational database.

Chapter 6: Authentication and Authorization—AWS Identity and Access Management

1. C. While each of the other answers represents possible concerns, none of them carries consequences as disastrous as the complete loss of control over your account.

2. B. The Action element refers to the kind of action requested (list, create, etc.), the Resource element refers to the particular AWS account resource that's the target of the policy, and the Effect element refers to the way IAM should react to a request.

3. A, B, C. Unless there's a policy that explicitly allows an action, it will be denied. Therefore, a user with no policies or with a policy permitting S3 actions doesn't permit EC2 instance permissions. Similarly, when two policies conflict, the more restrictive will be honored. The AdministratorAccess policy opens up nearly all AWS resources, including EC2.

4. B, C. If you don't perform any administration operations with regular IAM users, then there really is no point for them to exist. Similarly, without access keys, there's a limit to what a user will be able to accomplish. Ideally, all users should use MFA and strong passwords.

5. A, B. X.509 is the standard protocol for SOAP requests, but access keys are used for S3 and Amazon Mechanical Turk requests. Passwords are never used for encryption, just authentication, and key pairs are generally used only for EC2 instances or for authenticating signed URLS for CloudFront distributions.

6. D. The top-level command is `iam`, while the correct subcommmand is `get-access-key-last-used`. The parameter is identified by `--access-last-key-id`. Parameters (not subcommands) are always prefixed with `--` characters.

7. B. IAM groups are primarily about simplifying administration. It has no direct impact on resource usage or response times and only an indirect impact on locking down the root user.

8. C. X.509 certificates are used for encrypting SOAP requests, not authentication. The other choices are all valid identities within the context of an IAM role.

9. A. Key Management Service manages encryption infrastructure but isn't FIPS 140-2 compliant. Security Token Service is used to issue tokens for valid IAM roles. And Secrets Manager handles secrets for third-party services or databases.

10. B. AWS Directory Service for Microsoft Active Directory provides Active Directory authentication within a VPC environment. Amazon Cognito provides user administration for your applications. AWS Secrets Manager handles secrets for third-party services or databases. AWS Key Management Service manages encryption infrastructure.

11. A. Identity pools provide temporary access to defined AWS services to your application users. Sign-up and sign-in is managed through Cognito user pools. KMS and/or CloudHSM provide encryption infrastructure. And credential delivery to databases or third-party applications is provided by AWS Secrets Manager.

12. A, D. You IAM policies will be as effective as ever, even if outsiders know your policies. Since even an account's root user would never have known other users' passwords, there's no reason to change them.

13. B. IAM policies are global—they're not restricted to any one region. Policies *do*, however, require an action (like create buckets), an effect (allow), and a resource (S3).

14. B, C. IAM roles require a defined trusted entity and at least one policy. However, the relevant actions are defined by the policies you choose, and roles themselves are uninterested in which applications use them.

15. D. STS tokens are used as temporary credentials to external identities for resource access to through IAM roles. Users and groups would not use tokens to authenticate, and roles are used to define the access a token will provide, not the recipient of the access.

16. C. Policies must be written in JSON format.

17. B, D. The correct Resource line would read "Resource": "*". There is no "Target" line in an IAM policy.

18. B. User pools provide sign-up and sign-in for your application's users. Temporary access to defined AWS services to your application users is provided by identity pools. KMS and/ or CloudHSM provide encryption infrastructure. And credential delivery to databases or third-party applications is provided by AWS Secrets Manager.

19. C, D. An AWS managed service takes care of all underlying infrastructure management for you. In this case, that will include data replication and software updates. On-premises integration and multi-AZ deployment are important infrastructure features, but they're not unique to "managed" services.

20. B, C, D. In this context, key usage monitoring is only useful to ensure that none of your applications is still using an old key that's set to be retired.

Chapter 7: CloudTrail, CloudWatch, and AWS Config

1. B, D. Creating a bucket and subnet are API actions, regardless of whether they're performed from the web console or AWS CLI. Uploading an object to an S3 bucket is a data event, not a management event. Logging into the AWS console is a non-API management event.

2. C. Data events include S3 object-level activity and Lambda function executions. Downloading an object from S3 is a read-only event. Uploading a file to an S3 bucket is a write-only event and hence would not be logged by the trail. Viewing an S3 bucket and creating a Lambda function are management events, not data events.

3. C. CloudTrail stores 90 days of event history for each region, regardless of whether a trail is configured. Event history is specific to the events occurring in that region. Because the trail was configured to log read-only management events, the trail logs would not contain a record of the trail's deletion. They might contain a record of who viewed the trail, but that would be insufficient to establish who deleted it. There is no such thing as an IAM user log.

4. B. CloudWatch uses dimensions to uniquely identify metrics with the same name and namespace. Metrics in the same namespace will necessarily be in the same region. The data point of a metric and the timestamp that it contains are not unique and can't be used to uniquely identify a metric.

5. C. Basic monitoring sends metrics every five minutes, while detailed monitoring sends them every minute. CloudWatch can store metrics at regular or high resolution, but this affects how the metric is timestamped, rather than the frequency with which it's delivered to CloudWatch.

6. A. CloudWatch can store high-resolution metrics at subminute resolution. Therefore, updating a metric at 15:57:08 and again at 15:57:37 will result in CloudWatch storing two separate data points. Only if the metric were regular resolution would CloudWatch overwrite an earlier data point with a later one. Under no circumstances would CloudWatch ignore a metric update.

7. D. Metrics stored at one-hour resolution age out after 15 months. Five-minute resolutions are stored for 63 days. One-minute resolution metrics are stored for 15 days. High-resolution metrics are kept for 3 hours.

8. A. To graph a metric's data points, specify the Sum statistic and set the period equal to the metric's resolution, which is in this case is five minutes. Graphing the Sum or Average statistic over a one-hour period will not graph the metric's data points but rather the Sum or Average of those data points over a one-hour period. Using the Sample count statistic over a five-minute period will yield a value of one for each period, since there's only one data point per period.

9. B. CloudWatch uses a log stream to store log events from a single source. Log groups store and organize log streams but do not directly store log events. A metric filter extracts metrics from logs but doesn't store anything. The CloudWatch agent can deliver logs to CloudWatch from a server but doesn't store logs.

10. A, D. Every log stream must be in a log group. The retention period setting of a log group controls how long CloudWatch retains log events within those streams. You can't manually delete log events individually, but you can delete all events in a log stream by deleting the stream. You can't set a retention period on a log stream directly.

11. A, C. CloudTrail will not stream events greater than 256 KB in size. There's also a normal delay, typically up to 15 minutes, before an event appears in a CloudWatch log stream. Metric filters have no bearing on what log events get put into a log stream. Although a misconfigured or missing IAM role would prevent CloudTrail from streaming logs to CloudWatch, the question indicates that some events are present. Hence, the IAM role is correctly configured.

12. B, D. If an EBS volume isn't attached to a running instance, EBS won't generate any metrics to send to CloudWatch. Hence, the alarm won't be able to collect enough data points to alarm. The evaluation period can be no more than 24 hours, and the alarm was created two days ago, so the evaluation period has elapsed. The data points to monitor don't have to cross the threshold for CloudWatch to determine the alarm state.

13. B. To have CloudWatch treat missing data as exceeding the threshold, set the Treat Missing Data As option to Breaching. Setting it to Not Breaching will have the opposite effect. Setting it to As Missing will cause CloudWatch to ignore the missing data and behave as if those evaluation periods didn't occur. The Ignore option causes the alarm not to change state in response to missing data. There's no option to treat missing data as Not Missing.

14. C, D. CloudWatch can use the Simple Notification Service to send a text message. Cloud-Watch refers to this as a Notification action. To reboot an instance, you must use an EC2 Action. The Auto Scaling action will not reboot an instance. SMS is not a valid Cloud-Watch alarm action.

15. A. The recover action is useful when there's a problem with an instance that requires AWS involvement to repair, such as a hardware failure. The recover action migrates the same instance to a new host. Rebooting an instance assumes the instance is running and entails the instance remaining on the same host. Recovering an instance does not involve restoring any data from a snapshot, as the instance retains the same EBS volume(s).

16. B. If CloudTrail were logging write-only management events in the same region as the instance, it would have generated trail logs containing the deletion event. Deleting a log stream containing CloudTrail events does not delete those events from the trail logs stored in S3. Deleting an EC2 instance is not an IAM event. If AWS Config were tracking changes to EC2 instances in the region, it would have recorded a timestamped configuration item for the deletion, but it would not include the principal that deleted the instance.

17. B, C, D. The delivery channel must include an S3 bucket name and may specify an SNS topic and the delivery frequency of configuration snapshots. You can't specify a Cloud-Watch log stream.

18. D. You can't delete configuration items manually, but you can have AWS Config delete them after no less than 30 days. Pausing or deleting the configuration recorder will stop AWS Config from recording new changes but will not delete configuration items. Deleting configuration snapshots, which are objects stored in S3, will not delete the configuration items.

19. C, D. CloudWatch can graph only a time series. METRICS()/AVG(m1) and m1/m2 both return a time series. AVG(m1)-m1 and AVG(m1) return scalar values and can't be graphed directly.

20. B. Deleting the rule will prevent AWS Config from evaluating resources' configurations against it. Turning off the configuration recorder won't prevent AWS Config from evaluating the rule. It's not possible to delete the configuration history for a resource from AWS Config. When you specify a frequency for periodic checks, you must specify a valid frequency, or else AWS Config will not accept the configuration.

Chapter 8: The Domain Name System and Network Routing: Amazon Route 53 and Amazon CloudFront

1. A. Name servers resolve IP addresses from domain names, allowing clients to connect to resources. Domain registration is performed by domain name registrars. Routing policies are applied through record sets within hosted zones.

2. C. A domain is a set of resources identified by a single domain name. FQDN stands for fully qualified domain name. Policies for resolving requests are called routing policies.

3. D. The rightmost section of an FQDN address is the TLD. `aws.` would be a subdomain or host, `amazon.` is the SLD, and `amazon.com/documentation/` points to a resource stored at the web root of the domain server.

4. A. CNAME is a record type, but it's not a category. TTL, record type, and record data are all category names.

5. C. An A record maps a hostname to an IPv4 IP address. NS records identify name servers. SOA records document start of authority data. CNAME records define one hostname as an alias for another.

6. A, C, D. Route 53 provides domain registration, health checks, and DNS management. Content delivery network services are provided by CloudFront.

7. C. Geolocation can control routing by the geographic origin of the request. The simple policy sends traffic to a single resource. Latency sends content using the fastest origin resource. Multivalue can be used to make a deployment more highly available.

8. A. Latency selects the available resource with the lowest latency. Weighted policies route among multiple resources by percentage. Geolocation tailors request responses to the end user's location. Failover incorporates backup resources for higher availability.

9. B. Weighted policies route among multiple resources by percentage. Failover incorporates backup resources for higher availability. Latency selects the available resource with the lowest latency. Geolocation tailors request responses to the end user's location.

10. D. Failover incorporates backup resources for higher availability. Latency selects the available resource with the lowest latency. Weighted policies route among multiple resources by percentage. Geolocation tailors request responses to the end user's location.

11. A, D. Public and private hosting zones are real options. Regional and VPC zones don't exist (although private zones do map to VPCs).

12. A, B. To transfer a domain, you'll need to make sure the domain isn't set to locked and an authorization code that you'll provide to Route 53. Copying name server addresses is necessary only for managing remotely registered domains on Route 53. CNAME record sets are used to define one hostname as an alias for another.

13. B. You can enable managing remotely registered domains on Route 53 by copying name server addresses to the remote registrar's admin interface. Making sure the domain isn't set to locked and requesting authorization codes are used to transfer a domain to Route 53. CNAME record sets are used to define one hostname as an alias for another.

14. C. You specify the web page you want used for testing when you configure your health check. There is no default page. Remote SSH sessions would be impossible for a number of reasons and wouldn't definitively confirm a running resource in any case.

15. A. Geoproximity is about precisely pinpointing users while geolocation uses geopolitical boundaries.

16. A, D. Users on a single corporate campus or accessing resources through a VPN will not benefit from the distributed delivery provided by CloudFront.

17. C. API Gateway is used to generate custom client SDKs for your APIs to connect your backend systems to mobile, web, and server applications or services.

18. A. Choosing a price class offering limited distribution is the best way to reduce costs. Non-HTTPS traffic can be excluded but not through the configuration of an SSL certificate. Disabling Alternate Domain Names or Compress Objects Automatically won't reduce costs.

19. C. Requests of an edge location will only achieve lower latency after copies of your origin files are already cached. Therefore, a response to the first request might not be fast because CloudFront still has to copy the file from the origin server.

20. B. RTMP distributions can only manage content from S3 buckets. RTMP is intended for the distribution of video content.

Chapter 9: The Reliability Pillar

1. C. 99.95 percent availability translates to about 22 minutes of downtime per month, or 4 hours and 23 minutes per year. 99.999 percent availability is less than 30 seconds of downtime per month, but the question calls for the minimum level of availability. 99 percent yields more than 7 hours of downtime per month, while 99.9 percent is more than 43 minutes of downtime per month.

2. A. The EC2 instances are redundant components, so to calculate their availability, you multiply the component failure rates and subtract the product from 100 percent. In this case, 100% − (1% × 1%) = 99.99%. Because the database represents a hard dependency, you multiply the availability of the EC2 instances by the availability of the RDS instance, which is 99 percent. In this case, 99.99% × 99% = 98.99%. A total availability of 99 percent may seem intuitive since it's the availability of each component, but because the redundant EC2 instances have a hard dependency on the RDS instance, you must multiple the availabilities together. A total availability of 99.99 percent is unachievable since it's well above the availability of any of the components. 97 percent would represent the total application availability if the EC2 instances were hard dependencies instead of redundant components.

3. B. DynamoDB offers 99.99 percent availability and low latency. Because it's distributed, data is stored across multiple availability zones. You can also use DynamoDB global tables to achieve even higher availability: 99.999 percent. Multi-AZ RDS offerings can provide low latency performance, particularly when using Aurora, but the guaranteed availability is capped at 99.95 percent. Hosting your own SQL database isn't a good option because although you could theoretically achieve high availability, it would come at the cost of significant time and effort.

4. B, D. One cause of application failures is resource exhaustion. By scoping out large enough instances and scaling out to make sure you have enough of them, you can prevent failure and thus increase availability. Scaling instances in may help with cost savings but won't help availability. Storing web assets in S3 instead of hosting them from an instance can help with performance but won't have an impact on availability.

5. B. You can modify a launch template by creating a new version of it; however, the question indicates that the Auto Scaling group was created using a launch configuration. You can't modify a launch configuration. Auto Scaling doesn't use CloudFormation templates.

6. A. Auto Scaling strives to maintain the number of instances specified in the desired capacity setting. If the desired capacity setting isn't set, Auto Scaling will attempt to maintain the number of instances specified by the minimum group size. Given a desired capacity of 5, there should be five healthy instances. If you manually terminate two of them, Auto Scaling will create two new ones to replace them. Auto Scaling will not adjust the desired capacity or minimum group size.

7. A, D, E. Auto Scaling monitors the health of instances in the group using either ELB or EC2 instance and system checks. It can't use Route 53 health checks. Dynamic scaling policies can use CloudWatch Alarms, but these are unrelated to checking the health of instances.

8. B, C. Scheduled actions can adjust the minimum and maximum group sizes and the desired capacity on a schedule, which is useful when your application has a predictable load pattern. To add more instances in proportion to the aggregate CPU utilization of the group, implement step scaling policies. Target tracking policies adjust the desired capacity of a group to keep the threshold of a given metric near a predefined value. Simple scaling policies simply add more instances when a defined CloudWatch alarm triggers, but the number of instances added is not proportional to the value of the metric.

9. A, D. Enabling versioning protects objects against data corruption and deletion by keeping before and after copies of every object. The Standard storage class replicates objects across multiple availability zones in a region, guarding against the failure of an entire zone. Bucket policies may protect against accidental deletion, but they don't guard against data corruption. Cross-region replication applies to new objects, not existing ones.

10. C. The Data Lifecycle Manager can automatically create snapshots of an EBS volume every 12 or 24 hours and retain up to 1,000 snapshots. Backing up files to EFS is not an option because a spot instance may terminate before the cron job has a chance to complete. Cloud-Watch Logs doesn't support storing binary files.

11. D. Aurora allows you to have up to 15 replicas. MariaDB, MySQL, and PostgreSQL allow you to have only up to five.

12. B. When you enable automated snapshots, RDS backs up database transaction logs about every five minutes. Configuring multi-AZ will enable synchronous replication between the two instances, but this is useful for avoiding failures and is unrelated to the time it takes to recover a database. Read replicas are not appropriate for disaster recovery because data is copied to them asynchronously, and there can be a significant delay in replication, resulting in an RPO of well over five minutes.

13. A, C. AWS sometimes adds additional availability zones to a region. To take advantage of a new zone, you'll need to be able to add a new subnet in it. You also may decide later that you may need another subnet or tier for segmentation or security purposes. RDS doesn't require a separate subnet. It can share the same subnet with other VPC resources. Adding a secondary CIDR to a VPC doesn't require adding another subnet.

14. A, D. Two EC2 instances each with 2 private IP addresses would consume 100 IP addresses in a subnet. Additionally, AWS reserves 5 IP addresses in every subnet. The subnet therefore must be large enough to hold 105 IP addresses. 172.21.0.0/25 and 10.0.0.0/21 are sufficiently large. 172.21.0.0/26 allows room for only 63 IP addresses. 10.0.0.0/8 is large enough, but a subnet prefix length must be at least /16.

15. A, D. Direct Connect offers consistent speeds and latency to the AWS cloud. Because Direct Connect bypasses the public Internet, it's more secure. For speeds, you can choose 1 Gbps or 10 Gbps, so Direct Connect wouldn't offer a bandwidth increase over using the existing 10 Gbps Internet connection. Adding a Direct Connect connection wouldn't have an effect on end-user experience, since they would still use the Internet to reach your AWS resources.

16. B. When connecting a VPC to an external network, whether via a VPN connection or Direct Connect, make sure the IP address ranges don't overlap. In-transit encryption, while useful for securing network traffic, isn't required for proper connectivity. IAM policies restrict API access to AWS resources, but this is unrelated to network connectivity. Security groups are VPC constructs and aren't something you configure on a data center firewall.

17. A, C. CloudFormation lets you provision and configure EC2 instances by defining your infrastructure as code. This lets you update the AMI easily and build a new instance from it as needed. You can include application installation scripts in the User Data to automate the build process. Auto Scaling isn't appropriate for this scenario because you're going to sometimes terminate and re-create the instance. Dynamic scaling policies are part of Auto Scaling.

18. D. By running four instances in each zone, you have a total of 12 instances in the region. If one zone fails, you lose four of those instances and are left with eight. Running eight or 16 instances in each zone would allow you to withstand one zone failure, but the question asks for the minimum number of instances. Three instances per zone would give you nine total in the region, but if one zone fails, you'd be left with only six.

19. C. 99.99 percent availability corresponds to about 52 minutes of downtime per year. 99 percent, 99.9 percent, and 99.95 percent entail significantly more downtime.

20. A, C. Because users access a public domain name that resolves to an elastic load balancer, you'll need to update the DNS record to point to the load balancer in the other region. You'll also need to fail the database over to the other region so that the read replica can become the primary. Load balancers are not cross-region, so it's not possible to point the load balancer in one region to instances in another. Restoring the database isn't necessary because the primary database instance asynchronously replicates data to the read replicas in the other region.

Chapter 10: The Performance Efficiency Pillar

1. A, B, D. ECUs, vCPUs, and the Intel AES-NI encryption set are all instance type parameters. Aggregate cumulative cost per request has nothing to do with EC2 instances but is a common key performance indicator (KPI).

2. A, B, C. A launch configuration pointing to an EC2 AMI and an associated load balancer are all, normally, essential to an Auto Scaling operation. Passing a startup script to the instance at runtime may not be necessary, especially if your application is already set up as part of your AMI.

3. B. Defining a capacity metric, minimum and maximum instances, and a load balancer are all done during the Auto-Scaler configuration. Only the AMI is defined by the launch configuration.

4. A. Long-lived, more complex web applications and processes requiring in-depth monitoring and tracking are both more suited for EC2 instances, while processing transactions is a strength of Lambda.

5. D. RAID optimization is an OS-level configuration and can, therefore, be performed only from within the OS.

6. C. CloudFront and S3 Transfer Acceleration deliver low latency but not resilience. RAID arrays can deliver both, but only on EBS volumes.

7. A. Neither S3 Cross-Region Replication nor EC2 Auto Scaling use CloudFront edge locations, and the EBS Data Transfer Wizard doesn't exist (although perhaps it should).

8. B. Scalability is managed automatically by RDS. Indexes, schemas, and views should be optimized as much as possible.

9. C, D. Automated patches and updates are benefits of a managed service like RDS, not of custom-built EC2-based databases.

10. A, C. ElasticSearch isn't likely to help with a graphics workload. CloudFront can help with media transfers, but not with graphics processing.

11. C. The Application load balancer works on layer 7. The Classic Load Balancer isn't optimized for layer 4. There is no such thing as a Dynamic Load Balancer.

12. A, B, D. CloudDeploy is not a good source of CloudFormation templates.

13. A. There is no default node name in a CloudFormation configuration—nor is there a node of any sort.

14. B, D. Terraform and Ansible are not directly integrated with OpsWorks.

15. A, C. There are no tools named CloudWatch OneView or AWS Config Dashboards.

16. A, B. Advanced permission from AWS is helpful only for load testing operations. A complete record of your account's resource configuration changes would make sense in the context of AWS Config, but not CloudWatch.

17. D. CloudTrail tracks API calls. CloudWatch monitors system performance. CodePipeline is a CI/CD orchestration service.

18. B, C. Varnish and Nginx can both cache data but are not integrated into ElastiCache.

19. A, D. In many cases, Memcached will provide faster service. Redis configuration has a rather steep learning curve.

20. B. Read replicas based on the Oracle database are not possible.

Chapter 11: The Security Pillar

1. A, C. A password policy can specify a minimum password length but not a maximum. It can prevent a user from reusing a password they used before but not one that another user has used. A password policy can require a password to contain numbers. It can also require administrator approval to reset an expired password.

2. B. The Condition element lets you require MFA to grant the permissions defined in the policy. The Resource and Action elements define what those permissions are but not the conditions under which those permissions are granted. The Principal element is not used in an identity-based policy.

3. A, D. IAM keeps five versions of every customer managed policy. When CloudTrail is configured to log global management events, it will record any policy changes in the request parameters of the CreatePolicyVersion operation. There is no such thing as a policy snapshot. CloudTrail data event logs will not log IAM events.

4. B. When an IAM user assumes a role, the user gains the permissions assigned to that role but loses the permissions assigned to the IAM user. Because the role can perform the Run-Instances action in the us-east-1 region, the user, upon assuming the role, can create a new instance in the us-east-1 region but cannot perform any other actions.

5. A. Granting a user access to use a KMS key to decrypt data requires adding the user to the key policy as a key user. Adding the user as a key administrator is insufficient to grant this access, as is granting the user access to the key using an IAM policy. Adding the user to a bucket policy can grant the user permission to access encrypted objects in the bucket but doesn't necessarily give the user the ability to decrypt those objects.

6. C. VPC flow logs record source IP address information for traffic coming into your VPC. DNS query logs record the IP addresses of DNS queries, but those won't necessarily be the same IP addresses accessing your application. Because users won't directly connect to your RDS instance, RDS logs won't record their IP addresses. CloudTrail logs can record the source IP address of API requests but not connections to an EC2 instance.

7. C, D. Athena lets you perform advanced SQL queries against data stored in S3. A metric filter can increment based on the occurrence of a value in a CloudWatch log group but can't tell you the most frequently occurring IP address.

8. A. The Behavior finding type is triggered by an instance sending abnormally large amounts of data or communicating on a protocol and port that it typically doesn't. The Backdoor finding type indicates that an instance has resolved a DNS name associated with a command-and-control server or is communicating on TCP port 25. The Stealth finding type is triggered by weakening password policies or modifying a CloudTrail configuration.

The ResourceConsumption finding type is triggered when an IAM user launches an EC2 instance when they've never done so.

9. A, C. The AWS Config timeline will show every configuration change that occurred on the instance, including the attachment and detachment of security groups. CloudTrail management event logs will also show the actions that detached and attached the security group. Although AWS Config rules use Lambda functions, the Lambda logs for AWS managed rules are not available to you. VPC flow logs capture traffic ingressing a VPC, but not API events.

10. D. The Security Best Practices rules package has rules that apply to only Linux instances. The other rules contain rules for both Windows and Linux instances.

11. C, D. You can use an IAM policy or SQS access policy to restrict queue access to certain principals or those coming from a specified IP range. You cannot use network access control lists or security groups to restrict access to a public endpoint.

12. A, C. HTTPS traffic traverses TCP port 443, so the security group should allow inbound access to this protocol and port. HTTP traffic uses TCP port 80. Because users need to reach the ALB but not the instances directly, the security group should be attached to the ALB. Removing the Internet gateway would prevent users from reaching the ALB as well as the EC2 instances directly.

13. B. A security group to restrict inbound access to authorized sources is sufficient to guard against a UDP-based DDoS attack. Elastic load balancers do not provide UDP listeners, only TCP. AWS Shield is enabled by default and protects against those UDP-based attacks from sources that are allowed by the security group.

14. A, C. WAF can block SQL injection attacks against your application, but only if it's behind an application load balancer. It's not necessary for the EC2 instances to have an elastic IP address. Blocking access to TCP port 3306, which is the port that MySQL listens on for database connections, may prevent direct access to the database server but won't prevent a SQL injection attack.

15. B, D. Both WAF and Shield Advanced can protect against HTTP flood attacks, which are marked by excessive or malformed requests. Shield Advanced includes WAF at no charge. Shield Standard does not offer protection against layer 7 attacks. GuardDuty looks for signs of an attack but does not prevent one.

16. A, D. You can revoke and rotate both a customer-managed CMK and a customer-provided key at will. You can't revoke or rotate an AWS-managed CMK or an S3-managed key.

17. D. Customer-managed customer master keys (CMKs) can be rotated at will, while AWS-managed CMKs are rotated only once a year. RDS lets you use a customer-managed CMK to encrypt data, while DynamoDB requires you to use an AWS-managed CMK. RedShift is not designed for highly transactional databases and is not appropriate for the application. KMS stores and manages encryption keys but doesn't store application data.

18. B, D. To encrypt data on an unencrypted EBS volume, you must first take a snapshot. The snapshot will inherit the encryption characteristics of the source volume, so an unencrypted

EBS volume will always yield an unencrypted snapshot. You can then simultaneously encrypt the snapshot as you copy it to another region.

19. B. You can enable encryption on an EFS filesystem only when you create it; therefore, the only option to encrypt the data using KMS is to create a new EFS filesystem and copy the data to it. A third-party encryption program can't use KMS keys to encrypt data. Encrypting the EBS volume will encrypt the data stored on the volume, but not on the EFS filesystem.

20. A, D. You can install an ACM-generated certificate on a CloudFront distribution or application load balancer. You can't export the private key of an ACM-generated certificate, so you can't install it on an EC2 instance. AWS manages the TLS certificates used by S3.

Chapter 12: The Cost Optimization Pillar

1. C. The Free Tier provides free access to *basic* levels of AWS services for a new account's first *year*.

2. A. The Standard storage class provides the most replicated and quickest-access service and is, therefore, the most expensive option. Storage rates for the Standard-Infrequent and One Zone-Infrequent classes are lower than Standard but are still more expensive than Glacier.

3. B. Cost Explorer provides usage and spending data. Organizations lets you combine multiple AWS accounts under a single administration. TCO Calculator lets you compare the costs of running an application on AWS versus locally.

4. D. Cost Explorer provides usage and spending data, but without the ability to easily incorporate Redshift and QuickSight that Cost and Usage Reports offers. Trusted Advisor checks your account for best-practice compliance. Budgets allows you to set alerts for problematic usage.

5. A, B, D. There is no such thing as a specially hardened organization-level VPC.

6. B, C. Trusted Advisor doesn't monitor Route 53 hosted zones. Proper OS-level configuration of your EC2 instances is your responsibility. Trusted Advisor monitors your EC2 instances for lower than 10 percent CPU and network I/O below 5 MB on four or more days.

7. B. TCO Calculator helps you compare on-premises to AWS deployments. Trusted Advisor checks your account for best-practice compliance. Cost and Usage Reports helps you analyze data from an existing deployment.

8. A. Monitoring of EBS volumes for capacity is not within the scope of budgets.

9. A, B. You're actually allowed only two free budgets per account. Cost allocation tags are managed from the Cost Allocation Tags page.

10. D. Spot instances are not appropriate for long-term use. Since it's possible to schedule an RI to launch within a recurring block of time, provisioning other instance configurations for the summer months will be wasteful.

11. C. Payment options (All Upfront, Partial Upfront, or No Upfront), reservation types (Standard or Convertible RI), and tenancy (Default or Dedicated) are all necessary settings for RIs. Interruption polices are relevant to spot instances, not reserve.

12. C. The more you pay up front, the lower the overall cost. There's no option called Monthly.

13. B, D. Containers do tend to launch more quickly than other compute models and do make it easy to replicate environments, but those are not primarily cost savings.

14. B. Standard reserved instances make the most sense when they need to be available 24/7 for at least a full year, with even greater savings over three years. Irregular or partial workdays are not good candidates for this pricing model.

15. D. There are three request types: Request, Request And Maintain, and Reserve For Duration. A spot instance interruption occurs when the spot price rises above your maximum. A spot fleet is a group of spot instances launched together.

16. A. Workload completions, manual restarts (which, technically, don't exist), and data center outages are never referred to as interruptions.

17. B. A spot instance pool is unused EC2 instances matching a particular set of launch specifications. Spot maximum and spot cap sound good but aren't terms normally used in this context.

18. A. The Spot Advisor only covers guidance for instance compute specifications and instance type.

19. D. The command is `request-spot-fleet`. The `--spot-fleet-request-config` argument points to a JSON configuration file.

20. C. The availability zone, target capacity, and AMI are all elements of a complete spot fleet request.

Chapter 13: The Operational Excellence Pillar

1. C, D. It's a best practice to organize stacks by lifecycle (e.g., development, test, production) and ownership (e.g., network team, development team). You can store templates for multiple stacks in the same bucket, and there's no need to separate templates for different stacks into different buckets. Organizing stacks by resource cost doesn't offer any advantage since the cost is the same regardless of which stack a resource is in.

2. A, B. Parameters let you input custom values into a template when you create a stack. The purpose of parameters is to avoid hard-coding those values into a template. An AMI ID and EC2 key-pair name are values that likely would not be hard-coded into a template. Although you define the stack name when you create a stack, it is not a parameter that you define in a template. The logical ID of a resource must be hard-coded in the template.

3.   C. When using nested stacks, the parent stack defines a resource of the type `AWS::CloudFormation::Stack`, which points to the template used to generate the nested stack. Because of this, there's no need to define a VPC resource directly in the template that creates the parent stack. There is also no need to export stack output values because the nested stacks do not need to pass any information to stacks outside of the nested stack hierarchy. For this same reason, you don't need to use the Fn::ImportValue intrinsic function, as it is used to import values exported by another stack.

4.   A. A change set lets you see the changes CloudFormation will make before updating the stack. A direct update doesn't show you the changes before making them. There's no need to update or override the stack policy before using a change set to view the changes that CloudFormation would make.

5.   C. To use Git to access a repository as an IAM user, the developer must use a Git username and password generated by IAM. Neither an AWS access key and secret key combination nor an IAM username and password will work. Although SSH is an option, the developer would need a private key. The public key is what you'd provide to IAM.

6.   D. You can allow repository access for a specific IAM user by using an IAM policy that specifies the repository ARN as the resource. Specifying the repository's clone URL would not work, as the resource must be an ARN. Generating Git credentials also would not work, as the user still needs permissions via IAM. There is no such thing as a repository policy.

7.   A. CodeCommit offers differencing, allowing you (and the auditors) to see file-level changes over time. CodeCommit offers at-rest encryption using AWS-managed KMS keys but not customer-managed keys. S3 offers versioning and at rest-encryption, but not differencing.

8.   B. The `git clone` command clones or downloads a repository. The `git push` command pushes or uploads changes to a repository. The `git add` command stages files for commit to a local repository but doesn't commit them or upload them to CodeCommit. The `aws codecommit get-repository` command lists the metadata of a repository such as the clone URL and ARN but doesn't download the files in it.

9.   D. CodeDeploy can deploy from an S3 bucket or GitHub repository. It can't deploy from any other Git repository or an EBS snapshot.

10.   B. A blue/green instance deployment requires an elastic load balancer to direct traffic to the replacement instances. An in-place instance deployment can use an ELB but doesn't require it. A blue/green Lambda deployment doesn't use an ELB because ELB is for routing traffic to instances. There's no such thing as an in-place Lambda deployment.

11.   C. The AllAtOnce deployment configuration considers the entire deployment to have succeeded if the application is deployed successfully to at least one instance. HalfAtATime and OneAtATime require the deployment to succeed on multiple instances. There's no preconfigured deployment configuration called OnlyOne.

12.   B. The AfterAllowTraffic lifecycle event occurs last in any instance deployment that uses an elastic load balancer. ValidateService and BeforeAllowTraffic occur prior to CodeDeploy allowing traffic to the instances. AllowTraffic is a lifecycle event, but you can't hook into it to run a script.

13. A. CodePipeline stores pipeline artifacts in a S3 bucket. An artifact can serve as an input to a stage, an output from a stage, or both. A provider is a service that performs an action, such as building or testing. An asset is a term that often refers to the supporting files for an application, such as images or audio. S3 doesn't offer snapshots but does offer versioning for objects.

14. B, C. You can implement an approval action to require manual approval before transitioning to the deploy stage. Instead of or in addition to this, you can disable the transition to the deploy stage, which would require manually enabling the transition to deploy to production. Because CodePipeline uses one bucket for all stages of the pipeline, you can't create a separate bucket for the deploy stage. Even if you could, disallowing developers access to that bucket would not prevent a deployment, as CodePipeline obtains its permission to the bucket by virtue of its IAM service role.

15. A, D, E. A pipeline must consist of at least two stages. The first stage must contain only source actions. Since the templates are stored in CodeCommit, it must be the provider for the source action. The second stage of the pipeline should contain a deploy action with a CloudFormation provider, since it's the service that creates the stack. There's no need for a build stage, since CloudFormation templates are declarative code that don't need to be compiled. Hence, the pipeline should be only two stages. CodeCommit is not a valid provider for the deploy action.

16. B. A pipeline can have anywhere from two to 10 stages. Each stage can have 1 to 20 actions.

17. B. Automation documents let you perform actions against your AWS resources, including taking EBS snapshots. Although called automation documents, you can still manually execute them. A command document performs actions within a Linux or Windows instance. A policy document works only with State Manager and can't take an EBS snapshot. There's no manual document type.

18. A. The AmazonEC2RoleforSSM managed policy contains permissions allowing the Systems Manager agent to interact with the Systems Manager service. There's no need to install the agent because Amazon Linux comes with it preinstalled. There's also no need to open up inbound ports to use Systems Manager.

19. A, D. Setting the patch baseline's auto-approval delay to zero and then running the AWS-RunPatchBaseline document would immediately install all available security patches. Adding the patch to the list of approved patches would approve the specific patch for installation, but not any other security updates released within the preceding seven days. Changing the maintenance window to occur Monday at midnight wouldn't install the patch until the following Monday.

20. A, B. Creating a global inventory association will immediately run the AWS-GatherSoftwareInventory policy document against the instance, collecting both network configuration and software inventory information. State Manager will execute the document against future instances according to the schedule you define. Simply running the AWS-GatherSoftwareInventory won't automatically gather configuration information for future instances. Of course, an instance must be running for the Systems Manager agent to collect data from it. The AWS-SetupManagedInstance document is an automation document and thus can perform operations on AWS resources and not tasks within an instance.

Index

Note to the Reader: Throughout this index **boldfaced** page numbers indicate primary discussions of a topic. *Italicized* page numbers indicate illustrations.

A

A records, 173
AAAA records, 173
accelerated computing instances, 24–25
access
    IAM. *See* Identity and Access Management (IAM) service
    instances, 33–35
    S3 objects, **54–57**
access control lists (ACLs)
    network. *See* network access control lists (NACLs)
    S3 object rules, *55*
access keys in IAM, **129–130**, 135
ACM (Amazon Certificate Manager), 57, 270
actions
    Auto Scaling, **203–204**, *203–204*
    CloudFormation stack policies, 302
    CloudWatch alarms, **157–158**
    IAM policies, 125–126
    NACL rules, 79, 81
    permission statements, 250
    pipelines, **314–315**
    Systems Manager, **316–318**
AfterAllowTraffic hooks, 311
AfterBlockTraffic hooks, 311
AfterInstall hooks, 311
Agent, CloudWatch, **153–154**
alarms
    CloudWatch, **155–158**, **201–202**
    CodeDeploy, **312**

ALB. *See* application load balancer (ALB)
alerts
    billing, 279
    CloudWatch events, 158
    outages, 208
alias records, 174
ALL distributions in Redshift, 111
AllAtOnce deployment configurations, 310
Amazon Aurora
    database resiliency, 206
    description, **100–101**
    multi-AZ with, **109**
    RDS replicas, 107
Amazon Certificate Manager (ACM), 57, 270
Amazon Machine Images (AMIs), 23, 250
Amazon Resource Names (ARNs), 134
Amazon Web Services (AWS) overview
    CLI, **15**
    CLI example, 39–40
    cloud, **6–11**
    exam essentials, **17**
    exercise, **17**
    platform architecture, **11–13**
    regions, 25–27
    reliability and compliance, **13–14**, *14*
    review questions, **18–19**
    service level agreement, **14**
    software development kits, **15**
    summary, **16**
    support plans, **15–16**
    technical support and online resources, **15**

AmazonEC2ReadOnlyAccess policy, 134

AmazonEC2RoleforSSM policy, 317

AMIs (Amazon Machine Images), **23**, 250

API (application programming interface) in S3, 50

API Gateway Service, 11

Application integration category, 7

application load balancer (ALB)

    Auto Scaling, 199

    cloud-native applications, 194–195

    Elastic Load Balancing, 229

    traditional applications, 193

Application management category, 7, **10–11**

application problems, detecting, 142

application programming interface (API) in S3, 50

application specification files in CodeDeploy, **311–312**

ApplicationStart hooks, 311

ApplicationStop hooks, 310

approval action for pipelines, **315**

apps in Chef deployments, 232

appspec.yml file, 311

archives in Glacier, 58

ARNs (Amazon Resource Names), 134

artifacts, pipeline, **315–316**

As Missing option for CloudWatch alarms, 157

assessments in Inspector, 265

associations

    inventory, 320

    State Manager, 318

Athena, searching logs with, **260–261**, *260–261*

attaching elastic network interfaces, **73**

attributes

    DynamoDB, **113–114**, 116

    relational databases, **96–97**

audit reports in AWS Config, 158

auditing resource configurations, **262–263**, *262–263*

Aurora

    database resiliency, 206

    description, **100–101**

    multi-AZ with, **109**

    RDS replicas, 107

authentication

    CloudHSM, **133–134**

    Cognito, **132**

    exam essentials, **136**

    key management service, **133**

    Managed Microsoft AD, **132**

    overview, **131–132**

    review questions, **137–140**

    Secrets Manager, **133**

    single sign-on, **132–133**

    summary, **135**

authorization, fine-grained, **249–250**

auto-approval delays for patches, 318

Auto Scaling service

    application load balancer, 199

    CloudWatch alarms, 158

    cost optimization, **288**

    dynamic scaling policies, **200–203**

    DynamoDB, **115–116**

    EC2, **38**

    functions, 8

    groups, **199**

    health checks, **199–200**

    launch configurations, **197**

    launch templates, **197–198**

    manual, **200**

    options, 200

    overview, **197**

    performance, **220–222**

    scheduled actions, **203–204**, *203–204*

automated snapshots in RDS, **109–110**

automation
    infrastructure. *See* infrastructure
       automation
    Systems Manager actions, **316–317**
availability
    calculating, **192–193**
    cloud-native applications,
       194–195
    databases, 226–228, *228*
    description, 248
    designing for, **207–211**
    EBS volumes, 31
    increasing, **196**
    limits, **196**
    multi-AZ deployment, **108**
    Route 53, **176–177**
    S3, **52–53**
    serverless applications, **195–196**
    traditional applications,
       193–194
availability zone (AZs) in VPC service,
    71–72, *71*
Average statistics in CloudWatch, 149
AVG function in CloudWatch, 151
AWS. *See* Amazon Web Services (AWS)
    overview
AWS Config Compliance insight, 319
AWS Config service
    auditing resource configurations,
       262–263, *262–263*
    configuration history, **159**
    configuration items, **159**
    configuration recorder, **159**, **161**
    exam essentials, **162–163**
    functions, 10
    introduction, **142–143**
    monitoring changes, **161**
    overview, **158–159**
    recording software inventory, **161**
    review questions, **164–167**
    rules, **162**
    snapshots, **160**
    summary, **162**
AZs (availability zone) in VPC service,
    71–72, *71*

B

backdoors, finding, 264
backup and recovery
    options, **204–206**
    RDS, **109**
base tables in DynamoDB, 116
baselines, patch, 318
basic monitoring in CloudWatch, **147–148**
Basic plan, 15
bastion hosts in NAT, 87
BeforeAllowTraffic hooks, 311
BeforeBlockTraffic hooks, 311
BeforeInstall hooks, **310–311**
behavior
    CloudFormation stack updates, **301**
    EC2 instance configuration, **28**
    GuardDuty finding, 264
    Inspector analysis, 266
billing
    alerts, 279
    license fees, 23
    reports, 279
Billing and Cost Management
    Dashboard, 280
binary data type in DynamoDB, 114
block storage
    EBS. *See* Elastic Block Store (EBS)
       service
    volumes, 48
blue/green deployments, **309**
Boolean data type in DynamoDB, 114
bootstrapping, 28

boundaries, permissions, **251–252**

branches in Git, 304

Breaching option for CloudWatch
    alarms, 157

bring your own license (BYOL) model, 101

buckets
    AWS Config, 160
    S3 files, 49–58

budgets, **279–280**

build action in CodePipeline, **314–315**

build stage in CodePipeline, **313**

built-in insights in Systems Manager, **319**

burst capable (burstable) instances in
    RDS, **102**

Business plan, 16

BYOL (bring your own license)
    model, 101

C

CAA records, 174

caching in data operations optimization,
    237–238, *237*

calculator tools
    cost optimization, **282–284**
    Simple Monthly Calculator, 59
    TCO, 6

Center for Internet Security
    Benchmarks, 266

change management, AWS Config for,
    159, **161**

change sets for CloudFormation
    stacks, **301**

ChangeInCapacity setting in Auto
    Scaling, 201

Chef deployments, **232**

child tables in relational databases, 98

CIDR. *See* Classless interdomain routing
    (CIDR) blocks

classes for RDS instances, **102**

Classic Load Balancer, 229

Classless interdomain routing (CIDR)
    blocks, **69**
    IPv6, **69**, **72**
    overview, **68–69**
    secondary, **69**
    subnets, **70**

CLI. *See* Command Line Interface (CLI)

client-side encryption for S3 objects, **51**

Clock Speed instance type parameter, 219

cloud computing
    architecture, **5**
    optimization, **5–6**, *5*
    and virtualization, **4–6**, *4–5*

cloud-native application availability,
    194–195

cloud overview, **6–11**

CloudFormation service
    functions, 10
    overview, **296–297**
    stacks
        creating, **297**
        deleting, **298**
        exporting values, **300–301**
        infrastructure resource, **230–231**
        multiple, **298**
        nesting, **298–300**
        updating, **301–303**

CloudFront service
    functions, 9
    overview, **181–182**
    and S3, **226**

CloudHSM service, **133–134**

CloudTrail Events insight, 319

CloudTrail service
    data events, **144–146**
    event history, **144**
    exam essentials, **162–163**
    functions, 10
    introduction, **142–143**

logs
   integrity validation, **146**
   managing, **145–146**
   overview, **258–259**
   sending to CloudWatch logs, **154**
management events, **143**
review questions, **164–167**
summary, **162**
trails, **144–145**
CloudWatch service
   Agent, **153–154**
   alarms, **155–158, 201–202**
   dashboards, **235–236**
   exam essentials, **162–163**
   functions, **10**
   introduction, **142–143**
   logs, **152–154, 259–260**
   metrics
      basic and detailed monitoring,
         147–148
      expiration, **148–149**
      graphing, **149–150,** *149–150*
      math, **150–152,** *151–152*
      overview, **147**
      regular and high-resolution, **148**
   overview, **147**
   review questions, **164–167**
   summary, **162**
clusters
   EC2 placement groups, **37**
   ElastiCache, **237–238,** *237*
CMK (Customer Master Key), **51, 268**
CNAME records, **173**
CodeBuild server, **233**
CodeCommit repositories
   creating, **304**
   description, **233**
   interacting with Git, **305–307**
   overview, **303–304**
   security, **304**

CodeDeploy service
   agent, **308–309**
   application specification files,
      311–312
   deployment configurations,
      309–310
   description, **233**
   lifecycle events, **310–311**
   overview, **307–308**
   rollbacks, **312**
   triggers and alarms, **312**
CodePipeline tool
   continuous delivery, **313–314**
   continuous integration, **313**
   overview, **233,** *234*
   pipeline artifacts, **315–316**
   pipeline creation, **314–315**
Cognito authentication, **132**
cold HDD volumes, **32**
columns in relational databases, **96–97**
Command Line Interface (CLI)
   AWS
      description, **15**
      example, **39–40**
   IAM identities, **134–135**
   Route 53 example, **182–183**
   S3 example, **60–61**
Common Vulnerabilities and Exposures
   (CVEs), **265**
Community AMIs, **23**
compliance
   AWS, **13–14,** *14*
   Systems Manager, **320**
composite primary keys in
   DynamoDB, **113**
compression, data, **239**
Compute category, **7–8**
compute cost optimization, **284–288**
compute nodes in Redshift, **110–111**
compute optimized instances, **24–25**

conditions
    alarm thresholds, 155
    CloudFormation stack policies, 302
    permission statements, 250
confidentiality, 248
configservice command, 160
configuration recorder, **159**, **161**
configurations
    auditing, **262–263**, *262–263*
    AWS Config. *See* AWS Config service
    deployments, **309–310**
    EC2 instances, **25–27**, *26*
    infrastructure, **234–235**
connections in VPC service peering, 88
connectivity in resilient networks, **207**
consistency in databases, 226–227
constraints in relational databases, 98
content delivery network (CDN), 181
continuous integration and continuous
        deployment (CI/CD) in infrastructure
        automation, **233–234**
control plane operations, 143
convertible RIs, 285
cooldown periods in Auto Scaling, 201
cost allocation tags, 279
Cost and Usage Reports, **281**
Cost Explorer, **280–281**
cost management, **6**
cost optimization
    Auto Scaling, **288**
    budgets, **279–280**
    compute, **284–288**
    exam essentials, **289**
    introduction, **278–279**
    Lifecyle Manager, **288**
    monitoring tools, **280–281**
    online calculator tools, **282–284**
    Organizations, **281**
    review questions, **290–293**
    summary, **288–289**
    Trusted Advisor, **282**

CPUUtilization metric, 148–149, *149*
create-access-key command, 135
credentials
    CodeCommit, 305
    protecting, **248–249**
Cross-Region Replication (CRR),
    224–225
cryptocurrency, finding, 264
curl command, 34–35
custom deployment configurations, 310
custom rules in AWS Config, **162**
customer managed policies, 250
Customer Master Key (CMK), 51, 268

D

dashboards, CloudWatch, **235–236**
data backup and recovery, **204–206**
data compression, **239**
Data Definition Language (DDL)
        statements, 261
data distribution styles in Redshift, 111
data encryption
    data at rest, **268**
    data in transit, **270**
    Elastic Block Store, **269**
    S3, **269**
data events in CloudTrail, **144–146**
data operations optimization
    caching, **237–238**, *237*
    compression, **239**
    overview, **236**
    partitioning/sharding, **238–239**
data point to monitor in CloudWatch
        alarms, **155**
data points in CloudWatch metrics, 147
data points to alarm in CloudWatch
        alarms, 156
data striping, 223
data types in DynamoDB, **113–114**

data warehousing
  OLAP, 99
  Redshift, **110–111**
Database category, 7, **9–10**
database engines for RDS, **100–101**
database instances in RDS, 100,
  104–106, *105*
databases
  DynamoDB. *See* DynamoDB service
  exam essentials, **117–118**
  introduction, **96**
  nonrelational, **111–112**
  performance, **226–227**
  RDS. *See* Relational Database Service
    (RDS)
  Redshift, **110–111**
  relational, **96–99**
  resiliency, **205–206**
  review questions, **119–122**
  summary, **117**
DDL (Data Definition Language)
  statements, 261
deactivating unused keys, 129
Dedicated Host option, 26
Dedicated Instance option, 26
default routes in VPC service, **75–76**
default security groups in
  VPC service, **78**
deleting
  access keys, 130
  CloudFormation stacks, 298
  database columns, 97
  S3 objects, 205
delimiters in S3, **49**
delivery channels in AWS Config,
  159–160
delivery frequency in AWS Config, 160
dense compute nodes in Redshift, 110
density of servers, **284–285**
dependencies in traditional
  applications, 193

deploy action for pipelines, 315
deploying applications. *See* CodeDeploy
  service
deployments
  configurations, **309–310**
  creating, **308**
  groups, 308
  types, **308–309**
designing for availability
  99 percent availability, **208–209**
  99.9 percent availability, **209–210**
  99.99 percent availability,
    210–211
  overview, **207–208**
Desired capacity option in Auto
  Scaling, 199
destinations
  NACL rules, 79–81
  NAT, 83–87
  routes, 74–75
  security group rules, 77–78
detailed monitoring in CloudWatch,
  147–148
detecting problems, 142
detective controls
  Athena, **260–261**, *260–261*
  AWS Config, **262–263**, *262–263*
  CloudTrail, **258–259**
  CloudWatch, **259–260**
  GuardDuty, **264–265**, *265*
  Inspector, **265–266**, *266*
Developer plan, 15
Developer Tools, 233
differencing process in Git, 304
digest files in CloudTrail, 146
dimensions in CloudWatch, 147
Direct Connect service
  functions, 8
  resilient networks, 207
direct updates for CloudFormation
  stacks, **301**

Directory Service
   functions, 11
   tools, **132**
disk compression, **239**
DNS. *See* Domain Name System (DNS)
Docker host instances, 38
document data types in DynamoDB, 114
documents in Systems Manager, 316
Domain Name System (DNS)
   domains and domain names
      fully qualified domain
         names, **172**
      hierarchy, 171
      layers, **172**, *172*
      overview, **171**
      registrars, 172
      registration, 172, **174–175**
   exam essentials, **183–184**
   name servers, **171**
   namespaces, **170–171**
   overview, **170**
   record types, **173–174**
   review questions, **185–188**
   Route 53. *See* Route 53 service
   summary, **183**
   zones and zone files, **173**
durability
   databases, 227
   S3, **51–52**
dynamic scaling policies, **200–201**
DynamoDB service
   attributes and items, **113–114**
   Auto Scaling, **115–116**
   database resiliency, 206
   functions, 10
   introduction, **112**
   partition and hash keys, **113**
   reading data, **115–117**
   reserved capacity, **116**
   throughput capacity, **114–115**

E

EBS. *See* Elastic Block Store (EBS) service
EBS-Optimized Available instance type
   parameter, 220
EC2. *See* Elastic Compute Cloud (EC2)
   service
ECUs instance type parameter, 219
effects
   IAM policies, 125
   permission statements, 250
EFS (Elastic File System)
   backup and recovery, **205**
   description, **59**
EIPs (elastic IP addresses), **82–83**
Elastic Beanstalk service, 8, **37–38**
Elastic Block Store (EBS) service
   backup and recovery, **205**
   data encryption, **269–270**
   functions, 9
   volumes
      Lifecyle Manager, **288**
      overview, **31–33**
      RAID-optimized, **223–224**
Elastic Compute Cloud (EC2) service
   Amazon Machine Images, 23
   Auto Scaling. *See* Auto Scaling service
   AWS CLI example, **39–40**
   CloudWatch alarms, 158
   exam essentials, **40–41**
   functions, 7
   instances, **22**
      accessing, **33–35**
      behavior configuration, **28**
      environment configuration, **25–27**,
         26
      free capacity, **27**
      launching, **27**
      lifecycle, **29**
      pricing, **28–29**

provisioning, 23
reserved, 285
securing, 35–37, *36*
service limits, 30–31
spot, 285–288
types, 24–25, 219–220
introduction, 22
related services, 37–38
resource tags, 30
resources cleanup, 39–40
review questions, 42–45
storage volumes, 31–33
summary, 40
Elastic File System (EFS)
backup and recovery, 205
description, 59
elastic IP addresses (EIPs), 82–83
Elastic Load Balancing (ELB) service
Elastic Compute Cloud, 38
functions, 8
Elastic Network Adapter (ENA), 228
elastic network interfaces (ENIs)
attaching, 73
IP addresses, 72–73
overview, 72
security groups, 76–78
ElastiCache clusters, 237–238, *237*
elasticity in cloud computing, 6
ELB (Elastic Load Balancing) service
Elastic Compute Cloud, 38
functions, 8
ENA (Elastic Network Adapter), 228
encryption
CodeCommit, 305
data at rest, 268
data in transit, 270
Elastic Block Store, 269–270
S3, 50–51, 269–270
endpoint addresses in AWS, 12
enforcing service-level protection, 258

engines for RDS, **100–101**
ENIs. *See* elastic network interfaces (ENIs)
Enterprise support plans, 16
envelope keys, 51
ephemeral ports in NACLs, 81
EVEN distributions in Redshift, 111
events
CloudTrail, **143–145**
CloudWatch logs, **153**
logging, 142
S3, 51
Eventually Consistent data in S3, **53**
eventually consistent reads in
DynamoDB, 115
ExactCapacity setting in Auto Scaling, 201
expiration of CloudWatch metrics, **148–149**
exporting CloudFormation stack values,
300–301
external connectivity in resilient
networks, 207

F

failover routing in Route 53, **178**
fault tolerance in Trusted Advisor, 282
Files section for application specification
files, 312
filters
budgets and costs, 279–281
CloudWatch logs, **153**
IAM policies, 126
findings
GuardDuty, **264**
Inspector, 266, *266*
fine-grained authorization, 249–250
firewalls
security groups, 78
Web Application Firewall, 267
fleets, spot instance, **286–287**
flow logs in VPC, **259–260**

foreign keys in relational databases, 98
FQDNs (fully qualified domain
    names), **172**
free capacity for instances, **27**
full access commits, 304
fully qualified domain names (FQDNs), **172**

G

gateways
    API, 11
    Internet, **73–74**
    NAT, 36, *36*, **86–87**
    Storage Gateway service, 9, **59**
    VPC, **73–74**
general purpose instances, **24**
general-purpose SSD (gp2) storage in
    RDS, **103–104**
geolocation routing, **178**
geoproximity routing, 180
Git-based repositories. *See* CodeCommit
    repositories
Glacier service
    functions, 9
    Select feature, **57**
    storage, **57–59**
global inventory associations, 320
global secondary indexes (GSIs) in
    DynamoDB, **116–117**
graph databases, 112
graphing CloudWatch metrics, **149–150**,
    149–150
groups
    Auto Scaling, **199**
    CloudWatch logs, 153
    deployments, **308**
    IAM, **130–131**
    patch, 318
    placement, **37**
    security, 35, **76–78**, **81–82**, 267

GSIs (global secondary indexes) in
    DynamoDB, **116–117**
GuardDuty, **264–265**, *265*

H

HalfAtATime deployment
    configurations, **310**
hard dependencies in traditional
    applications, 193
hash keys in DynamoDB, 113, **113**
health checks
    Auto Scaling, **199–200**
    Route 53, 174, **177**
healthy instances in custom deployment
    configurations, 310
help forums, 16
hierarchy, DNS, 171
high availability in RDS, **108–109**
high-resolution metrics in
    CloudWatch, **148**
history
    AWS Config, **159**
    CloudTrail events, **144**
hooks
    application specification files, 312
    lifecycle events, **310–311**
hosted zones
    DNS, 173
    Route 53, **175–176**
hostnames in DNS, 171
hosts
    databases, 227
    DNS, 172
    NAT, 87
    S3 objects, **56–57**
    virtual machines, 4, *4*
hot partitions in DynamoDB, 113
HTTPS access in security group
    rules, 77

I

Identity and Access Management (IAM)
service. *See also* authentication
credentials, **248–249**
enforcing service-level protection, 258
fine-grained authorization, 249–250
functions, 10
identities
access keys, **129–130**
command-line example, **134–135**
exam essentials, 136
groups, **130–131**
overview, 125, *125*
policies, **125–126**
review questions, 137–140
roles, 36, 131
summary, 135
user and root accounts, **126–129**, *128*
managed policies, 250
overview, **248**
permissions boundaries, **251–252**
roles, 252–258, *257*
S3 object policies, 55–56
identity pools in Cognito, 132
Ignore option in CloudWatch, 157
implied routers in VPC, 74
in-place deployments, 308–309
inbound rules
NACLs, 79–80
security groups, 76–77
indexes in DynamoDB, **116–117**
Infrastructure automation
CI/CD, **233–234**, *234*
CloudFormation, 230–231
third-party, **232**
infrastructure configurations
load testing, **235**
overview, **234**
visualization, **235**

inline policies, **250**
input/output operations per second (IOPS)
in RDS, **103**, 106
INSERT statements in SQL, 99
insights in Systems Manager, **318–319**
Inspector service, **265–266**, *266*
instance classes in RDS, **102**
Instance Storage instance type
parameter, 219
instances
cloud computing, 5
EC2, **22**
accessing, **33–35**
behavior configuration, 28
configuring, **25–27**, *26*
free capacity, 27
launching, 27
lifecycle, **29**
pricing, **28–29**
provisioning, **23**
securing, 35–37, *36*
store volumes, **33**
types, **24–25**
EFS
reserved, **285**
spot, **285–288**
NAT, **87**
performance, **219–220**
RDS, 100, **104–106**, *105*
role policies, **253–256**
Systems Manager, 317
INSUFFICIENT_DATA state for
CloudWatch alarms, 156
integrity
description, 248
log file validation, **146**
Intel AES-NI instance type
parameter, 220
Intel AVX instance type parameter, 220
Intel Turbo instance type parameter, 220

Internet Corporation for Assigned Names
　　and Numbers (ICANN), 171
Internet gateways, **73–74**
interruptions
　　CloudFormation stack updates, 301
　　spot instances, 286
inventory
　　AWS resources, 142–143
　　recording, **161**
Inventory Manager, **319–320**
invoke action for pipelines, **315**
IP addresses
　　ENIs, **72–73**
　　instances, **33–35**
　　NAT, **83–87**, *86*
　　prefixes for CIDR blocks, 68–69
　　subnets, 70
　　VPC, **82–83**
IPv6 CIDR blocks, **69**, 72
IPv6 Support instance type parameter, 220
items in DynamoDB, **113–114**

J

jump hosts in NAT, 87

K

KEY distributions in Redshift, 111
Key Management Service (KMS)
　　data at rest, 268
　　description, **133**
　　EBS volumes, 32, 269
　　EFS, 270
　　functions, 10
　　S3, 51
　　service-level protection, 258
key pairs for EC2 instances, **37**
key-value pairs in nonrelational
　　databases, 111

keys
　　DynamoDB, **113**
　　IAM, **129–130**
　　nonrelational databases, 111
　　relational databases, 98
Kinesis Streams, 239
KMS. *See* Key Management Service
　　(KMS)

L

Lambda service
　　deployments, 309
　　EC2, 38
　　functions, 8
　　logs, 259
　　server density, 285
　　serverless applications, **195–196**
large objects in S3, **49–50**
latency
　　databases, 227
　　Route 53, **178**
launch configurations in Auto Scaling,
　　197, 220–222
launch templates in Auto Scaling, **197–198**
launching instances, **27**
layers in Chef deployments, 232
leader nodes in Redshift, 111
licensing considerations in RDS, **101**
lifecycle
　　CodeDeploy events, **310–311**
　　EC2 instances, **29**
　　S3 objects, **53–54**
Lifecycle Manager
　　backup and recovery, 205
　　cost optimization, **288**
limits
　　EC2, **30–31**
　　Trusted Advisor, **196**, 282
list-access-keys command, 135

list document type in DynamoDB, 114
load balancing
    ALB. *See* application load balancer
       (ALB)
    EC2, 8, **38**
    and network optimization, **227–230**,
       228
load testing, **235**
local routes in VPC, 74–75
local secondary indexes (LSIs) in
    DynamoDB, **117**
logical IDs in CloudFormation, 297
logs and logging
    CloudTrail
       integrity validation, **146**
       managing, 145–146
       overview, 258–259
    CloudWatch, **152–154**, 259–260
    events, 142
    S3 objects, **51**
    searching, **260–261**, *260–261*
low-latency access, 11–13
LSIs (local secondary indexes) in
    DynamoDB, 117

M

m out of n alarms in CloudWatch, 156
magnetic storage in RDS, 106
main route tables in VPC, 74
maintenance items in RDS, **110**
managed instances in Systems
    Manager, 317
Managed Microsoft AD authentication, **132**
managed policies, **250**
managed rules in AWS Config, **162**
management events in CloudTrail, **143**
manual Auto Scaling, **200**
map data type in DynamoDB, 114

MariaDB database engine
    description, 100
    multi-AZ with, 109
Marketplace AMIs, 23
master database instances in RDS, 107
math for CloudWatch metrics, **150–152**,
    151–152
MAX function in CloudWatch, 151
Maximum option in Auto Scaling, 199
Maximum statistics in CloudWatch
    metrics, 149
Memcached engine, **237–238**
Memory instance type parameter, 219
memory-optimized instances
    EC2, 24–25
    RDS, 102
METRICS function, 152
metrics in CloudWatch
    basic and detailed monitoring,
       147–148
    expiration, **148–149**
    graphing, **149–150**, *149–150*
    log filters, **153**
    math, **150–152**, *151–152*
    overview, **147**
    regular and high-resolution, **148**
MFA (multifactor authentication), 249
Microsoft SQL Server, 101
MIN function in CloudWatch, 152
Minimum option in Auto Scaling, 199
Minimum statistics in CloudWatch
    metrics, 149
mirrored sets of data, 223
missing data in CloudWatch alarms, **157**
monitoring
    availability, **176–177**
    AWS Config changes, **161**
    CloudWatch, **147–148**
    cost optimization, **280–281**
multi-AZ deployment, **108–109**, 206

multi-tier architecture for resilient
    networks, 207
multifactor authentication (MFA), 249
Multipart Upload feature, 50
multiple CloudFormation stacks, **298**
multiple relational database tables, 97–98
multivalue answer routing in Route 53,
    178–179
MX records, 173
MySQL database engine
    description, 100
    multi-AZ with, 109

N

NACLs. *See* network access control lists
    (NACLs)
name servers in DNS, **171**
namespaces
    CloudWatch, 147
    DNS, 170–171
NAPTR records, 174
NAT. *See* network address translation (NAT)
nesting CloudFormation stacks, **298–300**
network access control lists (NACLs), 35
    overview, **79**
    rules, **79–81**
    security groups, 81–82, 267
network address translation (NAT)
    devices, 84–85
        EC2 instances, 36, *36*
        route table configuration for,
            85–86, *86*
        gateways, 86–87
        instances, 87
        overview, 83–84
network boundaries
    access control lists and security
        groups, 267

description, **267**
Shield, **268**
Web Application Firewall, **267**
Network Load Balancer, 229
Network Performance instance type
    parameter, 220
Network Reachability in Inspector, 266
Networking category, **7–9**
NetworkOut metric, 150, *150*
networks
    optimization and load balancing,
        227–230, *228*
    resilient, **206–207**
nondatabase hosting, 227
nonrelational databases, **111–112**
Not Breaching option for CloudWatch
    alarms, 157
NS records, 174
null data type in DynamoDB, 114

O

objects
    S3
        accessing, **54–57**
        lifecycle, **53–54**
    storage, 48
OK state in CloudWatch alarms, 156
OLAP (online analytic processing), **99**
OLTP (online transaction processing), **99**
on-demand pricing model for EC2
    instances, 28
one-to-one NAT, 84
One Zone-IA class storage pricing, 58
One Zone-Infrequent Access storage class,
    52–53
OneAtATime deployment configurations,
    309–310
online analytic processing (OLAP), **99**

online resources
  cost optimization calculator tools,
      282–284
  support, **15**
online transaction processing (OLTP), **99**
operational excellence
  CloudFormation. *See* CloudFormation
      service
  CodeCommit, 303–307
  CodeDeploy, 307–312
  CodePipeline, 313–316
  exam essentials, 320–321
  introduction, 296
  review questions, 322–325
  summary, 320
  Systems Manager, 316–320
operations in permission statements, 250
OpsWorks Chef deployments, **232**
OpsWorks Puppet deployments, **232**
optimization
  cloud computing, 5–6, *5*
  data operations. *See* data operations
      optimization
option groups in RDS, **101**
Oracle, multi-AZ with, 108
Organizations for cost optimization, **281**
OS section in application specification
    files, 311
outbound rules
  NACLs, 80–81
  security groups, 77–78
output artifacts in pipeline, 316
overriding stack policies, **303**

P

parameters in CloudFormation, 297
parent stacks in CloudFormation, 298
parent tables in relational databases, 98

partition keys in DynamoDB, **113**
partition tolerance in databases,
      226–227
partitioning
  data operations optimization,
      238–239
  OLAP, 99
password policies, 128, 249
PAT (port address translation), 85
patch groups, 318
Patch Manager, 317–318
peering in VPC, **87–88**
pentests, finding, 264
PercentChangeInCapacity setting in Auto
    Scaling, 201
Percentile statistics in CloudWatch
    metrics, 149
performance efficiency
  Auto Scaling, 220–222
  compute services, **219**
  data operations, **236–239**, *237*
  databases, **226–227**
  EC2 instance types, 219–220
  exam essentials, 240–241
  infrastructure automation, 230–233,
      234
  infrastructure configurations, 234–236
  network optimization and load
      balancing, 227–230, *228*
  overview, 218–219
  review questions, 242–245
  serverless workloads, **222–223**
  storage, **223–226**
  summary, 239–240
  tracking, 142
  Trusted Advisor, 282
permissions
  authorization, 249–250
  boundaries, **251–252**
  roles, 252

Permissions section in application
specification files, 312
persistence, finding, 264
Personal Health Dashboard insight, 319
physical IDs in CloudFormation, 297
Physical Processor instance type
parameter, 219
pipelines, **313–316**
Pivotal Greenplum Database technology,
227
placement groups, **37**
point-in-time recovery in RDS, 109
policies
Auto Scaling, **200–203**
CloudFormation stacks, **302–304**
IAM, **125–126**
managed, **250**
passwords, 249
roles, **253–256**
routing, **177–179**
pools for spot instances, 286
port address translation (PAT), 85
port ranges
NACL rules, 79, 81
security group rules, 77
PostgreSQL database engine, **100–101**
power user commits in CodeCommit, 304
prefixes
CIDR blocks, 68–69
S3, **49**
presigned URLs for S3 objects, **56**
Presto technology, 227
preventing CloudFormation stack updates,
303–304
prices
EC2 instances, **28–29**
S3 and Glacier, **58–59**
spot instances, 286
primary database instances in multi-AZ
deployment, 108

primary ENIs, 72
primary keys in relational databases, 98
primary private IP addresses, **72–73**
primary resources in failover
routing, 178
principals
CloudFormation stack policies, 302
identities. *See* Identity and Access
Management (IAM) service
S3, 55
private AMIs, 23
private IP addresses, **72–73**
private subnets, 75
Processor Architecture instance type
parameter, 220
profiles, instance, **253–256**
projected attributes in DynamoDB, 116
protocols
NACL rules, 79–80
security group rules, 77
provisioned IOPS SSD, **106**
provisioned throughput in DynamoDB,
114
provisioning instances, **23**
PTR records, 174
public IP addresses, **82**
public subnets, 75
publishers, SNS, 157
Puppet deployments, **232**

Q

queries
DynamoDB, 116
nonrelational databases, **112**
relational databases, **98**
Route 53, 259
Quick Start AMIs, 23
QuickSight, 281

R

RAID-optimized EBS volumes, **223–224**
range keys in DynamoDB, 113
RDS. *See* Relational Database Service (RDS)
read capacity units (RCUs), 114–115
read only commits, 304
read replicas in RDS, **106–108**, 238
reading DynamoDB data, **115–117**
recon, finding, 264
record types, **173–174**
recording software inventory, **161**
recovery options, **204–206**
recovery point objective (RPO)
    availability design, 209–210
    RDS, 109
recovery time objective (RTO)
    availability design, 209
    RDS, 109
Redis engine, **237–238**
Redshift storage, **110–111**
Reduced Redundancy Storage (RRS), 52
regions
    availability, 195
    AWS, **11–13**
    configuring, **25–27**
registrars, domain name, 172
regular-resolution metrics in
    CloudWatch, **148**
Relational Database Service (RDS)
    automated snapshots, **109–110**
    backup and recovery, **109**
    database engines, **100–101**
    database resiliency, 206
    functions, 9
    high availability, **108–109**
    instance classes, **102**
    licensing considerations, **101**
    logs, 259
    maintenance items, **110**

option groups, **101**
overview, **99–100**
read replicas, **106–108**
storage, **103–106**, *105*
relational databases
    columns and attributes, **96–97**
    multiple tables, **97–98**
    OLTP and OLAP, 99
    Structured Query Language, **98–99**
Release Notes page, 234
reliability
    Auto Scaling. *See* Auto Scaling service
    availability, **192–196**
    AWS, **13–14**, *14*
    data backup and recovery, **204–206**
    databases, **205–206**
    designing for availability, **207–211**
    exam essentials, **211–212**
    introduction, **192**
    resilient networks, **206–207**
    review questions, **213–216**
    summary, **211**
replacement in CloudFormation stack
    updates, 301
replicas, read, **106–108**, 238
replication, cross-region, **224–225**
reports, billing, 279
repositories. *See* CodeCommit repositories
request types for spot instances, 286
Reserve Instance (RI) Utilization
    template, 281
reserve pricing model for EC2
    instances, 28
reserved capacity in DynamoDB, **116**
reserved instances in EC2, **285**
resiliency. *See* reliability
resilient networks, **206–207**
resource groups, 319
resource records in DNS, 173
resource tags in EC2, **30**

ResourceConsumption finding, 264
resources
    auditing configurations, **262–263**,
       262–263
    CloudFormation stack policies, 302
    IAM policies, 125
    inventory, 142–143
    permission statements, 250
retention periods in RDS, 109–110
RI (Reserve Instance) Utilization
    template, 281
roles
    assuming, **256–258**, *257*
    IAM, **36**, **131**
    instance profiles, **253–256**
    overview, **252–253**
rollbacks in CodeDeploy, **312**
root accounts, **126–129**, *128*
root users, 125, 249
rotation of IAM access keys, **129**
Route 53 service
    availability monitoring, **176–177**
    command-line example, **182–183**
    description, **174**
    DNS management, **175**
    DNS queries, 259
    domain registration, **174–175**
    exam essentials, **183–184**
    failover routing, **178**
    functions, 9
    geolocation routing, **178**
    health checks, **177**
    hosted zones, **175–176**
    latency routing, **178**
    multivalue answer routing, **178–179**
    review questions, **185–188**
    routing policies, **177–179**
    summary, **183**
    traffic flow, **180**, *180*
    weighted routing, **178**

route tables
    NAT devices, **85–86**
    VPC, **74–76**
routes
    Route 53 routing policies, 174, **177–179**
    VPC peering, 88
RPO (recovery point objective)
    availability design, 209–210
    RDS, 109
RRS (Reduced Redundancy Storage), 52
RTO (recovery time objective)
    availability design, 209
    RDS, 109
rules
    AWS Config, **162**
    network access control lists, **79–81**
    security groups, **76–77**
Run Commands in Systems Manager, **317**
run-instances command, 39
Runtime Behavior Analysis in Inspector,
    266

S

S3. *See* Simple Storage Service (S3)
Sample count statistics in CloudWatch
    metrics, 149
scalar data types in DynamoDB, 113
scaling and scalability
    Auto Scaling. *See* Auto Scaling service
    cloud computing, **5–6**, *5*
    databases, 227
    DynamoDB, **115–116**
    read replicas, 107
scaling out, 220
scans in DynamoDB, 116
scheduled actions in Auto Scaling,
    203–204, *203–204*
schemaless databases, 111
SDKs (software development kits), **15**

searching in logs, **260–261**, *260–261*
second-level domains (SLDs), 172
secondary CIDR blocks, **69**
secondary indexes in DynamoDB,
　116–117
secondary private IP addresses, **72–73**
secondary resources in failover
　routing, 178
Secrets Manager, **133**
security
　AWS Config, 158
　data encryption, **268**
　detective controls. *See* detective controls
　EC2 instances, 35–37, *36*
　exam essentials, **271**
　IAM, See Identity and Access
　　Management (IAM) service
　introduction, 248
　network boundaries, **267–268**
　repositories, **304**
　review questions, 272–275
　summary, 270–271
　Trusted Advisor, 282
Security and identity category, 7, **10–11**
Security Best Practices in Inspector, 266
security groups
　EC2 instances, **35**
　network, **267**
　VPC, **76–78**, **81–82**
security problems, detecting, 142
Security Status checklist, 125, *125*
Security Token Service, 254–255
SELECT statements in SQL, 98
sending CloudTrail logs to CloudWatch
　logs, 154
server-side encryption in S3, **50–51**
Server-Side Encryption with Amazon
　S3-Managed Keys (SSE-S3), 50
Server-Side Encryption with AWS KMS-
　Managed Keys (SSE-KMS), 51

Server-Side Encryption with Customer-
　Provided Keys (SSE-C), 51
serverless applications with Lambda,
　195–196
serverless workload performance,
　222–223
servers
　density, **284–285**
　name, **171**
service level agreements (SLAs), **14**
service-level protection, enforcing, **258**
service limits
　Elastic Compute Cloud, **30–31**
　Trusted Advisor, **282**
Session Manager, **317**
set data type in DynamoDB, 114
sharding, **238–239**
Shared Responsibility Model, 13, *14*
shared tenancy model, 26
Shield service, **268**
Simple Monthly Calculator, *59*, 282–283
Simple Notification Service (SNS)
　CloudTrail notifications, 259
　CloudWatch alarms, 157
　functions, 11
Simple Object Access Protocol
　(SOAP), 128
simple primary keys in DynamoDB, 113
Simple Queue Service (SQS)
　functions, 11
　queues, 258
simple scaling policies, **200–201**
Simple Storage Service (S3)
　architecture, **49–51**
　availability, **52–53**
　backup and recovery, **204–205**
　and CloudFront, 226
　command-line example, **60–61**
　cross-region replication, **224–225**
　durability, **51–52**

encryption, 50–51, **269**
exam essentials, **61–62**
functions, 9
introduction, **48–49**
objects
    accessing, **54–57**
    lifecycle, **53–54**
pricing, **58–59**
review questions, **63–66**
summary, **61**
Transfer Acceleration, **225–226**
Simple Systems Manager (SSM), 316
Simple WorkFlow (SWF) Service, 11
single sign-on (SSO), **132–133**
size of Auto Scaling groups, 199
SLAs (service level agreements), **14**
slash notation for CIDR blocks, 68
SLDs (second-level domains), 172
snapshots
    AWS Config, **160**
    EBD volumes, 32
    RDS, **109–110**
Snowball storage, **59–60**, 239
Snowflake technology, 227
SNS (Simple Notification Service)
    CloudTrail notifications, 259
    CloudWatch alarms, **157**
    functions, 11
SOA records, 174
SOAP (Simple Object Access
    Protocol), 128
software development kits (SDKs), **15**
software inventory, recording, **161**
solid-state drives (SSDs) for EBD
    volumes, **31**
sort keys in DynamoDB, 113
source action
    NACL rules, 79
    pipelines, **314**
source/destination checks in NAT, 87

sources for security group rules, 78
Speed Comparison page for Transfer
    Acceleration, 225
SPF records, 174
spot instances, **285–288**
spread groups, 37
SQL (Structured Query Language),
    98–99
SQS (Simple Queue Service)
    functions, 11
    queues, 258
SRV records, 174
SSDs (solid-state drives) for EBD
    volumes, **31**
SSH
    instance launching, **27**
    root access through, 266
    security group rules, 77
SSM (Simple Systems Manager), 316
SSO (single sign-on), **132–133**
stacks
    Chef deployments, 232
    CloudFormation
        creating, **297**
        deleting, **298**
        exporting values, **300–301**
        infrastructure resource, **230–231**
        multiple, **298**
        nesting, **298–300**
        updating, **301–303**
    Simple Monthly Calculator, **283**
Standard class storage pricing, 58
standard instances
    multi-AZ deployment, 108
    RDS, **102**
starting configuration recorder, **161**
State Manager, **318**
stateful firewalls, **78**
states for CloudWatch alarms, **156**
static website hosting, **56–57**

statistics for CloudWatch metrics,
　149–150, *149–150*
StatusCheckedFailed_System metric, 158
StatusCheckFailed_Instance metric, 158
STDDEV function, 152
stealth, finding, 264
step scaling policies, **202**
stopping configuration recorder, **161**
storage
　databases, 99
　EC2 instances, 24–25, **31–33**
　nonrelational databases, **111**
　performance, **223–226**
　RDS, **103–106**, *105*
Storage category, 7
Storage Gateway service
　description, **59**
　functions, 9
streams for CloudWatch logs, **153**
stress testing, **235**
strongly consistent reads in DynamoDB, 115
Structured Query Language (SQL), **98–99**
subdomains in DNS, 172, *172*
subnets
　NAT devices, 85–86
　VPC, 70–72, *71, 75*
subscribers, SNS, 157
SUM function in CloudWatch, 152
Sum statistics in CloudWatch, 149
support plans, **15–16**
SWF (Simple WorkFlow) Service, 11
Systems Manager
　actions, **316–318**
　compliance, **320**
　insights, **318–319**
　Inventory Manager, **319–320**
　overview, **316**
　Patch Manager, **317–318**
　Session Manager, **317**
　State Manager, **318**

T

tables
　DynamoDB, 115
　nonrelational databases, 111
　relational databases, **97–98**
tags
　cost allocation, 279
　EC2, **30**
target groups in application load balancer,
　194
target tracking policies in Auto Scaling,
　202–203
TCO (Total Cost of Ownership)
　Calculator, 6, **283–284**
TDE (transparent data encryption), 101
technical support, **15**
templates
　Auto Scaling, **197–198**
　CloudFormation. *See* CloudFormation
　　service
tenancy in EC2 instances, **26–27**
test action in pipelines, **315**
third-party automation, **232**
thresholds for CloudWatch alarms, **155**
throughput capacity in DynamoDB,
　114–115
throughput-optimized HDD volumes, **32**
time ranges in CloudWatch metrics, 150
time to live (TTL) in caching, 237
TLDs (top-level domains), 171–172
TLS (Transport Layer Security), 270
top-level domains (TLDs), 171–172
topics in SNS, 157
Total Cost of Ownership (TCO)
　Calculator, 6, **283–284**
total lifecycle costs, 59
tracking performance, 142
traditional applications, availability in,
　193–194

traffic flow in Route 53, **180**, *180*
trails for CloudTrail events, **144–145**
Transfer Acceleration, **225–226**
transparent data encryption (TDE), 101
Transport Layer Security (TLS), 270
triggers in CodeDeploy, **312**
Trojans, finding, 264
troubleshooting, AWS Config for, 159
Trusted Advisor
   cost optimization, **282**
   limits, **196**
Trusted Advisor Recommendations
   insight, 319
trusted entities in IAM, 131
TTL (time to live) in caching, 237
TXT records, 174

U

UnauthorizedAccess, finding, 265
updating CloudFormation stacks, **301–303**
URLs for S3 objects, **56**
user accounts, **126–129**, *128*
user pools in Cognito, 132

V

ValidateService hooks, 311
validation of log file integrity, **146**
vaults in Glacier, 58
vCPUs instance type parameter, 219
Version section in application specification
   files, 311
versioning
   backup and recovery, **204–205**
   S3 objects, **53–54**
Virtual Function (VF) interface, 228
Virtual Private Cloud (VPC) service
   CIDR blocks, **68–72**

elastic IP addresses, 82–83
elastic network interface, 72–73
exam essentials, 89–90
flow logs, 259–260
functions, 8
Internet gateways, 73–74
introduction, **68**
NACLs, 79–82
NAT, 83–87, *86*
peering, 87–88
public IP addresses, 82
review questions, **91–94**
route tables, **74–76**
security groups, 76–78
subnets, **70–72**, *71*
summary, 88–89
virtual private clouds (VPCs)
   configuring, **26**, *26*
   regions, 13
   resilient networks, **206–207**
virtualization, 4–6, *4–5*
VM Import/Export, 38
volumes
   EC2 instances, **31–33**
   Lifecycle Manager, **288**
   RAID-optimized, **223–224**
VPC. *See* Virtual Private Cloud (VPC)
   service
Vulnerability and Penetration Testing
   page, 235

W

WAF (Web Application Firewall), **267**
warehousing
   OLAP, 99
   Redshift, **110–111**
warm-up time in Auto Scaling, 202
WCUs (write capacity units) in
   DynamoDB, **114–115**

Web Application Firewall
    (WAF), **267**
website hosting for S3 objects,
    56–57
weighted routing in Route 53, **178**
Well-Architected page, 16
whitelisting in security group
    rules, 76
widgets in dashboards, 235
write capacity units (WCUs) in
    DynamoDB, 114–115

Y

Your Security Credentials page, 128, *128*

Z

zones and zone files
    DNS, **173**
    hosted, **175–176**
    VPC, **71–72**, *71*

Comprehensive Online Learning Environment

Register to gain one year of FREE access to the comprehensive online interactive learning environment and test bank to help you study for your AWS Certified Solutions Architect - Associate (SAA-C01) exam.

The online test bank includes:

- **Assessment Test** to help you focus your study to specific objectives
- **Chapter Tests** to reinforce what you've learned
- **Practice Exams** to test your knowledge of the material
- **Digital Flashcards** to reinforce your learning and provide last-minute test prep before the exam
- **Searchable Glossary** to define the key terms you'll need to know for the exam

Go to `http://www.wiley.com/go/sybextestprep` to register and gain access to this comprehensive study tool package.

Register and Access the Online Test Bank

To register your book and get access to the online test bank, follow these steps:

1. Go to `bit.ly/SybexTest`.
2. Select your book from the list.
3. Complete the required registration information including answering the security verification proving book ownership. You will be emailed a pin code.
4. Go to `http://www.wiley.com/go/sybextestprep` and find your book on that page and click the "Register or Login" link under your book.
5. If you already have an account at `testbanks.wiley.com`, login and then click the "Redeem Access Code" button to add your new book with the pin code you received. If you don't have an account already, create a new account and use the PIN code you received.